THE TEENAGE LIBERATION HANDBOOK:

It's primarily a practical handbook, bursting with clever strategies, valuable resources and wise guidance on how to design an interest-driven self-education. It was the sole inspiration for our family to take on an endeavor we thought was out of the question. If you've ever considered the idea of homeschooling, no matter how remotely, read this book.
    -- Griff Wigley in *Whole Earth Review*

An irreverent and thought-provoking guide....very thorough and highly entertaining.
    --*Home Education Magazine*

[Llewellyn's] enthusiasm for learning, her great faith in kids, and the wonderful educational possibilities she presents will make her book tantalizing reading for teens who can't make it in school but have the discipline and the passion to learn on their own.
    --American Library Association *Booklist*

Inspiring and very practical....helps teenagers see that they can take control of their lives and make adolescence, instead of the stereotypical period of boredom, alienation, and rebellion that we are accustomed to, a time of interesting discoveries, real learning, and meaningful work.
    --Susannah Sheffer, editor of *Growing Without Schooling*

Every autodidact should get down on their knees in gratitude to Grace Llewellyn for her commitment to education in the true sense of the word. Every house that has a teenager should also have a copy of The Teenage Liberation Handbook*....important and magical.*
    --Kendall Hailey, author of *The Day I Became an Autodidact*

Packed with information for young people who want more than schools can offer....an invaluable and unique resource....A former middle school English teacher, Llewellyn knows how to speak directly and persuasively to young readers, and even those who do not decide to leave school after reading her book will have a hard time viewing formal education in quite the same way again....Llewellyn presents a credible and appealing case for becoming self-taught....This is a fascinating, frightening, and exhilarating book that is sure to prove controversial among parents and teachers. At the very least it will open eyes and minds. At the most it might open whole new worlds of possibilities for its young readers
    --*Voice of Youth Advocates* Magazine *(VOYA)*

Cover design based on a painting by David Sherrets. Most interior illustrations
from the Dover Pictorial Archive series.

Llewellyn, Grace
        The teenage liberation handbook : how to quit school and get a real life and

    education/ by Grace Llewellyn.

        p.   ; cm.

        Included bibliographical references (p.   ) and index.
        ISBN 0-9629591-0-3

        1. Self-culture. 2. Home schooling--United States. 3. Education (Secondary)--
United States. 4. High Schools--United States--Controversial works.
I. Title.

LC32   371.3'944 [20]

10 9 8 7 6 5 4   Printed in the U.S.A.

THE
TEENAGE
LIBERATION
HANDBOOK

How to Quit School
and
Get a Real Life
and Education

Grace Llewellyn

Lowry House   *   Eugene, Oregon

For Heather.

For Shira, John M. and John R., Ross, Shawni, Matt, Aaron G., Andy, Brian, Jeff, Demian, Rick, Noah, Kris, Amy, David, Chris, Karen, Morgen, Aaron R., Aaron Z., Susan, Marc, Melissa, Young, Amanda, Beanie, Josh, Kartik, Jason G., Jason V., Yu, Laura, Becky, Lesley, Clara, and Emile. No strings.

And for the dream of the wild horses.

Thanks

This book has been nurtured and built by many people. To adequately acknowledge them, I'd need at least a hundred pages. What follows, therefore, is inadequate.

In writing this book, I stood on the shoulders of a giant. John Holt's visionary, compassionate books on education and unschooling opened my eyes and clarified my beliefs. He died in 1985, two years before I even heard of him. Nevertheless, like most people whose lives are changed by his books, I think of him as a personal friend. Without his work this book wouldn't have been possible. I wouldn't have thought of it, let alone written it. Many of my ideas throughout this book are built directly on his.

Next, I am extremely grateful to the homeschooling community--the thousands of people who have taken John's ideas and turned them into reality. Without their examples, my book would be flat, hypothetical, and utopian. They give the rest of us a beginning sense of what's possible without schools.

More than a hundred teenagers filled out my lengthy questionnaire on unschooling, some in great detail. I am especially grateful to Anne Brosnan, Joshua Smith, and Kim Kopel, who took time to write me long, informative, and entertaining letters.

During her driving trip around the country, never-schooled Anita Giesy stopped in Oregon and fascinated me for days with descriptions of unschoolers nationwide and stories from "inside" the homeschooling movement.

Parents who wrote me especially insightful letters include Jj Fallick, Gwen A. Meehan, Bonnie Sellstrom, Michaele Maurer, Bea Rector, Penny Barker, Theresa Lui, and David R. Graham.

I am grateful, also, to the many families who invited me to their homes. Of these, I am most grateful to the wonderful family whose invitation I accepted--the Raymonds of Port Townsend, Washington: Kath, Dan, Seth, Vallie, and Lydia Grace.

The generous people at Holt Associates gave me permission to use material from *Growing Without Schooling* magazine, and it is this material which helps me to show, again and again, what a range of activities is possible for a person unrestricted by school.

And in a general sense, all of us who support homeschooling or unschooling are indebted to the families who spent (and continue to spend) years of their lives working for fair homeschooling laws.

I thank the college admissions officers and professors who shared their opinions and advice, and the people from various organizations who patiently answered my questions and sent information.

However. I don't want my thanks to *incriminate* these helpful people. Many whom I quote share my faith in teenagers and wholeheartedly support unschooling in the same sense I do. Others might be less completely in agreement with me. For instance, just because a college admissions officer expresses enthusiasm about unschooled applicants doesn't mean he endorses my entire philosophy, and it doesn't mean he's not equally enthusiastic about *schooled* applicants. A few of the unschoolers and homeschoolers whom I quote will undoubtedly think I am out of hand when I insist that you do not necessarily need to learn higher math or even read a lot to have a worthwhile life. Several homeschooling parents who have helped me might think I underestimate the parents' role in a teenager's education. And in a general sense, this book does have more than its share of sassy rebellious moments. The sass and rebellion is all mine, except where you detect it within somebody else's directly quoted words. I was born with these unfortunate qualities; just ask my mother. To sum up, the opinions of this book, except where otherwise stated, belong to me.

Also:

I want to make it abundantly clear that this book is not a personal attack on schoolteachers. There would be little point in that, since I was a teacher myself and continue to hold the same ideals that sent me into teaching in the first place. Anyway, I want to publicly thank my teachers who dealt in excellence despite the complex set of difficulties all schoolteachers face. Foremost among these is Jerry Vevig, choir director extraordinaire, who blessed me and hundreds of other teenagers with the opportunity to work incredibly hard and sound exquisite. Others who especially inspired or encouraged me include Mrs. Darnell, Mrs. Welch, Mrs. Anderson, Mr. Jenkins, Mr. Ah Fong, Mr. Smith, and Mr. Coughlin. (I can't bring myself to write their first names. I don't even *know* most of their first names.)

Also, the teachers and administrators with whom I worked at the Colorado Springs School were not only brilliant, but also generous and wise. I was especially inspired by Bruce Hamilton, Ava Heinrichsdorff, Tom Howes, Karen Huff, Pat Musick, Gary Oakley, Hela Trost, and Charlie Tye. It is very much in spite of these people, rather than because of them, that I wrote this book.

Finally, I am grateful to friends and family who have supported my work in various ways:

Many pointed out resources that I included in this book. Others, like my teaching colleague Gary Oakley, encouraged me and/or talked at length with me, helping me clarify ideas.

I am immensely indebted to people who carefully read the manuscript or parts of it, helping me identify and fix many weaknesses: Heiko Koester, Clement Cheung, Kris Shapiro, Dick Ruth, and the trusty Llewellyn pack: Ned, Richard, Heather.

For support both personal and intellectual, I thank Richard, Heather D., Colleen, Heather, Kelly, Heiko, and especially Ned. I thank my housemate Caroline Diston, who kept me sane and happy by bringing me warm dinners and hot tea and coaxing me away from my computer to go dancing--any joyous overtones you detect in these pages have a lot to do with living around her. And from my heart, I thank my parents, whose love, trust, and support has buttressed so much of my life.

*I recognize June by the flowers, now. I used to know it by review
tests, and restlessness.*

--Lisa Asher, unschooled teenager,
in *Growing Without Schooling* magazine

*What is life? It is the flash of a firefly in the night. It is the breath of
a buffalo in the winter time. It is the little shadow which runs across
the grass and loses itself in the sunset.*

--Crowfoot,
Blackfoot warrior and spokesman.

Contents

PART THREE
--THE TAILOR-MADE EDUCATIONAL EXTRAVAGANZA--

PART FOUR
--TOUCHING THE WORLD: FINDING GOOD WORK---

PART FIVE
---THE LIVES OF UNSCHOOLERS---

first, a nice little story

On a soft green planet, a smiling baby was born in an orchard resplendent with every kind of fruit in the universe. The baby's parents called her Tanika, and Tanika spent her days roaming the warm wet ground on hands and knees. Spotting a clump of gulberries off in the distance, she'd crawl after it and crush the sweet fruit in her mouth, red juice staining her brown chin and neck. A muavo would fall fatly from the high crown of the muavo tree, and she'd savor its golden tang. Each day revealed new wonders-- bushapples, creamy labanas, the nutty crunch of the brown shrombart. The orchard's fruit sparkled in the dew and sun like thousands of living moist jewels against the green fragrance of cushioning leaves.

As her eyes grew stronger Tanika lifted her gaze. The opulent branches above her hung heavy with fruits she'd never dreamed of, globular and glistening. Tanika's mother and father wandered the orchard too, sometimes, and she watched them reach out easily and take a shining cluster here, a single green satinplum there. She'd watch them eat and imagine being tall enough to roam and reach so freely as they.

Sometimes one of them would bend down and give Tanika one of those fruits from up there in the moving leaves. Fresh from the branches, it intoxicated her, and her desire to know and taste all the fruits of the orchard so consumed her that she began to long for the day she could reach that far.

Her longing strengthened her appetite, and the fruit strengthened her legs, and one day Tanika crawled to the base of a mysterious bush at the edge of the stream that watered the orchard. She leaned carefully forward and braced her arms as she positioned her feet. Unsteadily she rose and groped for the shrub's pale fruit. Tugging knocked her off balance and she sat down hard in an overripe muavo, but she barely noticed the fruit squishing under her thighs: in her hands she grasped a fruit thin-skinned and silver, fresh and new. She pressed it to her nose and face before she let her teeth puncture it.

No sooner had she tossed the smooth pit into the stream, than she heard a rustling behind her. A jolly bespectacled face grinned down at her.

"Well, well, well! You're a mighty lucky little girl! I've come to teach you to get the fruit down from the tall trees!"

Tanika's happiness unfurled like a sail. She could hardly believe her good luck. Not only had she just picked and eaten her first bush fruit, but here was a man she didn't even know offering to show her how to reach the prism of treats high above her head. Tanika was so overcome with joy that she immediately rose to her feet again, and plucked another of the small moonish fruits.

The jolly stranger slapped the fruit from Tanika's wrist. Stunned, she fell again and watched her prize roll into the stream. "Oh dear," said the man, "You've already picked up some bad habits. That may make things difficult." The slapping hand now took Tanika's and pulled her up. Holding on this way, Tanika stumbled along behind the stranger.

She wanted to ask questions, like, "Why didn't you just show me how to pick those berries hanging above the bush where I was?" But she kept her mouth shut. If she was going off to pick the high fruit, she guessed it didn't matter where, or that she'd sacrificed her one beautiful moonfruit. Maybe they were going to a special tree melting with juicing fruits, branches bent almost to the ground, low enough for her outstretched fingers. Yes! That must be it. Excitement renewed, she moved her legs faster. The stranger grinned and squeezed her hand.

Soon Tanika saw the biggest, greyest thing she'd ever laid eyes on. In quiet fascination she tripped along as they stepped off the spongy humus of the orchard floor onto a smooth sidewalk. "Here we are!" beamed the guide. They entered the building, full of odd smells and noises. They passed through a pair of heavy black doors, and the man pushed Tanika into a loud, complicated room full of talking children and several adults. She looked at the children, some sitting on the floor, some crawling about or walking. All of them had trays or plates in front of them heaping with odd mushy lumps of various colors. Also, some of the children were busy coloring simple pictures of fruits, and some wore pins and tags on their shirts displaying little plastic pears and mistbulbs. Baffled, Tanika tried to figure out what the children were doing in such a dark, fruitless place, what the lumpy stuff was, and above all, why her guide had stopped here on their way to the bountiful tree.

But before she had time to think, two things happened. First, one of the kids took something metal and used it to scoop a lump of dull pinkish stuff into his mouth. Tanika opened her mouth in panic to warn the kid. Maybe there was something wrong with him; he was much bigger than she was, old enough to know better. But just as she began to yell, a new hand, slick, pulled her up again. "OK, Tanika," said the cheery woman that went with the hand, "This is the cafeteria. We're looking forward to helping you grow, and we're certain we can help you to pick tree fruit, as long as you do your part."

Tanika felt confused. She didn't see what this place could have to do with picking gulberries, and at the moment she was particularly hungry for more of that shining moonfruit. But she had no time to think. The slick-hand woman put Tanika on a cold chair at a table. "Here," she said, and nudged a box of crayons and a black outline of a plum at her. "Today you will color this, and it will help you get ready for eating tomorrow." Tanika started to feel foolish. She'd never guessed that learning to pick fruit would be so complicated. She colored the plum with all the colors in the box, trying in vain to make it round and enticing like the fruits of the orchard.

The rest of the day passed in a daze. Tanika was made to color more of the pictures, and to her disgust most of the children ate the formless mush on the plates in front of them. Some of the fat and greasy children asked for more and stuffed themselves. Whenever this happened, the adults ran in and put gold stars all over the kid's arms and face. Many things happened-- children fought, napped, sat quietly fidgeting with the stuff. Finally, the jolly man took Tanika's hand and led her out of the dark building. As her bare feet met the orchard grass, she caught the scent of ripe labana. She asked the stranger if he would get one for her, but he merely laughed.

Tanika was far too confused to put any of her questions into words. By the time they arrived at the tree where Tanika slept with her parents, the evening light had turned the leaves to bronze, and she was exhausted. Too tired to look for fruit, she fell asleep and dreamed fitfully.

In the morning her mind was clear. She still wanted to reach the high fruit, but she did not want to go back to the noisy smelly dark cafeteria. She could already reach the bushfruit; maybe in time she'd grasp the high fruit too.

But when the spectacled person arrived, he told her that she'd never reach the trees without many years in the cafeteria. He explained it--"You can't reach them now, can you?" and "Your parents can reach them. That's because they went to the cafeteria. I can reach them, because I went to the cafeteria." Tanika had no time to think this through, because he'd pulled her to her feet again and they were off. She hadn't had time to find breakfast, and her stomach rumbled painfully.

Tanika went in the room and sat down politely. "Please," she asked one of the adults, "Can you help me pick tree fruits today? That's why I'm here, and also today I didn't have time for breakfast."

The tall lady laughed. "Well, well, well! Aren't we cute! *Tree* fruit! Before you're ready for tree fruit, you have to prepare!" She disappeared behind a curtain and returned carrying a tray with a scoop of greenish stuff. Tanika jerked back. She looked around wildly for an escape route. Out of the corner of her eye she saw a boy watching with soft dark quiet eyes. The lady grabbed her hand.

"Don't be afraid, Tanika," she laughed. "How will you ever work up to eating tree fruit if you can't handle plate fruit?" She put the tray on the table, and took the metal thing, spooning up a piece of the stuff and holding it in front of the small girl. Tanika pushed the spoon away violently. Then she put her head down on the table and cried.

The lady's voice changed. "So you're going to be a tough one, Tanika? Just remember, you're only hurting yourself when you refuse to eat. If you want to succeed, you'd better do as we ask." She walked away.

When Tanika stopped crying, her stomach was desperately empty. She sat up and looked at the tray. She was afraid of the stuff. She bent down to smell it and caught a faint, stale whiff of limbergreen berry. The smell, even distorted, was a familiar friend. She picked up the spoon and ate her first bite of cafeteria food.

Tanika was relieved. Although the goop was slimy, far too sweet, and mostly tasteless, it wasn't nearly as bad as it looked. And it did seem to be made from limbergreen berries. She ate it all, and felt a little better. The lady came back. "Very good," she smiled. She stuck a green star on the back of Tanika's hand. "We'll do some more exercises and then later on you can try something new to eat."

Hours later, Tanika had been the apple in "Velcro the Stem on the Apple," and had drawn a muavo tree and listened to an older student explain what fruits contained vitamins P, Q, and Z. Apparently she had done all these things right, because the lady came back and put more green and gold stars on her hands and cheeks. Some of the children looked at her angrily, though, so perhaps she'd done something wrong.

At this point a man rang a little bell. Immediately all the children sat down at the tables and folded their hands neatly. A girl grabbed Tanika's hand and shoved her onto a chair. Then six children walked into the room carrying stacks of trays. They put one in front of each child, and Tanika saw that each tray contained five purple and blue wafers. "Yum!" said the girl next to Tanika, "Violetberry cakes!" Tanika jumped. She'd seen her parents eat violetberries, and also seen the accompanying ecstasy on their faces. She easily pictured the graceful coniferous trees on which they grew.

She picked up a wafer. It was warm, but not with the gentle warmth of the sun. She put it in her mouth. Dry, sandy...she chewed obediently but sadly. This was it? Disappointment sank her stomach and she put the cake down, mentally crossing violetberries off her wishlist forever.

In the end Tanika was made to eat the violetberry cake--all five hunks of it--before the spectacled man would lead her out the door. Her stomach throbbed all the way home. That night she crawled into her mother's arms and sobbed. Her mother rocked her, then whispered something to Tanika's father. He disappeared, and returned a minute later with an armload of tiny, glowing violetberries.

"It's time," said her mother sweetly, "For your first fresh violetberries."

Her father dangled them teasingly above her lips, but Tanika only cried harder. The berries' fragrance, though delicate and sweet, clashed with her distended heavy stomach. She was far too full, and it was violetberries' fault. Both parents teased and offered, but they finally gave up. The mother laid Tanika down to rest alone, and the two adults stood whispering while the moon rose, worry in their voices.

At the cafeteria the next day the adults met Tanika with an unpleasant stare. "You're making things difficult for yourself," scolded the woman with slick hands, "Your parents have reported that your attitude at home is not meeting standards for girls your age. You need to eat *much* more thoroughly." A girl brought a plate crowded with dried out, wrinkly little fruits. Tanika ate them, tough and tasteless. Her stomach hurt again. After they dissected a preserved bushapple, she ate another tray full of canned gulberry. Then she went back home and slept.

Days passed, and months. Tanika ate obediently and earned lots of stars. There was a picture of a bright green tree painted on one of the walls, and when the whole roomful of children ate their food quickly, the adults had them play a game. They taped three or four cut-out paper fruits to the tree, and then the kids were made to take turns jumping or reaching to try to take them. Whoever reached a fruit got to keep it, and also was called a winner and plastered with dozens of gold stars.

One day when the spectacled man walked her home he told her the cafeteria would be closed for two days for cleaning. He handed her a little white carton and said, "Be sure to eat all of this while I'm gone, and I'll pick you up in two days."

As he waddled away, a strange inspiration seized Tanika's brain. She touched her swollen belly and flung the carton away. Out of it tumbled cakes, red mush, hard little biscuits smelling flatly of labanas.

When she woke the next morning her stomach rumbled and she got up to look for breakfast. Leaving the clearing, she accidentally kicked a biscuit. Out of habit, she picked it up and almost put it in her mouth, then caught herself and aimed instead for a bush full of gulberries. Furtively she snatched a handful and crushed them to her lips. Sweet and wild, they made her want to sing.

Tanika's father saw her then, and called excitedly to her mother. Both of them ran to their child and squeezed her. "Look what you've learned at the cafeteria!" cried her mother. "My baby is growing up!"

"Be sure to eat all your homefood," said her father, "So you won't be behind when you go back." Then his tone of voice changed. "What's that?" he said. He sprinted off and grabbed up the white carton. Tanika watched in horror as he searched the orchard floor. A few minutes later he returned with everything--biscuits, cake, mush.

Tanika ate it all.

The cafeteria opened again and Tanika went back. Every day she ate faster, and gradually stopped resisting, even in her own mind. One day she reached the highest paper fruit on the painted tree. All the adults patted her head and she could barely see her brown skin under all the gold stars. She started walking to the cafeteria every day by herself. The adults started giving her food for the evenings, and usually she'd eat it like they said. One day, walking home, she flung her hands to the sky and they touched, accidentally, a muavo hanging down from its branch. Tanika jumped back. "I can pick it," she said slowly, "It worked." She thought for a minute. The cooks had said it would happen, someday, if she ate what they gave her and jumped as high as she could during the tree game.

Tanika gracefully severed the muavo from its stem, examined it, and tossed it neatly into a shadow.

She wasn't hungry.

the note to parents

Against the advice of lots of people, I didn't write this book for you. I wrote it for teenagers. I wrote it for teenagers because I wished that when I was a teenager someone had written it for me. I wrote it for teenagers because my memory and experience insist that teenagers are as fully human as adults. I wrote it for teenagers because I found an appalling dearth of respectful, serious nonfiction for teenagers. In short, I wrote it for teenagers because they are the experts on their own lives.

No, I have not forgotten your child's "place." I know that if you want to, you can probably prevent him from leaving school. I have written this book anyway, in the hope that after careful thought, you will see fit to honor the choice he makes.

Yes, if your son or daughter leaves school, it will change your life. If the experiences of pioneering homeschoolers can predict your future, you will see family relationships deepen; a teenager without eight hours of school and homework has time to make friends with her parents. You will see family relationships heal, uncomplicated by displaced anger about school. You will feel less harshly evaluated according to teenage fashion magazine standards. Depending on your own background and schooling, you may undergo a period of depression, anger, and bitterness. *You* went to school, after all, and in contrast to your children's unexpected freedom you may feel overwhelmed by a sense of loss--all the things you could have done with that time, all the choices you never thought you had, all the labels that stuck when schoolpeople put them on you. This funk, if you get it, will eventually give way to a new sense of freedom--at least mine did. You can't change the past, but you can change the present. You can peel the labels off, you can start making real choices, you have the rest of your life to *live*.

Homeschooling parents of teenagers are rarely *teachers*, in the school sense of the word, and this book never suggests that you forsake your own career or interests in order to learn calculus (etc.) fast enough to "teach" it. Healthy kids can teach themselves what they need to know, through books, various people, thinking, and other means. (A freshly unschooled person may at *first* be a lousy learner; like cigarettes, school-style passivity can be a slow habit to kick.)

Nevertheless, you will probably find yourself more involved than before with your son's or daughter's education. If you have helped with or supervised your children's homework, or stayed in close touch with their teachers, homeschooling need not drain your energy any more than that. Your role will change, however. No longer is it your job to nag or lecture; instead, you answer questions and help find people or resources to answer the questions that you can't answer. Instead, when your daughter starts sketching castles, you introduce her to the architect you know or tell her about the lecture on medieval life that you saw advertised in the paper.

If an unschooled teenager doesn't need *teaching* from you, what does he need from you? *Parenthood*, of course, and all the love and stability therein.

Also, help with logistics, as implied in the castle example above. Few people can immediately take complete responsibility for their educations after being forcefully spoonfed for years. Please be willing to make some phone calls to set up meetings or lessons, to tell your kid about events or resources he might not otherwise know about, to draw a map to the planetarium or explain how to use the university library. Also, you will need to accompany your son or daughter through your state's homeschooling legal requirements. Fortunately, every state has support groups to help you make sense of this process.

Also, trust. When you tell your daughter about that upcoming lecture on medieval life, make it clear that you are simply passing along information, not giving an *assignment*. If you don't believe in her, it won't work. If you give up on her, snoop, push, or frequently anxiously inquire into the status of her algebraic knowledge, you will destroy any chance you had for a healthy family relationship, *and* you will send her right back to school, where there is so much less to lose.

Part of trusting means respecting your teenager's need for transition time. As chapter 12 of this book points out, new unschoolers often need time to work through a flood of feelings about school and life, *before* they can start attending to things "intellectual" or "academic." Ride out the storm with your child. Offer your support, your ideas, your arms. Don't rush him.

Do I expect you to swallow all this? Not now; not by reading this short note. Later, *yes*. I expect you to change your mind in favor of unschooling by 1) reading John Holt's books *Freedom and Beyond, Instead of Education, Teach Your Own*, and *Escape From Childhood*, 2) reading literature by parents who have "homeschooled" their teenagers--especially Nancy Wallace's *Child's Work* and Micki and David Colfax's *Homeschooling for Excellence*, 3) getting to know homeschoolers near you (like people, they come in all varieties; don't give up if you're put off at first), 4) reading *Growing Without Schooling* magazine, 5) reviewing your own adolescence and your present life, and 6) humbly observing your teenaged child, allowing for the possibility that he might be a *person*....like you.

As for the rest of this book, you are a welcome guest. From time to time, you will find the words of other parents and adults, some of which may reassure you. Depending on your perspective, you may detect an overall tone of intoxicating hope or dangerous insubordination. Mostly, you will find piles of information you do not need: stuff that is common knowledge to adults but not so familiar to teenagers who have spent most of their lives secluded from the world and its array of wonders.

Finally, on a different note: if you are already disillusioned by your child's "education," or even sympathetic to the cause of unschooling, and if you live with a Stuck or Depressed teenager, I hope this book can be your ally in offering her or him some vision for healthy, self-directed change.

Best wishes.

about this book

Did your guidance counselor ever tell you to consider quitting school? That you have other choices, quite beyond lifelong hamburger flipping or inner-city crack dealing? That legally you can find a way out of school, that once you're out you'll learn and grow better, faster, and more naturally than you ever did in school, that there are zillions of alternatives, that you can quit school and still go to A Good College and even have a Real Life in the Suburbs if you so desire? Just in case your counselor never told you these things, I'm going to. That's what this book is for.

What it's not:

This is not a book about the kind of "homeschooling" in which you stay home all day and hang a chalkboard in the family room and write essays designed by your father and work geometry problems assigned by your mother.

There are some good things to say about that kind of homeschooling, especially for young children who haven't yet acquired basic reading, writing, and math computation skills. There are also some bad things to say about it. In this book I will say little about it.

Most people who do fantastic unschoolish things with their time *call* themselves homeschoolers, because it keeps them out of trouble and it doesn't freak out the neighbors. Anne Brosnan put it well in a letter to *Growing Without Schooling* magazine:

> When an adult comes up and asks, "Why aren't you in school?" you're supposed to soften it by saying, "My mom (or dad) teaches me at home." If you say, "I don't even *go* to school. So far, I've taught myself everything I want to know," they think you've run away from school or are a lunatic. Whereas the other way, they think your parent's a teacher and you get private lessons.
>
> The usual adult person in America thinks it's terribly hard to teach yourself something, and if you want to learn something, you've got to find somebody to teach it to you. This leads to the idea that kids are dumb unless taught or unless they go to school.*

---

* *Growing Without Schooling* #73

If you quit school, you too will probably wish to call yourself a homeschooler, at least when you talk to the school board. But that doesn't require bringing the ugliness of school into your home, or transforming your parents into teachers. Nor, for that matter, does it require that you stay home. The idea is to catch *more* of the world, not less. To avoid these kinds of connotations, I usually use the term *unschooling*. But be aware that many people who talk about *homeschooling* mean the same thing I do when I say *unschooling*.

This is not a book specifically about Christian homeschooling, although most Christians will find it as useful as anyone else. I point this out because many people associate homeschooling with fundamentalist Christianity and Fear of Darwin. Many homeschoolers *are* fundamentalist Christians, which has some heavy impact on what they do instead of *school* school. Many others, however, are agnostics, mellow Christians, Jews, pagans, atheists, and Buddhists. Help yourself to any religious belief you like, but in these pages I won't be suggesting that you read your Bible instead of a biology book.

What it *is*:

This book is a wild card, a shot in the dark, a hopeful prayer.

This book wants you to quit school and do what you love. Yes, I know, that's the weirdest thing you ever heard. Hoping to make this idea feel possible to you, I tell about teenagers who are already living happy lives without school, and I offer lots of ideas and strategies to help you get a real life and convince your adults to cooperate.

"Excuse me?" you interrupt, *"Quit school? Right. And throw away my future and pump gas all my life and get Addicted to Drugs and be totally lost in today's world. Right."*

If you said that, please feel free to march straight to the nearest schoolperson and receive a bushel of gold stars, extra credit points, and proud smiles. You've learned exactly what they taught you. After you get tired of sticking stars to your locker, do please come back and read further.

This book is built on the belief that life is wonderful and schools are stifling. It is built on an impassioned belief in freedom. And it is built on the belief that schools do the opposite of what they say they do. They prevent learning and they destroy one's love of learning.

Of course, there are hundreds of other books with similar premises. Some of these books go on to suggest that if certain changes were made, or smarter teachers were hired, schools would be good places. Other books say compulsory schools are *fundamentally* bad places and society, or at least individual people, should abandon them. This book agrees with that, but it doesn't stop there.

This is a *practical* book--a book for individual teenagers, a real-life handbook meant to be used and acted on. I have no hope that the school system will change enough to make schools healthy places, until it makes school blatantly optional. But I have plenty of faith that *people*--you, your friends--can intelligently take greater control over their own lives. So this book bypasses the rigid, uncreative red tape of that System and instead speaks directly to you.

If school didn't make people so stupid, this could be a very short handbook. But unfortunately, most of the teenagers I've known and worked with--like the teenager I was, eight years back--are more clueless than preschool children when it comes to knowing how to ask and answer important questions. So, much of this book is about access--how to do this, find that out, what your choices are and how to take advantage of them.

Whom it's for:

As the title gently implies, this is a book for *teenagers*, though their parents and little brothers are welcome too. If you are nine and want to use this book to get free, more power to you. If you are eleven and think of yourself as a teenager, that's fine with me too.

Is this book for *all* teenagers? Here are four answers.

If you are like me, this book is definitely for you. When I was in school, people asked me if I liked it. Sometimes I said yes. Sometimes I said no. I didn't think about it much, because I figured it didn't matter. Whether I liked it or not, I knew (or thought I knew) there were no other options. I believed in school in an abstract sense--education, learning, great writers and poets and thinkers and all that. My grades were good. I hated homework--and rarely did any--but I felt constantly guilty, rather than proud, about this. I wasn't offended by the disrespect my peers and I lived with, because I'd never imagined that it was *possible* for adults to treat me differently.

Usually, I thought I'd be fine if only I was a senior instead of an eighth grader, or if only I went to some artsy boarding school instead of boring Capital High School. I liked about half of my teachers, but felt no enthusiasm for their classes. I craved Friday afternoons and June. Except for choir, my life in school was dreary and uninspired, but I had nothing to compare it to. I'd never heard of homeschooling, let alone unschooling, and dropping out was not on my List of Possibilities in Life. I wonder now, sometimes with bitterness, how things might have been different if I had heard then of the possibilities beyond school. The first wave of the unschooling movement caught some people about my age, and I envy them.

Very definitely, this book is *not* just for people who are labeled gifted. I make this point because in these pages you will run into a lot of examples of unschooled teenagers who do rather impressive things with their time. I don't want you to be intimidated by them, only inspired. They don't live brilliantly because they are smarter than you; they live brilliantly because they have the time and encouragement they need. Many of them did very badly in school before their parents set them free.

If you have already considered leaving school--as a "dropout" or anything else, of course this book is for you. If you have been feeling guilty or inadequate because of your "failure" in school, perhaps I can knock some optimistic sense into you. Perhaps I can get you to think of yourself as *rising* out instead of *dropping* out. [*] The way we think of ourselves makes all the difference.

If you truly enjoy school and all of its paraphernalia more than anything else you can possibly imagine doing, I suppose I'm not writing for you, because I don't understand you. I'm not sure you exist, but if you do, we live in different universes. I used to think everyone was strong willed and independently inclined. Now I'm not sure. Sometimes I think perhaps school really does completely destroy that fierce, free spirit in some people. Other times my mother half convinces me that some people are naturally docile and passive. Maybe I have something to learn about docility. Or maybe I have a healthy aversion to something dead in people that should be alive.

However, I invite you to have a look at this book anyway. Even if it doesn't change the way you think about school, it might make you aware of some useful opportunities and resources--things you can do with your life in *addition* to school. After you finish your homework, naturally.

Of course, some places we call school are less schoolish than others. I feel pretty strongly that even the most alternative school, *as long as it is compulsory*, is not a healthy place to be. But I'd be an idiot to say every single school is bad for every single person. If you go to a humane school, and love it, even in May, and have a gut feeling that it's a good and healthy place, stay there. I hope I never tell anyone to ignore their gut feelings. I always listen to mine, and usually act on them. Of course, you have to make sure you're not confusing fear and deeply imbedded guilt with your true feelings.

Why I wrote it:
Just in case you are dying to know.

When I went to college, I knew from the start that I wanted to be an English teacher. I had always loved to read and write, but I had rarely enjoyed any of the work I had done in my English classes. In my naivete, I blamed this on my teachers. Several of them were obviously very intelligent, interesting, and creative people, but their classes were nevertheless dull, and as I said, I thought this was their fault. I knew I would be a different kind of teacher.

My own classes would be dynamic, entertaining, and always engaging. I would love the stimulation of being around "learning" all my life, and my students would shower me with continual gratitude for rescuing them from the brain-death of their previous existence.

Student teaching took some of the sparkle out of that arrogance, but I chalked up my victims' lack of complete enthusiasm to my inexperience and

---

[*] I got this terminology from Herb Hough's letter in *Growing Without Schooling* magazine #79.

lack of adequate time to prepare. (Somehow, I assumed that later I'd have more time to prepare.) Yes, a few of them said I was the best teacher they'd ever had. Most of them just turned in most of their homework on time and looked at me funny when I rhapsodized about writing. I did not find a real teaching position for the autumn after college graduation, and I ended up substitute teaching in the public schools of Oakland and Berkeley, California.

Subbing put me in the position to see the ugliest aspects of school, and my life-long tendency to rebel against or at least make fun of authority surfaced and grew. In between sending students to the office for calling me a "white bitch" or for pinching me or for loudly interrupting too many times, I'd sit and despairingly ponder the meaninglessness of these huge inner-city schools. I still felt that with determination, I could make a difference. However, I began to realize that working with the kinds of administrators I most often encountered could only be an uphill battle. Furthermore, for many of these students it was probably too late--schools had so crushed their "love of learning" that I could hardly hope to inspire all of them to write or think or discover wonderful things.

After that school year, I took a break to travel in Peru and then spent three months substituting in the homogeneous, well-behaved schools that I grew up in in Boise, Idaho. I still felt that I wanted to teach kids to read and write but I began to yearn to escape the rigidity and dullness of public schools. I began contemplating starting my own tiny, inexpensive, independent school. I imagined a group of about ten students who spent their time taking field trips and hanging out in someone's basement making movies or writing novels. While I was brainstorming and researching the logistics of setting up something like this, I first stumbled across the writing of John Holt. By that time I'd heard of homeschooling but dismissed it, as most people seem to, as the activity of a bunch of scaredy-cat fanatics afraid their kids would find out about evolution and condoms if they went to school. John Holt's writings threw a bright new light on the subject, and on the whole concepts of school and learning.

Essentially, he argued that learning is a *natural* process that happens to anyone who is busy doing something real for its own sake, and that school destroys and confuses this process. Although most of his ideas had never occurred to me, they immediately made so much sense that I felt as though I'd thought of them myself. His books were eloquent yet simple, by far the wisest words I had ever found about education. I realized that although a tiny school like the one I'd envisioned might be a good alternative for students, I wasn't equipped to start it--I didn't have any real expertise, and I didn't know anything worth teaching besides how to embroider, go backpacking, bake bread, dance a little, play the piano, and maybe write. I realized how few skills I had, and that the few skills I *did* have hadn't come from school. I knew about a lot of things from reading and keeping my ears open, but few of the books that had shaped my mind had been assigned or recommended in school. I felt freshly angry about having given up ballet (instead of school) in junior high, and about having pushed that biggest love of mine, dancing, into a mostly-neglected cupboard. Mainly, I felt flooded by a sense of loss and bitterness--all that time I'd *wasted* sitting and staring out windows when I could have been out traveling, learning, growing, *living*.

I determined to start living my life, then and there. I packed up and migrated to Taos, New Mexico, where I slept on the mesa in a house made of bottles and wind, and feasted every morning on sky and space and sage-scent. (At the same time, I supported my little sister's decision to quit high school.) I spent as much time as I could dancing.

I continued to read John Holt, but I eventually decided to teach anyway. After all, school was going to exist whether I wanted it to or not, and I figured I might as well jump in and make it the best experience I could. Anyway, I didn't know *how* to do anything that I wanted to do more. I still felt that public school was a horrendous institution, but I daydreamed about finding a private school that was humane and lively.

I found a position teaching seventh and eighth grade English at The Colorado Springs School, in Colorado Springs, Colorado. I was thrilled. A small, independent school, it believed firmly in experiential education--"learning by *doing*"--and my colleagues and the administrators were wonderful people: flexible, enthusiastic, imaginative, intelligent, funny, and warm. With only nineteen students, I'd have the chance to know each of them well. It seemed so different from public school that I looked forward to it with great excitement.

The year did go smoothly in most regards. However, I began to feel that this small school was not essentially healthier than ordinary public schools for most of its students. Naturally, they received more individual attention than they would have in public school, but some of them experienced an uglier flip side of that individual attention: we teachers seemed to see or otherwise find out nearly everything about students' lives, and then to hound students endlessly about things that were none of our business--missing homework assignments, social conflicts, messy notebooks. Even when we were not inclined to pry or push, students had little privacy, no way to escape our eyes.

Furthermore, this small, "caring," "creative" school was fundamentally the same as any ordinary public school, because *it controlled students' lives*. It continually dictated to them how to use their time. So what if they were role playing the lives of the early colonists instead of just reading the dry words of their American history textbook? These cute "experiential" activities we teachers took pride in had the same effect any schoolwork does. They stole kids' time and energy, so that John-the-math-genius-and-artist had no time to build his geometric sculptures, so that Andy couldn't pursue his fascination with well-made knives and guns, so that Kris and Chris and Rick and Young didn't have enough time to read, so that Shira--a brilliant actress and talented musician--was threatened with having to drop out of her outstanding chorale group if she missed any homework assignments.

In some ways, in fact, CSS seemed *more* harmful than public school. Homework was excessive, leaving students little freedom even at home. Lots of parents expected the school to help turn their offspring into lawyers and Successful Executives, and the school catered to this image enough that it put tremendous pressure on kids.

But despite all this, I decided to stay with teaching, and I brainstormed ways to make my classroom as healthy as possible. I wanted to give my students as much freedom within the realm of language arts as I could, so I devised an independent study program complete with an innovative "All A's" grading system borrowed from Richard E. Koop of Gulf Middle School in Florida. The assistant headmaster, a courageous, warm woman, gave me her blessing, saying that since I obviously had the kids' needs and growth foremost in my mind, she'd support my experiment.

I began my second year of teaching with high hopes that soon plummeted. Four or five people who loved to write (enough to do so in their spare time and vacations) thrived in the program. It gave them official time to do what they wanted to do anyway--write novels or collections of short stories or long long essays--rather than drain their energy with arbitrary assignments of arbitrary lengths fit into arbitrary schedules. But most of my students saw it as just another way to make them do something they really didn't want or need to do, at least not every day. So much for freedom.

After I had felt dismal for a while because my curriculum hadn't dramatically changed the nature of school, we went on a week-long field trip to Washington, D.C. Conflict was inevitable; the teachers who designed the trip naturally wanted to take as much advantage as possible of all the things to see and do in the area, so our schedule was hectic and demanding. At one point, the students were scolded for slouching and whispering during a dull evening lecture after a particularly exhausting day. As students exploded in their own defense, and one of my favorite students said sincerely that he wanted to go home, my mind reeled. It was perfectly fair, I thought, to expect people to behave wonderfully in any situation they chose freely to be part of. If I went to a movie and talked all through it, I'd deserve to get kicked out. If I didn't feel like sitting quietly, I shouldn't go in the first place. But our students hadn't been given any choice as to whether they wanted to sit through a lecture, or even whether they went to Washington, or, for that matter, whether they sat in English and science every day.

That night I lay in bed agitating till four AM. Although I hadn't upbraided our students on that particular evening, I had certainly done so countless other times, for similar and sometimes less justifiable reasons.

I called Holt's writings up in my mind and admitted to myself that he was right--school was a bad place, a *controlling* place, and I wasn't going to change anything by being there. I could see that some of my students were fed up with school, but I knew they had no clue as to other possibilities. And so the seeds of this book sprouted in my brain. Also, in the back of my head I knew I could not continue to teach, but at first I refused to look this knowledge in the face. The prospect of life without my "career" was frightening and uncertain. However, I started looking at the world with a fresher, more honest perspective. While bustling along the sidewalk and scolding students for dawdling, I thought longingly how I would enjoy spending a leisurely week in D.C. with a few of my students, talking with the homeless who camped across from the White House, roaming the Smithsonian for days, taking time out for skateboarding and sky staring.

Back in Colorado, my convictions strengthened daily. I noticed an Emerson quote on the "Civil War" bulletin board, and I shivered: "If you put a chain around the neck of a slave," it said, "the other end fastens itself around your own." The final catalyst came the Friday I read Thoreau with my classes. Nearly everything he said seemed to pertain to the whole school issue, but one fragment in particular of "On the Duty of Civil Disobedience" lodged itself in my brain.

After explaining that he would not pay his taxes as long as they supported such evils as slavery, Thoreau had written:

> If any tax gatherer, or any other public officer, asks me, as one has done, "But what shall I do?" my answer is, "If you really wish to do anything, resign your office." When the subject has refused allegiance, and the officer has resigned his office, then the revolution is accomplished.

That was that. Forced to face my own responsibility, I resolved first to quit teaching, and then to write this book. John Holt and a few others had written a stack of excellent books on unschooling, but I felt that teenagers needed their *own* book, one to tell them they weren't wrong to hate school, and to make them aware of alternatives.

The rest of the teaching year was horribly difficult and odd. In the classroom I vacillated between the easy going, honest human being I wanted to be, and the businesslike teacher I knew I had to be if my class was to function. One day I'd sit laughing with my students, talking about a story one of them had written, ignoring their gum (against school rules) or "off-task" behavior. The next day I'd hand out detentions for "swearing," tardies, and of course any rude, sarcastic, or otherwise "inappropriate" statements. In my confused inconsistency, I imagine I was a more frightening authority figure than a military-style teacher would have been; sometimes it seemed that no sooner had students let down their guard and begun to relate to me as a real person, than I would snap nervously back into teacher mode and bitch at them for "disrupting."

I could not tell my students about my raging opinions with a clean professional conscience, but I couldn't *not* tell them with a clean moral conscience. A friend sent me a button that said "Free the Kids," and I wore it. Some days I was afraid that by writing I'd lose all my friends and even the trust of my students themselves. I finally told two students what I was up to, and of course had some guilty professional twangs about doing so. But I desperately hoped that I would finish, and that my book would find its way into my students' hands, in time for them to decide whether they wanted it to make a difference in their lives.

How to use it

Notice that it's divided into five parts. The first tells why you should consider leaving school. The second tells how to get ready to do it. The third and fourth suggest ideas for how to do it once you're doing it. The fifth describes people who have already lived without school. I put it in the best order I could, but you can read it diagonally if you like. If you are already convinced that school is not the place for you, you may wish to skip the first section altogether, or skim it quickly. On the other hand, if this way of thinking is completely new to you, go as slow in Part One as you need to, to consider whether my statements make sense in your life.

Don't forget to share this book with your friends, or suggest that they find themselves a copy.

I recommend dozens of books, as well as other resources. For many books, I tell only the title and author, because that's all you need to track them down easily. For other books, I mention the publisher and date, which can be useful information if you're using interlibrary loan. When the publisher is small and obscure, I give an address as well.

When I give prices for books or other items, they are 1990 or 1991 prices. Like beanstalks, they will go up. If you order something without first checking with a supplier, ask them to bill you for the extra.

There is a lot of information in your hands. Don't feel obligated to follow up on all of it, or most of it. Don't let it overwhelm you. Don't feel you should read everything I recommend. Let it guide you to a few important things and let the rest go. The silences and spaces in your "education" are as necessary as your activity.

On the other hand, this book does not tell everything that's possible. Don't be limited by my suggestions, just use them as beginning points. Someday I may revise this book, so I'd welcome your recommendations for resources, or news of your own activities, or any other responses.

One more thing. All of us rise or sink to other people's expectations of us. Our society seems not to believe in teenagers enough to expect much of them. This book may shock you, therefore, when it tells how to plan a trip around the world, or when it suggests you start a business or become seriously involved in some academic field you love. But you're no imbecile--I'm certain because at fifteen *I* wasn't an imbecile. I didn't *know* much, but if the right information and some freedom had come my way, I could have soared. I hope that this book can provide some of that "right information" for you, and that it also helps you find the freedom you need.

GWS means *Growing Without Schooling* magazine. More details in the bibliography.

When I mention ages of particular teenagers, I mean their ages at the time that they wrote to me or to *GWS*.

Enjoy your flight....and tell me where you land.

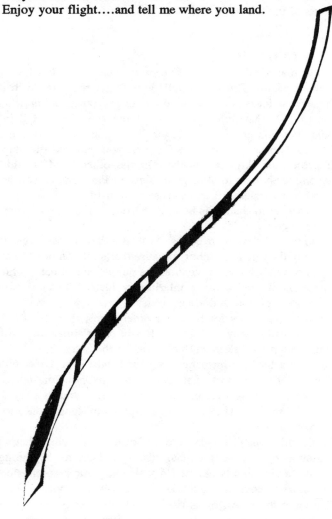

Part One

making the decision

sweet land of liberty

How strange and self-defeating that a supposedly free country should train its young for life in totalitarianism.

> *"No, David, wait until after class to use the bathroom."*

> *"Unfortunately, your daughter would rather entertain the class than participate appropriately."*

> *"Good morning, class. Please open your textbooks to page thirty. Thank you. John, you need to open your book to page thirty."*

> *"Carter, if I have to ask you again to sit down, you'll be taking a trip to the office."*

> *"Miguel, you are not in math. Please put it away. Remember, fifteen percent of your grade in my class comes from participation and attitude."*

> *"Ladies! Gentlemen! Let's keep the noise down in the halls."*

> *"I'd love to hear what you have to say, Monty, but you need to raise your hand first."*

> *"Tonight you need to finish the exercises on page 193 and read the next section."*

> *"Marisa, I need a written explanation as to why you didn't turn in your homework today."*

> *"Laura, put away the book. If I catch you again it's a zero for the day, and that's not something you can afford."*

What do you think of when you hear the word "freedom?" The end of slavery? The end of the Berlin wall? A prisoner tunneling his way out of solitary confinement in Chile with a spoon? An old woman escaping her broken body in death? Gorillas dancing in the jungle instead of sulking behind bars? When I hear the word "freedom," I remember the sweetest sunlight pouring over my teenaged cheeks on the first sleeping-in mornings of summer vacations.

Do you go to school? Yes? Then...

You are not free.

The most overwhelming reality of school is CONTROL. School controls the way you spend your time (what is life made of if not time?), how you behave, what you read, and to a large extent what you think. In school you can't control your own life. Outside of school you can, at least to the extent that your parents trust you to. "Comparing me to those who are conventionally schooled," writes twelve-year-old unschooler Colin Roch, "Is like comparing the freedoms of a wild stallion to those of cattle in a feedlot."[*]

The ultimate goal of this book is for you to start associating the concept of freedom with *you*, and to start wondering why you and your friends don't have much of it, and for you to move out of the busy-prison into the meadows of life. There are lots of good reasons to quit school, but to my idealistic American mind, the pursuit of freedom encompasses most of them and outshines the others.

If you look at the history of "freedom," you notice that the most frightening thing about people who are not free is that they learn to take their bondage for granted, and to believe that this bondage is "normal" and natural. They may not like it, but few question it or imagine anything different. There was a time when many black slaves took a sort of pride--or talked as if they took pride--in how well-behaved and hard-working they were. There was a time when most women believed--or talked as if they believed--that they should obey and submit to their husbands. In fact, people within an oppressed group often internalize their oppression so much that they are crueler, and more judgmental, to their peers than the oppressors themselves are. In China, men made deformed female feet into sexual fetishes, but *women* tied the cords on their own daughters' feet.

Obviously, black and female people eventually caught sight of a greater vision for themselves, and change blazed through their minds, through laws, through public attitudes. All is not yet well, but the United States is now far kinder to people of color and mammary glands than it was 100 years ago. What's more, these people are kinder to *themselves*. They dream bigger dreams, and flesh out grander lives, than picking cotton for the master or fixing a martini for the husband.

Right now, a lot of you are helping history to repeat itself; you don't believe you *should* be free. Of course you *want* to be free--in various ways, not just free of school. However, society gives you so many condescending, false, and harmful messages about yourselves that most of you wouldn't trust

---

[*] in *Growing Without Schooling* Magazine (*GWS*) #78.

yourselves with freedom. It's all complicated by the fact that the people who infringe most dangerously and inescapably on your freedom are those who say they are helping you, those who are convinced you need their help: teachers, school counselors, perhaps your parents.

Why *should* you have freedom?

Why should anyone? To become human, to live fully. Insofar as you live what someone else dictates, you do not live. Choice is a fundamental essence of life, and in the fullest life, each choice is deliberate and savored.

Another reason you should be free is obvious. You should learn to live responsibly and joyfully in a free country.

Recently, schoolpeople talk a lot about "experiential education." Educators have wisely realized that the best way to teach anything includes not only reading about a subject, but also practicing it. For example, my colleague Gary Oakley taught science by having students rehabilitate a polluted pond. Naturally, learning this way sinks in deeper than merely reading, hearing lectures, and discussing. It means participating--*being* a scientist or musician rather than watching from the outside.

What the educators apparently haven't realized yet is that experiential education is a double-edged sword. If you do something to learn it, then what you do, you learn. All the time you are in school, you learn through experience how to live in a dictatorship. In school you shut your notebook when the bell rings. You do not speak unless granted permission. You are guilty until proven innocent, and who will prove you innocent? You are told what to do, think, and say for six hours each day. If your teacher says sit up and pay attention, you had better stiffen your spine and try to get Bobby or Sally or the idea of Spring or the play you're writing off of your mind. The most constant and thorough thing students in school experience--and learn--is the antithesis of democracy.

When I was in sixth grade, I had the good fortune to learn that democracy in the "real world" is not a crime, at the same time that I learned (not for the first time) that democracy in schools *is* a crime. Two of my friends and I were disgusted by the state of our school lunches. After finding mold on the rolls one day and being generally fed up with the cardboard taste of things, we decided to take action. Stephanie and Stacey started a petition. Its purpose was a bit misspelled and unclear, but at the top it said something that meant, "Sign below if you are tired of revolting lunches, and put a check by your name if your roll was moldy on Tuesday." People signed the petition during lunch; we had three pages or so of sloppy signatures on wrinkly notebook paper.

Apparently some teachers got wind of what we were up to, and Miss Petersen (fake name) told Stephanie to give her the petition. After Miss Petersen looked at it through stern eyeglasses, she said she'd have to turn it over to the principal. Stephanie and I panicked. We held a secret meeting that afternoon in the hills and looked at each other with sick scared faces. We tried to convince ourselves that young criminals got off easily.

The next day Miss Petersen was moving a piano down the hall. Our brave friend Kelly walked by in his line on the way in from lunch. He saw the petition sitting on the piano, and he snatched it up. Miss Petersen didn't see him. He returned the petition to me. Go, team.

Stephanie and Stacey were summoned to the principal. He demanded to have the petition back, but since they didn't yet know about the Recovery, they said earnestly that Miss Petersen had it. He lectured them for their disrespect of authority, and said there was nothing wrong with the lunches, and that he didn't want to *ever* hear anything about petitions again, was that clear?

I took out my sky blue stationery with the mushrooms on it and wrote a letter to the governor. I apologized for not typing and for the wrinkliness and bad spelling of the petition. Then I explained why it was important that our lunches improve. I didn't say anything about the trouble we were in at school; I didn't want him to know how bad we were. I looked him up in the phone book, got his address, guessed on the zip code, and mailed it off. I was afraid he would report me to the principal, but I was ready to sacrifice myself for the cause.

The week after school was out, my father brought the mail in with a strange face. "Grace," he said, "Are you personally acquainted with Cecil Andrus?"

I tore the letter open. The governor said not to worry about my handwriting, that he would have responded sooner had I mailed the letter to his office instead of his house, and that he sympathized with my plight. He told me that school lunches weren't in his control, but he gave me the address of the people who could make a difference. Best--and most surprising--of all, he congratulated me on my "good citizenship" and encouraged me to keep on speaking up when something wasn't right in the world. During the next six years, the memory of that experience often helped me keep my hope and sanity while my friends and I were silenced, subtly and blatantly, again and again, by "authority."

Ah yes...

Authority.

Regardless of what the law or your teachers have to say about this, you are as human as anyone over the age of eighteen or twenty-one. Yet, "minors" are one of the most oppressed groups of people in the U.S., and certainly the most discriminated against legally.

It starts at home. Essentially, your parents can require you to do almost anything and forbid you to do almost anything. Fortunately, most parents try hard not to abuse this power. Yet, from a legal standpoint, the reason schools have so much tyrannical power over you is that they act *in loco parentis*--in place of the parent. As legal parental substitutes, they can search your locker or purse, tell you to be quiet, read your mail (notes), sometimes hit or "spank" you, speak rudely to you, and commit other atrocities--things I hope your parents would not do with a clean conscience, and things no sensible adult would do to another adult, for fear of losing a job or ending a friendship.

Many teenagers, of course, do clash with their parents to some extent. But most parents like and love their children enough to listen to their side, grant more freedom as they grow, back off when they realize they're overbearing, and generally be reasonable. The schools may do this with *some* "rebellious" students, but not usually, and not after a second or third "offense." Schools are too big, and the adults in them too overworked, to see "rebels" as people--instead, they'll get a permanent-ink "bad person" label and unreasonable treatment. Even in a small private school, authority is often unyielding and unfairly judgmental.

When I was substitute teaching in Oakland, California, one day they told me I could have a month-long job teaching choir and piano while the regular teacher had a baby. As it happened, I did have a fairly substantial musical background and could have handled at least that aspect of the job just fine. But the administrators showed no interest in my musical knowledge--all they wanted was someone who could maintain order for a month. When the principal introduced me to the choir class, one of the students raised his hand and asked, "Since she's not a music teacher, what are we supposed to do if she's not any good?"

The principal launched into a tirade about how it doesn't matter what you think of her teaching, you'll do exactly what she says and I don't want to hear about any problems from any of you; the state board of education decided she was good enough to be certified and that's all you need to know. Etc.

One of the worst things about this sort of arbitrary authority is it makes us lose our trust in natural authority--people who know what they're doing and could share a lot of wisdom with us. When they make you obey the cruel and unreasonable teacher, they steal your desire to learn from the kind and reasonable teacher. When they tell you to be sure to pick up after yourselves in the cafeteria, they steal your own natural sense of courtesy.

Many times, I have heard teachers resort defiantly to the proclamation that "The bottom line is, they need to do what we tell them because they're the kids and we're the adults." This concept that teenagers should obey simply because of their age no longer makes any sense to me. I can't figure out what it is based on, except adults' own egos. In this regard, school often seems like a circus arena full of authority-craving adults. Like trained animals, you are there to make them look good, to help them believe they are better than you.

But maybe you're not yet convinced. The sudden proclamation that you deserve to be free sounds too glib, too easy. Let's turn the question upside down:

Are there any good reasons you *shouldn't* have freedom?

Since schools supposedly exist to help you learn, the only legitimate answer they could offer is that you have to sacrifice freedom for the sake of learning. If learning and freedom were incompatible, having to choose would be tragic. But learning is NOT dependent upon school or upon slavery. If this doesn't strike you as obvious, I hope it will by the time you're finished reading chapter 2.

A wise friend of mine, who grew up in Germany under Hitler and later did time in American prison camps, startled me with a different reason you shouldn't have freedom. First, he agreed that schools are the antithesis of freedom. Then he said, but how can you really appreciate the freedom that comes with adulthood in a democracy, if you never know what it's like to live without it? I thought a lot about what he said, but I ended up deciding that a twelve year experiential lesson in bondage doesn't make freedom seem *precious*; it makes it seem *impossible*. It also misrepresents the nature of learning. After school, too many people continue to slap chains on themselves. Before school, nobody is so self-hating. Maybe after we abolish compulsory schooling in the twenty-first century we can set up voluntary month-long camps where people sit at desks and obey, just so they realize how lucky they are not to live their lives that way, just so they promise themselves to always live in celebration of their freedom.

Maybe you believe you aren't ready for freedom?

On some level, no one ever is; it's not a matter of age. People of all ages make mistakes with their freedom--becoming involved with destructive friends, choosing college majors they're not deeply interested in, buying houses with rotten foundations, clearcutting forests, breaking good marriages for dumb reasons. People cause tremendous pain and disaster, and you will never be so wise or perfect that you don't do stupid things. Sure, teenagers make mistakes. So do adults, and it seems to me adults have a harder time admitting and fixing theirs. While you are young, perhaps you are more likely to break your arm falling off a horse, but you are less likely to cause an oil spill or start a useless war. The only alternative to making mistakes is for someone to make all your decisions for you, in which case you will make their mistakes instead of your own. Obviously, that's not a life of integrity. Might as well start living, rather than merely obeying, before the age of eighteen.

Part of my work in writing this book involved contacting all the unschooled teenagers I could find. I asked them, each, as part of a questionnaire, what they considered the greatest advantages of unschooling. Almost unanimously, they agreed: *freedom!* Here are some typical comments:

"You can spend your time and energy doing things you like."

"I don't have to raise my hand to speak."

"Not being forced to do certain uninteresting subjects. Not sitting around for six hours doing something I don't like."

"Having time to do what I want."

"[In school] you had to have *permission* to go to the bathroom!"

"I feel sorry for the kids who have to go to 'prison' for 6-8 hours a day. I felt like we were the victims of a mass production enterprise."

"We are able to do so many things (go to the zoo, ride bikes, etc. etc.) while other kids are just sitting in classes and desks being bored..." (One reason this unschooler's sane parents kept her out of school was they "didn't like the idea of kids staying inside on sunny days.")

"Time, Time, Time. I have my life back for my own use. I am no longer having to wait and wait and wait for everyone else. I can concentrate on what I want to learn. I can work on my computer as long as I like. Or if I want to spend a lot of time diagramming sentences one day and no time again for two days, it's all right. Also we can travel and in general control our own lives! It is great!"

"I'm *free*!"

John Taylor Gatto, the 1991 New York State Teacher of the Year, puts it thus: "It is absurd and anti-life to move from cell to cell to the sound of a gong for every day of your natural youth in an institution that allows you no privacy and even follows you to the sanctuary of your home demanding that you do its 'homework.'"[*]

And in *GWS* (*Growing Without Schooling* magazine) #65, Lisa Asher writes about a day spent visiting her old high school:

....Despite the freedom that I have now, I feel limited by my past. I spent a total of 86 months in public schools, attending for at least part of every grade but seventh. There are still two years before I would graduate, but I don't plan to go back. I am angry with society for the time they made me waste. I wish I could have the time back again, and learn the way I feel I should have.

---

[*] John Gatto's speech as published in *The Sun*, June 1990 (Chapel Hill, NC), and also reprinted in *Utne Reader*, September/October 1990.

Near the end of the day, the hallways empty as the kids leave early to go to the beach. They have to come back tomorrow, and I don't. I don't have to get up at five to catch a bus at quarter to seven. I don't have to stay up 'til one studying for a test on something I don't care about, don't need, and am going to forget the minute the bell rings. I will not have to struggle with locks that the school is allowed to open anyway, fight my way through throngs of kids who once spent hours learning how to walk quietly in line, eat a sixty-cent lunch not fit to feed to pets, let alone growing teenagers and children. I won't be fighting for space in a tiny mirror mounted on a graffiti-plastered wall in the girls' room, where the door has been taken off the hinges to expose any tell-tale cigarettes. I won't be sleeping through classes where I am supposed to be learning math, doodling through classes where I am supposed to be learning history, or daydreaming through classes where I am supposed to be learning French.

I'll be sitting at home reading a book. Since I am not in school, perhaps I will learn something.

Chapter 2

school is
not for learning

"My schooling not only failed to   teach me
what it professed to be teaching, but prevented   me from
being educated to an extent which infuriates me when I think
of all I might have learned at home by myself."
--George Bernard Shaw, *Everybody's Political What's What*

"Schools and schooling are increasingly irrelevant to the great
enterprises of the planet. No one believes anymore that
scientists are trained in science classes or politicians in civics
classes or poets in English classes. The truth is that schools
don't really teach anything except how to obey orders."
--John Taylor Gatto, New York State Teacher of the Year 1991. *

"Men are born ignorant, not stupid; they are made stupid by
education."
--Bertrand Russell

"I very strongly believe that no homeschooler, or anyone else
for that matter, has a prejudice against learning something,
until someone makes them learn it."
--Unschooler Anne Brosnan, in *Growing Without Schooling (GWS) #76*

"An average second grader is a person slightly smarter than an
average third grader, because they've had a year less of
school."
--eighth grade student at The Colorado Springs School, May 1990

        The consensus is overwhelming. After dozens of nearly identical,
predictable conversations with friends and acquaintances, I'm no longer certain
this chapter is necessary.
        "Do you think you learned a lot in school?" I'd ask.

---

* John Gatto's speech as published in *The Sun*, June 1990 (Chapel Hill, NC), and also
reprinted in *Utne Reader*, September/October 1990.

"Oh no, of course not," came the typical reply, "I mean, I memorized a lot of facts for tests, but I don't remember any of it except a few things I was really interested in."

The unschooled teenagers who responded to my questionnaire offered similar comments. "The one thing I didn't do in school," wrote Jason Lescalleet, 14, "was learn."

Becky Cauthen, 14, remembers school: "I had to sit and wait for others to complete their work."

Patrick Meehan, 14, said "Many teachers seem to dislike students who ask questions."

Benjamin Israel Billings, 16, said, "I have never had a liking for regimented things and school is so strict that I found more pressure to get good grades (cheating, copying and lucky guessing) than to learn my subjects."

Indeed, many of these teenagers had quit school because of "lack of learning" or intellectual boredom.

Once out of school, things improved. I asked unschooled teens how they would rate their "academic" knowledge and skills in comparison to that of their schooled peers. Most of them felt like Kevin Sellstrom, 14, who said, "Far superior. More knowledgeable in most subjects including common sense."

Many teenagers angrily complained that school had wasted their time. Without it, they said, "you learn more in less time." Jason Lescalleet says that out of school "I get to learn instead of sitting with my head down."

This common sense we all seem to share--people don't need school to learn--is proved in a more
academic and official way by the work of Dr. Brian Ray's *Home School Researcher*. Ray and other researchers have shown that homeschoolers' academic test scores are consistently higher than school students'. [*]

Why don't people learn in school?

The most basic and overwhelming reason shoots us right back into the last chapter. Our brains and spirits are the freest things in the universe. Our bodies can live in chains, but our intellects cannot. It's that simple. The mind *will* be free, or it will be dead. It can be numbed, quieted, and restrained so that it memorizes names of Portuguese explorers and plods through grades one to twelve. If it is fiercely alive and teamed up with a forgiving spirit, it may find a way to be free even in school, and stay awake that way. But these strategies are defenses, not full-fledged learning. Albert Einstein, as compassionate and insightful as he was brilliant, said

---

* Information from National Home Education Research Institute, 25 West Cremona St., Seattle, WA 98119; (206) 283-3650. Especially see their 1986 publication *A comparison of home schooling and conventional schooling: With a focus on learner outcomes*.

It is, in fact, nothing short of a miracle that the modern methods of instruction have not yet entirely strangled the holy curiosity of inquiry; for this delicate little plant, aside from stimulation, stands mainly in need of freedom; without this it goes to wrack and ruin without fail. It is a very grave mistake to think that the enjoyment of seeing and searching can be promoted by means of coercion and a sense of duty.

There are other reasons school prevents learning too--fear of "bad" grades, lack of faith in one's abilities (usually due to previous unpleasant experiences with grades--including A minuses), an occasional uninformed teacher, illogical or inherently dull teaching methods and books, lack of individual attention, oxygen-starved classrooms.

These problems are the ones the educators can see. They exhaust themselves seeking solutions--hiring the smartest teachers they can get, searching the ends of the earth for easier ways to learn spelling, providing counseling services, buying textbooks with technicolor photographs, working hard on "anticipatory sets" (the beginning part of lessons which are supposed to "grab students' attention"). Most of these educators--especially when they are teachers rather than superintendents of school boards--do some good. If lots of people continue to go to school, I hope that the idealistic educators continue their efforts. These efforts make school more pleasant, the same way that clean sheets and warm blankets make a prison more pleasant than do bare scratchy mattresses with thin covers.

Their efforts cannot, however, make you free. Even if they encourage you to write research papers on topics that interest you, even if they reduce the amount of homework they assign, they cannot encourage you to joyfully follow your own intellectual mysteries, except in your spare time after your homework. To do so would be to completely undermine the basic structure of the schools.

Because they can never make you free, schools can never allow you to learn fully.

Love of learning

If you had always been free to learn, you would follow your natural tendency to find out as fully as possible about the things that interest you, cars or stars. We are all born with what they call "love of learning," but it dives off into an elusive void when we go to school.

After all, school does not help you focus on what you love, because it insists that you devote equal time to six or so "subjects." While interviewing an unschooled actress for *GWS* #73, editor Susannah Sheffer made an astute observation: "It's funny that people think kids should be well-rounded but don't seem to have the same expectations of adults. Adults seem to realize you can't do everything." In *Walden*, Thoreau laments, "Our lives are frittered away by detail," and admonishes, "Simplicity, simplicity, simplicity! I say, let your affairs be as two or three, and not a hundred or a thousand."

Of course, quitting school doesn't guarantee that you are going to learn more in *every* subject than you did in school. If you hate math in school, and decide to continue studying it outside of school, it's possible that you won't enjoy it any more or learn it much better, although being able to work without ridicule at your own speed will help. You *will* see a dramatically wonderful change in the way you learn about the things that interest you. What's more, you will find out that you are interested in things that haven't yet caught your attention, and that you can love at least some of the things which repulsed you in school.

Beyond the love and pursuit of something specific, there's another quality you might also call love of learning. It's simple curiosity, which kills more tired assumptions than cats. Some people move around with their ears and eyes perked open like raccoons, ready to find out something new and like it. Do everything you can to cultivate this characteristic; it will enliven your life immeasurably.

However, curiosity is another stubborn quality that thrives on freedom; therefore, school squishes it. Curiosity is an active habit--it needs the freedom to explore and move around and get your hands into lots of pots. It needs the freedom to watch TV with the remote control and flip through the channels at will. It needs the freedom to thumb through *Science News* and stop only where you want to. It needs the freedom to browse through your library's whole shelf of poetry. It needs the freedom to visit the zoo solo, spending an hour with the prairie dog colony and walking right past the giraffes, or vice versa.

Curiosity puts itself on hold when it isn't allowed to move at its own pace. I am thinking of the week-long field trip our middle school took to Washington, D.C., and of how my own curiosity took a nap during most of our "guided tours," even at the "fun" places like Williamsburg and Jamestown, and how I raced around excitedly when we had an unleashed day at the Smithsonian.

On the up side, the ironic truth is that everyone loves to learn--or at least did as a baby, and can get to be that way again. As John Holt points out, "Children do not need to be made to learn about the world, or shown how. They want to, and they know how." In fact, it could all add up to a great opening line the night you decide to break the news to your parents: "Mom, Dad, I'd really like to quit school because I'd rather learn."

Report Cards Vs. Freedom

Schools do have a few K-Mart quality substitutes for freedom. They know that if you dry up people's love for learning, you will certainly dry up their learning itself, unless you come through with a handy replacement: Pressure. Threats. Bribes. Tests. A's, B's, C's, D's, and F's. Yes, indeed, school does have one way to make you learn that you might NOT easily duplicate in a free life. Without an exam on Friday, maybe you wouldn't learn how to solve differential equations. Without a twenty-five dollar prize from

Mommy, maybe you wouldn't memorize the periodic table in order to get an A in chemistry. Maybe the pressure of grades and all the expectant hoopla surrounding them *do* help you to learn more.

Temporarily.

The day after the test, or the week after school's out, will you even take time to kiss your fact collection goodbye as it floats off on the breeze? In the long run, pressure is an ineffective substitute for curiosity and freedom to pursue those things you love, because people only remember and think about things they use or care about.

A lot of teachers believe learning depends on grades, because they are only used to seeing education take place in the forced environment of school. Physicist Frank Oppenheimer had a clearer head, putting massive energy into non-school learning environments (he started the Exploratorium, for example). About learning without grades, he said, "People built fires to keep warm long before Galileo invented the thermometer."*

Furthermore, the emphasis schools put on grades *prevents* healthy learning, even if it coaxes you into quickie learning.

Report Cards vs. Learning

Bad grades start a vicious circle. They make you feel like a failure. A sense of failure cripples you and *prevents* you from succeeding. Therefore, you continue to get bad grades and continue to be stifled. Of course, bad grades are relative--in many families B's are bad grades, especially if the First Born Son did better or Uncle Harold went to Yale. Feeling like a failure is a self-fulfilling prophecy, which is why most high-school dropouts make statistics that the schoolpeople love to quote. Think about it. Would you continue to enjoy (and improve at) skateboarding or hiking if someone scrutinized your every move, reported to your parents, and acted as if you'd never succeed in life if you didn't finesse your double kick flip before Friday, or add ten pounds to your pack and reach the pass by noon?

Obviously, we all need both privacy and respect to enjoy (learn) any activity. By privacy, I don't mean solitude. I mean freedom from people poking their noses into your business or "progress."

People assume that grades tell how smart you are, but of course they don't. They mostly reflect how well you cooperated by doing what your teachers said. They also reflect whether your teachers like you. Grades don't mean you can't read, write, or think. They don't show whether you can find out how to do something you believe in and then follow through and do it. They don't show the most fundamental aspect of intelligence--whether you learn from your experiences and "mistakes." They don't show whether you live with courage, compassion, intelligence, curiosity, or common sense. Even in an objective scientific sense, grades and test scores are not accurate

---

* See Hilde S. Hein, *The Exploratorium: The Museum as Laboratory* (Smithsonian Institution Press, 1990).

measurements of your intelligence. (A very interesting book on the subject of intelligence measurement is *The Mismeasure of Man*, by Stephen Jay Gould.)

The world and its complex terrible wonderful webs of civilization are far bigger and older than our nineteenth-century factory-style compulsory schooling system. There is room for all kinds of people--those who love books, and those who'd rather build things and take them apart all day, not just for an hour in woodshop or autoshop. There's room for those who would rather wander dreaming on a glacier, and perhaps awaken the rest of us with some truthful words in the tradition of Thoreau, Ed Abbey, Annie Dillard. There's room for those who want to make lasagna and homemade French bread and apple pie all day. None of these callings are better or worse than others. None mean failure as a human being, but they may likely cause "failure" in a dull system that you never asked to be a part of in the first place.

Furthermore, bad grades and other consequences of not doing your "work" punish you for what you *do* do (making friends, reading extracurricular novels) as much as for what you don't do. Tell me why, if you want to spend two days following badger tracks, you should be penalized for your choice with "zeroes" in five or six gradebooks and a truancy to boot.

Good grades are often equally dangerous. They encourage you to forsake everything worthwhile that you might love, just to keep getting them. When schoolpeople give you good grades, you give them your unquestioning loyalty in return. It makes me think of the Algonkian Indians who gave Manhattan Island to the Dutch in exchange for six dollars' worth of trinkets. We are not talking here about fair bargains; we are talking about manipulation and colossal rip-off.

Good grades, moreover, are addictive. You start to depend on them for your sense of self-worth, and then it becomes nearly impossible to do anything that will jeopardize them. When you have good grades, you have something to lose, and so you stop taking risks. The best things in life come from taking risks. My little sister, who is smarter than I am, always got bad grades. She also has an easier time being honest and direct with people than I do. I think these two bits of data are closely connected. The system never gave her any gold stars, so she didn't feel obligated to give it any soft false silent agreement in return. (On the other hand, she ended up with plenty of unnecessary failure-complex to work through.)

Finally, **grades confuse the meaning of education.** Patrick Meehan, 14-year-old unschooler, wrote me, "Giving grades puts the wrong focus on learning. It points a student toward competition and learning for the wrong reasons: to make grades rather than to become educated."

Some more ways that schools prevent people from learning:

Schools require passivity. When I taught language arts and history, I learned far more about them than I ever had in school and--in some ways--even in college. That's because teaching is an active role: seeking out and selecting readings, designing assignments, evaluating others' work. Sitting and doing those assignments and receiving those grades is the bottom of the learning ladder.

Schools cram you too full too fast. I don't mean they challenge you. I mean they throw too much busywork in your face. Being in school is like being incredibly hungry and sitting at Burger King eating too much, too fast to be satisfied, and then puking it up. Good learning, like good eating, is not only mental and physical, but also spiritual. Generally, you can satisfy the craving only in calm. If you don't have sufficient time or peace to digest knowledge, it only gives you a headache.

Schoolpeople care more about appearances than about learning. Just before a field trip, an administrator I worked with talked to students about "expectations." "We just want you to look nice," she said, "that's the most important thing." I don't think she heard herself, or quite meant to say that, but I couldn't forget it--as it says in the Bible, the mouth speaks what the heart is full of. In my own classroom, I forever harped on the way students sat. It didn't matter how well they could concentrate curled up on the couch; I was petrified that another adult would walk in and decide I was Incompetent. So most days students sat with their feet flat on the floor, stiff-spined, uncomfortable and trying to learn anyway.

School isn't challenging enough if you're academically inclined. It's not merely that school is too easy; you are not necessarily a straight-A student and in fact may feel overwhelmed by piles of homework. But so much of it is busywork with no connection to the molten cores of physics, mythology, philosophy. It also doesn't help that most of your fellow students would rather *not* be reading Milton.

Schools present learning backwards, emphasizing answers instead of questions. Answers are dead ends, even when they're "correct." Questions open the galaxies. In *Organic Gardening*, October 1982, Robert Rodale wrote,

I've been out of school for over 30 years, yet no matter how I manage to arrange my life, I still keep learning. In fact, I seem to learn faster the further in time I get from my school experience....

When you are in school, you are asked the questions, and are expected to be able to find the answers. Presumably, when you are sufficiently filled up with correct answers, you are educated, and then released.

I now believe, though, that real learning occurs when you become able to ask important questions. Then you are on the doorstep of wisdom, because by asking important questions you project your mind into the exploration of new territory. In my experience, very few people have learned how important is the asking of good questions, and even fewer have made a habit of asking them. Even in my own case, I had to wait until I'd almost totally forgotten the experience of schooling to be able to switch my mind into the asking as well as the answering mode...

School asks you to get stressed out attaining mediocrity in six or so subjects rather than be amazing at one or two you love. Some schools and educators *believe* in cultivating students' uniquenesses, but without major structural changes, they can't. As long as focusing on algebra means you get a C in psychology, or as long as you get lectured for falling asleep in history on mornings after late gymnastics meets, you are being pushed away from excellence toward anxious shoddiness.

Schools are overly obsessed with and manipulative of the learning process. Take lesson plans, for instance. A proper lesson plan is supposed to include an "anticipatory set" (attention getter), a purpose statement, a diagnostic check (a few questions to see how many people already know how to organize a five-paragraph essay, or whatever), "input" (lecture, filmstrip, etc.), monitoring ("Johnny, now that I've explained how to organize a five-paragraph essay, please remind the class what your first paragraph should accomplish"), modeling (reading the class a five-paragraph that got an A), guided practice (everyone begins essaying while you stroll around and answer questions), and independent practice (they finish the essay that night instead of watching the sparrows on the windowsill).

This kind of planning reflects some sense and logic, I admit. But two danger signals zap my little brain. First, all this strategy is just a mild substitute for Pressure. It's not necessary to manipulate someone if they already want to do or learn what you want them to do or learn. In other words, all this scientific bullshit is only necessary because education professors know how unpleasant it is to sit in school all day. The will to freedom rears its stubborn head again. Therefore, they try to mix your head around a little to make it work.

Second, messing with your mind this way is harmful and foolish the same way that it is harmful and foolish to try to "manage" nature. After centuries of idiocy, people are finally learning to respect the complexity and self-regulation of nature. No longer does America assume that we can help deer by killing off all the wolves, or help forests by putting out all of their fires. We are beginning to acquire a bit of necessary humility, beginning to see that when we interfere, we usually ruin.

We need to develop a similar respect for the natural processes of human minds. The most difficult thing most people ever learn to do is talk. Yet, everyone learns it on their own, without a teacher or a briber or a threatener or props or games. In families where adults read to children and read in front of children, leave all kinds of books around for children to look at, and answer their children's questions about reading, people learn to read with the same pleasure and confidence that accompanies their acquisition of speech. In general, people learn and grow as long as they are not prevented from doing so.

School won't answer the door when real chances to learn come knocking. There's nothing wrong with planning and setting goals--they help us to accomplish big things like writing books or pulling off a bike trip across Turkey. But life is unexpected. Sometimes it offers us something more glorious than what we'd planned, and we lose if we're not ready to let go of our agenda. Christians call it surrendering to the will of God. Eastern mysticists call it letting go of ego, floating in the flow. Whatever you call it, school has little room for it.

For example: in Washington, D.C., our self-imposed schedule demanded that we visit the Capitol for a predetermined length of time and then proceed directly to the next attraction. This schedule left no time for what might happen on the way into the Capitol. What did happen was that on the steps, five students and two teachers stopped to talk to a Vietnam vet fasting for U.S. reconciliation with Vietnam. He'd swallowed nothing but juice for seventy days. We listened to him with awe. At one point he asked, "Do you know what constitutional amendment guarantees me the right to sit here and talk about this?" Young, who always had the answers to all the questions, said, "The first!"

"Very good," pronounced another teacher, who at that moment had arrived on the scene. We all jumped. What did "very good" have to do with anything? She continued: "And which amendment prohibited slavery?" "The thirteenth," answered Young. "Exactly! And with that, let's be on our way," suggested our chaperone brightly. The rest of us looked at each other in vague incredulity; the disruption of learning was more awkwardly obvious than usual. Then we trudged up the steps behind her.

(By the way, this event also makes a perfect example of the way teachers and administrators are not allowed to be themselves in school, being required instead to fulfill ridiculous authoritarian roles. The woman who disrupted our fascination was as curious and human as any of the rest of us, but at the moment she felt a particularly strong responsibility to keep us on schedule. Later she told me she wished she could have encouraged a longer conversation.

I understood her position exactly, thinking of all the times I'd told students to come away from the window and sit at their tables, knowing whatever they saw or dreamed out the window was more important than writing a short story they didn't want to write.)

In general, school screens us off from reality--no matter how we define reality. Is reality in books, in the intellect? School censors more than it reveals. Does reality lurk in raw adventure? In religion? In culture? In friendship and community? In work? School just gets in the way.

Not only does your actual time in school block out learning, but it also prevents you from learning outside of school. It drains your time and energy. After you write your descriptive essay and review your Spanish verbs and it's time for bed, how are you supposed to think or write the poem you were imagining in history? How are you supposed to find energy to want to go outside and look at the newly sprung buds on the cottonwood tree?

School wouldn't be nearly so oppressive if it didn't demand center stage in your life. More times than I can count, I've heard adults tell teenagers, with apalling arrogance, that if they don't start getting their homework in on time, they'll have to quit drama, or chorale, or hockey, or their job, or sleeping over at friends' houses, or whatever it is that they love. Imagine a concert pianist getting ready for a performance. As she throws on her coat, her husband blocks the doorway. "Oh, honey," he says, "I'm afraid I can't let you go. You haven't prepared next week's menus, and you've left the music room in a mess. Until you get your priorities straight, you'll just have to stay at home."

Finally, schools play a nasty trick on all of us. They make "learning" so unpleasant and frightening that they scare many people away from countless pleasures: evenings browsing in libraries, taking an edible plants walk at the nature center, maybe even working trigonometry problems for the hard beauty and challenge of it. Luckily (and ironically), many things we learn from are not *called* "learning experiences" by schools, so we don't attach that schoolish learning stigma to everything. But by calling school "learning," schools make learning sound like an excruciatingly boring way to waste a nice afternoon. That's low.

*

Well, perhaps you I hear you say, *Indeed I do not learn much in school, but I do learn a little. If I quit, I won't learn anything.*

Forgive my rudeness, but that's upside-down-thinking. As John Holt said, if it's the medicine that makes you sick, *more* medicine will just make you sicker. And if you quit taking it, you'll get well.

You wouldn't suggest that you can't learn without school, if school hadn't torn your faith in yourself in the first place. Before you went to school, you taught yourself to speak. After you leave school, you will teach yourself how to live on your own and how to find out answers to questions that interest you. Even now, you learn on your own, every time you do *anything* of your own free will--kicking a soccer ball, falling in love, playing on computers, riding horses, reading books, thinking, disobeying rules.

In school, too, you already teach yourself; you just do it in the company of people who take the credit for your progress. I talk a lot with my brother Ned about education. He got marvelous grades in high school, won a city-wide contest sponsored by Hewlett-Packard, and went on to graduate from Caltech with a degree in electrical engineering. He learned in school, he says, because of the reading he did and the questions he thought about. Teachers had little to do with it. If the laboratory equipment and other resources in high school had been high quality, it could have helped immensely--but it wasn't, so it couldn't. He was in school, but in school he taught himself. And he learned more at home, on his own--building a computer, taking things apart, messing around.

Yes, when your teacher talks he shares his knowledge, which may be high quality fascinating knowledge or low quality dull knowledge. But your teacher cannot bridge the gap between what you know and what you want to know. For his words to "educate" you, you must welcome them, think about them, find somewhere in your mind to organize them, and remember them. Your learning is your job, not your teachers' job. And all you need to start with is desire. You *don't* need a schoolteacher to get knowledge--you can get it from looking at the world, from reading, from watching films, from conversations, from reading, from asking questions, from experience. As John Holt says in *GWS* #40, "The most important thing any teacher has to learn, not to be learned in any school of education I ever heard of, can be expressed in seven words: *Learning is not the product of teaching.* Learning is the product of the activity of learners..."

In fact, in today's information-laden USA, anyone who has acquired basic skills in reading, writing, and math computation can learn nearly anything they want to, on their own. Books, libraries, generous and knowledgeable people, and other resources make this possible. Young or old, anyone can in fact become an expert in a field they love, if they are not restrained and occupied by the petty nonsense of school or meaningless work. Part of learning is often contacting and receiving help from others, but learning does not require a boss, a rigid schedule, a schoolroom, or most of the other things schools provide. Nor does it require a whip. Until school destroys the joy and naturalness of learning, young children revel wide-eyed in the intricacies of their world, learning to talk without teachers, asking questions, growing. In her book *Wishcraft*, Barbara Sher says:

> All the people we call "geniuses" are men and women who somehow escaped having to put that curious, wondering child in themselves to sleep. Instead, they devoted their lives to equipping that child with the tools and skills it

needed to do its playing on an adult level. Albert Einstein was playing, you know. He was able to make great discoveries precisely because he kept alive the originality and delight of a small child exploring its universe for the first time.

Well, but what about all the things school has to make me learn?

What about them? The good things schools have are equipment and teachers. The bad things they have are schedules, grades, compulsory attendance, authority, dull textbooks, busywork, sterile atmospheres, too much homework, and teachers. You do not need to go to school to have teachers (or helpers, tutors, mentors) or equipment. If you want school teachers and equipment without school, maybe you can swing it. See chapter 19.

But what about all the mysterious techniques and scientific approaches they use to make me learn? Don't teachers know a lot more than I do about learning?

Hell no. Most teachers know about classroom management--how to threaten, manipulate, or cajole a class into quietly doing its work. Many can explain things clearly. Some even overflow with true enthusiasm for their subject, so that a few students are infected with a love of that same subject. All this, however, is a sorry substitute for the recognition that you have a mind of your own and are capable of using it. Teachers would be infinitely more helpful if they knew a lot and cheerfully answered questions, dispensed wisdom, and pointed out resources--but only when you asked them to.

As for all those mysterious techniques, relax. Nothing happens in school that can't happen elsewhere, and in fact most of what happens there is nothing but a shadow of real world learning. After all, nothing complicated takes place in school. In order to "learn," you are made to read, write and receive criticism on written work, do other exercises and have them corrected, listen to a teacher talk, discuss ideas or information with teachers or with classmates under teacher supervision, conduct laboratory experiments, receive individual attention, and "do" things, fashionably called "experiential education." Almost all of these school things you can do on your own. Substitute "wise adult" for "teacher," and you don't need school for *any* of them. Let's have a quick, demystifying, analytical look at these schoolish methods, one by one.

Reading:

Which has more books, a school or a library?

Which has better books, a school or a library?

Where are you made to read deadly textbooks?
a) the library, b) school, c) while exploring a bog

Where can you read at your own pace, for your own pleasure, without being tested and tricked and otherwise disrupted?
a) the library, b) school, c) a bog, d) a and c

Enough said.

Writing:
Perhaps you've always bought your pens and pencils from a machine at school. I'm here today to tell you that they can also be found at the corner drugstore. Paper too. Yes, it's true. And what more do you need to write without school?

In school, you write five-paragraph persuasive essays (although who ever heard of a five-paragraph persuasive essay showing its face in *Harper's* or *The Atlantic?*) and short stories and essay test answers and poems and whatever else your teachers demand of you. Out of school, you can do all of the above and whatever else you demand of yourself.

Don't you need a writing teacher to write? Well, no, probably not. If you read frequently and you have something to say, most of the logistics will take care of themselves. If you *don't* have something to say, you don't need to write. (I'm not being sarcastic. Why chatter on paper just to chatter on paper?) The reason many teenagers struggle violently with writing is that like most people, they are not burning with desire to communicate something particular in writing on a weekly basis.

Even if they are burning with that desire from time to time, they know that their five-paragraph essay is destined for their teacher's and maybe classmates' eyes only. When you're communicating with just twenty people, it often makes more sense to simply talk.

Sure, you may be confused about grammatical rules or mechanics. Books and occasional people can clear it all up for you. You don't need six years of "English" to make sense on paper.

On the other hand, if you are a serious future novelist or journalist, you might want to enroll in a writing workshop or course--but you will find the quality and seriousness you need in a college or independent course, not in school.

Doing exercises and having them corrected:
Many courses--especially math--consist mainly of working problems and having them checked. Sometimes--especially in math--working these problems is truly necessary for absorbing course material. In others, exercises are busywork--assigned arbitrarily so you don't feel you're "getting away" without doing anything.

When exercises seem valuable to you, take heart. Doing algebra problems in bed at ten AM produces exactly the same effect as doing them at ten AM in a classroom. Decent math books (which is to say, Saxon books and a few others) are clearly written. Most have answers in the back. When they don't, you can usually find a separate answer key.

Listening to Your Teacher Talk:
When you have a knowledgeable and/or wise and/or funny teacher, listening to her weave stories and lectures can be delightful. Assuming, that is, that she feels "allowed" by other schoolpeople to be herself and say what she truly knows and thinks. Unfortunately, this is seldom so, since most schoolpeople always worry about offending any of the parents who might re-elect them, and therefore strive to keep their teachers as mousy and un-opinionated as possible.

This is one of the fundamental badnesses of schools (and politics): almost everyone lives in fear of their superiors because their superiors live in fear of their constituents (voters, i.e. parents). Therefore, all the interesting ideas get censored:

Your teacher can't say, "Wait a minute. What's fueling this so-called war on drugs?" because Johnny's mother will call the principal outraged in her assumption that a teacher (of all people) is encouraging drug use, and the principal will worry that the superintendent will hear about it, and ask the teacher to please not talk about drugs in a deviant way. Your teacher probably can't say, at least not with force and conviction, that the United States isn't perfect or that the government still cheats Native Americans, or that children have no rights in this country or that Thoreau, Martin Luther King Jr., Ghandi, and many other heroes all believed in and acted on one's duty to peacefully break unjust laws. Ridiculous as it seems, schoolpeople would rather keep your head and mouth empty and uncontroversial than risk their jobs by giving teachers free rein. "No one is fired for hiding the truth from children," writes John Holt, "But many are fired for telling the truth."

Jessica Vitkus puts her finger on a lot of it when she describes one of her days as a substitute teacher:

We're talking about the upcoming marriage of Romeo and Juliet. And this girl who keeps pulling fuzz balls off her sweater points out that it's kind of gross that a 14-year-old girl would be getting married. "Had you even kissed a boy when you were 14?" she asks me. Obviously, part of me would really love to take off my shoes and sit on the floor and tell the class how my first kiss (I was in eighth grade) was nothing like Juliet's and that I don't think people fall in love at first sight. Those are some of the things I think about when I read. But they're the kind of thoughts I save for my friends. And in the classroom, I can't act like a friend because it's hard (and not too effective) to tell a friend to be quiet or that she may not go to her locker. Harsh as it may sound, teachers and students are not equals, and I have to maintain a certain distance. This also means that I can't 100 percent act like myself--which to me is the hardest thing about teaching. I smile at the girl to let her know that I heard her question, but I don't answer it. She gets the hint.*

When your teacher is *not* so knowledgeable, wise, funny--or confident that she can keep both her job and her honesty--listening to her lecture lag along is worse than watching *A Nightmare on Elm Street* for the ninth time.

And if you are especially on top of things, I bet you have figured out by now that people lecture in other places besides Your High School History Room.

If you like, go listen to one or ninety talks outside of school. There are lectures at local colleges and universities, libraries, museums, etc., and courses to be audited at colleges and universities. (Most college professors are *expected* to be controversial or at least original.)

However, a hunch tells me that although most people are moved by an occasional dynamic or profound speaker, few want to spend lots of hours every day on their butts soaking in someone else's words. It's not only too passive for most of us--more passive than reading--but also too slow.

Class discussion:
Exploring ideas with people interested in similar subjects is undoubtedly one of life's finest wines, as well as a stimulating way to "learn," and thus please all the adults who need you to do that in ways they understand. Especially when you want to clarify, resolve, or broaden your opinions, you must talk. Many of the best books, institutions, organizations, etc., began in, or fed on, talk. For example, J.R.R. Tolkien and C.S. Lewis met regularly to talk about their work in a small writers' group they called The Inklings.

Unfortunately, the difference between most "classroom discussions" and real, honest talk is equivalent to the difference between stale Wonder Bread and the rich warmth, sweetness, and complexity of homemade cinnamon rolls.

Imagine instead: you and your friends in front of a fire, feet on the sofa, planning how to get CFC-produced polystyrene foam banned in your city. Inventing an ideal society. Improvising haiku on the spot. Debating why Hamlet did what he did. Deciding what kind of research to carry out with your shared science lab. Considering the pros and cons of gun control. Why settle for a dismal school version of the real thing?

Experience:
Like many cumbersome terms that issue from schoolpeople's jaws, "experiential education" is an inflated, fancy term referring to a simple concept: learning by doing. School examples are learning government by experimenting with student governments and courts, or learning about

---

* Jessica Vitkus, "Hello, I'm Your Substitute Teacher," *Sassy* magazine, March 1991, p. 37.

literature partly by giving readings of students' own sonnets. The school I taught at deservedly attracts many students because of its experiential emphasis, consisting mainly of purposeful travel. Obviously, learning Spanish by staying with a family in Madrid beats learning Spanish by merely drilling in a classroom. Learning architectural design by sketching adobe buildings throughout the southwest beats learning architectural design by merely reading textbooks.

The Educators are on to something here. They figured out that life and the world are exciting, so they would try to squeeze a little more of it in between desks, chairs, walls, schedules, limited resources and transportation, and standardized tests. Lucky for you, if you quit school, you are automatically swimming in that whole big world that you call living and they call "experiential education."

By the way. An absurdity in the concept of experiential education is that "doing" has to be organized in some particular scientific-schoolish way in order for "learning" to take place. Worse, teaching this way implies that the experience would be unimportant if it were not engineered to generate "education" also. As you and I know, there would be little meaning in building and programming a computer solely to learn about electronics or math. Rather, knowledge about these subjects would happen naturally as a by-product of all the fun you were having if you just happened to want to build and program a computer. But the Educators haven't yet got their priorities straight. They hang on to an awful habit of thinking that school is reality and the universe only exists to make school "more educational." Instead, of course, the big wet world is reality and school should serve only to help us live better lives in that reality, not to block it off.

Individual attention:
If you attend a small school, or have enrolled in small classes, you may also be lucky enough to receive frequent individual attention from teachers. Everyone has a different learning style, and many people prefer to learn directly from people rather than from books. "When I want to learn something," says my friend Lesly, "I don't like to go read a book; I want someone to show me how to do it." Private conversations, whether they focus on your next screenplay, on why you messed up on half the equations on yesterday's algebra, or on how to sew a straighter seam, can be truly helpful.

One of the things that kept me going at CSS was my class schedule in which I met daily with most of my 26 students to discuss their writing. Though these conferences rarely strayed from the "point," they also enabled me to know each student well, making the whole thing a lot more human and a lot more fun. In fact, individual instruction is probably the only valuable instruction most of us get in school.

If you attend a typical public school, as I did, your teachers can only fantasize about having personal contact with all of their students. But if you're accustomed to it and you like it, you will like a full-blown relationship with a mentor better. And if there are particular teachers you especially like, you can likely continue those relationships, either in an informal way or perhaps by hiring them as weekly tutors. Anyway, when adults aren't giving you grades, it's much easier to learn from them and enjoy their company without guilt or anxiety.

*

End of analysis. School did not invent these activities and does not own them; they can be found outside of school in much fresher, juicier form. Schools have no monopoly on learning, or even on "school" methods of learning.

In the end, the secret to learning is so simple: forget about it. Think only about whatever you love. Follow it, do it, dream about it. One day, you will glance up at your collection of Japanese literature, or trip over the solar oven you built, and it will hit you: learning was there all the time, happening by itself.

chapter 3

what
school is for

If schools get in the way of learning, why do we have them? Why did anyone ever think they would work?

Compulsory schooling in this country started because of some lofty, beautiful hopes for democracy, unfortunately mixed up with a lethal dose of arrogance and tainted with a few other impurities. Thomas Jefferson, John Adams, and other early American leaders argued that in a democracy, people needed to have knowledge and wisdom in order to make decent decisions together. Also, they hoped America could be a country where "everyone" (meaning all the white boys who hadn't immigrated too recently) had an equal chance to succeed. Thus, they all needed a chance to learn and read and grow as children, rather than be packed off to factories for hard labor, rather than be shut off from the world of books and ideas.

People hadn't always thought this way; in most of the old kingdoms of Europe, no one particularly wanted Johnny to learn to read, because Johnny's purpose in life was to herd cows and do what the king said. In England, compulsory school for poor people had started in the fifteenth century, but not in support of democracy. Instead, the idea was to train the destitute for jobs so that rich people wouldn't have to support them with tax money.*

In other words, the ideals that led to American public education were idealistic and revolutionary ones. How wonderful if the people who held them could have been democratic enough to trust others to make the most of an opportunity.

If so, we might have had one bonanza extravaganza of an educational system, one in which children were legally guaranteed their basic material needs--shelter and food--until a certain age--sixteen, eighteen, twenty-two, whatever--and allowed to freely explore the physical and cultural worlds. Libraries and books could have been accessible to all. Tutors and academic specialists could have been paid by the government to answer people's questions, to teach them more intensely when a student wanted that. Apprenticeships could have been available, as well as open laboratories staffed

---

* See Lawrence A. Cremin, *American Education: The National Experience 1783-1876* (Harper and Row, 1980), Harry G. Good, *A History of American Education* (Macmillan, 1962), and Lawrence Kotin and William F. Aikman, *Legal Foundations of Compulsory School Attendance* (Kennikat Press, Port Washington, NY, 1980).

by scientists ready to let young people assist in their research. Children and teenagers could have roamed around sticking their hands into frog ponds, bread dough, and art supplies. They could have invented gadgets, cataloged fossils, and written poetry at will.

Instead, the people who thought up American education believed in no one but themselves. They did not trust children to learn, and they did not trust the "lower classes" to want their children to learn. I doubt any kind of intellectual freedom even occurred to them. They believed that in order to have education, it would have to be forced. Thus came compulsory schooling. They modeled the American system on the German one, which never pretended and was not intended to create a democracy.

Another reason we have schools even though they prevent learning is that schools are intended not *only* for learning. They have other purposes too, somewhat less charming.

Although compulsory schooling was begun in this country mainly in hopes of educating people worthy of democracy, other goals also imbedded themselves in the educational system. One was **the goal of creating obedient factory workers who did not waste time by talking to each other or daydreaming.** Historian Lawrence A. Cremin writes, "...There was one educational problem that proved ubiquitous wherever factories did appear, and that was the problem of nurturing and maintaining industrial discipline." Cremin goes on to explain that before the industrial revolution, people had scheduled their lives in harmony with the seasons, holidays, and their own preferences. But factories

> required a shift from agricultural time to the much more precise categories of industrial time, with its sharply delineated and periodized work day. Moreover, along with this shift in timing and rhythm, the factory demanded concomitant shifts in habits of attention and behavior, under which workers could no longer act according to whim or preference but were required instead to adjust to the needs of the productive process and the other workers involved in it....The schools taught [factory behavior], not only through textbook preachments, but also through the very character of their organization--the grouping, periodizing, and objective impersonality were not unlike those of the factory. [*]

This industrial indoctrination continues full force in schools today, turning out people who conveniently obey authority, don't think too much, and work hard for little reward.

---

[*] *Lawrence A. Cremin, American Education: The National Experience 1783-1876* (Harper and Row, 1980), pp. 350-1.

Another early goal of American education was religious; in fact, the first compulsory education act came in 1642 in Massachusetts, one of the strictest puritan colonies. According to the puritans, "that old deluder Satan" kept "men from the knowledge of the Scriptures." Though we no longer officially learn to read in order to read the Bible, schools preserve some rather smelly leftovers from this influence. The puritan assumption that everyone would emerge from school with the same religious beliefs evolved into the secular idea that school should produce people who all think alike in a general sense.

(The middle colonies and Southern colonies, which were not focused around religion, did not have compulsory education until centuries later. They were a much more diverse group of people and had no desire to lose that diversity.*)

When schools started educating everyone--girls and Native Americans and new immigrants as well as white boys--they took on another, related purpose. For all of its idealism about democracy, America wasn't ready to treat people respectfully or equally. **Schools took on the task of stamping out "minority" and other differing cultures.** "The Indian schools were like jails and run along military lines, with roll calls four times a day," says Sioux medicine man Lame Deer in *Lame Deer, Seeker of Visions*. He goes on to lament:

> The schools are better now than they were in my time. They look good from the outside--modern and expensive. The teachers understand the kids a little better, use more psychology and less stick. But in these fine new buildings Indian children still commit suicide, because they are lonely among all that noise and activity. I know of a ten-year-old who hanged herself....When we enter the school we at least know that we are Indians. We come out half red and half white, not knowing what we are.**

Schools also exist to provide babysitting: preventing teenagers from competing in the job market or running loose in the streets. Like other school purposes, this goal stands smack in the way of learning; it translates mainly into an unforgivable waste of time. If we could scrap it, school could surely teach everything more efficiently, not "reviewing" year after year, and you'd finish in half the time. When adults go to workshops, there is usually little of the educational hanky-panky and muddle and time wasting you get in school. Unschooler Jessica Franz, 12, wrote me, "I feel that I am about at the same level as the kids at my grade although I do 'school'

---

* See Lawrence Kotin and William F. Aikman, *Legal Foundations of Compulsory School Attendance* (Kennikat Press, Port Washington, NY, 1980).

** John (Fire) Lame Deer and Richard Erdoes, *Lame Deer, Seeker of Visions* (Washington Square Press, 1972).

only occasionally as opposed to six or seven hours a day." Her comment is echoed by the experiences of thousands of other unschoolers who spend little formal time on academics but know much much more, and get better scores on standardized tests than the average schooled student.

Contrast school's use of time with the way people study for the GED. The GED actually tests a higher level of knowledge than what school teaches; supposedly one third of high school *graduates* would fail it. Nevertheless, when high school dropouts want to take it, they are typically coached for sixteen to twenty-four hours over a period of four to six weeks. Books that prepare people to take the GED suggest around thirty home-study sessions, each about one to three hours. That's all they need, *not* four years sitting at a desk with someone else's bubble gum stuck underneath.

I am reminded of a conversation my colleagues and I had with a parent when I was teaching. We had suggested that this man's son skip the eighth grade and go directly into the ninth, since he was extremely bright, competent, socially adept, and "responsible" in doing his schoolwork. At first, the father had some qualms. He was worried that his son would miss some of the "building blocks" of courses such as math, science, and foreign language. No, said the teachers, Jasper (fake name) would miss nothing important by skipping a grade.

That information was good for Jasper, since he was allowed to skip eighth grade and save himself a year of "nothing important." But the implications of that conversation are horrendous. Year after year, you attend school for many reasons. You may think the most important reason is learning, but in reality you are receiving "nothing important" in exchange for your twelve years of drudgery. Sure, schools teach some potentially helpful skills and information. But the amount of good stuff is insignificant next to the piles of inanity, and furthermore, the meat of most year-long courses could be covered in a good two or three day session.

Schools didn't *begin* in order **to provide millions of jobs for teachers, administrators, maintenance people, and office workers,** but since they provide those jobs now, that is one of their main purposes. It is probably the one that will kick hardest if lots of young people get hip and quit. Yes, it would be tragic for all those people to be out of work. But why must you provide their livelihood with the skin of your souls? The government pays them to do dirty-work; it might as well pay them to do good work--help in libraries and museums, provide teaching and tutoring to people of all ages who ask for it, read to blind and elderly people. In the meantime, it shouldn't be your burden.

Why do we stand for it? Why do most people believe unquestioningly in compulsory education?

Because they are mystified, shamed, and intimidated into believing in it, that's why.

Schoolpeople talk in specialized, complicated language, as if learning were a specialized, complicated process. "Mastery learning," they say, "Criterion-referenced testing, multicultural education, prosocial behavior, expository teaching, and stanine scores. So there." They pretend--and believe-- that what they do is all very tricky and difficult.

Teachers take themselves very seriously when they do things like design courses and lesson plans. They try to sound very scientific when speaking to students and talking about students. (Remember, I know because I was a teacher. I didn't just see it, I did it. It's a tremendously addicting power trip.)

Indeed, all their complicated undertakings *are* probably necessary to induce *forced* learning. They are also necessary in order to make schoolpeople themselves feel important. But none of it should intimidate you. Most of what teachers actually know about teaching has to do with classroom management (a.k.a. "discipline"). In other words, most of what they know is stuff that obviously wouldn't matter if you were learning what you want to learn.

Ben Gipson, a college student who plans to teach high school psychology, life management, and reading skills, and who was a student delegate to an NEA (teachers' union) convention, wrote an essay which was printed in the December 1990 *NEA Today*. Gipson wrote arguing that it is best to major in education rather than in the field one hopes to teach: "Not only is a child's thinking different from an adult's, but a five-year-old's is different from a seven-year-old's. If you haven't studied Piaget, Kohlberg, and Erikson, you won't really know that."

Oh, you won't? Well, no, not if you bury your nose in books and never think about your own childhood or talk with kids.

But schools push you beyond intimidation; they *shame* you into believing you need them. By giving out grades, they cancel people's faith in their perfectly good brains. Once you accept a report card's verdict that you're not so smart, you're hardly in a position to say you don't need school. If they happen to decide you *are* smart, you have the opposite problem--your ego is addicted. You "succeed" in school, so why risk leaving it for a world where you might not get straight A's?

It boils down to something called "blaming the victim:" school blames you instead of itself for your intellectual influenza. After first grade, you forget about your heaping supply of natural curiosity. When they tell you the reason you don't do your schoolwork well enough is that you have no drive, curiosity, or love of learning, you start believing them. By the time they tell you that if you can't make it *with* school, you certainly can't make it *without* school, you're really lost.

Obviously, schools need you to believe that you couldn't learn without them. Once they convince you of this, through intimidation and shame, it's over; you submit without much argument to twelve years of it. You become susceptible to the illogical kind of line one of my colleagues fed his students when they didn't finish their math: "OK, don't turn in your homework. Grow up and be a junkie."

The good part is that once you recognize their game for what it is, you can think about it clearly and start trusting yourself again.

So, dear reader, here we are at the end of another chapter. I invite you to sit down with your feet up and reflect upon your values and goals. Do they mesh with school? Are you tickled pink to have your mind programmed into Obedient Worker mode? To cash in your cultural heritage for Mainstream American Suburbia-think? To be babysat thirty-five hours every week?

Yes? Good girl. Good boy. Just put your feet back down, sit a little straighter, please, and do not look to the left or right.

No? Uh-oh. Welcome. Read on.

schoolteachers: the People vs. the Profession

This book has no intention of lessening your appreciation for the people who teach school. Yet, my commentary in this chapter is both sweet and sour. On one hand, I want to acknowledge the wonderful qualities teachers have, and to explain a few difficult and ironic aspects of their profession. In general, it is not teachers' faults that School Is Bad--although if they all quit there would be no more school. On the other hand, I want to point out some less healthy aspects of common teacher personalities, to help you understand some of the guilt-dynamics you may feel at school, and to help you give yourself permission to leave.

Most teachers are generous, intelligent, beautiful people. Some are very talented or knowledgeable in their fields and would make great mentors or tutors outside the constraints of school. Many have given up chances to make lots of money because they believe in teaching even though it pays poorly. Especially if they are men, they sometimes endure years of being hassled by their families--"Why don't you find a *real* career?" In any grip-on-reality contest, your average schoolteacher would win four times as many trophies as your average Gillette or Exxon executive.

Most teachers and other people in schools believe they are doing the Right Thing. They are not preventing democracy, freedom, and education on purpose. When they do purposely prevent freedom, they think it is in your best interest, so that you'll be ready to work hard and "succeed" in your afterlife. Respect their good intentions.

A few teachers are amazing enough to conquer. In their classes, something strong and beautiful happens, despite all the unpleasant forces of the opposition. The classic example is Elliot Wigginton, who started an oral history program in Georgia. His students write the famous *Foxfire* books and magazines. These books enlighten the whole world both about the richness of Appalachian culture and the capabilities of teenage journalists.

Jerry Vevig, my own high school choir director, is not so famous but was also an extraordinary teacher before he got promoted. Whenever I entered his room--for 6:30 A.M. practice, jazz choir, or concert choir--I forgot I was a high school student and instead became a serious artist in likeminded company. He wasn't always nice, and usually made us sing fifteen minutes into our lunch break, but he treated us like musicians, not kiddies, and he knew his stuff. I especially remember once when "The Capital Singers" performed for a huge business Christmas banquet at The Red Lion--one of our twenty performances that month. The adult audience ignored us while we set up microphones. But when Carl rolled the first lush chords over the piano, all the talking hushed, and when Ronelle sang the first ripe note of the opening solo, a man dropped his fork. We were for real. Mr. V. brought out our best, and we loved him for it. I don't want to deny that some teachers can make wonderful things happen in school. I just know that the odds are way against them.

Also, just because someone teaches doesn't mean they're mentally "in league" with the school system. Many teachers start teaching in the first place because they think school is a bad place and they hope to make it better.

Unfortunately, most of these teachers either end up quitting or else compromising their ideals--the system is so much bigger and stronger than they are. Still, a lot of teachers have a few years of passionate vision in them. Don't assume, because schools squash you, that teachers *want* to squash you. For most teachers, as well as students, the world will be a more chocolate place when school is not compulsory and full of administrative backwash.

Which brings me to a different point. Not all teachers want to run your lives, but they have no choice. They *must* "manage" you. It is their *job* to give you F's if you don't do "your" work, to report your absences, to make you be quiet, to assign homework, to enforce school rules they don't personally believe in, such as You Have to Wear Socks With Tennis Shoes, and No Leaning Back in Your Chair. No teacher could keep a job if she said, "It doesn't matter whether you do the homework tonight. If you'd prefer to spend more time doing something else, please do. You won't get a zero, and I won't be disappointed in you." Teachers' job descriptions leave no way for them to treat you with the respect they would show their friends.

I can illustrate my point in a backwards way by telling you about a day I just couldn't do the job. I was substitute teaching physics. One of the people in the class, a 14-year-old-boy, was a good friend of mine. Because he was there, I came in the door as myself, not Miss Llewellyn. The class zoomed way out of control. Airplanes flew into the chalkboard; everyone talked while I gave the assignment; two boys in dark glasses put their feet on their desks, leaned back, crossed their arms, and grinned. Any other day, I would have snapped into the role they'd created for me. I was good at it. "Ladies and *gent*lemen," ran my usual substitute talk, "*Where* is your self-respect. Mr. Washington and Mr. Garcia, please remove the glasses. Yes, it's difficult, I know. I'll wait. If any of you would care to visit the office, you can let me know by sending another airplane in this direction. Any questions?"

But with Otto's perceptive eyes on me, I couldn't bring myself to say the words. In his presence, they seemed suddenly so petty and artificial. They had nothing to do with Grace Llewellyn. I did a lousy job that day because Otto brought a sudden flash of a deeper reality. What that says about the days I *could* do my job is unpleasant indeed.

Something that surprised me when I started teaching was that my fellow teachers were terrific people. Almost all of them. That hurt my brain a little. I remembered having a lot of mean, stupid teachers in school--was I wrong? Or had the teaching profession changed radically in five years?

The truth didn't strike until I substitute taught for a few months in my own former junior high and high school, rubbing my adult shoulders with the very same people who used to grade my tests and ask me not to read novels during their brilliant lectures. All of *them* were terrific people too--in my adult company. From the glimpses I caught of them in their classes, and the student conversations I overheard in the halls, some were apparently still mean and stupid in their classrooms.

I started wondering how many teenagers thought *I* was mean and stupid when I stood in front of a classroom. And over the next few years, I came to believe firmly: the majority of teachers are amazing, intelligent, generous and talented *people*. But the role they are forced to play in school keeps them from showing you these beautiful sides of themselves. Their talent and energy is drained instead by their constant task of telling people what to do.

Not everything about teachers is terrific, of course. Like a lot of other kinds of people, they have their weak points as well as their good qualities. And some of the things for which we praise teachers most loudly are the ways they cause the most harm.

For instance, many teachers seem to have an inborn desire to run other people's lives (also known as "help people"). Even if it were tolerable that others should run our lives, teachers are rarely any good at doing so, being as fully human as their students.

It makes sense that controlling sorts of people would gravitate toward teaching. It's a great profession for people who wish they were a king or God. Me, for example. When I was six or so I used to love to play school. I was the teacher. I called it Pee-Wee. My brothers, the students, were usually unenthusiastic but I was older and I could bribe or force them into it. I choreographed dances and made them learn, pinching them when they lost the beat. In general, I didn't feel my own life was enough territory--I wanted to design theirs too (just like my teachers got to design *my* life, I might add). It is this controlling and designing quality that disturbs me again and again in teachers--including myself--and in administrators. The most dangerous people in life are often those who want most to help you, whether or not you want their "help." "She's the sort of woman who lives for others," wrote C.S. Lewis, "You can tell the others by their hunted expression."

Teaching also turns you into an automatic Authority Figure. It is ideal work for anyone who likes to feel superior. No one questions much where your authority comes from, or how much is deserved.

Moreover, being a teacher is a perfect way to get attention and praise for being selfless and generous. Do you know anyone who loves to suffer nobly, as long as someone's watching and feeling sorry for them? A lot of teachers do. They thrive not on money, but on the brownie points they get for staying up all night to grade quizzes, for bringing their advisees Halloween candy, for earning abominable salaries, for driving across town in a blizzard to rent *The Story of English* on video, for explaining fractions thirty times to Suki on Friday afternoon, for neglecting their own favorite sports in order to coach basketball. Unfortunately, people who are good at suffering and working hard in public are also good at giving other people guilt trips.

One of the most dedicated, popular, and brilliant teachers I've known worked hard to arrange a weekend outdoor-film festival for Colorado Springs School boarding students. It was optional, and few went. The teacher was sad and disappointed in students for showing so little enthusiasm. I wondered how he would feel if his boss expressed disappointment in *him* if he missed a free U2 concert. Another teacher responded to his frustration with wisdom: "We have to provide a wide array of activities for them," she said, "But not be so personally invested in them that we get hurt when they'd rather do something else."

What do we need instead of people who love to sacrifice themselves for others? We need people who do what they most love, and do it well, and let others hang around or join in unforced, and share their knowledge instead of hoarding it. This behavior requires *true* generosity, because it allows other people to be equals, not helpless victims.

Another unfortunate aspect of teacher personalities is a limited perspective. Most have not worked at other kinds of jobs, beyond summers at a cash register. Like you, they have spent all their lives in school. This leaves them almost incapable of imagining their students' potential futures. They can't help but communicate to you their narrow sense of the possibilities in life.

Finally, there is nothing wrong with teaching, only with teaching in the conditions of compulsory school. Lots of people do learn certain things best by being taught or shown. So don't limit yourself by assuming that a teacher in school is the same as a teacher out of school. A teacher out of school--in a martial arts studio, a book discussion group, or a community education French class--can be himself and teach from his heart. Also, since you are not required to undergo his teaching, you will stay only if his method works for you.

When choice, freedom, and individuality are introduced into a teaching situation, it can be great for everyone involved. That's why I love my new work giving dance lessons. The old issues of guilt simply don't come up. If people want to learn middle eastern dance and swirl sequined veils, and if they like my teaching and my dancing, they pay me to teach them. If they stop liking it, they quit, or perhaps look for a different teacher. I don't stress out or take it personally--everyone learns differently. No one takes my ex-students to court for truancy or gives them an F. Those of us who stay in class are empowered by our common goal and our common success.

chapter 5

The Power and Magic of Adolescence vs. The Insufferable Tedium of School

Youth is the time to go flashing from one end of the world to the other both in mind and body; to try the manners of different nations; to hear the chimes at midnight; to see sunrise in town and country; to be converted at a revival; to circumnavigate the metaphysics, write halting verses, run a mile to see a fire, and wait all day long in the theatre to applaud 'Hernani.'
--Robert Louis Stevenson, *Crabbed Age and Youth*.

If you ever read any anthropology, one of the first things you notice is that primal cultures simmer up all of their mystery and magic and power and ask their teenagers to drink deeply.

A sixteen-year-old Dakota boy fasts until an empowering vision overtakes him. A newly-menstruating Apache girl becomes the goddess White Painted Woman in an intense, joyful theatrical ritual which lasts four days. All over the planet, traditional cultures provide various ritual experiences to adolescents, bringing them into contact with the deepest parts of themselves and their heritage.

There is danger and pain, as well as beauty and exultation, in some of these traditional ways of initiating people into adulthood. I don't want to make any shallow statement that we've got it all wrong because we don't ask pubescent boys to endure three days of biting wasps.

But I would like you to reflect for a minute on the contrast between the way *our* society initiates its young and the vivid undertakings of the primal world.

What do you get instead of vision? You get school--and all of the blind passivity and grey monotone it trains into you.

For an institution to ask you, during some of your most magical years, to sit still and be good and read quietly for six or more hours each day is barely even thinkable, let alone tolerable. How do you feel when the sun comes out in March and makes the most golden day imaginable, but you have to stay in and clean your room?

In case you've lost touch with your burgeoning beauty, let me remind you that that's exactly what's going on, for at least six years of your teenaged schooling. Adolescence is a time of dreaming, adventure, risk, sweet wildness, and intensity. It's the time for you to "find yourself," or at least go looking. The sun is rising on your life. Your body is breaking out of its cocoon and ready to try wings. But you have to stay in--for *such* a long time--and keep your pencils sharpened. School is bad for your spirit, except the pep club kind.

It's no accident, I'm sure. The way our society is set up now, something's got to prevent visionary experience. Otherwise, ninety percent of the American monoculture would shatter.   People who are fully and permanently awakened to the wildness and beauty in and around them make lousy wage-slaves. On the other hand, people who are *not* distracted by a wellspring of spiritual and sexual yearnings can assemble clock radios or automobiles very quickly.

More importantly, unawakened people are less likely to *question* the things in our society which are horrifically dull and ridiculous. The point of seeking any kind of visionary experience is to *see*. When vision comes to you, eternity is its black velvet backdrop. Everything else comes out on the stage to sing and dance. Some of it fits in with the grandeur of that backdrop, and some of it only clashes, looking ugly and cheap. You end up wanting to adjust your life so that it's full of stuff that fits in with eternity, and not crammed with things that don't matter.

Therefore, one reason many primal cultures can confidently guide their young toward visionary experiences is that they're not worried. They don't have to worry that the visions will show anything horrible about the society itself. If there *is* something going wrong with the cultural state of affairs, they want to know, so they can fix it.

In this culture the opposite is true. When you have a messy house, you don't offer a magnifying glass to your guests. You probably don't even open the curtains and let the light in.

If we did teenaged visions, democracy would get a boost, but the powers of Mass Production and Rat Racing Consumerism would take a dive. We would see that far too much of what we accept as "reality" is a blasphemy against true reality. Since our consumptive culture is out of balance with the rest of the universe, it would look mighty bad under the inspection of visionary young people. Get it? The US of A does not invite its young to seek visions, because those visions would force a Big Change.

No force of dullness and ignorance is strong enough, however, to stop you from seeking. Eternity, God, Goddess, whatever you call it--is too strong. It will get in, though it has to battle school and other strongholds of society. Writers and artists bring us some inklings, though when school introduces us to them, it nearly destroys their potency.

The Big Mystery creeps in through all your fascinations with the unknown--music with heavy pulses and strange lyrics, sexual fantasies and experiences, the occult, drugs (including alcohol). Obviously, some of these things can be taken to unhealthy excess. Drug abuse is a disease. Drug *use*, however, is often the sign of someone's intense spiritual quest. Hallucinogens can be an easy, though risky, way to tap into visionary experience. There are other ways, healthier though more difficult--through trance and fasting, for instance.

Unfortunately, most adults refuse to acknowledge the powerful impulse behind any of these activities, labeling them as "bad," as if that would make them go away. Why? Their own visionary tendencies got cancelled out by society at sweet sixteen. Misery, as they say, loves company. It is *incredibly* painful for an emotional cripple to be around someone who is emotionally free. And so most adults would rather pretend desperately to visionary teenagers that the world is nothing more than green lawns, white socks, and recently sanitized carpets.

Visionary tendencies come in dark and light, or a combination thereof.

Some teenagers want dark experiences. They walk in cemeteries at night. They write stories about suicide; they obsess on black clothing and Pink Floyd lyrics. None of it means they are "bad" or twisted. When they are finished playing with the dark, they will understand the light much better. If they are ignored or ridiculed, maybe they will do something drastic, but their search is usually only an earnest attempt to understand the depths.

Others gravitate toward the light--daytime psychedelic colors, long solitary hikes. They determine to become a dancer or artist instead of something "realistic." If their family is sedately Catholic, maybe they go to the Assembly of God and speak in tongues. If their family goes to the Assembly of God, maybe they climb a hill and offer flowers to Apollo.

Schools--and many parents--lie a lot at this point, telling you you're out of touch with reality. The truth is, you're out of touch with the expectations and patterns of an *un*real, man-made industrial society. You are *in* touch with the reality that counts. Look at the milky way some night and think about it. You'll know. In *Lame Deer, Seeker of Visions*, a Sioux Medicine man talks about the reality of "the white world" versus the deeper reality of artists and Indians:

> Artists are the Indians of the white world. They are called dreamers who live in the clouds, improvident people who can't hold onto their money, people who don't want to face "reality." They say the same things about Indians. How the hell do these frog-skin[*] people know what reality is? The world in which you paint a picture in your mind, a picture which shows things different from what

---

[*]   "Frog-skins" are dollar bills.

your eyes see, that is the world from which I get my visions. I tell you this is the real world, not the Green Frog Skin World. That's only a bad dream, a streamlined, smog-filled nightmare.

Because we refuse to step out of our reality into this frog-skin illusion, we are called dumb, lazy, improvident, immature, other-worldly. It makes me happy to be called "other-worldly," and it should make you so. It's a good thing our reality is different from theirs.[*]

Furthermore...

Schools--and this society they represent--go beyond blocking your visionary tendencies. They further cripple you by making fun of you, as if you were not quite human, the new niggers. Why? Probably because every hierarchical society seems to need niggers to put down, and women and African-Americans won't take it anymore. When someone puts *you* down, you want to put somebody else down.

(Dr. Seuss, reliable social commentator, wrote a story called "King Looie Katz." King Looie Katz makes Fooie Katz carry his long proud royal tail around. So Fooie Katz sticks his own nose in the air and makes another cat haul *his* tail. Pretty soon all the cats in Katzenstein are walking around carrying the tail of the cat in front of them...except the very last little cat, who doesn't have anyone to carry his.

That little cat, who is a bit like you, takes action. He yells "I Quit" and slams down the tail in his paws. Everybody else follows suit. The story concludes:

And since that day in Katzen-stein,
All cats have been more grown-up.
They're all more demo-catic
Because each cat holds his own up.[***]

Food for thought.)

Another reason adults make fun of you is that they're jealous. Teenagers are beautiful and fresh; the perfume of a flower is concentrated in the bud. Yes, many teenagers are awkward, pimpled, or strangely tall and thin. Far more adults, however, are awkward (having forgotten how to use their bodies), sallow-skinned (too much sitting in air-conditioned offices) and predictably heavy (not enough skateboarding).

** John (Fire) Lame Deer and Richard Erdoes, *Lame Deer, Seeker of Visions* (Washington Square Press, 1972).

*** "King Looie Katz," in Dr. Seuss (Theodor Geisel), *I Can Lick 30 Tigers Today, and other stories* (Random, 1969).

A healthy adult society would acknowledge the beauty of youth, make up some good poems about it, and then not think about it too much. There are certainly more productive activities in life than fixating on the rosy cheeks you'll never have again. But since we do not have a healthy adult society, we get all bent out of shape over it, create a cult of young-beautiful-people-in-magazines, and punish real live teenagers by telling them they are ugly.

Just in case you do figure out that you are beautiful, we make sure that you can't appreciate it, by telling you that you are confused and overly emotional during these traumatic years and for pete's sake don't go and make any decisions for yourself, and don't let loose and have any free wild experiences with life. Dogs in mangers, we turn the power of adolescence into a weak disease. Teachers sit in the teachers' lounge and laugh about you behind your backs.

Isn't he cute, they say. Poor Kristy, with no idea of how she sticks out in that magenta skirt. This, from people who are overweight, in ruts, out of touch with their dreams, insecure, and otherwise at least as imperfect as the subjects of their conversation. Thank god I'm not that age any more, says Mrs. Wallace, leaning her double chin over her desk. We read tacky cute articles in *Family Circle* called "How to Survive the Terrible Teens: An Owner's Guide." The owner being the parent, of course. *School*, yes, is something to survive, but being a teenager is something that flies.

We force you to act younger than you are, legally withholding your ability to control your own life. The *World Book* encyclopedia says, "Most teenagers mature psychologically at the rate set by their society. As a result, psychological adolescence normally lasts at least as long as the period of legal dependence." Certainly, there is no *biological* limitation to teenage independence. In other times and places, teenagers have commonly married, raised children, held jobs, operated businesses, and occasionally ruled countries.

It seems you're talking about more than just schools here. Aren't you getting off the point a bit?

Yes, school is not the only bad guy in the war against whole adolescence. But it *is* our culture's deathly substitute for powerful growing experiences. It *is* the way we take your time so you don't explore your own inklings of truth. It *is* the place where you learn to be passive instead of active. Quitting school isn't going to guarantee you a healthy, passionate adolescence, but at least it will remove the biggest obstacle against that flowering.

chapter 6

and a few other Miscellaneous Abominations

Aside from the previously described Big Reasons to quit school, there are dozens of random miscellaneous ones, also important, like

School puts you into intense, forced contact with people who are only your own age. It discourages you from making friends with other people. If you don't like being shut up with your peers all day, that doesn't mean you're socially maladjusted. Why should you prefer the company of hundreds of people your own age to a healthy mix of more diverse people? Adults have been around longer than teenagers. Therefore, they have experiences and perspectives that teenagers lack.

When adults aren't your schoolteachers (and therefore have no control over you), most will treat you like real people. Outside of school, if you're busy doing something, most adults won't think of you as a "kid"--at least not for long. You will learn from them, and they will learn from you. Also, you can have friends younger than yourself.

School socializes you into narrow roles. Girls wear makeup. Boys play football. Girls giggle. Boys stammer and grunt. All teenagers are incapable of serious thought--unless they're nerds or at least "different."

School labels people, putting them into limiting categories. Schools have lots of people. When we have to deal with large quantities, sorting things into categories helps us to make sense of them. Most people tend to use this survival mechanism in school, so everyone ends up with hundreds of conveniently labeled acquaintances. According to the unspoken rules of most schools, you are one thing or another. You are an artsy fartsy drama freak *or* a cheerleader-type, not both. Your school life is autoshop class *or* college prep, not both.

It's not easy to cross these boundaries, so many people never try. Out of school, you can forget them. I heard from an unschooling ballet dancer who milks goats, from an unschooling fisherman who listens to progressive rock, plays dungeons and dragons, and is an Eagle Scout. No categories there.

School teaches frenzy. When adults get turned loose after college, lots of them go to bookstores and buy self-help books. These books help them unlearn the lessons of school. Slow down, they say. Concentrate only on the important things. Don't give yourself guilt trips for not Doing Everything. Live your life the way *you* want to live it. If you quit school now, maybe you can reclaim this childhood wisdom before you sprout wrinkles, and save thirty dollars or so in self-help books.

If you go to school, you almost have to be a jerk to other people, to yourself, or to both. When other people are jerks, life loses a bit of its sheen. When *you* are a jerk, life loses a lot of its sheen. Yet school sometimes gives you no choice.

A simple example is my day in May at the natural history museum, a school field trip. The tour guide and the teachers told the students to sit quietly and listen to the tour guide. The tour guide stood in front of the exhibits, blocking them. She rambled dully, as tour guides are prone to do. The exhibits, on the other hand, were stunning and infinitely more "educational" than any dry-rot lecture or textbook.

The students had two choices. They could show the expected "respect" to the tour guide and sit quietly, bored as bureaucrats, disrespecting themselves. Or they could show "disrespect" and disobedience to the guide and stand up, walk around, and look and learn. Andy did. Andy got scolded. I hate remembering.

Schools create meaningless, burdensome problems for you to solve. School claims to be a system which is accountable to the larger world around it. In other words, what you learn in school is supposed to help you make sense of the rest of the world. In good moments, you do learn useful information. But much of your time in school is spent simply learning how to get along in *school*. Schoolpeople impose elaborate homework policies, consequences, and language--"You're earning an F. That's a problem. How are you going to solve it?" They call things like grades and homework your "responsibility," without giving you the slightest choice in accepting that responsibility.

Schoolpeople justify their actions by saying they're teaching you to be responsible and "follow through" later in school and later in life. But all of this is so different from "real life" that it's ridiculous. In "real life," you *choose* what to take responsibility for. Under circumstances of freedom, following through is a completely different game from the one you play in school.

Schools give you an incurable guilt trip. Last year at school we watched a videotape as part of a study skills unit. It was about getting good grades. You *should* get good grades, the speaker kept saying. If you are capable of an A, he said, but you only get a C, that ought to be unacceptable to you. Maybe, he added, not quite joking, you ought to make yourself sleep on the floor that night.

In a parent-teacher conference, a wealthy, "successful" father complained about Jill's (fake name) C's and B's. "I wouldn't care if she couldn't do the work," he said, "I'm just angry that she doesn't. Why does she throw her talent away?" As if C's and B's meant that one was doing nothing with one's life. It all boils down to a guilt trip if you spend your energy on what you care about, and pats on the head if you forget who you are and do what you're told.

Schools blame victims. In other words, they inflict all manner of nasty experiences and expectations on you, and then tell you it's your fault for not liking it. They blame *you* for *their* problems. An advice column in *Scholastic Choices*, March 1990, ran this letter:

> I'm 13 and I want to quit school. I think it's boring. Besides, my teachers are all mean. I think I could get a job on a farm and make a living that way. What should I do?

Easy enough to answer--"Quit school, of course. It *is* boring. Teachers *are* mean, though it's part of their job to be that way. Work on a farm if you *want*, but as a 13-year-old you shouldn't have to worry about earning a living." The king of the advice column, however, had different ideas:

> ....The way you write and express yourself tells me that you are smart, though unhappy, and are blaming your dissatisfaction on things outside of yourself. [In other words, you should be blaming your dissatisfaction on yourself.] You don't feel bored because school is boring or teachers are mean. You don't feel secure or comfortable with yourself. If you can't settle these feelings in a year or so, counselors can help you learn to understand your feelings more clearly.

No comment.

There's more to life. You yearn. I grow furious and heartbroken when I think on this one too long. You know: life is NOT the color of linoleum halls or the drab hum of industrial lighting or the slow ticking of the clock. Look at the stars. Look hard at the faces of people throwing frisbees in a park, singing in church, passing the potatoes, planting tomatoes, fixing a kitchen table or the engine in an old pickup. Look at a baby or a piece of handcarved furniture or a three-hundred-year-old tree or a pebble or a worm or the sweater your grandmother knitted for you. Perhaps school's greatest danger is that it may convince you life is nothing more than an institutionalized rat race.

School, of course, is not the only big gray institution our country relies on to suck the spirit out of its people. Hospitals, big office buildings, and numerous governmental interferences pull the same trick. But school is the first such institution most of us endure, and it wears down our resistance to the later ones. It makes them seem normal; it makes us feel greedy or idealistic or stupidly poetic when we hear our hearts telling us, "It shouldn't be like this! I'm better than this! I was made for more wonderful things."

School conditions you to live for the future, rather than to live in the present. In *Growing Without Schooling* magazine #39, Marti Holmes, mother of a 16-year-old, wrote: "Homeschooling has not closed any doors that I can see, and has provided rich, full years of living (rather than 'preparing for life')." Contrary to the teachings of school, you are not in dress rehearsal. More than anything else, this book is about living--*now,* as well as twenty years from now. Quit school before it convinces you life is nothing but a waiting game, an *ugly* waiting game. "We are always getting ready to live, but never living," wrote Emerson. Don't let the schoolpeople write that on your tombstone.

chapter 7

But
Miss Llewellyn...

Panic strikes your hungry heart. You cry out:

I want to be free....But I also want to go to college and get a good job! My friends are all in school, and what would I do without football?

Yeah, there are a lot of buts. They all have answers. Let's look. One at a time.

But I want to go to college and get a good job!

Fine. Neither depend on graduating from high school. For college, see chapter 31. As far as jobs go, yes, there is plenty of prejudice against "drop-outs," and if you refer to yourself as one, forget it. If, on the other hand, you call yourself a homeschooler or explain exactly what you did instead of school, and why, employers will most likely smile approvingly.

However...be prepared to change your thoughts about what you want out of life. School shapes so much of your mind that when you leave it, you may no longer feel certain that you want college--or you may feel *more* certain. You may grow different ideas as to what kind of work you want to do, and your definition of a "good job" may change. Furthermore, by quitting school and beginning to make independent choices, you run the risk of turning into a person who sculpts creative, fulfilling ways to earn money without reporting to a boss.

Does school actually prepare you for the world of work? If you plan to have a peon job all your life, then yes, school will break your spirit ahead of time so you don't fight when you get nothing wonderful out of adulthood. For that matter, school will condition you to accept *any* kind of work you don't love, whether as an M.D. or a secretary.

School, however, does not prepare you to identify your own dreams and make them come true.

But I have to learn school subjects--math, history, literature, etc.-- because they will make me into a Proper Citizen!

Yes, investigating all these subjects will probably make you a better citizen.

Going to school all day and Obeying Authority as if you lived in a dictatorship will make you a worse one.

What's a patriot to do? Quit school and learn all that juicy stuff and do your best to prevent bad stories (histories) from repeating themselves. Read widely and thoughtfully. The more you do, the less all of us will need to worry about our future. Education, as they call it, should make you a more intelligent voter, and more importantly a good *leader* in any situation--serving on a city planning committee, nudging your aunt Marcia to recycle her beer cans. Certainly, the more informed and thoughtful a group of citizens are, the wiser decisions they ought to make as a group.

True, people who don't go to school might end up knowing different types of things from schoolteenagers, depending on their interests. This, too, is a sign of good citizenship. A community is made more intelligent if its people bring many different perspectives and a wide expanse of knowledge. If you wind up knowing more about Jacques Rousseau than Martin Luther King, or Hopi farming practices instead of the structure of DNA, or motorcycle engines instead of computers, your citizenship will be as intact as the Jones's. *More* intact, actually, because you'll like what you know, and you'll keep it in mind whenever you think about anything.

Furthermore, I don't know about ingraining it in your brain that any sort of learning is your *responsibility*. Your life and time belong to you and the universe, and only to the government to the extent that the government is in harmony with the universe. Anyway, lots of heavily "educated" people are rotten citizens. So read to feed your hungry head, not to fulfill some pinched sense of duty.

> *But my school has a good choir!*
> *I live to play football!*
> *And what about me? I want to be Miss Drill Team U.S.A.!*

This one's tough. Some schools do offer outstanding performing and sports opportunities that are difficult to find elsewhere. My own melodious memory of singing with and playing piano for two outstanding choirs in high school almost compensates for the lackluster hours I spent enduring everything else. Almost, but not quite. If you truly love your opportunity to belong to a school team or performing group, consider two things:

First, you *can* leave school and continue to participate in these activities--either at school itself or elsewhere. Chapters 26 and 27 expound on this topic. Chapter 19 contains specific information about participating in school just as much as you want to--i.e. marching band and photography but no math, English, or anything else.

Second, if you can't replace the activity, or participate in it without being enrolled in school full-time, is it terrific enough that it makes up for the drudgery of the rest of school? If you want to play professional football, maybe so. Everyone makes trade-offs; millions of adults live somewhere without liking it because it offers them work they do like. But if you'd have as much fun playing hockey with an independent league as playing school football, get clear. Cash in your shoulder pads for freedom.

But in school I learn lots of facts!

It's much easier, and far more delectable, to get them from an encyclopedia, *Harper's* "Index," or Trivial Pursuit answer cards.

But what if all I want to do instead of school is watch TV all day?

Well. Don't misunderstand me. I hereby go on record as a bona-fide TV hater. I plan to never own one, although a VCR would be nice. I would turn heartsick and give up if this book led to a cult of TV parasites who soaped instead of schooled, and I personally would rather be stuck going to junior high all day than force-fed channel zero for six hours.

However, I don't worry. If you think what you want most is to soak in sit-coms all day, probably all you really need and want is the mandatory vacation described in chapter 12. After a week or so of TV, you'll feel restless and ready to move on. If you don't yet have any ideas, you'll be ready to find some. Furthermore, I'm convinced that addiction to TV is a by-product of schooling. School doesn't encourage you to take action. Once you get used to sitting passively all day, it's hard to be a Person with Initiative. But school doesn't really kill your brain; it only sends it into deep freeze. After it thaws, you'll want more than TV.

But what if I don't get along with my parents and don't want them to be my teachers?
        OR
But what if my parents both work and can't stay home to homeschool me?

If unschooling or homeschooling depended on parents to be teachers, I'd never write a book about it. Lots of teenagers get along with their parents (especially teenagers who don't go to school) but lots don't. And no matter how well you get along with your parents, that doesn't mean you'd like them to direct your education. I would have *hated* for my parents to be my "teachers" in the school sense. The conflicts and power struggles we already had could only have intensified.

On the other hand, I would have loved to be an "unschooler," in charge of my own education. If my parents and I had known about unschooling and tried it, I think they would have been wise and trusting enough to let me explore independently. Likely, our relationship would have improved since I would have felt better about my own life. But I would have fiercely resisted any well-meant parental attempts to control my learning.

So, once and for all, let's get this straight: I am not talking about turning your parents into your main teachers, *unless that is specifically what you and they want to do.* Your teachers can be yourself, books, basketball courts, adults you talk to or write letters to, your friends, museums, plants, and rivers.

I heard from several unschoolers, by the way, whose parents both worked away from home. Not only that, but in *Growing Without Schooling* Magazine (*GWS*) there are occasional letters from parents with *younger* children who stay home without adults during the days--and like it, and don't die. More importantly, the majority of teenaged homeschoolers who wrote me said that their parents played a minor role in their educations. They answer questions when asked, talk a lot, and sometimes share their expertise *when the teenager is interested.* In other families, the parents really do get involved, learning right along with their children, but that happens more often at younger ages. Both the parents and teenagers who contacted me seemed to share an understanding that a teenager is old enough to direct his own education and activities.

To be sure, there are families where the parent takes over the role of teacher and principal--sometimes in a very authoritarian way. The idea repels *me*, but if you like it that's your business.

But I love outsmarting authority!

I sympathize; there's great satisfaction in beating someone at their own game. If you're a fighter and a rebel, however, there are worthier causes than school. Outsmart the big businesses who destroy rainforests and ozone. Outsmart the lying politicians. Get out in the world where we need you.

And understand this: petty though school is, it has more power to break your spirit than these bigger forces do. That's because its *business* is breaking you. The more you rebel, the more they'll tell you you're a failure with F's and suspensions on your permanent record. When they do, no matter how tough you are, you'll have a hard time believing in yourself. Out in the real world, the opposite comes true. No matter how hard you work against a wrongdoing corporation or government, they can never flunk you. Instead, the madder you make them, the more successful you know you are.

Understand this, too: the ultimate way of outsmarting school is to leave it and start learning.

(Of course, quitting school doesn't necessarily mean you're anti-authority. Lots of very authority-respecting Christians do it. It just means you're anti-*abuse* of authority, and perhaps anti-*fake* authority.)

But I'm lazy! If no one makes me learn, I won't.

How do you know you're lazy when you've never had the chance to choose what to work at?

If you call yourself lazy, your biggest job in unschooling will be remembering, glimmer by glimmer, how much you loved to learn before school took that love away. Frogs, wheels, words, blocks, dogs--when you were a little kid, the world dazzled you. Also, you will need to allow yourself to admire ("learn") the things that still sparkle in your kaleidescope, whatever they are.

And laziness shouldn't be confused with zen-like tranquility--"lazy" travelers who hang out in a little Peruvian village for a week will soak up the life and ambience of Peru far more than the typical tourist who in one week sucks in Macchu Picchu, three market towns, four museums, two ancient ruins, and one horseback ride along the Urubamba river. People who find ways to get out of the "rat race" or the obscene commercialism attending Christmas improve the quality of their lives by deliberately avoiding frantic, mindless activity. The same goes for learning: watching the sky for two hours will do more for anyone's cortex than a harried afternoon of longitude worksheets.

But my friends are in school!

Ah yes. The big one. So get your friends to quit with you. See your school friends on evenings or weekends when they're finished with their homework. Make new friends through your interests. (Jeff Richardson, 14-year-old unschooler, comments, "You don't need to go to school to have a lot of friends. I meet a lot of friends through skateboarding. Even if you don't know a skater that's going down the street you say 'Hey dude! Come here!' You automatically have something in common. I've met a couple of homeschooling skaters before too.") Read chapter 14, which exists solely to coach you along in the social department.

Anyway, stop and think about it. We are social creatures, yes--but not *institutional* creatures.

How much communication do you usually have with your friends on school? Except at lunch and potty breaks, you are rarely supposed to talk with them. If you have friends in some of your classes, you see them--but I'm not sure this is the way to build trust, compassion, generosity, and other qualities integral to healthy friendship. In some courses you compete for A's with the other students. Your discussion is overseen and censored by a teacher. Working together is called cheating. What really gets cheated is your ability to help each other climb.

And remember: your enemies are in school too. Adults control and humiliate teenagers, and teenagers even things out for themselves by controlling and humiliating each other. Few people emerge from school's obsessive popularity and conformity contest without scars.

But there's nothing better to do!

One of my favorite and usually most profound students gave this sloppy slogan as the reason he'd stay in school even if he didn't have to. He explained a bit by saying that he was too young to have a job and anyway all his friends were there, so he could neither work nor socialize. Indeed, without a meaningful alternative and good company, school might seem the least of several evils.

Yes, this society is hostile and unwelcoming to teenagers, and laws do prevent teenagers from working for money in certain situations. However, with a small carton of creativity and confidence, you'll dream up an infinite number of enjoyable and enlightening alternatives. That's what parts Two, Three, and Four of this book are for.

But it's easy to go to school--I don't have to think for myself!

To you, I have nothing to say. Stay right there at your graffiti-adorned desk. When you turn eighteen, proceed directly into the army. Be all that you can be, according to somebody else.

Miss Llewellyn, you're not being nice.

Sorry. You're right. By the way, you can call me Grace.

Who would consciously stay in school just to avoid thinking for themselves? No one, probably. And if everything we did was based on conscious, rational choice, life would be simple indeed. Dull, too.

But we are not such rational creatures. Until we face them, fears from our subconscious can ruin our lives. If you don't tingle at the thought of quitting school, please look inside and figure out why. Think hard about whether you're afraid of independence. It's natural to be scared of facing the drums in your own dancing shoes; if you think for yourself, you have no one but yourself to blame for your successes and failures.

Adults, too, hide from the chance to direct their own lives and minds--which is why a lot of them stay in "safe" jobs they detest all their lives, idly fantasizing about the career risk they will take when the kids are grown, or the adventures they will seek once they retire.

Yes, when we live in dreams, we can imagine our "futures" in tissue-wrapped perfection. When we get out of dreams into the present, we find no such perfection. Instead, we find life. It's scary stuff. But it's *real*. Acknowledge your fear, but don't give into it. Dance bravely and brightly. Learn to be a human bean and not instant mashed potatoes.

chapter 8

class dismissed

Tanika has been in the cafeteria a long time now. She is heavy; she feels clogged; her cheeks are greasy; but she understands that these conditions are part of life.

She helps to serve the trays of food now. Sometimes she is asked to assist in convincing a reluctant new pupil to eat. She is especially good at this since she can testify how she felt the same way once, but now realizes how wrong she was. She enjoys telling how she has learned to take control of her eating habits.

Tanika takes considerable pride in her achievements. Last year, for instance, she won a prize during testing week for eating a pint of processed moonfruit strips in less than a minute. It is true that she threw the prize--a jar of gulberry puree wrapped in pink paper--into the stream, but no one else knows and Tanika never thinks about it.

"You are a fantastic eater!" the spectacled man said to her just last week.

At home she barely notices the trees and their fruit. She has so many more pressing, more important things on her mind--planning the welcoming picnic for children who have moved to the orchard from other parts of the planet, inventing a creative new way to serve gulberries, eating her homework.

Today she is coaching an annoying little girl who has so far refused to eat. However, Tanika knows she didn't have time for breakfast, and so she patiently lifts a spoonful of limbergreen berry pudding to the child's face.

But the little girl does not open her mouth. Instead, she pushes the spoon away violently, so that its contents splat on the floor. Then she puts her head down on the table and cries as if everything, *everything* is lost.

Suddenly, something unfurls deep inside of Tanika. Life comes fast sometimes. She looks up. She notices that there are no windows in the cafeteria. Out of the corner of her eye she catches a boy watching with soft dark quiet eyes. She turns her head and watches him back. He stands, and she sees that he is lean, as if he has not eaten all of his food. He asks her something with those eyes. She trembles in limbo.

Tanika swallows. A strange inspiration has seized her brain. Touching her swollen belly, she grabs the small girl's hand and walks quickly toward the door. The boy is at her side in an instant and swings the baby to his hip. In the blurred background, a cook lifts a confused, suspicious mouth. They race through the dark hallways. They push the heavy black doors open and burst out onto the spongy humus. They escape their shoes. It has just rained; the sky is dark and translucent but streams of sunlight catch the glittering leaves and soak into their hair.

Tanika runs forward, slipping her brown body out of its cafeteria smock. She gracefully severs a muavo from its stem, and, kneeling, gives it to the little girl. The little girl sucks at it like a monkey in paradise.

The boy laughs. He leaps like a gazelle and captures a cluster of mazina berries. He hands them to Tanika. She smiles and hands them back. She had a big lunch, and she isn't hungry. But there is tomorrow, and a whole orchard resplendent with every kind of fruit in the universe.

Part Two

the first steps

chapter 9

your
first
unassignments

I did it. I decided not to go to school anymore. NOW WHAT???

First, celebrate your audacity with deep chocolate ice cream.

Second, consult your parents. You might get this over with after dinner tonight, or you might acclimate them slowly to the idea. See chapter 10.

Third, decide what legal or official steps to take, if any. Read chapter 11. Contact a local support group (see Appendix B) and ask for their advice. If it turns out you live in an area where homeschoolers are tortured by the school districts, perhaps you should continue to attend school until you've enrolled in an umbrella school or filed the necessary paperwork. In other areas, all you'll need to do is get your parents to write a letter announcing your actions. Of course, if you're legally old enough (16 in most states), you can just plain quit.

After you've settled with parents and legalities, you're free. Now the real fun begins. The first big thing you need is a vacation, but that needs a whole chapter to itself, so I'll first suggest some smaller things you may wish to do in the beginning of your unschooling career:

-Subscribe to *Growing Without Schooling* magazine (complete information in bibliography). If you do, you will immediately have access to unschooling/homeschooling friends all over the country. The magazine is dominated by letters from parents concerning younger children, but there are usually articles and letters by teenagers too. Also, *GWS* publishes a directory of many of its subscribers, which you can use to contact others. Teenager Sylvia Stralberg commented in *GWS* #80,

> *GWS* has been a source of great comfort to me in the past few months. As I read about other kids who are homeschooling and benefiting from it, I no longer feel guilty about my decision to leave school. I rather feel proud of myself and excited about what the future will bring.

-Join a local homeschool organization, such as the one that helps you out when you need legal advice. If your group needs help, consider volunteering. Meet other homeschooled/unschooled teenagers through this group.

-When you start to wish your friends had more time to spend with you, become a pernicious influence in their lives. Phone them up after dinner to remind them to do their homework. Get them a copy of this book. Propose that they help you start a science co-op or a bakery. During school hours, of course.

-Think about your space. You don't necessarily need any new or fancy equipment, but you do need a place where you feel comfortable, happy, and organized. Likely, you already have a desk or homework corner in your room. Take the time now to make it wonderful. Hang posters. Find a place to keep notebooks, library books, and other paraphernalia. Make sure you have a cozy chair by a window where you can sit and read or write. Consider potential laboratory space, workshop space, studio space, a corner for a museum or collection. Sacrifice a few dollars to an office supply store, for a desktop organizer, file folders, whatever.

What will you call yourself?

Think about the words you will use to talk about yourself. Some of the potential vocabulary includes "self-taught," "autodidact," "doing independent study," "tutored at home," "dropped out," "dropped in," "homeschooled," "unschooled," "lifeschooled," "not going to school, just living my life..." Each term has different implications and connotations, as you will discover when you start talking to other people about your new life.

One of my students noticed my ears perk up when she said she had a friend who didn't go to school. However, when she explained that her friend "went to school at home," writing reports and reading books prescribed and overseen by her mother, my ears plunked down again.

"I am not really interested in that sort of homeschooling, but in unschooling," I told her.

She stared incredulously. "*Un*schooling?" she sneered, "There's a name for that. It's called dropping out."

On *that* term--"dropping out"--John Holt wrote, "It is interesting to note that even the people who hate school most, get the least from it, see it most clearly as a profoundly stupefying and alienating experience, still use this word to describe leaving this unreal and useless situation. I urge them to stop using this phrase, and point out that it is 28 or so years since I was last in an educational institution, and I have not been out of the world; one does not disappear into outer space when one steps out the door of a school building. Indeed, it might make more sense to speak of dropping *in*." * And Herb

---

* John Holt, "Notes for a Talk to Students," *GWS* #74

Hough wrote in *GWS #79*, "Self-learning upwardly mobile students...do not drop out of school--they rise out."

A mother wrote me about neighbors who snooped into her family's unschooling: "People were often nosey, insensitive. [The kids] learned to deal with it by saying that they were tutored. People shut right up! Rich people aren't harassed?!"

Ben and Theressa Billings, 16 and 13, felt slighted by the term "unschooling." Theressa wrote me, "I don't like it when you call homeschooling 'unschooling' because we do schoolwork just like all our peers."

A mother and father told me that although they thought of themselves as *un*schoolers, they had good friends who taught school, and therefore called themselves *home*schoolers to lessen any defensiveness.

As I said in the introduction, I don't care for the term "homeschooling"--it makes me imagine people who keep an overhead projector in the living room. But there's nothing inherently wrong with the term "school;" in the beginning it was a Greek word--"scole"--that meant *leisure*. Learning in Greece (for boys, anyway) was so pleasant--spending free time strolling along and talking with philosophers--that the word for leisure came to have educational connotations.

Advice

Finally, listen to the teenagers who wrote me with suggestions for new unschoolers:

"Relax!...Don't think you aren't learning enough if you aren't sitting for seven hours in a desk."

"If school is your problem, start by taking a six week vacation."

"Get rid of any guilt feelings--unschool yourselves psychologically first--expand, the sky is the limit."

"Enjoy what you are doing now and you will truly 'learn'!"

"Do things *you* are interested in. Explore your interests. Try to use yourself as a guide."

"Sometimes when kids start homeschooling they're a little overcome by their freedom and spend it mostly watching television...I just say that an unschooling life has got to grow on you, and...when you get out of school take advantage of your freedom and do the things you wanted to when you were in school and thought you didn't have time. (Hopefully that's not watching television!)"

"Try to find the things you like to do the most and then pursue them and forget about academic subjects for awhile."

"Don't get locked in the house--no matter how much you love your parents, you need to get out or the days will get longer."

and finally...

"Party on!"

chapter 10

the perhaps delicate parental issue

Most unschooled people have, in the past, been out of school because of their *parents'* beliefs. This is where the book in your hands tries to dream something new--that *you*, because of *your* initiative and *your* yearning, march in front of your own parade.

> *Lovely*, you say, *but what that means is that I have to convince my parents that unschooling is a good thing for me and them.*

Yes.

Fortunately, with a little care and planning, you will probably be able to help them see the light. Ideally, it will go well enough that your parents support and encourage you without too much entangling themselves in your hair, and become so inspired by you that their own lives become richer and braver.

First, though, let's confront some fears *you* might have about unschooling and parents:

Your fears

What if I don't get along with my parents? Won't unschooling just make it worse?

I have some comfort to offer you. Unschooling generally seems to make parents into allies and friends rather than disciplinarians and authority figures. At least, dozens of unschooling parents and teenagers have told me so. Kacey Reynolds, 16, gave a typical comment: "I must have missed something in Jr. High, because there was a turning point somewhere where my peers have stopped loving and started hating their parents. I'm glad I missed it."

Joel Maurer, 13: "My mom likes me better than when I was in school."

Tabitha Mountjoy, 14: "My parents and I have a really good relationship with each other. I think that being home educated helps and I love having them around."

A mother: "Most of our friends with teenagers seem to either not know their kids very well, or else to not like them very much. They seem to think of the teenage years as something to endure, or survive. I'm very thankful to both know and like [my son]."

Another parent wrote in *Growing Without Schooling (GWS) #26,*

> Have other parents noticed a very easy adolescence with unschooled kids? I think that my 15-year-old son's early acquaintance with responsibility for his own actions has made it unnecessary for him to rebel and fight for independence. He is willing to accept my judgement at times because it is offered as one adult to another and not as a restriction on a kid who doesn't know anything.

Judy Garvey wrote in *GWS #70*, "Homeschooling is so much easier than having to deal with children who have been in school all day."

Many unschoolers told me that once they left school, all kinds of family arguments and hostilities just disappeared. It makes sense; no more quarrels about grades or homework, no more need to take revenge on parents for what happens at school.

If you still have doubts, think of activities you would enjoy away from home--volunteering, apprenticing, babysitting while you read or do math.

My parents have always hounded me about my schoolwork. I'm afraid if I quit school they'll be even worse, since they won't have any teachers to help "control" me.

Make sure when you discuss unschooling with them that they understand your need for independence. Make a point of talking with them often about your activities. Show them what you accomplish, or keep a daily log that they are welcome to read. If you admit your concerns as well as your joys, they will see that you are in touch with reality, and won't need to preach constantly. Ask their advice when you can--they will feel valued and it will encourage them to give up their controlling role in favor of a softer advisory one. *You* set the tone. More details in the section "Beyond yes."

The Gentle Art of Persuasion

You know your parents. I don't. What causes giggling in one family might cause slamming doors in another. Perhaps your relationship with your parents is warm and trusting enough that you can simply bring your ideas up casually at the dinner table with confidence that they'll understand and support your decision to quit school. On the other hand, maybe you hide this book under your mattress and KNOW they'll say NO before you finish your first sentence. Most likely, you fit somewhere between these two extremes, and you should find at least some ideas in this chapter that enable you to convince your parents and then live happily with them for some more years.

Unless you know that your parents will agree easily, I suggest a bit of structure, planning, and method. There are lots of ways you could organize this. You might start by asking them to attend a homeschoolers' meeting with you, or by leaving books on homeschooling laying around the house in conspicuous places. What follows is a detailed explanation of *one* way to do it. It is rather formal, because formal procedures get most adults to sit up and pay attention.

1. Before you talk to them, know what you're talking about.

Do some background investigation so that you can discuss homeschooling and unschooling with some confidence and expertise. I recommend a) reading a sample issue of *Growing Without Schooling* magazine, b) skimming through *Homeschooling for Excellence*, by David and Micki Colfax, c) reading at least a few chapters of a John Holt book--preferably *Teach Your Own, Instead of Education*, or *Freedom and Beyond*, d) contacting a local homeschooling support group and asking them briefly for their suggestions as to legal and logistical procedures, e) acquainting yourself with an actual unschooled teenager, preferably a fairly independent one.

2. Write a proposal.

Even if you're not sure exactly what you want to do once you're free, your parents can't help but be favorably impressed by a thoughtfully written plan of action. Also, writing the proposal will challenge you to think about some important questions, which will both prepare you to talk with your parents and also clear your vision as to what it is you hope to do with your new life.

In the proposal, include the following:

-Your reasons for wanting to leave school. Tell stories from your own school experiences, without exaggerating. If you don't think your perspective is enough, quote other people too. John Holt always works. You might want to reread chapters 1 through 7 of this book.

- What you would like to do instead. Don't commit to anything too specific, because your mind will surely open and change after you're accustomed to freedom. However, do give a fairly specific possible plan of action, so your parents know you've really thought about it. For example, you might say something like:

> I recognize that when I'm out of school, I might find new interests or goals, and that might lead me to change my activities. But since I am very interested right now in dance, this is what I'd like to start focusing on. My ideas are to
>
> -keep taking ballet lessons
> -start taking African jazz dance lessons
> -begin volunteering at the Center for the Performing Arts in exchange for free passes to dance performances

-read the following books: Doris Humphrey, *The Art of Making Dances*, Joan Brady, *The Unmaking of a Dancer,* Isadora Duncan, *My Life,* Walter Terry, *How to Look at Dance.*
-practice at home at least one hour daily
-audition for the next musical sponsored by the Little Theater
-work out an apprenticeship or internship at my dance studio, preferably as a teacher of pre-ballet classes

-Your academic plans. You might handle this in two ways: you could say that you *want* to keep studying all of the major academic subjects--math, science, literature, social sciences, perhaps foreign language--because you want to go to college, or whatever. Explain how you might study each of these. Or, you could say that you would prefer to discontinue the formal study of some or all of these subjects, in order to have more time for focusing on your interests. Sweeten this by saying that you are willing to compromise, if you are. Also, point out ways in which your interests encompass academic subjects. If your plan is to ride horseback through the ghost towns of Idaho, remind them that you will be doing history, geography, and P.E. all day long. If you write a magazine article about it afterward, you are also doing English. If you take photos or make sketches, that's art. If you plan how far to ride each day and how long it will take, that's math, though basic. If you ask questions and read up on the lay of the land you pass through, that's geology. If you cook your meals on a campstove, that's home ec. The bigger you live, the more "academics" get automatically kneaded into your days.

-How you see your parents' roles in your new life and education. This will be especially important, since most people think of homeschoolers as being taught by their parents. If you want to work independently, say so. If you want their help in finding resources or in making decisions, say so. If you think you may need a lot of help from them, say so. Obviously, you need to be considerate of their own needs and lives. If they are busy people, suggest alternate ways of getting the help you need--from other adults, former teachers, tutors, books, relatives. You may want your parents to be heavily involved or barely involved in your education. Your parents themselves may be excited and flattered at your including them, or they may feel burdened and frightened. If both your parents work outside your home, assure them that other unschooled teens do just fine that way. If they don't like the thought of your being home alone all day, point out your plans for apprenticeships, volunteering, or other away-from-home activities. Likely, this won't be an issue--after all, teenagers are the nation's babysitters.

-A statement that you will need a vacation at the beginning of your unschooling career to recover from school. If your parents are difficult to convince, you don't want to shock them by sleeping through the first two

weeks of unschooling. If you plan to take a purging break (and I hope you do--see chapter 12), let them know from the outset.

-A tentative outline of the legal or official steps you will need to take together. Depending on what state you live in, you may need to think these procedures through carefully later, but for your parents' introduction, you can be somewhat general. Use the advice given to you by local unschoolers.

-A bibliography. It need not be fancy, but do include a short list of books or articles you think might be helpful. There are plenty of books for you to check into listed in the bibliography at the end of this book.

3. Role play.
Imagine all the questions and arguments your particular parents might come up with, and decide how you can most honestly and thoughtfully respond to them. Also, imagine all the secret fears they might have that could prevent them from supporting you. The more you understand about your parents' values and lives, the better.

To get you started, here are some of the obvious questions some parents I know might bring up, along with ideas for possible responses:

You've never done very well in school, even with all those teachers around to prod you along. How am I supposed to believe you could quit school and actually learn anything on your own?

If you've ever been interested in anything--in school or out--and gone after it in an independent way, remind them of that. If you've developed an interest but not developed it due to lack of time, point out that more time will help you to follow through. Explain that in order to learn, you must have the freedom to explore things that interest you. Ask them if they are any good at learning things on command. Ask them to think about the ways they learn--now, not in their ancient past.

Acknowledge that unschooling would require them to trust you to learn and grow independently, and that at first this might be very difficult for them. If you wish, tell them you could unschool on a trial basis.

You might want to share with them some of the words of parents who wrote me about their unschooling experiences:

Bea Rector wrote from Arizona while her 12-year-old daughter Aurelia was performing in Yellowstone with a singing and dancing troupe called Kids Alive. "Trust kids to want to learn," she says, "They don't need to be forced. If given a good example and encouraged to follow their own interests, they'll work for the knowledge needed to be 'successful' adults."

A formerly frustrated Brooklyn parent wrote to *Growing Without Schooling* #32,

[My daughter] wouldn't let me tutor her and she wouldn't do all the educational things I had planned, like go to museums and stuff. She hung around in her bathrobe and drew pictures all day. For nearly three years. Summers, too.

Well, you should see her art work today. Fantastic!

Gwen A. Meehan wrote me a year after she'd taken her son Pat, then 13, out of school:

Pat had asked me after fourth grade to please, please let him stay home and learn. My reaction was the same as most people's: (1) I didn't dream that it was, in fact, a legal option, (2) I couldn't imagine his not having daily, active social interaction with the other students, and (3), selfishly, "there goes any time I might have for my own projects." I'm not even mentioning the sheer terror at the idea of being his official "TEACHER." Parenting is responsibility enough. (Turns out I was only spooking myself all the way around! It has been a piece of cake!)....

I should have listened then. If I had, we could have avoided so much pain and so much lost self-esteem. I don't know if I'll ever see again the relaxed, happy, confident, healthy young person who went so happily into kindergarten...."

I'm not qualified to teach you, or *I don't have time to teach you.*
Point out that you're not asking them to be your teachers (unless you are), that you can pursue your interests on your own and in the company of people with similar interests. Remind them that you know how to read, make friends, use the phone, write letters, and look up books at the library. Ask them if they always need teachers when they become interested in a subject. If you currently ask them for help with homework, and expect to continue to ask for a similar amount of help, acknowledge this. Tell them that most "homeschooling" parents do not *teach* their children, but rather allow them to learn on their own. Here are some testimonies on that subject:
"...[My parents] used to be very involved but this year I have mainly been doing my own work with just a little help and *lots* of encouragement from them."--Tabitha Mountjoy, 14.
"We're available whenever she needs us or is searching for answers. We suggest, support, make things available but trust her to search for herself what *she's* interested in."--Linda J. Savelo, mother of 13-year-old unschooled Andrea.
Maria Holt wrote in *GWS #35* after ten years of homeschooling her sons:

The most important thing I want to impress upon people about our family school is this: WE NEVER TAUGHT ANYTHING. My husband refused to allow it. The closest I came to "teaching" our four sons was during the evening reading-aloud session. We've waded, mulled, or stormed through the *Old Testament, War and Peace*, and *Moby Dick*, among many, many other classics. It was never required to come and listen, and one of our sons gave it up, preferring to read to himself. We provided for and supported the boys--never taught them. Their studies grew out of their own interests. They used all the local libraries and we sent for books from the state library. At one time, they spent months just fixing up an old fishing boat. We never really know *what* they were learning! My husband says we won't know the success or failure of our home schooling for a very long time, if *ever*. We always said they'd "graduate" from the home school when the direction of their lives was outward from home. And that is what has happened..."

She tells about the two who decided to go to college, and then continues,

The youngest...worked during his last two years at home at a local restaurant to earn money for flying lessons. (He had taught himself to read through a stamp collection and magazines about flying. He is a good historian. His specialty is the American Civil War, which, for him, developed from the stamp collection.) Now, at 18, he has been hired as a flight instructor at a respected flying school at Bradley Field in Hartford, Connecticut.

On a similar note, Ruth McCutchen writes in *GWS #52*:

The most frequent response that I get nowadays to the statement that my children are homeschooled is, "Really? How wonderful! I admire you, but I could *never* do that! I just don't have what it takes, etc. etc." When I tell them that *I* don't do it, the *children* do and explain a bit what I mean, I'm met with incredulity....

Now that Deborah, Rebekah and Abigail are 17, 15, and 12, I find more and more that they really are doing it on their own. They long ago reached the point of asking me more questions that I *don't* know than ones that I *do*.

Ruth goes on to describe her girls' interests, including geography, math, anatomy, quilting, clarinet, writing penpals, Bible prophecy, ancient history, physics, Latin, drawing, maps, and current international events.

David and Micki Colfax, in *Homeschooling for Excellence*, write: "In homeschooling, the children typically teach themselves, with the parents appropriately relegated to the job of suggesting courses of study and being available to answer questions--an uncomplicated process..."

And in her book *And the Children Played*, Patricia Joudry writes, "Some people think that if you're going to educate your children at home, you have to be constantly at the ready with blackboard and pointer. Not a bit: you have to do something much harder than that. Mind your own business."

I can believe you'll do fine in chemistry and history because you've always liked them, but what about learning Spanish?

You could either promise to do Spanish first every day, in order to relieve their anxiety, or you could try to help them understand that you don't need to learn Spanish now, that if and when you want it, you can learn it. You may decide to compromise at first, by structuring your academics quite a bit, but chances are, your parents will mellow in time. Ideally, they will be able to share the perspective of Rachel Diener, who wrote me about her 13-year-old son,

> His education is entirely self-directed--that is, he chooses what he wants to learn and how and when he wants to learn it. As a result, if compared with his peers, he is far ahead in some areas (computer knowledge, electronics, vocabulary) and behind in some others (math computation, handwriting skills). He and I are both satisfied with this. I think if he is allowed to focus on his strengths and pursue them to the limit rather than plodding along trying to remediate his weaknesses, he will be a happier and more successful person.

Far more important than the fears your parents will express are the fears they won't express. Your job is to guess what these fears might be, think them through, and then bring them up during your upcoming meeting without directly accusing your parents of thinking this way. Here are some things your parents might feel but not be able to say:

I had to go to school and suffer. It would be too painful to see you go free when it's too late for me.

Realize that if your parents agree with your feelings about school, that might force them to admit to themselves that a lot of their own schooling was a waste of time. Recognize that they are likely to feel a rush of despair and sense of loss over this, and that they may avoid these feelings by denying that there's anything wrong with school--yours or theirs.

The solution is grand and beautiful, though perhaps difficult. Unschooling is a statement of faith in human nature. By living your life as proof that you can learn and grow without an institution's control, you show them that they can do the same. If they had childhood interests which they've squelched, it's not too late to reclaim them. If they hate their jobs, they can find ways to replace them with work they love. Don't preach or be condescending to your parents about this, but find ways to support their interests. If your mom says she always wished she had time to plant a flower garden, bring her library books full of flower gardens, or offer to help with planting and weeding.

I'm afraid you want to be so independent that you won't need me. That makes me feel insecure.

Don't force your parents to say this. Just point out that you value and need their support, that you can't succeed without their blessing, that unschooling helps to destroy barriers in other families and likely will in yours too. Assure them that you'll let them know what you're doing. Tell them you'll need their advice in certain areas. Make them feel important. They are.

I'm afraid of what my friends, boss, or colleagues will think.

Don't force your parents to bring this one up either; they won't want to sound mundane or insecure when you are discussing the lofty principles of trust, freedom, and learning. And obviously, you mustn't say you know they want you to stay in so they can avoid shame and embarrassment. That's an accusation, and then they have to defend themselves against you instead of supporting you. (Anyway, you *don't* know this, any more than they know the inside of *your* brain.) Instead, take away their fear without ever mentioning it.

Tell your parents about some of the people who have been "successful" without school. (Chapter 40 is a good start.) Likely, your parents have even heard of the Colfaxes getting into Harvard. You could agree to use terminology that your parents find comfortable--perhaps "doing independent study" rather than something brash like "unschooling" or, god forbid, "dropping out." If you are college bound, tell your parents they can say so to anyone who asks.

Once you are an actual unschooler, keep making it easy for them by being articulate, presentable, funny, intelligent, interesting, and expert--at least as much as you can be these things without compromising yourself. In general, give them every opportunity to be proud of you and the unschooling movement.

4. Schedule a meeting.

In choosing a time, ask yourself: when are your parents in the best mood? When are you most refreshed and articulate? When are they most likely to trust you? (Just after they see your report card? Just before they see your report card? After you scrub the toilet? After you read *Paradise Lost* even though your English teacher never mentioned it?) It's probably best at this point not to tell them exactly what you'll be discussing. Don't sound too mysterious or choked up, though, or they'll do nightmares on your behalf until the meeting. Just say, "Could we set a time this week to sit down and talk? There's something I'd like to discuss with you."

5. Hold the meeting:

-In everything you say, give your parents the benefit of the doubt. Believe that they want the best for you, and that therefore they'll probably cooperate as soon as they truly understand what you want. *Don't* put them on the defensive by assuming that they're going to fight.

-Introduce the subject, not by saying that you are asking them if you can deschool yourself, but by saying you are interested in the subject of homeschooling and would like to share some of your ideas with them. Tell them you don't want any sort of answer from them during the meeting, but that they are free to ask questions and bring up any points for discussion. Throughout the meeting, continue to focus on presenting information rather than asking permission.

-Give them each a copy of your proposal, keeping a copy for yourself also, and then read through it together, stopping for discussion whenever someone wants to ask a question or make a comment. If you decided not to write a proposal, then you should have at least thought through the same issues so you can discuss them intelligently.

-Have paper and pencil ready. If they ask you something you don't have an answer for, don't panic or try to fake it. Instead, write the question down and tell them you'll think about it and get back to them. Obviously, you strengthen your case by following through.

-Bring evidence of your interests to remind them that you are not just a student, but a person. This evidence could be photographs, books you've enjoyed, ski poles, rocks, vintage clothing, scrapbooks.

-Capitalize on your talents. If you are an actor or storyteller, present scenes from a typical day at school. If you are a writer, write a poem or story that expresses your plight.

-If you don't have any talents, capitalize on that. Everyone has talents, of course, but if yours are hidden or underdeveloped, point out that unschooling will allow you to discover and build them. Talk about the ways you want your life to change when you are out of school.

-Have library books on hand for them to look at. I recommend: Nancy Wallace, *Child's Work*, David and Micki Colfax, *Homeschooling for Excellence*, and John Holt, *Teach Your Own, Freedom and Beyond,* and *Instead of Education.* I also recommend copying the speech John Gatto gave when he accepted one of his awards for New York City Teacher of the Year. See the bibliography for all of these. You might even choose a passage to read aloud during your meeting. Help them realize that in letting you out of school they have intelligent company and moral support.

-If you've already met unschoolers through local support groups, consider inviting a parent and/or unschooled teenager to the meeting. (Make sure your parents know ahead of time that you'll have guests.) You might wish, instead, to invite these people to your second meeting, by which time your parents are likely to have lots of questions.

-Encourage them to ask questions. Do not be glib or patronizing. Essentially, in asking to unschool, you are asking your parents to honor your uniqueness and to take you seriously. Return the favor.

-Conclude the meeting by asking them to think about your ideas, and by scheduling another meeting about a week later.

6. Hold your second meeting.
Ask them for their response to your ideas. If they say yes, great. If they say maybe, work through their hesitations until you get to yes.

What if worse comes to worst and they say no?

Grieve and moan on your best friend's shoulders. Throw darts. Do whatever you do in the face of disaster.

When you're ready to deal with it, here are some strategies for round two:

Beyond no
1) Ask your parents why they said no. See if you can strike a compromise. Ask them if there's anything you can do that would get them to say yes.

2) Suggest a trial run. You could start unschooling in the middle of August, so they have a couple weeks to see how you manage. Also, that would allow you to recover from the previous school year. You could agree that if they're not satisfied with your way of educating yourself, that you go to school. A drawback to this sort of timing is that you may feel cheated out of your normal summer vacation, and thus not as exhilarated as you would if you quit in, say, October. Also, the whole idea of being watched and evaluated runs contrary to the idea of pursuing interests because you *want* to. Still, you could probably psyche yourself into it and make it work.

3) Continue to read up on the subject of unschooling and education in general, and keep giving your parents articles and library books. Read aloud to them or make tapes they can listen to in the car. *GWS* is full of stories of one parent convincing the other parent to unschool after enough exposure to *GWS* and John Holt.

4) Ask them to attend a local homeschoolers' meeting or fair with you.

5) Become pen pals with one of the teens listed in *Growing Without Schooling*. Keep your parents posted on your friendship.

6) Help them *feel* what you feel. Ask them to attend school with you for a day, and to take notes and do the homework just as if they were a student. Or, without sounding threatening, ask them to think about how they want to be treated when *they* are powerless. For example, when they are old do they want you to take their choices seriously, or would they like you to abandon them to a "nursing home" or other institution?

7) Befriend as many unschoolers and their families as possible. When you meet some your parents might like, invite them to dinner. Be sure they know what they might be getting into.

8) When you have a choice of topics for research papers, etc., write on unschooling. Show your parents your work.

9) See if any of your parents' friends or relatives can understand your side. If they can, ask them to intervene on your behalf.

10) Ask them again to think hard about their own ways of learning and their own past, and whether they think school was truly good for them, and how much they learned in it.

11) Watch *Dead Poets' Society* with them. At heart, it's a movie about unschooling; at heart, unschooling is all about "seizing the day."

12) If you can, survive spiritually by focusing more on your life outside of school and not worrying too much about your grades.

13) When you sense the timing is right, ask them to reconsider.

Beyond yes

After they say yes, you want to live with them in harmony. Try to be tolerant of your parents' worries, especially at first. If they are a bit overbearing, don't panic--they'll relax. If they ask you to study in a fairly rigid way at first, try to cooperate--many unschooling families start this way and then slowly come to their senses, abandoning unnecessary structure.

You might show them this bit of wisdom, written by Donna Richoux in *GWS #52*:

> Over the years I've had a few long phone calls from parents who are concerned about the lack of academic interest shown by one of their children. Among other things that cause them worry is the fact that the child will show an interest in something and the parent will arrange for a chance to follow up on it--lessons, a visit--and shortly thereafter the child loses interest.
>
> Somewhere in these conversations I've said something like: how would YOU feel if someone older than you--say your mother, or mother-in-law--lived with you now and always worried about whether you were OK, whether you read too little or too much, and whether she should do something to fix you up? Suppose she got upset because you signed up for a course somewhere and then dropped out? Suppose she MADE you continue?
>
> The parents laugh ruefully in recognition. "That would be awful. I'm always signing up for things and dropping out," they say.
>
> There are many good reasons for dropping out of an adult education class--the brief exposure was enough to satisfy one's curiosity, something about the teacher turns one off, one has less time than one expected because of other changes in one's life. Aren't we lucky that, as adults, we CAN quit? Nobody tells us we have to finish what we begin, or worries about what that says about us. So maybe it's reasonable to extend that same privilege to our children.

Or show them Gwen Meehan's comment on working with her son Pat, 15:

> I was all full of the things I was going to help Pat explore academically this year, but it has been abundantly clear that that route would lead nowhere. He

might cooperate wanly in order to placate his father and me, but he wouldn't really learn anything.

If your parents just can't relax, find yourself an adult advisor, mentor, or tutor whom your parents respect. Chances are, once they see that this adult doesn't get bent out of shape over your choices, they'll back off.

If they *still* watch you too closely, turn the tables on them with a friendly (if possible) sense of humor. Watch them back. Take notes on how well they seem to be learning, and how well they use what they learn. Give them progress reports. Once they get the message, stop.

Most importantly, continue to do all you can to support and encourage *their* dreams. If your independence inspires them to dramatically change their own lives, don't freak out. Stand behind them and beam.

chapter 11

The Not Necessarily Difficult Legal Issue*

As I write, homeschooling is legal in all fifty states.

However:

-In a few states it is quite regulated. In these states, homeschoolers are still working for better laws. They could use your help. There's no better way to learn "American Government."

-Even where homeschooling is now easy, it wasn't always. In the seventies and eighties, schools and courts harassed a lot of families. Lucky for you, homeschoolers did not give up. Instead, they banded together, spoke the truth, suffered, and eventually won supportive laws. Thanks to their very hard work, you aren't likely to face any serious hassle from your school district, let alone a court trial. Don't take their struggle for granted--and be ready to stand up for your freedom if you need to.

-If laws can change for the better, they can also change for the worse. If a lot of people wanted to quit school all at once, schoolpeople would panic about losing their jobs, and would therefore lobby for tighter restrictions on homeschooling. There are millions of schoolpeople, and they might win.

On the other hand, growing numbers of people support homeschooling. When homeschoolers are so obviously living intelligently and happily, and when their average test scores are higher than school students' average test scores--even though these tests narrowly reflect mainly *school* methods of learning--legislators and courts look rather silly requiring them to go back to school "for their own good." Truth is on your side.

This chapter will give you some basic pointers and information on the legal aspects of homeschooling. Yes, I am shifting my terminology a little. In this chapter, I will mostly use the euphemism "homeschooling" rather than "unschooling." Unschooling is not a legally recognized term, and probably never will be. Don't use it when you talk to schools, courts, or legislators; it will piss them off or at least confuse them.

("Homeschooling" implies that *somebody* is teaching you, even if it's "only" your parents. That's easier for arrogant professional educators to swallow. Of course, you *do* have guiding adults in your life, but no one should

---

*The information in this chapter is as accurate as I could make it. However, it is not intended as *official* legal advice, which I am not qualified to give. Legally, only an attorney has the right to give legal counsel.

be bossing you about. Gradually, tactfully, start letting people know that you are responsible for your own education. But don't strut around acting as if you don't need no help from nobody. It's not true, and it will earn you enemies.)

General stuff you need to know to understand homeschooling legalities:

1. Education laws are the business of each state, not of the federal government. Therefore, Californians and Iowans face completely different sets of regulations.

2. Every state has statutes, or written laws, on compulsory education. These laws now have specific provisions for homeschooling. In some cases they define homeschooling as a type of private school. You can get a copy of your state's most recent statutes by writing the state department of education--addresses at the end of this chapter. (You needn't write a fancy business letter--a postcard will do. Just request a copy of all statutes pertaining to homeschooling, and any guidelines they have for homeschoolers. If you don't want them to know who you are, use a fake name and your grandmother's address.)

Most departments will respond quickly and sweetly, sometimes with heaps of advice, including the phone numbers of homeschooling organizations. The Indiana State Attendance Officer sends a friendly, no-nonsense letter to prospective homeschoolers, concluding: "That's all there is to it. If you have any questions at all, please let me know. I will help you in any way I can." Vermont mails a thorough, encouraging package of information which includes ideas for "home" education such as specific opportunities at local museums. Alternatively, you can look up statutes at a law library or request them from a local representative.

3. In some states, statutes are clear and precise, and readily understandable. In others, they are vague. In any state, the statutes are only *part* of the law. The other major part is the way courts interpret statutes. The less precise your state's laws are, the more room a court has to play with them. Therefore, if you want to really understand homeschooling law you need to both read your state's statutes AND find out if any court cases have applied them in surprising ways. Ways to keep up on court cases include 1) reading the *Journal of Law and Education*, as described in this chapter's section on law libraries, 2) reading *Growing Without Schooling* magazine (*GWS*) or the newsletter of the National Homeschooling Association. Both contain legal updates including court cases in all states, and 3) staying in touch with a local support group.

4. We do, supposedly, live in a democracy. The people who pass the statutes are your local elected representatives--not the state senators and representatives who work in Washington D.C., but the state legislators who work in your state capitol. These people are supposed to represent the choices of the people who elect them. Technically, that's not you, because you're not old enough to vote. However, any politician with foresight pays attention to

the opinions of thoughtful future voters. Obviously, your parents' voices count too. See the end of this chapter for suggestions on changing legislation.

5. No law is an issue until someone tries to enforce it. The vast majority of homeschoolers are perfectly legal. However, in restrictive areas, some people do break laws in order to homeschool. Sometimes, schoolboards ignore them. Sometimes, schoolboards simply don't know about homeschooling families. Until Mr. Mint registers Junior Mint for kindergarten, they don't know he exists. If a schoolboard does get upset over your actions, it may first ask you to return to school, and then perhaps try to take you to court.

Often, by the way, schoolboards are completely misinformed about homeschooling laws, and think they have much greater power than they do. If worse comes to worst and you are taken to court, one thing you can do in preparation is attend a few other trials--not necessarily homeschooling trials--just to demystify the whole thing a bit.

What do the statutes say?

Laws change frequently, and they are different in every state. Within state laws, separate districts have varying policies and attitudes. Therefore, I cannot tell you exactly what you are expected to do in your particular district this year, and whether you should cooperate with or defy the local authorities. Instead, I'll discuss a few aspects of current statutes and fortify you with a lot of addresses--people near you who can give precise information. Addresses of state departments of education are at the end of the chapter. In Appendix B, you'll find addresses of homeschool support groups.

Most statutes specify that you must register with the state or a local board, be in "homeschool" for a certain number of days and a certain number of hours, and that you keep attendance records. Some statutes ask that you keep records such as logs, portfolios of written work, and even written evaluations of progress (like grade reports); in some states, you must show these records to certain officials. (Be creative with unsavory regulations. If your state requires a progress report, write it yourself and have the parents sign it.) None of these requirements should cause problems. Attendance in school can certainly include educational field trips, such as your kayaking expedition around Prince William Sound.

Other requirements may be more bothersome:

1. One requirement in most state's homeschooling laws is that parents provide instruction in the same areas schools do--math, language arts, science, art, history, health, etc. Don't panic when you read this stipulation. Remember that by pursuing your interests, you will automatically include some of these subjects. On the leftover ones, you can either leave them out and probably not get caught, or else you can study them in a way that you find interesting. There are so many ways to explore any subject that you can almost certainly end up with a legal program that you like, even if it includes subjects you used

to hate. See the rest of this book, especially chapters 16 and 17, for ways to design a program you can love and everyone else can accept.

And remember: the laws don't ask you to imitate school *methods*. Textbooks, for instance, are not required; nor are grades or book reports. School activities take most of their shape from rigid schedules, bureacratic logistics, and limited access to the outside world. There's no point in lowering your intellect to that level.

2. Because people just don't get it about self-education and insist on believing that homeschoolers are taught by their parents, some statutes say a lot about parents' qualifications. Iowa and Michigan, the strictest states in many respects, require that a homeschooling parent hold a teaching certificate. However, Iowa compulsory attendance laws do not apply to anyone "who is over the age of fourteen and is regularly employed," or *"whose educational qualifications are equal to those of pupils who have completed the eighth grade* [italics added]. " Also, homeschoolers are currently working to change these laws, by showing that teacher certification is not necessarily related to teacher *qualification*. (Most prestigious private schools couldn't care less whether their teachers are certified.) By the time you read this, certification may no longer be necessary.

In other states, your parents face different educational requirements. For instance:

In Pennsylvania and North Carolina, one parent must hold at least a high school diploma, GED diploma, or college degree. In Ohio, one parent must have a diploma, GED diploma, another "equivalent" credential, or else must consult regularly with someone who has a bachelor's degree. In South Carolina, the parent must both have a high school diploma or equivalent, *and* pass a basic skills test.

In West Virginia, a parent must both have a high school diploma or equivalent *and* have formal education at least four years beyond you. In other words, if you are a ninth grader, one of your parents needs to have completed a year of college. In New Mexico, one parent must hold a bachelor's degree, although the state superintendent can waive this requirement. In Tennessee, your parent must have a bachelor's degree if you have reached ninth grade-- otherwise a diploma or GED equivalent. Arizona parents must pass a basic competency test in reading, grammar, and math.

In North Dakota, if your parent does not qualify for a teaching certificate, he or she must pass the National Teacher's Examination *or* you can spend one hour a week with a certified teacher. (In many cases the district enrolls you half-time and pays for this contact.)

Other states have similar arrangements, where parents without teaching certificates or college degrees must consult with a certified teacher. Sometimes, these states pay for this consultation by enrolling you in local schools and paying a teacher-consultant.

3. In some states, there are clear-cut statewide guidelines; follow them and you have automatic legal approval. In others--such as Delaware, Idaho,

and West Virginia--you are supposed to request permission, often from local or county boards. However, these boards usually have specific guidelines to follow in granting approval, and their decisions can be challenged.

4. In California, you can easily register your home as a private school; also, in many districts you can homeschool through an independent study program, which is a branch of the public school system.

5. Many states require you to take standardized tests. The following states require yearly testing: Arkansas, Minnesota, New Mexico, North Carolina, North Dakota, Oregon, South Carolina, South Dakota, and West Virginia.

These states also require standardized testing, but not every year: Alaska, Arkansas, Georgia, Pennsylvania, Tennessee.

In Massachusetts and Nebraska, certain officials can require testing in individual cases.

In various other states, you are required to submit some type of annual "assessment." Standardized testing is one of your choices, but you can also elect an alternate method, such as having a certified teacher evaluate your progress.

In some states that require testing, very low scores can send you back to school. In Colorado, for instance, if the composite score on your test is at or below the thirteenth percentile, you are first given the chance to take another test; if your scores are *still* below the thirteenth percentile, you may be required to go to school until the next testing period. In Arizona, if your scores are low the county school superintendent can ask an independent evaluator to talk with your family and look at your whole homeschool situation and decide whether you should continue it.

6. In some states, you can start homeschooling and then notify your local authorities. In others, you must first notify them and wait for their response before leaving school.

7. And in Kansas you must conduct a tornado drill three times yearly. There's no place like home.

How to find more specific legal information:

The more you know, the more powerful your position. That's one major purpose of anyone's education, of course--but as an unschooler living on the edge, you have a real chance to put this truth into action, *now*.

1. Contact a local homeschooling group.

This is the single most important thing you can do for your legal education. These groups can share the lessons learned by all of their members and contacts. They have had experience dealing with local laws and school boards, and can offer you invaluable advice. Many groups publish guides to local laws.

Indeed, most homeschooling groups are far more knowledgeable and helpful--not to mention cheaper--than lawyers. This situation won't likely change soon--generally, homeschoolers are an enterprising bunch of people and take the initiative for doing their own legal research. They don't call on the help of lawyers except when absolutely necessary. Therefore, lawyers have little incentive to become expert on homeschool law.

There are homeschooling groups in every state, and you can communicate by mail if not in person. Addresses in Appendix B. Some of the groups near you may be so strongly opinionated as to religious or other "truths" that you feel alienated by them. However, even many fundamentalist Christian homeschooling groups are very helpful to less religiously oriented unschoolers.

2. Johnny Homeschooler In the Law Library

I got up my nerve to go in and you can too. Law libraries exist at law schools and court houses, and sometimes elsewhere. To help you decide what to look for and how to make sense of it, I recommend the excellent book *Legal Research: How to Find and Understand the Law,* revised edition, by Attorney Stephen Elias (1986, Nolo Press, 950 Parker Street Berkeley, CA 94710). Also, tell law librarians what you need and ask for their help. You will not find a great wealth of information on homeschooling, because it's a relatively new, unexplored legal territory. I do recommend the following resources:

-Journal of Law and Education (published four times a year), especially the section entitled "Recent Developments in the Law," which summarizes court cases. In the three latest issues I found two paragraphs on homeschooling issues. In one, a Pennsylvania court had ruled in favor of a homeschooling family since the statute's definition of a "qualified tutor" was vague, leaving interpretation up to local superintendents. The court thought that this practice "allowed arbitrary and discriminatory application." In the other instance, a Michigan family had lost a case because they did not have a certified teacher.

-Legal Foundations of Compulsory School Attendance, by Lawrence Kotin and William F. Aikman. (Kennikat Press, Port Washington, NY, 1980. Financed by a grant from the National Institute of Education, Department of Health, Education, and Welfare.) Clear yet technical, this book helped me to understand the broad picture and the trends which have led to compulsory school attendance laws. Imaginatively, it also discusses the possibility of *repealing* these laws. If you choose to work with a lawyer, she should read this book.

However, most lawyers charge money for the time they spend reading something for you. Therefore, you might instead read it yourself and summarize important points for your lawyer. Or read it and a few other books--and be your own lawyer. (It's legal to be your own lawyer. You can't be anyone else's, however, unless you have a license to practice law.)

3. Other sources of information:

Various homeschooling magazines and national organizations monitor the legal news. Probably the best source of nationwide legal information is *GWS*, which prints updates of laws and reports on court cases.

A good book is Stephen Arons' *Compelling Belief: The Culture of American Schooling* (McGraw-Hill Book Company, 1983), which examines some of the reactions school districts and courts have had to homeschooling.

An Ounce of Prevention

If you live with a bit of diplomacy, you shouldn't have to actually deal with courts or hostile school boards. Legal technicalities, after all, are not the only factor which affects your right to homeschool; unspoken social rules are even more important and fundamental. The following suggestions are especially important if you live in one of the greyish states where people have to request permission to homeschool. However, they can help maintain peace and goodwill anywhere.

1. Trust, as much as you can.

Don't turn a peaceful situation into a war. Until they prove otherwise, assume that the people in your school are your allies. Assume that they want you to have the best possible education, and that therefore they will cheer you on. Teachers and even administrators will likely support you unless you put them on the defensive.

Most of the teens I heard from said they'd never been hassled, and that the schools basically ignored them as long as they fulfilled local requirements. In most cases this involved little more than sending in a short statement every September briefly outlining their plans. Some reported that their local schools were not just neutral, but helpful and supportive. Thirteen-year-old Anne Brosnan, for instance, wrote me: "The school is perfectly happy with us, and we've never been to court. About twice a year a lady comes from Babylon Schools to visit us, and she's really nice and we like her. We don't take tests and she just makes sure we are 'pretty smart'!!"

A California mother wrote in *GWS* #35 about what happened after she explained to the local principal why she planned to take her daughters out of school:

> The principal agreed with me completely about my observations and said he would support my endeavors in any way he could. His support was not just official, but warm and genuine...The district agreed to send me any non-consumable materials I needed. The principal said my children could partake of school activities if they wanted as long as fulltime students weren't bumped from the class and the teacher was agreeable....

Of course, there is no guarantee they'll be nice. A few teenagers wrote me about minor trouble they'd had: "'They' still feel they own us," 15-

year-old Todd Brown wrote about his school district in Virginia, "The local principal has forbidden us and some other nonschooling friends from taking driver's ed. Also in the past he has been unreasonable and even downright rude." A parent wrote me that local school officials "enjoy control and power, and their lack of awareness and support causes problems."

Sometimes schoolpeople simply talk arrogant nonsense--"We...were informed that no parent could teach a child to read...," Californian Bonnie Sellstrom told me about the early stages of homeschooling her now-teenaged sons, "We did put Gary in the independent [homeschool] program with the principal's approval and he was able to complete second and third grade while his schoolmates completed first grade."

2. Keep your ship together. At the same time that you radiate friendliness and expect your schoolpeople to be nice, **give them every reason you can to hate the idea of messing with you**--especially if you live in a state with difficult homeschooling laws. Some of these reasons could be:

-Get your community on your side. If the schools think you're all alone, they might move in for the kill. But if they see that your community supports you, they'll realize the odds are against them and stay off your case. And your community *will* support you if you give them the slightest reason to do so. In most situations, people love to root for any underdog with the guts to beat a system.

How to win that community support? Be visible. With some of your free time, start a project that is terrific for everyone--a tree planting campaign, a theater production for kids, a teen-to-senior-citizen adoption program, a neighborhood newsletter. Smile. Take lessons from neighbors, in exchange for work. If you keep to yourself, your community may think you are arrogant and standoffish, that you consider yourself (but not other people) "too good" for the schools. That will get their hackles up for sure. Of course, if you *do* consider yourself better than other people, no amount of fakey goo will make your neighbors like you.

-When you start homeschooling, in addition to fulfilling state requirements, have a lawyer write a polite but firm letter to your district, explaining your actions and a summary of recent court decisions regarding homeschooling. Unless your lawyer knows a lot about homeschooling (and few do), you can save money by researching and preparing this summary yourself, and simply having her finalize and sign it.

-Or: when you start homeschooling, write a very detailed, typed paper explaining your actions, your plans, your reasons, a brief history of homeschooling, and a summary of local laws and recent national court decisions. Mail it to the schoolboard. (In some states, you are required to submit a written plan anyway; by making it long and detailed, you help establish yourself as a force to be reckoned with.)

Forget everything you ever learned about good writing being direct and simple; make it as long and flowery as you can. Unfortunately, bad confusing writing impresses most bureacrats more than clear writing does. Toss in plenty of jargon like "learning style," "individualized education program," "experiential education," "writing across the curriculum," and "neuro-linguistic programming." Don't say you've been growing mushrooms; say you've been "learning mycology through experiential education." Borrow a textbook on educational psychology from a college library to get some juicy terms, or have a teacher-friend help.

In *GWS* #44, Lisa Boken wrote about working with and learning from boatbuilders, day care centers, an herb shop, and a health food store. "We call this," she explains, "for the benefit of the public school authorities, Reality Centered Learning. We give everything we do with the kids a buzzword like that..."

Follow up by keeping a detailed portfolio of everything you do--your writing, your art, extensive lists and journals of books you read and places you go.

-In general, stay informed on homeschooling issues. If you have to attend meetings with school officials, take the initiative for politely educating them on homeschooling--don't let *them* preach to *you*.

3. Understand what the schoolpeople have to lose: money and pride. Don't carelessly say or do things that increase their losses.

Money: if you quit by the dozens or hundreds, teachers and other schoolpeople will panic about their jobs, reasonably enough. Schools are given money based on the number of students enrolled in them--usually about $3,000-4,000 per year per student. Therefore, each person who quits causes his school to lose that much money each year. Some states and districts work out programs where they continue to enroll homeschoolers, giving them access to certain classes and services in return. These programs could be developed much further, helping both the schools and homeschoolers financially. However, if the homeschooling movement continues to grow rapidly, teachers *will* eventually lose jobs.

Pride: quite aside from the homeschooling movement, the teaching profession has long suffered from a general feeling of not being respected or taken seriously enough. Teachers do face injustice--they are not trusted with enough independence or creativity in the classroom, they are swamped with inane clerical details, students and parents viciously blame them for things that are beyond their control, and their pay is low compared to other careers that require similar qualifications. All of this discourages teachers from living with healthy humility and honesty; instead, it encourages them to be generally defensive and overly concerned with their reputations.

To teachers of this unfortunate mentality, homeschooling feels like an additional slap in the face, even a challenge to do battle. After they wear themselves out convincing the public that they are knowledgeable, indispensable professionals, homeschooling families come along and say, "We don't need you. Our kids will have better educations without you."

(Of course, there are many earnest teachers whose self-esteem is intact enough that they can see clearly. They are not puffed up with superficial pride, and will be glad to see you escape to learn freely, even though they may nevertheless worry about money.)

Teachers have formed several very powerful unions, which not only work for higher salaries but also lobby for laws which help them. Obviously, favorable homeschooling laws do *not* help them. So far, the NEA (National Education Association) and other unions have not felt threatened enough by homeschooling to really fight hard. But as homeschooling continues to rise and shine, they *will* fight hard. Already, for the past three years they have included a head-in-the-sand statement in their annual resolutions: "The National Education Association believes that home schooling programs cannot provide the student with a comprehensive education experience."*

If I belonged to the NEA I would be embarrassed by such a careless declaration. Nationwide, homeschoolers' standardized test scores are above school kids', even though these tests don't reflect the variety of learning methods and subjects available to homeschoolers.** Then there's that term "comprehensive." Of *course* homeschooling can't offer a comprehensive education. Neither can school. "Comprehensive" is a huge word. It approaches infinity. No one should toss it around so glibly.

Furthermore, in order to try to get comprehensively educated even in their confused understanding of the term, you can't have time to be comprehensively *alive*. The underlying message is that schoolpeople prefer quantity over quality. Their statement implies, "Homeschoolers can not be trusted to force enough worksheets, textbooks, and multiple choice quizzes on their children, in the fields of English, biology, chemistry, algebra, geometry, art appreciation, history, health, geography, French, and Physical Education." Anyway, if those NEApeople themselves were "comprehensively educated," they would have done their homework and learned that homeschoolers are far beyond their petty ideas of education.

But of course the NEA has to make their statement, silly as it is. If we had somehow gotten ourselves into a nutrition predicament similar to our education predicament, by this time all kids would be eating three meals a day at state run cafeterias, where millions of cooks, waitresses, and other cafeteriapeople earned salaries. If sad parents suddenly got smart and brought their kids home for blueberry pancakes, those cafeteriapeople would lose no time issuing proclamations that parents without degrees in nutrition are unfit to feed their own children.

Teachers' money and pride panics are not your fault; they are the natural and fitting consequences of an arrogant profession which has preyed for a century on the nation's young. However, you may want to generously do

* *NEA Today*, September 1990, p.18.
** See the journal *Home School Researcher*. Information available from NHERI, 25 West Cremona St., Seattle, WA 98119; (206) 283-3650.

something to alleviate the problem. With tact, you can make things easier for both you and the schoolpeople, at least in the short run. If you want to ease the money panic, you can look for a way to stay partially enrolled in school so they get their dollars (chapter 19). If you want to ease the pride panic, you can avoid making public statements that accuse teachers of incompetence. In your conversations, focus instead on the structural problems of schools, and point out that the system prevents teachers from teaching to their best ability. No honest teacher will disagree with you there.

Beyond information: what are you going to do?

-In most cases in most states, you can simply obey the law and be a happy "homeschooler" free in the world.

-If local laws are difficult, here are some options:

1) If you are legally old enough, drop out of school. For all practical purposes, you can be an "unschooler" or homeschooler, eating nonstop intellectual candy if you so desire. Colleges and employers won't mind, especially if you call yourself a homeschooler.

2) Enroll in a correspondence school, or just a couple correspondence courses. *I* wouldn't, because it's too much like school. But it might help you convince the Authorities you are serious, especially at first. Also, you can enroll in college correspondence courses and begin earning college credit this way. (Correspondence schools are just school by mail. They have preplanned courses and textbooks. They send you assignments; you do them and mail them. Then they mail you criticism and grades, and often award credit.) There's a list of some correspondence schools in Appendix C. For a very detailed list of available college and high school level courses, see *Peterson's Independent Study Catalog*.

3) Enroll in a long distance "umbrella school." Unlike correspondence schools, these schools usually encourage you to learn as creatively and independently as you wish, and do not provide set curriculums or correspondence teachers. They do not require you to study anything; their function is mainly to help you keep records and to handle negotiations with your local schoolpeople when necessary. Usually, they charge a flat fee which can seem expensive--but if it solves your legal worries and thus sets you free, it's money very well spent.

The Home Based Education Program of Clonlara school, in Michigan, is probably the most widely used umbrella school. It offers as much or as little structure as you want, although it does not actually provide textbooks. It can give you copies of the same curriculum guidebooks public schools use, formats for record keeping, and a high school diploma. If you like, Dr. Pat Montgomery, the director, will handle all of the negotiation with your school district, and she and other staff will answer your questions over the phone or through mail. Currently, the program costs $350 per year, for everyone in a single family. Clonlara has had a campus-based school since 1967, and the home-based program since 1979. Address: The Home Based

Education Program, Clonlara School, 1289 Jewett, Ann Arbor, MI 48104. Similar schools listed in Appendix C.

4) Enroll in a program that combines some of the elements of a private school with homeschooling. There aren't yet many important or successful schools of this type, but more will undoubtedly form. Furthermore, you can try to get one started in your own state if you can find an interested certified teacher.

Here is one example of an inexpensive program that works. It could provide a model, or more direct help, for someone near you to follow:

A few certified teachers in Washington wanted to support homeschooling, so they started The Family Academy in Seattle, which trains certified teachers to work respectfully with homeschoolers. "Our goal," states their literature, "Is to help the homeschool family succeed."

The local teacher works mainly as a consultant, helping to plan academic programs and locate books and other resources. Also, through the Academy, homeschoolers have access to science fairs, scholarships, group activities, and other opportunities. Participants can receive high school credit, diplomas, and transcripts.

The administrators of Family Academy are interested in building other chapters across the country. If you or a certified teacher you know would like more specific information, contact them for more information: Family Academy, 14629 20th SW, Seattle, WA 98166, (206) 246-9227.

5) Simply stop going. If you are part of a large, chaotic school district, nobody may ever have time to figure out you're missing. The same can hold if you've freshly moved to a new area--how does a school know it owns you unless you tell them? Many homeschooling families, particularly in rural areas, never register their children in school to begin with, so the schools never realize they exist. If you never have to deal with school officials, well, you escape all the potential paperwork and nonsense they may ask you and your parents to complete.

Of course, if you try this method, you and your parents may have a constant feeling of "hiding," a perpetual fear of being caught. Also, if you *are* caught, the schoolpeople may be especially hostile and vindictive since you didn't ask their almighty permission in the first place.

If and when they notice your absence, revert to plan 1, 2, 3, 4, and/or 6. Or hide--take off to another state or country. Actually, I'm not joking. It's been done by people who lived in the vicinity of especially vicious school districts. I wouldn't recommend doing this without your parents' blessing, except in an extreme situation beyond the realm of usual healthy experience.

6) Enroll in a homeschool insurance program, *before* you get into legal hot water. (They won't take you if you're already in trouble.) As I write, there's only one major program, but others may form soon. The Home School Legal Defense Association, run mainly by Christian lawyers, prefers to think of their organization as a homeschoolers' "union," but it works like an insurance program. After you join, if anyone brings legal action against you

the HSLDA will provide attorneys or other legal assistance at no additional cost. Generally, this means *they* work as your attorneys.

The HSDLA has a *strong* fundamentalist Christian overtone, but they don't require any particular religious conviction of their members. Because some non-Christian homeschoolers have felt uncomfortable supporting or working with the HSDLA, an alternative organization may spring up soon. Meanwhile, more information from HSLDA, P.O. Box 159, Paeonian Springs, VA 22129, (703) 882-3838.

7) Work to change the laws. Contact your representatives: write, phone, visit. You can make very specific suggestions on legislation, or you can simply help teach them about homeschooling, by describing your own life and education. This is one of the main ways homeschoolers have so far had legal success: by getting to know their representatives and showing them how wonderful homeschooling is.

If you're up for more, write a bill that would make homeschooling more possible, and then ask your local representative to sponsor it. If your state has difficult laws, homeschoolers are probably already working on a bill. Hook up with them and see how you can help. An important change that most statutes need is an acknowledgment that homeschooled teenagers have the right to teach *themselves*--so the Authorities won't poke their noses into your parents' qualifications and schedules.

Two related statutes would also be most helpful. First, consider writing (or supporting) a bill that allows people of any age to take the GED. Second, work on "educational choice" legislation that gives tax credits to people who want to educate their children outside of the public schools. (Minnesota has such a law, and Oregon had a bill on the 1990 ballot, though it didn't pass.) Make sure that these credits are available to homeschoolers as well as private school students.

The way this works is that if you choose to homeschool or go to private school, the state tax people give *you* most of the money they would have otherwise given to the public school. You use this money to help pay tuition at a private school, or to buy supplies for homeschooling. Through legislation like this, you could get several thousand dollars a year--which could obviously make a substantial improvement in your attic laboratory.

A potential drawback: schools may become more reluctant to share their resources with you. If you decide to write a bill like this, consider aiming for a compromise, where homeschool students might give up around $500 of their rebate, and then be legally entitled to use certain school resources. See chapter 19 for more information on using school resources.

If you plan on working on homeschooling legislation, see *The Story of a Bill*, by Howard Richman, which tells how Pennsylvanian homeschoolers won a very helpful homeschooling law. You could base your own efforts on Richman's detailed account. Available from John Holt's Book and Music Store, address in Appendix C.

State departments of education

Alabama
Dept. of Education
State Office Bldg Rm 483
501 Dexter Avenue
Montgomery, AL 36130
(205) 261-5156

Alaska
Dept. of Education
PO Box F
Juneau, AK 99811
(907) 465-2800

Arizona
Dept. of Education
1535 W Jefferson St
Phoenix, AZ 85007
(602) 255-4271

Arkansas
Dept. of Education
Arch-Ford Education
Bldg, Rm 304-A
4 Capitol Mall
Little Rock, AR 72201
(501) 682-4204

California
Dept. of Education
PO Box 944272
Sacramento 94244
(916) 445-2700

Colorado
Dept. of Education
State Office Bldg
201 E Colfax Avenue
Denver, CO 80203
(303) 866-6806

Connecticut
Dept. of Education
PO Box 2219
Hartford, CT 06145
(203) 566-5061

Delaware
Dept. of Public
Instruction
PO Box 1402
Dover, DE 19903
(302) 736-4601

District of Columbia
DC Public Schools
Presidential Bldg, Rm 1209
415 12th St, NW
Washington, DC 20004
(202) 724-4222

Florida
Dept. of Education
The Capitol, Plaza
Level 08
Tallahassee, FL 32399
(904) 487-1785

Georgia
Dept. of Education
Floyd Memorial Bldg,
East Tower, Rm 2066
205 Butler St, SE
Atlanta, GA 30334
(404) 656-2800

Hawaii
Dept. of Education
PO Box 2360
Honolulu, HI 96804
(808) 548-6405

Idaho
Dept. of Education
Len B Jordan Bldg,
Rm 200
650 W State St
Boise, ID 83720
(208) 334-3301

Illinois
State Board of
Education
100 N 1st Street
Springfield, IL 62777
(217) 782-2221

Indiana
Dept. of Education
State House, Rm 229
Indianapolis, IN 46204-2798
(317) 232-6610

Iowa
Dept. of Education
Grimes State Office
Building
Des Moines, IA 50319-0146
(515) 281-5294

Kansas
Dept. of Education
State Education
Building
120 E 10th St
Topeka, KS 66612
(913) 296-3201

Kentucky
Dept. of Education
Capital Plaza Tower,
1st Floor
Frankfort, KY 40601
(502) 564-4770

Louisiana
Dept. of Education
PO Box 94064
Baton Rouge, LA
79894-9064
(504) 342-3602

Maine
Dept. of Educational
Services
State House, Station
23
Augusta, ME 04333
(207) 289-5800

Maryland
Dept. of Education
Maryland State
Education Bldg
200 W Baltimore St
Baltimore, MD 21201
(301) 333-2100

Massachusetts
Dept. of Education
1385 Hancock St
Quincy, MA 02169
(617) 770-7300

Michigan
Dept. of Education
PO Box 30008
Lansing, MI 48909
(517) 335-4933

Minnesota
Capitol Square Bldg
550 Cedar St
St. Paul, MN 55101
(612) 296-2358

Mississippi
Dept. of Education
PO Box 771
Jackson, MS 39205
(601) 359-3513

Missouri
Dept. of Education
P.O. Box 480
Jefferson City, MO
65102
(314) 751-4446

Montana
Office of Public
Instruction
Capitol Bldg, Rm 106
Helena, MT 59620
(406) 444-3654

Nebraska
Dept. of Education
PO Box 94987
Lincoln, NE 68509
(402) 471-2465

Nevada
Dept. of Education
Capitol Complex
Carson City 89710
(702) 885-3100

New Hampshire
Dept. of Education
State Office Park
South
101 Pleasant Street
Concord, NH 03301
(603) 271-3144

New Jersey
Dept. of Education
CN 500
Trenton, NJ 08625
(609) 292-4450

New Mexico
Dept. of Education
Education Bldg
300 Don Gaspar Ave
Santa Fe, NM 87501-
2786
(505) 827-6635

New York
Office of Elementary,
Secondary, and
Continuing Education
State Education Dept.
Education Bldg
Annex, Rm 875
Albany, NY 12234
(518) 474-4688

North Carolina
Dept. of Public
Education
116 W Edenton St
Raleigh, NC 27603-
1712
(919) 733-3813

North Dakota
Dept. of Public
Instruction
State Capitol
Bismarck, ND 58505-
0164
(701) 224-2260

Ohio
Dept. of Education
Ohio Dept.s Bldg, Rm
808
65 S Front St
Colombus, OH 43215
(614) 466-3304

Oklahoma
Dept. of Education
Oliver Hodge
Memorial Education
Bldg, Rm 121
2500 N Lincoln Blvd
Oklahoma City, OK
73105
(405) 521-3301

Oregon
Dept. of Education
700 Pringle Pkwy, SE
Salem, OR 97310
(503) 378-3573

Pennsylvania
Dept. of Education
Harristown 2 Bldg,
10 Fl
333 Market St
Harrisburg, PA 17126
(717) 787-5820

Rhode Island
Dept. of Education
Roger Williams Bldg
22 Hayes St
Providence, RI 02908
(401) 277-2031

South Carolina
Dept. of Education
Rutledge Bldg, Rm
1006
1429 Senate St
Columbia, SC 29201
(803) 734-8492

South Dakota
Dept. of Education
Richard F Kneip Bldg
700 Governors Dr.
Pierre, SD 57501

Tennessee
Dept. of Education
Cordell Hull Bldg,
Rm 100
436 6th Avenue North
Nashville, TN 37219
(615) 741-2731

Texas
Education Agency
William B Travis
Bldg, Rm 2-104
1701 N Congress Ave
Austin, TX 78701
(512) 463-8985

Utah
Office of Education
250 East 500 South
Salt Lake City, UT
84111
(801) 533-5431

Vermont
Dept. of Education
State Office Bldg
120 State Street
Montpelier, VT 05602
(802) 828-3135

Virginia
Dept. of Education
P.O. Box 6Q
Richmond, VA
23216-2060
(804) 225-2023

Washington
Dept. of Education
Mail Stop FG-11
Olympia, WA 98504
(206) 753-6717

Wisconsin
Dept. of Public
Instruction
PO Box 7841
Madison, WI 53707
(608) 266-1771

Wyoming
Dept. of Education
Hathaway Bldg, 2nd
Floor
2300 Capitol Ave
Cheyenne, WY 82002
(307) 777-7673

chapter 12

the importance
of The Vacation

Before you start your new life, you have to let go of the old one.

There are loud cruel voices you must banish, before you can hear the sweet faint muses. There are harsh schedules you must cancel, before you can coax your natural rhythms back into place. Otherwise, no music.

Learning in school is swimming upstream against the current of your natural curiosity and rhythm. It takes exhausting effort, but it can be done. Unschooling is swimming downstream, still kicking and paddling and crossing over to investigate the shores, but without fighting. *If you don't give yourself time to turn around in the river, unschooling will be a miserable confusion. If you don't give yourself time to adjust, this book will not work for you.* Still facing upstream, you'll drift downstream. In other words, you'll be neither here nor there...and maybe you'll end up wanting to be back *there*, in school, because at least you know it's someplace.

The vacation I hereby suggest is your time to turn around--and rest-- *before* you make any effort to steer your course. If you *don't* take a vacation, you may start unschooling with the same frenzied guilty complexes that you've been schooling with. No fun.

Your vacation:

When you quit school, do nothing academic for at least, at the absolute minimum, a week. If you wish, however, write stories or journal entries about your past and your future. Dream, dream, dream. If you crave TV, watch it. If you crave sleep, indulge. Allow yourself to go through withdrawal. Pass no judgments. If you want to "work" on anything, work on forgiving and forgetting. Forgive yourself for everything. Forgive your teachers for everything. Forgive your parents for everything. Forget the lies school taught--forget that learning is separate from your life, that you can't teach yourself, that you are defined by your grades, and all other such nonsense. Detoxify. Purge.

Obviously, your parents need to know this vacation is coming. If not, they may anxiously pile textbooks around you and assign essays on The Reign of Queen Elizabeth. I don't know about you, but that sort of well-intentioned concern would certainly drive *me* back to school. If they don't think they can handle watching you do nothing for a week or so, visit your grandmother.

And after the vacation:

Unfortunately, I can't promise that all your school wounds will heal in one short week. The complete process of unschooling your spirit could take a month or even years. Anthony J. Hermans, 17, reflects, "It's not easy to learn to deal with excessive freedom--especially when you're used to something else." Judy Garvey, homeschooling parent and author of *How to Begin Homeschooling*, calls the transition process "flushing out." She points out in *GWS* (*Growing Without Schooling* magazine) #70 that it can involve a period of hating the mention of anything remotely connected to academics, or even a temporary lack of interest in *everything*.[*]

A few enemies may lurk in your gut, waiting to make life difficult. Fear, for example, may overwhelm you at first. Most of the structure in your world has suddenly evaporated, and not just for the weekend. Your time is yours, and you may feel dazed by the responsibility of that concept. Expect to be afraid; just don't give in to that fear. Where there's fear, say some wise women I know, there's power. No one feels afraid when they walk into a boring job for the fourteenth year, which is a sorry reason to do a boring job for fourteen years.

Another enemy is the guilt that blocks your natural curiosity. People who have never gone to school have never developed negative attitudes toward exploring their world. Unfortunately, you probably have. It's not your fault if you don't immediately want to run out and watch ladybugs with a magnifying glass. It might take time before your desire to learn surfaces from beneath the layers of guilt--the voices insisting *I should learn this, I have to learn that*. Give yourself that time. Don't push. You'll come around. Dan Raymond, Seth's father (chapter 41) told me he thought it would take a year before a new unschooler could do anything "real" and start going forward on his or her own.

Impatience, too: in chapter 3, I pointed out that schools helped 18th- and 19th- century factory owners by forcing people to shift from a natural, agricultural way of scheduling their lives to an artificial, industrial way. Quitting school, you can ease back into a healthy tempo, but you'll have to be more patient with yourself than factory owners are with their employees. Allow yourself to find a natural pace, even though that means you may slow down, stare into space more often, breathe easier. You won't necessarily accomplish less--most homeschoolers accomplish far more than their schooled peers--but it's O.K. if you *do* accomplish less. The meaning of life has to do with quality, not quantity.

The worst thing that can go wrong with your unschooling is lack of trust.

---

[*] You can order *How to Begin Homeschooling* by writing to RR1 Box 105, Blue Hill, ME 04614.

If your parents don't trust you, they will nag or look like they want to nag. If they see you watching TV they may assume that's all you'll ever do. It will drive you crazy. You'll wish you were back in school, where everyone *expects* you not to want to learn anything. Tell them how important their trust is. Continue to educate them about homeschooling. Share the stories in this chapter with them. Introduce them to other homeschooling families through your local groups. See chapter 10.

If the schoolboard doesn't trust you, that's not so bad because you don't have to see them every day. Still, it can force you into more structure and more subjects than you think are healthy. Don't worry too much about the school board. Learn how to be diplomatic. Don't piss them off.

The worst disaster by far is *you* refusing to trust yourself. You can suffocate yourself under a stack of guilt trips. If parents and teachers have not trusted you through a lot of your life, it is not your fault that you finally stopped trusting yourself too. It's their fault, but there's no point in revenge. Instead, work through it.

Help

If anyone is still on your case with things you "should" be doing, or nasty demonstrations of no trust, or if you find yourself tormented by guilt, school nightmares, or an inability to relax, *get some help*. Perhaps all you need is contact with other unschoolers. Maybe you need more intensive care, such as work with a counselor. On behalf of wise friends, I recommend co-counseling, although I am not myself a co-counselor.

I mention co-counseling because it is far less judgmental than some other forms of counseling and therapy; a traditional psychiatrist might start with the unhelpful assumption that your unschooling is the cause of your problems. Also, co-counseling is extremely empowering. Co-counselors work in pairs; each person performs two roles--counselor *and* client. (A session goes like this: first, one person is the counselor and the other the client. After a designated time period, such as an hour, you switch roles.) Furthermore, after you take a short, inexpensive* introductory course, it is free. According to co-counseling literature, it "assumes that everyone is born with tremendous intellectual potential, natural zest, and lovingness, but that these qualities have become blocked and obscured in adults [and teenagers] as the result of accumulated distress experiences (fear, hurt, loss, pain, anger, embarrassment, etc.) which begin early in our lives."

After you complete the "Fundamentals Class," available in nearly every city in the U.S., you can participate in any group of co-counselors. Co-counseling is open to all ages, and has special youth chapters and newsletters in some places. You can get more information by sending for the current issue of *Present Time*, $3 from Present Time, 719 Second Avenue North, Seattle, WA 98109. Each issue of this magazine not only gives a broad sense of the co-

---

* Some scholarships are available.

counseling movement, but also lists names and addresses of teachers and contact people all over the world.

*

An issue related to this business of guilt and trust is the question of structure--but we'll deal with that in chapter 16.

One relatively uncomplicated solution to some of these psychological difficulties is suggested by Judy Garvey and Jim Bergin, who have a 13-year-old son, in *GWS #76*: An apprenticeship or job outside the home, they say, is the best way to make the transition to unschooling. Because it is a structured use of time out in the world, it combats any feeling of "dropping out" or "failure."

*

Hey, Miss Llewellyn, if it's so complicated and difficult for some people to heal from school, why are you so optimistic? How do you know I can recover?

Partly because I've heard enough success stories. Partly because like many adults, I have recovered too. It wasn't until I was in college, but my brain did finally boomerang back from the land of grades, SAT scores, harried paper writing, boredom, obedience school, and busywork. The revival, by the way, happened mainly through conversations with friends, and mostly NOT because of any official college curriculum.

These stories and comments will help to illustrate the process:

Katrina Dolezal, 15, writes in *GWS #76*: "I think the best way to make the transition from public school to homeschool is to be allowed plenty of time to forget some of what was learned in school about how you should learn."

Sylvia Stralberg describes her vacation in *GWS #80*:

Things finally got so bad this year in eleventh grade that I said, "That's it--I'm not going back to school anymore," and I didn't. I had a few months of recuperation, which meant doing WHATEVER I felt like doing, be it baking, reading, cutting recipes, or watching a movie. I had a lot of guilt feelings during that time about not being in school, but fortunately I have wonderful parents who reassured me that what I had done was OK.

Rosemary Risley writes about her daughter in *GWS #76*:

Lora only read what she was forced to read when she was in school, and I would sometimes coerce her by reading one chapter out loud to her and then having her read the next to me. All of a sudden, during the summer between school and homeschool, she became an avid reader....I don't know how many books she read that summer, but I was amazed--it was as if now that she didn't have to, and she was free, she wanted to read. She has read over sixty books in each nine months of homeschooling. If we did nothing else these two years, I consider that a major accomplishment.

Judy Garvey writes in *GWS #76*:

Before children go to school in the first place, all of their natural learning systems are intact. This is what we can see in families who have homeschooled their children from the very beginning. However, once children are in school for about three years, they are forced to shift over to a very unnatural system to survive the emphasis on memorization and the daily stress, rigidity, and humiliation of classroom life...

Most children are very hurt and angry about what has happened to them and to their peers in school. As long as they stay in school that anger must remain under control. When they come home, it all begins to come out. It may show up in extreme highs and lows, negative emotional outbursts, or long periods of apparent depression.

Kathleen Hatley writes in *GWS #45*:

A change that pleases me very much this year was to watch our son Steve (12), who spent four years in public school, and who spent his first year of homeschooling asking for "assignments," become a more self-motivated learner. He became interested in mechanical drawing when I gave him a beginning drafting set and he spends a lot of time designing cars and space ships. He has discovered science fiction and reads Asimov, Bradbury, Heinlein and others with great enjoyment (he has always read a lot, but despises the school-type reading programs where one must answer questions to prove comprehension). We both enrolled in the IBM Systems computer course at the state Vo-Tech school and he thoroughly enjoyed that--the perfect classroom situation, in my opinion, no tests, no grades, just people voluntarily coming to learn about something which they were interested in, from a helpful expert in the field. Since Steve's career goals tend toward the technical at this point, he works real hard at mathematics, and at his request we added the Key Curriculum algebra and geometry series to his regular sixth grade math. He surprised me this year by informing me that he didn't want to take a summer break from his schoolwork!

Darlene Graham, a mother, started to feel like homeschooling was working after three years. In *GWS #37*, she advised, "Don't feel discouraged if your school program doesn't work like magic from day one. We have found that the longer our children were in public school, the harder it was for them to re-develop their own natural curiosity and creativity."

In *GWS* #64, editor Susannah Sheffer relates a conversation with Emily Keyes, 16. When she was in school, says Emily, she hated it and always got in trouble for not doing her homework. After eighth grade, her parents heard of homeschooling and decided to try it with both Emily and her younger brothers. After her mom took a class in homeschooling, she decided to try "natural learning," with no curriculum. Emily was lost at first:

> I still didn't know what to expect, or what I would want to do with the time, because back then I wasn't interested in much of anything. We decided to start homeschooling on the day that school started, and it should have been like any other day, except we didn't know what to expect of one another. We didn't know what mom was going to do, if mom was going to assign lots of stuff. My attitude was still so rebellious. I was so fed up with school that I felt I didn't want to learn anything. There was so much tension that first week.

> The change was very gradual. Your whole thinking changes. In school, everything's programmed for you, this is how you have to think, and then all of a sudden you're on your own, and you don't know what you want to do. It was so hard at the beginning, but I knew there was no way I would go back to school, and I think we all knew it would get better if we stuck it out.

Emily goes on to explain how eventually she discovered that she thinks mechanically and logically, and how she learned to fix machinery, to work with sound equipment, and to enjoy, among other things, early American history.

Arlean Haight writes in *GWS* #28:

> When we took the children out of school nearly two years ago, we had advice from several people, among them Dr. Pat Montgomery of Ann Arbor, Michigan [director of Clonlara--see chapter 11]. She told us if we would let the children follow their own interests, and just help them when they needed help, they would learn more than if we put them on a pre-planned curriculum.

> I respected Dr. Montgomery, and was grateful for her help. But I just couldn't see any glimmer of hope in Becky [14]. It seemed that seven years of public school had successfully stamped out any inclination she might have had to learn. By her own admission, she had learned to cram for tests, make A's and B's on her report cards, and promptly forget almost everything she had "learned." Whenever I allowed her free rein on "school," her one interest was mindless fiction--nothing of any value that I could see. Pat tried to encourage me, but I had the misgivings and insecurities that I see in so many other parents new to home-schooling. I was afraid Becky would learn nothing at all. So--we embarked on a "curriculum." It turned out to be just a duplication of

the old public school pattern. So I went pretty easy with it, still allowing her freedom, and limiting her fiction reading to what I felt was least objectionable.

But, Pat was right. It finally happened. This year Becky progressed from Louis L'Amour Western fiction to an interest in Western history, then to the history of the United States, and is now in the process of memorizing the Constitution word for word.

chapter 13

money, bicycles, and other Technical Difficulties

"We haven't the money, so we've got to think."--Lord Rutherford

"There is no wealth but life."--John Ruskin

Money

If your parents were paying full tuition at some gourmet private school before you quit, no problem. You can have plenty of private lessons, lab equipment, a library all to yourself, a high fashion set of drums, and money left over to vacation in Jamaica.

But you needn't be rich. Some homeschoolers spend under a hundred dollars per year on supplies. That's less than many school kids spend on *school* supplies.

Of course, if money is scarce at your house, you might not get lots of toys and the high fashion drums. On the other hand, you won't clutter up your life with things you end up feeling obligated to use.

The best money advice I can give, in fact, is to use your lack of money to help you. Let it help you focus your life around a few things that matter most to you. If you decide to be a naturalist and a photographer, spend your money there, not on a bunch of fancy math books you don't need. That way, you won't end up wasting *time* doing more math than you need.

Another way scarce money can be a blessing: you will be more creative and develop a clear understanding of what is necessary and fundamental to your interests. By figuring out what you don't need, you will also figure out what you do need. That's some of the best learning you can do about anything.

Also, remember that although you may lose a stingy little pond-full of "free" education--use of textbooks and equipment and such--you get an ocean of time in exchange. If you want, you can look at time as money. You can use it as an investment in your future (by volunteering in a field you dream of working in later) or as a way to get cash now (a job).

To make your money go as far as possible, here are strategies:

-Use school facilities and books. You will encounter the least resentment if you work out an arrangement where the school gets to officially enroll you (so they get money for you) in exchange for providing equipment and even allowing you to take the classes you want or attend events. For details on this sort of arrangement, see chapter 19.

-Buy only books you will use again and again. Get others through your school district (textbooks), as mentioned above, or libraries. Use interlibrary loan. If your district is not cooperative about loaning you books even though your parents' taxes support the schools, talk with individual teachers you trust about borrowing books from their classrooms. If they think you are going to run to the Authorities and say, "Miss Pickle loaned me a chemistry book, so there!" they won't do it, because they don't want to get in trouble. Be diplomatic and low-key.

-Trade your time for lessons or equipment. Try to do work that you learn from and enjoy, not just slave labor. For instance, Seth Raymond and his younger sister Vallie earned free pottery classes by running a kiln. His mother Kath told me, "Art and music teachers usually like kids who barter for lessons. If they're willing to work, they're more invested in what they're doing."

Along the same line, *GWS* (*Growing Without Schooling* magazine) #70 mentions a violin student who "is cataloging his [teacher's] records in exchange for the lessons the man is giving him."

-See Barbara Sher's book *Wishcraft* (Viking, 1979) for great ideas. One is holding a barn-raising, an event where people get together and tell what they have and what they need, and then team up to make each others' dreams come true with minimal cash.

-Use someone else's lab equipment for labs that require microscopes or other expensive equipment. (See chapter 21 for access to lab equipment.) However, about half the labs in most science books don't require expensive equipment, just beakers, graduated cylinders, graph paper, etc.

-If you want to learn to play the piano and don't have one, practice in a school or university practice room, or at someone else's house.

-Earn money in a way that brings you into closer contact with what you love. Finance your photography education by taking portraits of senior citizens and selling them, for example. If you take this approach rather than working at McDonald's, you win doubly--you not only earn money, you also gain experience. That way you won't feel resentful about having to "pay" for your own education--because paying for your education can be part of it.

-Find books and equipment at university and college used book sales, thrift stores, flea markets, and garage sales.

-Work for legislation that would give tax credits (like $3000 per student per year) for education outside public schools, including homeschooling. Minnesota passed a similar measure. Oregon had one on the ballot but turned it down. Most people oppose it because they think it discriminates against the poor whose parents couldn't afford to send them to private schools even with a $3000 discount. But for "homeschoolers," $3000 would make a tremendous difference, *especially* for poor people. In other words, this legislation gives your parents a tax refund to be used for equipment and resources for your homeschooling.

-Get a grant. A grant is when someone else gives you money to carry out a project. Look up "grants" at the library, and try especially to find an up-to-date book in the reference section.

The government is one source of grants; for instance, the National Endowment for the Humanities has a Younger Scholars program for people under 21. It gives $1800 to $2200 to each recipient, who carries out a research project of her choice in history, archaeology, or another humanities field. (See J. Robert Dumouchel's *Government Assistance Almanac*, Foggy Bottom Publications. Or, for information on this particular humanities grant, contact Division of Fellowships and Seminars, Younger Scholars Program, National Endowment for the Humanities, Room 316, Washington, DC 20506, (202) 786-0463.)

Transportation
If you are not legally old enough to drive:

-ride your horse, bicycle, or feet.
-if your area has good public transportation, use it.
-carpool with unschooling teens.
-if you volunteer or work on a regular schedule, ride with an adult who works at the same place.
-put up notices at the places you spend your time, explaining that you need rides. Offer to contribute gas money. If strangers offer you rides, be sure you know enough to trust them before you accept.
-invent an alternate means of transportation, preferably one which will not contribute to global warming and lung cancer.
-speak up for your right to drive.

If you *are* legally old enough to drive:
If you live in a state with one of those disgusting laws preventing "dropouts" from driving until they're 18, do what you can to change it. But don't worry on your own behalf--the law shouldn't affect you if you're a "homeschooler." Kathryn Blount, 15, in Texas, found that all she needed was a letter from a parent or tutor saying she was homeschooled (*GWS* #73).

Adults only
Vita Wallace writes in *GWS* (*Growing Without Schooling* magazine):

I am in a figure drawing class for adults...partly because I just couldn't stand the idea of being in a class labeled "for teenagers." My mother called the teacher before the class began to see if it would be all right if I signed up for it. He said that as long as I thought I could concentrate for two hours straight, I was welcome to try it. No one there has ever asked me how old I am, and I don't think they'd mind if they knew.

To be a Compleat Self-schooler, start developing some assertiveness. You will need it as you look for unorthodox ways to find things out, get things done, and join classes or groups that teenagers aren't usually part of. Realize that rules are usually flexible.

For example, a Middle Eastern dance troupe I belonged to had a rule that members had to be at least 20, but a 19-year-old danced blithely in our midst, and no one ever thought about it. When we got around to reviewing the troupe's constitution, we canned that rule. Many organizations have obsolete rules that no one cares about. If you set about your business believing (politely) that anything is possible, you will prove yourself right.

And other Technical Difficulties

One *GWS* reader had kids who were hassled when they hung out in the world during school hours. "Why aren't you in school," everybody's cousin wanted to know. The mom solved the problem by printing up "passes" that explained the kid was on an independent educational errand, complete with her administrative signature at the bottom. No more harassment.

Chapter Summary
Where there's a will, there's a way.

getting a social life without proms

Whenever I mention my work on this book, hardly anyone says, "But how would people learn anything without school?" Instead, they say, "But how will they make friends?"

The question kills me. Teenagers make friends in *spite* of school, not because of it. There is only one reason schools can claim to enhance social growth: thanks to compulsory education, schools are full of *people*.

Well. A good slice of birthday cake surpasses its beginnings in flour, sugar, milk, egg, and vanilla extract. Likewise, a healthy social life goes far beyond mere contact.

A healthy social life requires much more than indifferent daily acquaintanceship with 300 people born the same year you were. It starts with a solid sense of self-esteem and self-awareness. It builds in *time*--time to spend with other people in worthwhile, happy activities where no one loses, no one is forced to participate, and where conversation and helping one another are not outlawed. In other words, school fights hard to keep your social life from happening, even though defensive schoolpeople preach loudly that school is important for socialization.

(Actually, they're right. While school has little to do with social *growth*, it has everything to do with *socialization*. I think it was in *Growing Without Schooling* magazine that I read someone's clear explanation of that term: socialization means bringing an individual under the control of the group. School-style socialization makes a group of people obedient and easily manipulated by peer pressure or "authority"; it makes a nation of idiots who wish they were people on TV since they don't know who they themselves are.)

As for romance. Affection, intimacy, and passion really are not encouraged to take root in a linoleum room smelling of chalk-dust. A mystery-relationship belongs out in the big mystery-world.

So. School is detrimental to friendship and other social joys, insists your author. But where does that leave you? To have a social life, you at least have to start with raw material--other human beings. Since most of the people near your age are shut up in school, you do face a challenge. Now, you are not alone in your aloneness--*most* of the social structures of our society have broken down. In the last decade of the twentieth century, streets are seldom neighborhoods; family members rarely know each other well; adults' work environments require so much conformity that people cannot see who their colleagues are. Friendship and community do not happen automatically. But with a little effort, you *can* make them happen, just as adults do. Don't sit home and mope, and don't be unimaginatively convinced that you need school to have friends. Instead:

Create a new and better social structure.

When school is the structure of your life, you run into people all the time. When school is not the structure of your life, you can build a better social structure instead of inventing each day from scratch. This approach frees you from having to make a continual effort to spend time with people: if you always meet Josefina and Nazir to play music on Thursdays, then on Thursday you don't have to say to yourself, gosh I feel kind of like spending time with someone but I don't know quite whom to call, or what I feel like doing. Here are a few of the many possible strategies.

1. Set up regular, scheduled contact with friends. Start an important project with schooled or unschooled friends, and set regular times to work together two or three times per week. These projects could be anything-- writing a book, cleaning up a beach, starting a health information library, making a music video, rebuilding the engine of an old pickup.

2. If you prefer to work independently, you can still share *space* with friends. Your arrangement could be simple: school friends coming to your house to do their homework while you do your academic work, unschooled friends bringing a novel and lounging on your bed. Or your arrangement could be more complex: a workshop or other definite space in one of your homes where each of you kept ongoing projects and worked in the warmth of each others' company, with sunlight streaming through the windows and music in the background.

3. Start a business that puts you into frequent contact with people- -like custom-painting skateboards or tutoring Spanish.

4. Join clubs or organizations for people with similar interests. There are infinite possibilities, especially in a city: the Society for Creative Anachronism (see chapter 23), the Sierra Club, outdoor programs of universities, performance guilds, ultimate frisbee teams, Amnesty International, drum circles, mountain search and rescue, city planning committees.

There are important non-school organizations specifically for teenagers, too. Look into 4-H, church or temple youth groups, YMCA activities, hockey or soccer teams, scouts, youth symphonies and other musical groups, teen hotlines and support groups.

5. Start your own club--to work on environmental issues, cook desserts, undertake "projects" like those described in #1 above, whatever. Advertise your first meetings by posting fliers at or near a school, or by having friends post fliers, or by placing a classified ad in a school newspaper.

6. Get involved in a regular work situation (see Part 4 of this book) that provides contact with the kind of people you like to be around.

7. Take a class outside of school--dance, martial arts, bicycle repair.

8. Start a weekly study circle to explore a subject you're interested in--Zen Buddhism, Shakespeare, the history of your region. A book to check is Leonard Oliver's *Study Circles*. Also see Chapter 17, on salons.

Some things that happen to many unschoolers:

-They keep up their friendships with school friends, doing the same kinds of things with them that they used to. Sometimes, they feel frustrated because their school friends don't have as much free time as they do.

-They grow closer to their families and start liking their parents and siblings more than they used to.

-They have fewer acquaintances. They develop stronger, closer friendships. They appreciate not having to spend time around hordes of people they don't have a lot in common with.

-Their friends include adults and children as well as people their own age. They get over any former feelings that they can't talk with adults.

Jeremiah Gingold wrote in *GWS* (*Growing Without Schooling* magazine) #74:

I am friends with the adults who live in the house next door to us....Dick is interested in bicycling and philosophy and Crunch is interested in word games, movies, and sports. These are all things that I am interested in, which is one of the reasons I immediately became friends with them. The other reason is that they take me seriously and respect what I have to say about things. There are a few things that I talk to them about that I don't talk to most of my friends who are closer in age to me (I'm 13)--for instance, politics and education.

I don't think my friendship with them is very different from my friendships with other teenagers, except for the fact that we have better conversations. We often fool around with each other the way I would with friends my age. I think there are many things that I can learn from them, but that doesn't make me feel that they are necessarily superior to me. There are probably things that they can learn from me also. I do think that we have a very equal friendship, most likely because they respect me in the same way that I respect them.

Anne Brosnan, 13, wrote me:

My social life is much more rounded than school kids'; I talk to anyone and everyone the same. I've noticed that most kids will talk to anyone younger than them but only superficially, and hardly talk to adults at all except when spoken to. I don't believe in that and make a point of showing that I'll talk to anyone about anything. On the track team there's all ages and I'm friends with all equally. I don't make a point of talking to someone just because of closeness in age. For example, I talk to the little boys in kindergarten because we share a common hatred of the rock group "New Kids on the Block." And the coaches ask me quite important things such as make sure so-and-so is standing in the right lane, and sometimes they get so mixed up I have to remind them what they are supposed to be doing (they're grateful for it).

I have about thirty pen-pals and they range in age from about ten to fifty. I consider these my friends and my social life because you can be "social" through the mail. I may not have as *many* friends or acquaintances as other kids but it is not the amount but the quality of friendship that counts.

.....I've heard a whole lot about homeschoolers going back to high school for various reasons and the main one was to have more friends. But school isn't supposed to be about friends--the purpose of schools is to learn, or to be taught. However I never heard of a homeschooler going back to high school to get an education, because that is what they were doing before they went back to school. The stupidest reason I've heard of was a kid who wanted to go to high school so she could go to her prom. This, I think I shall refrain from commenting on....!

Anthony J. Hermans, 17, was out of school during seventh and eighth grades, though he is now in a private high school. He wrote me that unschooling "allows an individual to meet (and learn to deal with) a wide range of people rather than being largely restricted to one's 'peer' group....Homeschooling can provide an incredible boost in self reliance and esteem which all but eliminates peer pressure. I feel very little pressure from my peers as do other homeschoolers with whom I have conversed."

-Younger unschoolers--around 12 and 13--often appreciate not having to deal with the pressure of having "boyfriends" or "girlfriends" just to fit in and be popular. Older teenagers frequently feel that most of their schooled peers are immature, inexperienced, and uninteresting. They fall in love and make friends with people slightly older than themselves. Their relationships and friendships are strong and honest. In general, unschooling allows teenagers to stay "young" as long as they want, but also to "grow up" as soon as they are ready.

-They exchange letters with unschoolers and other people around the world. Sometimes, they travel to meet these people.

-Their friends are mostly people who share common interests. When I asked about the greatest advantages of unschooling, 15-year-old Michael Severini said, "I can spend more time with people who have the same interests I have."

-They grow more secure and feel better about themselves as a result of leaving the social world of school, a world which is often cruel, judgmental, and nosey. Suzanne Klemp, 15, comments, "My confidence has grown immensely--I am not judged for reasons such as clothes, money, or my looks....My social life is better than it ever was at school. I meet people at the YMCA [where she teaches ballet], ballet class, and I have adult friends."

-They do sometimes feel excluded from the bustling social activity at school. Most of them, however, feel that this social activity is shallow and unfulfilling. They don't *really* want it, but sometimes they do fantasize about it.

What else can you do if you feel lonely and isolated?

1. Take your feelings seriously. Human contact is crucial. Don't try to tell yourself it's not important to have friends. If you want to be in love, don't tell yourself that's silly. It's not.

In fact, our social needs are more important and basic than our intellectual and creative needs. If you let your social life end when you quit school, pretty soon you won't care much about learning and exploring the world. You'll want to get right back to your locker, because Tatiana will be rummaging in her locker next to you. Psychologist Abraham Maslow pointed out that people have a hierarchy of needs. Each of us has to feel a sense of belonging, love, acceptance, and recognition, *before* we can set out to fulfill "higher" needs such as intellectual achievement and complete self-fulfillment.

2. Don't romanticize your memory of school. School does provide contact with masses of people. It does not make friends for you, or even provide an environment that is good for making friends. Everyone who goes to school, and everyone who doesn't go to school, has times of overwhelming loneliness. Being in a crowd doesn't necessarily help.

3. Take responsibility for your own social life. Make an effort to stay in touch with former friends. If you aren't invited enough, do some inviting. Throw a party. If you're lonely, don't blame the universe, me, or yourself. Instead, do something about it.

4. Be sensitive to your friends' feelings about your changing life. If they stay in school, they may watch you with envy. They may overly romanticize *your* life, or feel intimidated by your independence and growing maturity. Quitting school *will* make you smarter and happier than you used to be, but it will not make you superior to your friends. Don't be arrogant; don't think that unschooling makes you the most interesting creature in the universe.

Don't feel apologetic for your happiness, but do reinforce your friends' trust in you by showing your interest in their activities. Go out of your way to let them know what you enjoy and admire in them. Don't talk more than you listen. But if they become hostile and defensive, and you can't work through this stuff together, it's time to seek out new friends who are not threatened by your growth.

5. Involve your old and new friends in your most important activities. Don't think of friendship as something that takes place only during French fries and mall shopping. Don't settle for boring, predictable friendships. Challenge each other. Get a little more honest as time goes by.

6. Go to school sometimes. Eat lunch there, be in the choir, be a t.a., go to assemblies. See chapter 19 for ways this can be worked out. If it can't be worked out, who will catch you if you eat with your friends? I know of a college student, majoring in sociology, who routinely eats in a high school cafeteria just to watch people interact in their high school ways. No one has ever noticed that she doesn't belong.

And you can always hang out at the schoolteenager hang-outs, if that's your style.

7. See your family in a new light. Cultivate your siblings and parents as friends.

8. Free yourself of schoolish prejudices. Don't cheat yourself out of potential friends because of the clothes they wear or the makeup they don't wear. A shared sense of taste and style is a legitimate part of some of your friendships, but there's no reason *all* your friends have to look like you, is there?

9. The best solution of all: *Get your friends out of school!* Let the vision spread....

chapter 15

adults
in a new light

Now that you don't have to *obey* teachers and principals and hall monitors with walkie-talkies, maybe you can start some healthy relationships with adults.

These relationships can take all kinds of shapes. Adults can be your friends, buddies, jogging partners, and other "equals." Since you already know about friendships among equals, I see no point in explaining How to Make Adult Friends. If you spend time around adults--in chess clubs or during political campaigns or wherever--you will make adult friends. Thirteen-year-old Mylie Alrich pointed out to me that when you don't go to school, "the line between 'kids' and 'grownups' is almost not there."

It is also valuable, however, to have *unequal* relationships with adults. To reach your fullest potential, you need mentors, role models, and teachers. That's not because you're a "kid." Adults also need mentors, role models, and teachers in order to reach *their* fullest potential. No one should be bossing you around or giving you unsolicited report cards, but these guides *can* help push and encourage you to do things you might not be gutsy, determined, or skilled enough to do on your own.

Teachers (and tutors)

are a fairly obvious role--people who explain their knowledge in a specific area. You may or may not admire them as people-in-general. You *do* need to admire their expertise in whatever they're teaching you, or else find a new teacher. Some teachers become *more* than teachers--mentors or role models or friends. But it is fine to have a teacher simply in order to learn a particular set of skills.

Teachers may not actually teach a *class* or formal lessons, of course. Jonathan Kibler writes in *GWS* (*Growing Without Schooling* magazine) #74:

> Besides my dad, there are three people in particular who have helped me learn more about computers. First, Mr. Warner was my 4-H Club instructor. He taught me the most commonly used BASIC words. He explained what the commands "PRINT," "GOTO," and "INPUT" meant. Also, he taught me about flow charts. Knowing about flow charts helped me to write my own programs. He also introduced me to some new programs. Before I met Mr. Warner I knew nothing about computers; I am very glad that I met him through 4-H.

> Second, Mrs. Penn is a computer instructor at a school. She goes to the same church as I do. When she found out that I was interested in computers, she

invited me to work on them with her. Almost every Sunday after church I go over to the school with her and work with the computers in the classroom. I play computer games and write programs. I enjoy these Sundays very much. Mrs. Penn has also lent me books about computers. Through her, I have gained more appreciation for what computers can do. I am happy that she takes the time to allow me to work with her.

When I first got my own computer, I didn't know how to work any of the software. I found out that one of the dads in my YMCA Trailblazer group, Dr. Loader, had the same computer and printer as I did. He offered to help me figure out some of the software. I had a lot of questions about word processing programs in particular. Dr. Loader happened to have a word processing program that was easy to use and he copied it for me. He also spent a lot of time answering questions for me over the phone--and in the beginning I had a lot of questions! He invited me over to his office so that he could better explain how the programs worked. Once he even came over to my house on his lunch hour to help me print a file. I'm really grateful for all the time he has given to me.

I'm really fortunate to have all of these friends who know about computers and are willing to help me.

Role models

are people you admire from afar. You watch what they do and figure out how they do it. You study them to see what you can learn from them. You can have role models in the career you hope to go into, or role models for life-in-general. By giving you a picture of what's possible, they help you to challenge yourself. They can be people you know--like your parents--or people in the news--like Sinead O'Connor or Sandra Day O'Connor. Role models don't have to know you exist in order for you to learn from them. Sometimes, other young people can be role models.

Other adult guides

Adults play many other helpful roles also. They can be spiritual leaders like gurus or rabbis or priests, experts you can ask for occasional advice or information, counselors, advisors. They can be teachers in unusual senses of the word:

In ancient Greece, philosophers wandered through the streets and countrysides with teenaged boys, engaged in dialogues about truth and beauty. In a talk at my college, Barry Lopez spoke about the Eskimo people, who have no word for "teacher" or "wise man" but instead recognize people who play the role of "isumataq." The *isumataq* does not teach or preach, but in his presence, wisdom is *revealed*. I mention these roles because they can help you to see and encourage nuances in your own relationships.

Mentors

The rest of this chapter is about mentors--people who pay a lot of attention to you and give you long-term help, advice, guidance, and support. Depending on their style, they might also kick your pants when they think you're not challenging yourself enough. In the *Karate Kid* films, Mr. Miyagi-- the trainer (*sensei*)--and his student Daniel give a great picture of mentorship in action.

Eileen Trombly provides another example in *GWS* #18:

> Amy, 14, has taken ballet lessons from an older woman in town and has developed a unique, warm relationship with her over the years. The woman is now in her eighties, still participates in dance, and has a very interesting past which she shares with Amy. The lesson is one-on-one so there is always much time for sharing and feeling relaxed in each other's company. The teacher was once a ballerina in the New York Ballet Troupe; owned a theater with her husband, who was in vaudeville; was daughter-in-law of a former Connecticut governor; and was acquainted with Anna Pavlova. She has much to offer in the way of experiences, and her polished yet friendly manner has served to influence Amy in a very positive way.

You don't *need* a mentor to have a nice life. Furthermore, not everyone who wants a mentor finds one. However, people who do have mentors say that the relationship helps them grow and succeed much more than they could on their own.

If you'd like to have a mentor, how can you find one? Patiently. Mentors are not as easy to find as adult friends, teachers, tutors, and role models. You can't just advertise in the help-wanted section--anyone who thinks of himself as a ready-made mentor is quite certainly *not* one. Likely, a mentorship will develop naturally out of other types of relationships:

If you have an intense interest in music, perhaps you take piano lessons, and over time, you grow closer to your teacher. Eventually, he may begin to take a more personal interest in you, and one day you realize you have a mentor.

After you've been leading tours at the science museum for a few months, the director asks you into her office for a cup of tea. It turns out she knows all about stars, and when you tell her you have been learning to identify constellations, she invites you on her next telescope outing. Two months later, you realize she has become your mentor.

There is no quick formula to follow; like most important human relationships, each mentorship will develop uniquely and at its own pace. In *Professional Women and Their Mentors*, Nancy Collins cautions:

> When you find the right mentor, you never actually say: "Will you be my mentor?" This is the number one rule of beginning the relationship....Mentor relationships take time to develop....The relationship seems to begin when the

mentor is both supportive and demanding, and the mentoree feels stretched and appreciated....

However, if you know someone whom you think would make a good mentor, you can certainly *encourage* the relationship in that direction. Tell them you admire their work. Show your appreciation for any time they spend with you. Ask for their advice. Watch for small ways to help them out. If they teach classes, sign up--and put focused energy into your work. If they enjoy the role you are quietly creating for them, they will soon start to take initiative for developing the relationship. If not, they'll back away. Be sensitive. Don't force.

If you don't yet know anyone you'd like to have as a mentor, get more involved in what you love. This way you can meet lots of adults-- potential mentors. Take a pottery class; volunteer at the zoo; join a writers' guild.

An ideal mentor is good at what she does, and other adults respect her. *Your* feelings toward her, however, are the most crucial. Nancy Collins writes, "In selecting your mentor, you should try to choose someone for whom you feel admiration, affection, respect, trust, and even love in the broadest sense."

Some of your former school teachers have excellent mentorship potential--as long as they have the time to develop an individual relationship with you. Also, of course, they must have some expertise. Forget teachers who are obsessed only with "teaching" itself, and not entranced with their subject. Avoid attaching yourself to someone who wants mainly to "help you grow up" or some such slobbery vague condescending controlling rot.

Don't forget old people. With time on their hands and a lifetime of experiences behind them, they can make splendid mentors, enriching their own lives and yours.

Also, mentors need not be sugary touchy-feely types who always encourage you to do what you feel like doing and who tell you everything you do is wonderful. I often work best with very demanding people, like Pat, my flamenco teacher, who snapped, "Again! Lift your chin! Bend your knees! Faster! Don't look at the floor!" But if you prefer the sugary touchy-feely type, that's fine too. Encouragement, recognition, and warmth may be exactly what you need.

Once you have a mentor, relinquish a little bit of control. Remember, you picked somebody you trusted, so now try the things they suggest. Take the risks they ask you to take. Let them push you onto your tightropes.

Finally, think about your end of the bargain. How can you return some of your mentor's generous energy? Offer to help by cleaning her house or typing her novel. Realize that you will never completely pay her back for her gifts, and that she won't ask you to, but that someday you can obliquely return the favor by sharing your own white-haired expertise with some wild teenager.

starting out:
a sense of
the possibilities

A Different Kind of Time

Don't be a factory. Do a few things well instead of everything poorly. Big undertakings--like starting a town orchestra or trying to find the ultimate physics theory--do take time. If you love your big undertakings, that time is never wasted.

A Different Kind of Structure

The homeschooling community talks a lot about structured education versus unstructured education. Although there is no such thing as a completely structured or a completely unstructured education, these terms are convenient and can make it easier for you to think about how you want to organize your unschooled life.

In a mostly "unstructured" education, you *let* life happen to you, keeping your eyes open and learning from whatever you happen to do. In a mostly "structured" education, you *make* life happen, setting goals and making plans. Which is best? That's a philosophical and religious question, and there are plenty of respectable votes on both sides.

An unstructured education frees you from unnecessary boundaries between life and learning. It allows you to calm your mind and to live on a healthy schedule, reading only when you are hungry. It invites you to soak up the universe by swimming in the river without telling yourself, "I should be thinking about the natures of the currents, and the names of the potential fish near my feet, and the dead poets who wrote about water." It meshes with the teaching of Zen masters, Indian gurus, and ancient Chinese philosophies, which ask their followers not to strive, not to battle life, but to let themselves be shaped and carried by its flow.

A structured education, on the other hand, is what you want if you are goal-oriented or if you enjoy being methodical. After all these years of living with other people's curricula, you can get a big thrill designing your own personalized education. Obviously, it can be as formal, rigorous and organized as you want, far more so than school if you so desire. You can set big or small goals for yourself such as finishing a math textbook by a certain date, writing a letter to your newspaper every week, writing and illustrating a children's book during October and November, completing an inventory of local tree species before Earth Day, phoning three people each day until you find an apprenticeship you like. If you take this approach, you *will* get things done. Barbara Sher's book *Wishcraft* (Viking, 1979) can help you set epicurean goals and reach them, although she writes about life, not just education, which may confuse you if you don't yet realize they're the same.

One more point about structure versus unstructure: don't assume that structure has to be *school*-style structure. Personally, I despise the idea of school-at-home, and the kind of schoolish schedule that would entail. But you can build your own structure centered around whatever you like. For some homeschoolers, structure consists of five or more hours of daily music practice. For others, it consists of a full-fledged computer programming business, or nonstop reading, or tinkering all day long with electronics.

One valuable kind of structure is goal-setting, which is explained in profound detail in the aforementioned *Wishcraft*. This is the sort of structure which serves your desires (I want to build a windmill so I will do this, that, and the other thing) instead of your sense of guilt (I should study chemistry every day for forty-five minutes). Obviously, you are going to learn plenty by setting out to achieve your goals; in the windmill department that's going to include physics, carpentry, geography, and probably history--for a start. If your goal is writing a book on unschooling, you're going to learn about the homeschooling movement, about the publishing industry, about word processing, about library research, about efficient versus inefficient original research, about law libraries, about words, and about fear--for a start. If your goal is to restore the neighborhood swamp to health, you'll learn about chemistry, biology, politics, economics, your own muscles, and organizing people--for a start.

If you are completely confused as to how to start structuring your life, here's one way: do "academics" for two hours each day--not necessarily lots of subjects, or the same ones every day. You are not going to dry up if you don't do 45 minutes every day of "social studies." Do some kind of "work" or project for four hours. In your leftover time, read, see friends, talk with mom and pop, make tabouli. Take Saturdays and Sundays off. Sound arbitrary? It is. I made it up, although it is based on a loose sort of "average" of the lives of a hundred unschoolers, most college-bound. Once you try this schedule for a month, you will know how you want to change it.

Quite possibly, you may need a structured plan because your state laws require that you submit one. If this is the case, read chapters 17 through 30 for ideas and then try two brainstorming techniques:

1. Make a list of the subjects you have to cover. For each, write down all the ways you can think of to "study" them, and a list of related books you think you might like to read. Also ask your family and friends.

2. Make a list of your most important interests. Then look at each one and figure out how academic subjects could be related to it. For instance, if you love horses, your horse list might look like this:

Language Arts/English: Read *National Velvet*. Write a profile of a local horse breeder. Write poetry or stories from a horse's point of view.

Social sciences: Conduct a study of various careers related to horses. Figure out why so many young girls are intensely interested in horses, by conducting a survey or another type of study. Read about the profound influence horses have had on cultures around the world, such as the culture of Plains Indian tribes. Stay on a working cattle ranch for a week.

Science: Learn about horse anatomy, diseases, and biology. Find out about the evolutionary history of horses. Learn to use a microscope to diagnose horse diseases.

Art: Draw horses. Make a saddle or other tack. Produce a documentary video on horse care or horse races.

You get the idea.

Here are some comments and morsels of advice from unschoolers on their experiences with school-style structure and other kinds of structured and unstructured learning:

In *GWS* (*Growing Without Schooling* magazine) #22:

This past year, we got away from correspondence schools altogether, ordered our own texts (for math only), and really got unschooled....My daughter (13) now studies totally independently, with only occasional help in algebra, or help with a Spanish conversation. Her progress is really astounding, too. She reads more than ever, and does about three times the work that she did in regular school--by choice. I guess that once we eliminated all the busywork, she discovered how much *fun* learning can really be. She is once again eager, sets her own schedule, and still manages to get so much done that it is truly astonishing. The changes in her have also been very beneficial, because, as she controls and uses her own time, it has matured her and made her very responsible and sensible.

In *GWS* #35 a brave mother writes about her teenagers:

"What do they do all day?" Why is it that I don't know? *Why is it that I don't care?* We don't keep journals or go on field trips or categorize the day's activities into subject areas. I can't stand the dead smell of all those fakey thought-up things.

Also in *GWS* #35, Borgny Parker wrote about unschooling her teenaged daughter Abigail:

We started off thinking that we would be following the public school day at home. That did not work well at all. Both David and I saw the need to keep our distance because we were putting Abi under the same pressures she was seeking to avoid. What evolved was our own blend of non-schooling, I guess. We saw Abigail take off in different directions by herself...

Gwen Meehan, mother of Patrick (who is quoted in several places in this book), wrote me:

Last year was licking wounds and healing time. We both put much more emphasis on structured learning. We "did History, English, Algebra" and other "school" things. It was fine and necessary for that time.

Over the summer, however, I read all my back issues of *Growing Without Schooling* which high-lighted homeschool information for older students. By the time I had finished, I realized the overwhelming consensus was: get off the formal education road entirely. Every parent and every child backed up the idea of simply letting the student direct his/her own education. My role would be "facilitator." I did not have to worry about "teaching a curriculum," no matter how loose.

This has been the proper direction for us. Patrick is developing wonderfully....

Other parents wrote:

"The only books we steadily use are math books, because math is easier to stick with if we use a specific book. I really prefer the Saxon method and he does too."

"Throw away the textbooks, tests, and timesheets."

Teenagers wrote:

"We study reading, math, language, spelling, social studies, and science. We stuck close to [our] textbooks for our first two years. This was no different than being in school, and caused a lot of stress for all of us. It was also *boring*!" (The writer now uses textbooks only for math.)

"If the school sends you a curriculum guide, ignore it. You'll learn a lot more going at your own pace."

"Don't try to imitate school. Take areas you are interested in and learn from there. Find adults who know about subjects you are interested in and learn from them."

"Don't schedule yourself too tightly. In school a lot of time is spent just moving from class to class, being counted, disciplined, organized. You don't need to structure everything. Be relaxed. Take time to talk. Take time to think. Do nothing sometimes. Ask questions. Don't force learning. Some days you're just not in the mood, other days you don't want to stop."

Don't sink to the level of school.

Dream the biggest dreams you can, and then follow them. Start a cultural exchange program for Japanese and American teenagers. Build a log cabin and furniture to go inside it. What you lack in skill and experience, you can make up for with time and patience. Don't rush.

Remember your adolescent power and magic.

Don't spend all your time on mental stuff. It's not natural. You have your whole life to be academic. You have only seven years to wiggle and pray in a teenaged body.

Life doesn't get worse, but it does get less intense. Things become less new, and hormones stop raging. So honor and treasure your passion while it lasts. I'm not telling you to act on your every whim or to do stupid things like get pregnant when you're not ready to be. I am telling you to cling stubbornly to your spiritual yearnings, not to be talked into any imitation reality, to fall in love with people, and, as Thoreau put it, to suck all the marrow out of life.

A Small Dose of Chinese Philosophy

Before I suggest specific things to do with your precious time, I want to throw the spotlight on the concept of balance.

Some things we do are *outward*--giving, producing, working, speaking, taking action. Others are more *inward*--receiving, consuming, relaxing, listening, being passive. To be healthy we need to balance both in our lives. No one speaks wisely without having first listened. No one can listen happily if they aren't heard also.

When it comes to structuring your life, people of any age need to combine what our society calls "working," or "real life," with "academics." I am going to redefine these general areas as *giving out* and *taking in*. Learning, or education, happens equally in both, to the degree that you are fully awake and present. It happens most, though perhaps subconsciously, when you are happy. It happens rarely in school. That is, learning about history or how to talk in Spanish happens minimally in school. Learning how to take orders and sit quietly--that happens continually.

Most people your age are forced into too much *taking in*. Restricted from working or otherwise contributing to society, forced to read and listen all day, young people are desperately dependent, useless, powerless, and passive. Your lives are out of balance.

On the other hand, many adults feel pressured to do nothing *but* give out--the workaholic executive who feels like a failure if he doesn't advance continually in his career, the classic-tragic mother who drives her four kids to ten kinds of lessons and cooks three color-coordinated, balanced meals daily and scrubs Junior behind the ears but has no time to take a photography class or digest her own food or soak in a bubble bath. These lives, too, are out of balance.

People *need* balance. If they don't find it in a good way, they'll get it in a superficial way that hurts themselves and the world around them. We call some of them yuppies--people who work at stressful, nice-money jobs but don't feed their minds and spirits enough, so they switch into another mode-- buy, buy, buy. Bad for personal growth and bad for the planet, which is what gets used up when people buy things they don't need or even deep-down want.

Conversely, teenagers who aren't allowed to affect the world or achieve independence in a good way often resort to vandalism, insulting their teachers, joining gangs, killing cats, yelling at their parents--anything to make a difference. School denies your basic need to touch the world, to contribute, to matter.

Many activities seem to cross the line between giving out and taking in. Traveling, for example, is active and takes work, but is usually more "taking in"--absorbing, enjoying, looking, listening--than "giving out." On the other hand, learning to write is considered academic, and schools rarely encourage you to direct your writing to a real audience, but actually, writing is essentially a way of speaking out and affecting the world.

The Chinese concept of Yin and Yang nicely expresses the relationship between these two ways of being. Yang contains the outward, aggressive, giving aspects of the universe and one's life. Yin contains that which is inward, passive, receiving. The sun is yang and the moon yin, a candlestick yang and a bowl yin, hardness yang and softness yin.

What society calls "education" is mostly a yin activity, while "work" is yang. And you may prefer to think of adolescence as a more yin time in your life than adulthood. Nevertheless, both ways of being are necessary for health and satisfaction. In fact, according to Chinese philosophy, most of our troubles--global, health, and societal--result from a stagnant imbalance of yin and yang.

It boils down to this: you need to have both of these kinds of activity- -"giving out" things like starting a business, directing a play, or volunteering at the local soup kitchen, and "taking in" things like watching the news, reading, or going to hear a historian speak at a local museum. Also, realize that "academics" are only one part of the yin you need. Leave yourself time to stare at the fishbowl or linger at dinner. When you escape school you'll undoubtedly want a more outward, active life that affects the world around you, but don't starve yourself by shutting off the inward flow. The *Tao Teh Ching* reminds us, "For all things there is a time for going ahead, and a time for following behind; a time for slow-breathing and a time for fast-breathing;...A time to be up and a time to be down." If you were a bike, you'd have at least ten speeds. Shift gears as needed.

What's Ahead

Part three, chapters 17-31, are mainly about what you can soak up, or "education," or the yin part of your unschooled life. Part four, chapters 32-38, are about touching the world, "work," yangish stuff. Mix and match.

Finally: I give you a lot of the suggestions in this book in order to bridge the gap of fear; you're so used to being told what and how to do everything that I figured I would hold your hand a bit. But only if you want your hand held. If you're ready to say, "I can figure out what I want and how to do it on my own," that's *fine*. Hesitate not. After all, you are the heroines and heroes on the edge of a frontier. Your choices will inspire the unschoolers who follow. Hold your heads high, and ride off into the sunrise.

Part Three

the tailor-made educational extravaganza

chapter 17

Your Tailor-Made Intellectual Extravaganza

From here through Chapter 31, this book puts access to academia in your lap. Before you ignore this advice, or--worse--before you approach it with determined despair because you "should," please listen: intellectual fervor is for everyone. Maybe you don't think so, because when they made you do worksheets in history, biology, or English, they stole from you the desire to investigate the past, marvel at caterpillars, or hear a good story. *Don't let them get away with it.*

Or maybe you don't think intellectual fervor is for you, because you think you know where your territory is, and it's anywhere--under the hood of a pickup, in the cosmetics section of a department store--except in academia. Wrong! The *universe* is your territory. You don't have to take a test to be allowed into the community of intellectuals. It doesn't matter whether you have four points or only one. In your grade average, that is. If you read slowly or have a small vocabulary, you can read slowly and like it, and you can ask a person or a dictionary about words you don't know. If your father does nothing after work but drink beer and watch TV, that doesn't ban you from the poetry section of the library. If *you* do nothing after school but drink beer (or Dr. Pepper) and watch TV, that doesn't ban you from the poetry section of the library.

Now that you're out of school, why bother at all? Why not just lie and write in your log book that you spent two hours yesterday reading *The Mind's I*, and that you collected coyote poop all morning today to see what they've been eating?

Why? Lots of reasons.

Because if you find out and soak up some of the conflicting mesmerizing shocking funny logical illogical beautiful sparks we call "knowledge" or "information," you will grow a broader mind, more capable of seeing the connections and relationships between things that make the world and life so mysterious and wonderful.

Because knowledge married to wonder shapes your mind into the interesting, lively kind of place you'd like to inhabit for the next eighty years, maybe even eternity.

Because if you don't know what's been said and thought and tried before you walked in the door, you may repeat someone else a few times before you contribute anything new. The world does need new contributions, which is one *good* reason the schoolboard has for wanting you to be educated.

Because it is more fun to be in the know than to be ignorant and confused.

Because if you know things and think about them, you'll free your mind of narrow prejudices and cruelties. (Another reason you do the rest of us a favor by getting educated.)

Because if you know why the Trojan War, the French Revolution, World War II and Vietnam were fought and what changes they led to, you can form your own opinion about what justifies war, and what kind of war can be justified. Being informed improves your citizenship.

Because if you're a budding pianist, you need to understand the tradition behind you--not only the great pianists and composers, but also the roots of music in fire and ritual and mystery. Whatever you love, you will love it more when you understand its history.

Because certain skills--skills you already have but should continue to exercise--reading, writing, and arithmetic--can give you control over your own affairs. You can write to friends, businesses, congressmen, the public. You can read about whatever you want to know about, you can manage your money. (This stuff was supposed to be "taught" thoroughly in grade school. Chances are it wasn't, so you may want to work more on it.) If you can go further and do algebra and calculus, you can design buildings, bridges, airplanes, computers.

Maybe, also, because you have to prove to the parents that your brain isn't mildewed from snooping around in the forest instead of sitting in Miss Enquist's biology class.

How does it work?

Getting educated in the big beautiful sense needn't ruin your day. If you devote two hours each night to reading and sometimes writing, conducting Scientific Experiments, or tackling other mental exercises, you will certainly learn far more, and far better stuff, than you have been learning in school. Of course, you may wish to spend more time on "educational" activities you love. But don't feel obligated. After all, you never spent a lot of time learning in school. As Micki and David Colfax (whose homeschooled sons went to Harvard) point out in *Homeschooling for Excellence,*

> The child who attends public school typically spends approximately 1,100
> hours a year there, but only twenty percent of these--220--are spent, as the
> educators say, "on task." Nearly 900 hours, or eighty percent, are squandered
> on what are essentially organizational matters.[*]

---

[*] David and Micki Colfax, *Homeschooling for Excellence* (Warner Books, 1988), p.46.

Academia in what you love

There are seven big fat chapters in this book which tell you how to study all the school subjects without school. They can help you both learn things you are already interested in and also discover that you like more intellectual stuff than you ever thought you did.

But at the same time, you can sweeten your life by giving your brain to the things that already have your heart. It's mostly a matter of realizing that there is no cement wall between the things we do and the things we learn. Rather than look for things to do that fit into a "subject," look at the things you already like to do and think about where they might take you if you didn't stop them.

For instance.

I have always loved ethnic textiles and costumes. I used to not have time to do anything about it, but now I keep a hefty scrapbook of pictures cut out mostly from *National Geographics*, showing the traditional costumes of cultures all around the world. I also collect textiles and costumes when I can afford to, and I make replicas of folk costumes, very very slowly. I don't think of this as anything academic--it's just something I enjoy--but if I were a teenager I would most certainly point it out to the schoolboard and colleges as an eminently respectable way of fulfilling my social studies requirement.

After all, this activity has put me into contact with all kinds of knowledge. For example, after I noticed that Apache moccasins resembled the footwear of the tribes who live along the Amur River in Siberia, I went to the library and found out that the ancestors of the Apache had migrated across the land bridge and down to the American southwest quite directly, without dillydallying along the way or mingling much with other people. Later, as I read folktales of the Amur tribes and heard people talk about Apache religion, I noticed more similarities between the two cultures, subtle things I wouldn't have picked up on if not for the earlier moccasin clue. I keep this connection in my head as one of the questions I'm going to investigate when I have time. Meanwhile, I used a book on Native American footwear to design a pair of Apache-style moccasins which I decorated with a fishy Siberian motif.

Also thanks to my interest in costume, I know the whereabouts of all kinds of countries and regions within these countries. (Throughout high school and college, I'd barely heard of these places--Tunisia, Bosnia, Sardinia, Turkestan, Rajasthan.) Through costume, I've learned a lot about history and the relationships between countries. Women's dress in Southeastern Europe, for example, reflects centuries of Turkish rule. An intense interest in folk and ethnic dance has grown up beside my love of costume. The way different cultures dress has taught me many things about the way they perceive the roles of men and women, and about the relationship between people and nature. My interest has also invited me to reflect on the value of the industrial revolution, which is largely responsible for the drab factory-made clothes we wear now-- and for other carelessly built aspects of our 20th-century lives. I could fill a few more pages with things I've pondered and learned about in connection with ethnic costume. I won't.

My interest in costume is not any more inherently cerebral than your interest in airplanes, skiing, Pink Floyd, cute boys on TV, church, baseball, computers, or dogs. Your scrapbooks, obsessions, daydreams, collections, conversations, questions, and reading can all bring you into contact with the lushest, most meaningful kind of academia.

Jaywalking in the Milky Way

Along that line, be aware of interdisciplinary studies. What are interdisciplinary studies? Usually anything with "studies" tacked onto the end-- American studies, Asian studies, bioregional studies, environmental studies, ethnic studies, urban studies, women's studies.

A single discipline provides *one* language, or set of questions, through which to look at *everything*. Conversely, an interdisciplinary "field" looks at one thing with a lot of languages. For example, in women's studies you might 1) read and criticize literature by women and about women, 2) study women's roles in history, 3) look at women's bodies from a biological point of view, and 4) look at contemporary female roles through sociology.

I encourage you to apply the interdisciplinary idea to whatever you love. Consider history, geography, literature, art, science, etc. as they relate to your interest. If you love cars, maybe you would like to find out the history of cars and other transportation, about the role of cars in literature and movies, about the symbolic role of cars in our culture, or even about the environmental damage they cause.

Who will screen your calls?

Your teachers used to. Some did a good job. Most were lousy. You need to figure out how it's going to happen now.

Huh?

The unpleasant flip side of living in an information age is that it's hard to know what matters and what doesn't. With millions of books to choose from, which one are you supposed to read?

One of the best things a good teacher does is bring you the worthwhile stuff instead of the bullshit. However, teachers are not usually very good at this role. First of all, they are bombarded with even more information than most people, and a lot of it is very cheap-imitation-style unappealing stuff the educational publishers want them to buy. They have little way of knowing what's worthwhile and what's junk, and little time to make thoughtful choices. Educational publishing is *mostly* junk, so they're likely to go wrong.

Also, the best books on any subject are hardly ever textbooks. Since teachers are supposed to live in the land of textbooks, they often don't read the best books or even think profoundly in their own fields. Too many social studies teachers, for example, have little feel for the life of other cultures or for the kinds of forces that go into national elections.

Teachers are often out of touch with the real innovations in their field, and have no sense of how their field connects to the world. (Remember, most teachers have done little besides go to school.) Teachers are not necessarily experts in their field. They do not even necessarily love their field. For these reasons, most teachers are not the best people to trust with the task of helping you choose resources. Every school has exceptions, of course. The Colorado Springs School is full of living arguments to the contrary, but then The Colorado Springs School, or anything like it, is not accessible to most people.

Who or what, instead of teachers, can help you to make sense of the heaps?

This book provides a start. It tells you a few good resources to get your hands on, both in general (chapter 20) and in specific subjects (chapters 21--30). It also tells you about reference works for each field--books that point out other good books. Sometimes the best reference works include the mail-order catalogs of specialty stores. In chapter 21, for example, you will be guided towards the catalog of The Exploratorium store.

Another most excellent friend you can have is *The Essential Whole Earth Catalog*, which seductively describes pretty much the best books in nearly every field. I do mean nearly every field, ranging from evolutionary biology to cheesemaking to boardsailing to Western spirituality. You should also use the earlier out of print *Next Whole Earth Catalog*. Both reside in most libraries, though I am addicted to owning my own.

If you become especially interested in a particular subject, ask for help from an adult who has a passionate relationship with it. See chapter 15.

Librarians can give penultimate advice.

After you've been independent for a while, you'll develop a knack for scanning your eyes over dozens of library books and magically choosing the one or two that will most reward your efforts.

By the way, if you are addicted to babytalk, you'll have to get over it. School textbooks are mostly written in babytalk, because their writers know you're not interested, and babytalk is the only possible way to keep your patience. Most popular books, high school textbooks, and newspapers are purposely written at about eighth-grade level. When you get into real books, some of them will be tough. As long as you're interested in the subject, the toughness will be worth it.

Of course, a lot can be said in simple, straightforward language, but complex subjects often require more difficult language. School tends to assign novels at higher reading levels, but otherwise doesn't challenge you much. Therefore, college reading comes as a big shock for a lot of freshmen. Most of the books I recommend in the next chapters are not especially difficult, but some do go beyond eighth grade level.

Some unschooled ways to learn anything

Throughout the upcoming chapters, you'll find heaps of specific suggestions for ways to learn without school. Chapter 18 is devoted to listing resources you can find in your community. Right now I will mention a few activities that can enhance your learning in any subject but don't fit in the "community" category.

-Create a small museum that relates to your interest--natural history, local art, archaeology, skateboarding. A helpful book is *Exhibits for the Small Museum: A Handbook*, by Arminta Neal (American Association for State and Local History, Nashville, 1976). In college I lived in a natural history interest house. We kept a little museum in a back room full of a charming disarray of rocks, shells, fossils, and dilapidated iridescent taxidermed birds. In other words, you don't have to be rich or famous or hired by the government to start your own museum.

-Write papers. The "What I Did on my Summer Vacation" essay is usually rot, especially since when your teacher reads it she doesn't have enough time to care about what it says. Writing a mandatory essay comparing and contrasting the French Revolution and the American Revolution is also usually just busywork. But when you get interested all by yourself in the similarities and differences between the two revolutions, writing a paper can be one of the best ways to develop and clarify your knowledge and opinions. Writing can be a sharp tool that helps you reflect and draw conclusions on any experience or topic. You can write much more precisely than you can talk, because you have time to organize and think through complicated arguments and ideas. For inspiration, find academic journals in fields you like.

If "papers" and essays are too strenuous for you, you can write your thoughts about what you learn in an informal journal.

-Read academic journals, but only if you're ready to be patient. These journals (magazines) are written by and for specialists--they do not attempt to entertain the general public or to explain anything in easy language. No eighth grade reading level here. If you're still interested, look in a college library, where you'll find magazines like *Studies in Soviet Thought*, *The Journal of Psychohistory*, *The Ukrainian Quarterly*, *Sport and Exercise Psychology*, *Energy Economics*, *Work, Employment, and Society*, *Asian Music*, *Research in African Literatures*, and *The Journal of Medicine and Philosophy*.

-Write letters to people and organizations, asking questions big or small. Especially write letters to people you admire. Be extremely polite, but not self-deprecating. Enclose a SASE--self addressed stamped envelope. (That means with *your* address on it.) If they respond and invite you to write again, go ahead. If you write to people who aren't terribly famous your chances of a thoughtful response are better--not because famous people are heartless, but because they are already swamped with mail.

Unschooler Chelsea Chapman writes in *GWS* (*Growing Without Schooling* magazine) #69:

I write to a former U.S. Olympic Equestrian Team trainer who writes to help me with training and riding our horses. I started writing to her last fall when we were having trouble with the training of our Norwegian Fjord colt. I got her address out of a newsletter put out by the Norwegian Fjord Horse Registry and sent her a letter asking how she dealt with *her* Fjord horses. She mostly writes and tells me stuff about her horses and training methods and tack.

-If you have a computer, find software that can help you learn what you want to learn. It need not be expensive; you can find lots in the public domain or you could buy ritzy commercial programs together with friends or other homeschooling families. Also see *How to Get Free Software*, by Alfred Glossbrenner (St. Martin, 1984). For more up-to-date information, hook into a computer network or ask computer-geek friends.

One of the best commercial sources is Broderbund, which sells a wide variety of educational software for all kinds of computers. Programs include Print Shop, the award winning Carmen Sandiego series (history and geography), and calculus, geometry, and physics tutors, as well as many others. Broderbund Software-Direct, P.O. Box 12947, San Rafael, CA 94913-2947, (800) 521-6263.

-Also if you have a computer, buy a modem and tap into a whole new global community through computer networks. Through networks, you can research an astounding variety of topics, find out the latest sports scores, participate in discussions on the Middle East or read tips on finding nude beaches.

CompuServe is one of the largest and most important networks; free introductory membership and information usually comes with modems; otherwise get information from CompuServe , 5000 Arlington Centre Boulevard, P.O. Box 20212, Columbus, OH 43220, 1-800-848-8990.

An especially innovative network is the WELL (Whole Earth 'Lectronic Link), put together by the amazing people who do the *Whole Earth Catalogs*. Their "conferences" include topics like the Grateful Dead and pretty much everything else. Have your modem dial (415) 332-6106 to sign up, or call (415) 332-4335 for information.

An idea whose time has come is Jim Mayor's Home-Education Computer Users' Group. Since forming an electronic bulletin board in June 1988 (HUG-BBS), Mayor has seen little activity and exchange take place, but the board remains open. This is your chance to converse with other homeschoolers--one conference is open solely to people under 18. It is also your chance to find access to programs that Mayor considers "genuinely good educational uses of the computer." For more information, call Jim Mayor at home (301) 253-5467, or let your computer talk to his--(301) 937-2302. Or write (send SASE): James Mayor, 26824 Howard Chapel Drive, Damascus, MD 20872-1247.

Networks will undoubtedly change, expand, and multiply in the next few years, so ask those computer-geek friends or a local computer shop for suggestions.

-Don't forget how to communicate without a computer. Form a study group to investigate a subject that interests you. Or consider hosting or joining a salon--a regular discussion session with friends or acquaintances, somewhere comfortable with good tea and scones. The *Utne Reader* proclaims:

> Salons may be the antidote to the atomized and over-mediated lifestyle that prevails in pre-millenial America. We need to get together and talk with each other about the things we care about and believe in. It's fun. It's hip. And it can change the world.*

-If you want to develop serious expertise in any academic area, find a copy of Ronald Gross's *The Independent Scholar's Handbook* (Addison-Wesley, 1982).

Keep your antennae unfurled

Most young children have a pretty good sense of what they like--but only in a *general* sense. They can't know about all the *specific* things they might like because they don't know about everything out there that coincides with their tastes. Long before I was six I loved ballet lessons and dressing up like a Gypsy and swirling around at home. I grew up taking ballet and occasional jazz and tap lessons, and I enjoyed them. But it wasn't until college that I discovered international folk dancing, which hit much closer to home-- and it wasn't until after college that I found belly dancing, which hit *all* the way home to my Gypsy heart.

The moral of the story, of course, is *keep looking*. Hela, a teacher and one of my heroines, says "Take a bite of everything so you don't miss something you could have loved." Ava, also a teacher and another of my heroines, makes a point of trying something new every year. Last year, when she was nearly 60, she took up sea kayaking.

A little Sermon

Probably it's sad if you quit school and don't read any challenging books, but it's not the end of the world and certainly not enough reason to despise yourself. How many adults you know find two hours each week, let alone each night, to edify their souls through "education?" OK, maybe some of them went to college and supposedly learned everything they ever needed to know there, but how much of that do they actually remember?

---

* You can read the whole excellent series of articles on salons in the March/April 1991 issue of *Utne Reader*. Available in libraries, or subscriptions from Utne Reader, PO Box 1974, Marion, OH 43306-2074, currently $18/year.

I hereby proclaim that you are nearly guaranteed to improve your intellect by quitting school--even if you don't make the slightest effort. With a healthy, relaxed (unschooled) brain, you will undoubtedly pick up useful and captivating knowledge about the universe simply by keeping your eyes open, watching some good movies, reading magazines in the dentist's office, and asking people to explain things they say that you don't understand. Most adults have forgotten what they learned in school, don't attempt to organize their education any more than this, and get along all right in the world. You don't have to be "educated" just to keep your heart beating and your car running.

Everyone has their own clock. Though I got mostly A's in high school, I learned little. I forgot things soon after tests because most of the curriculum meant nothing to me. So much for informed citizenship. However, as my interests have broadened in the few years since I've been out of college, I've effortlessly amassed quantities of useful knowledge in widely varied subjects. In other words, I suffered from a poor education when I was a teenager, but this poor education did not prevent me from opening my eyes and getting on with things a few years later. If you don't read now, you can read when your hormones wane.

chapter 18

beyond "field trips": using cultural resources

In order to go about acquiring this tailor-made intellectual extravaganza thing that you will call an "education" when talking to the school superintendent, you'll want to draw from a variety of cultural resources, including libraries, museums, and other palaces of wisdom. If you live in a big city your largest trouble will be choosing the prettiest palaces from a kingdom full of them. If you live in a rural area or smaller town, your choices will be limited--you have more natural and rural resources instead. But no matter where you live, information abounds. Once you know some ropes, you can find whatever you need.

The Public Library

is the most valuable resource for most people's educations. When this country gets its shit together, it will have much less school and much more library. In a library, you can learn whatever you want, but no one will try to make you learn anything. You can find treasure in even a small library; with either a librarian's guidance or a small dose of courage, desire, and knowledge, you can find REAL words: novels or poems that awaken your spirit, non-fiction that explains how to do anything--blow up a dam or build solar panels or make cream puffs or get a children's book published or choose a tennis racket or sew a seam or write a bill and find someone to help turn it into a law.

There are two ways to use the library: with an agenda and without an agenda. *I cannot overly stress the importance of having no agenda*, at least occasionally. School makes you think of the library as a place to go when you want specific information about a specific subject. That's one thing the library is for, of course.

But the library is also a smorgasbord of surprises. Sometimes, go to the library and walk into the shelves and see what's there. Forget the card catalog, and don't try to think what subjects you might be interested in. You don't have to read any books you find, or even check them out, but pick them up and read their back covers and flip through a few. Also, if your library has an oversize section (for large, tall books) poke around in them--that's where you find lavish art books, photographs of Balinese dancers, and other surprises.

Using the library *with* an agenda takes a bit more skill. Unfortunately, if you're like most teenagers and many adults I've worked with, you don't know how to use the library, even if you think you do. You'll spend a lot of time there, so check out the territory thoroughly:

1) **Sign up for a tour.** If you don't see one advertised, ask. That way you'll find out about all the things you'd otherwise never realize your library has. Ask whether your library has an introductory handout or a map. In school you are used to being kept in the dark as to the way things work. There is no particular reason for schoolpeople to want you to know how school works. Sometimes information is deliberately withheld from you--for instance, teachers have "teacher's editions" of textbooks, with all the answers and with background information to make them sound more intelligent than you.

The library is the opposite; it is all about access to information. Librarians *want* you to know how to use the library. It makes their jobs easier and more rewarding.

2) **Become intimate with the card catalog.** Yes, you've learned all about title, author, and subject cards every single year since fourth grade. However, many libraries now use a computerized system, much more fun and efficient (although those wooden drawers had great ambience). When you're looking up information by subject, get good at brainstorming for related terms--especially narrower or broader terms. For instance, if you type in "Snakes" and don't want to plow through all 943 listings, try "snakes mythology" or "snakes natural history" or "snakes pets" or "snakes North America." Conversely, if you type in "polka" and nothing comes up, try "folk dancing." Also, try different forms of the same word. If "runners" yields nothing, try "running." If nothing works, ask the librarian.

3) **Familiarize yourself with the cataloging system.** (Smaller libraries--which means most public libraries--use the Dewey decimal system; larger libraries--most college and university libraries--use the Library of Congress system.) This way, when you want information on a general topic, you can ignore the card catalog and march straight to the right shelf. When I want to look over a library's supply of books on dance, embroidery, folk songs, folktales, international costume, American Indian history, or gardening, I simply smile sweetly at all the people hunched over their computers and head right for the proper shelf. Since these are some of my main interests, I know where to find them, just as you know your best friends' phone numbers by heart, and can find their houses without maps.

Many libraries have handy little cards with the Dewey decimal system all broken down. Another way to do it is to use the card catalog to look up one book on the subject that interests you, and then go look at all the books shelved in that area.

4) **Peruse the periodicals (magazines) frequently.** Periodicals are more useful than books in many situations, especially when you're looking into a subject that changes or develops rapidly, like political issues or fabric

dyeing techniques. Learn to use the *Magazine Index* (on microfiche), as well as *The Reader's Guide to Periodical Literature*. (In some libraries, *The Reader's Guide* is now computerized.)

5) **Does your library have a local history section?** If so, it may include books by and about interesting locals, law records, yearbooks--your parents'?, photographs, newspaper clippings, and tape recorded interviews. When my brothers and I were dirty barefoot kids visiting my grandmother we used to love to make our way into the elegant local history wing of the public library to look at photos of our ancestors and a blueprint of my grandmother's house before she tore it up to make more room for animals.

6) **Check out the reference section in scrupulous detail.** Don't lose out by assuming it's just shelves of encyclopedias. A reference section is an opulent microcosm of bookish delights. The only way to know what it has is to slowly inspect its shelves. While hunting down books like *The Guide to Alternative Colleges and Universities* and *The New Improved Good Book of Hot Springs*, I've chanced upon other delights like *The Encyclopedia of Unbelief*, *The Art of Maurice Sendak* and *A Dictionary of Chivalry*. If you find a reference book you love, check to see if there's another copy on the regular shelves that can be checked out.

7) **Don't be embarrassed to use the children's and young adult sections.** Smart adults use them all the time. Not only do they yield some of the most charming stories of all time, but they also provide a splendid introduction to any subject. When you have gaps in your knowledge, like you've heard of Joan of Arc but don't know why people make such a fuss over her, chances are you don't need to read *Joan of Arc: The Image of Female Heroism*. Instead, check out a children's biography and get an understanding of the big picture. When the big picture tickles your curiosity, then pick up something dense and intense--you'll be ready for it. (You can also read encyclopedia articles for introductions to anything, of course. But children's books are brighter and often about the same length.)

8) **Realize that there are books about everything, not just "bookish" things.** (Actually, I don't know what "bookish" means. Good poetry, for example, isn't bookish-- it's life-ish.) There are books about car repair, winning teenage pageants, and saving the world. There are books about everything you've thought of plus everything you haven't thought of: books of Maori folktales and Zulu chants, Scottish folk songs and Southeast Asian recipes. Books by and about people who talk with gorillas and dolphins, books full of joyous reports by "survivors" of "death." Whatever it is, if people have put a name to it, then someone has written a book about it, and your library can get it for you.

9) That's another thing. Even if the book you want doesn't appear in the Catalog, your library can probably get it for you through **Interlibrary Loan**. Go to the reference desk and ask them. You'll have to fill out a form and probably pay money--in Eugene I have to pay two dollars every time I

want a book. When it's a book I really need or want to read, two dollars is a bargain.

10) Don't overlook the library's other treasures--**CD's, video movies, pamphlet files, career files, phone books** of New York City and other exotic ports, **newspapers, and bulletin boards.** Be sure to know where the **new books** sleep, and glance over them from time to time.

11) To become an advanced library user, see the excellent book *Knowing Where to Look: The Ultimate Guide to Research*, by Lois Horowitz (Writers' Digest Books, 1988).

College and University Libraries

If you live near a college or university, do not be afraid to use their libraries. If you feel strange about it, just remember, you *live* there. If it's a state university, your parents' taxes pay for it. College students are just visiting for four years or so--it's not their territory any more than yours. These libraries offer far more in the way of scholarly journals (in case you have the patience necessary to bushwhack through mortifying terminology), academic studies of things, art books, and literary classics. Most have separate libraries for math and science; some have separate law, architecture, art, map, education, or music libraries. Most also have special collections--books from a particular country, or on a particular subject.

These libraries tend to skimp on how-to books, children's books, *Seventeen Magazine*, mysteries, Harlequin romances, Gothic novels, and science fiction. They probably won't have a copy of *The Lorax*. Instead, they might have something with a convoluted title like *Speaking for the Trees: The Lorax and Environmental Debate in Oregon Schools*.

In an academic library, you can also use the **CD-ROM databases.** These are huge computerized indexes which can help you find access to very specialized information.

One CD-ROM database which can be especially helpful is ERIC, the Educational Resources Information Center, compiled for teachers and educational researchers. If you ask it to list instructional materials, it will list things like this: "Getting Started on a Research Project in Field Biology: Practical Guidelines for Students" or "The Complete Science Fair Handbook" or "Spelling Rules" or "Auto mechanics supplementary units." You can also use ERIC to look up a specific topic that interests you in the word/phrase index. By asking for "flamenco," I found a flamenco (dance) handbook.

Next, you copy down the ERIC number of any titles that interest you, and take these numbers over to the ERIC microforms files. You find the microforms for the articles you want, and then you sit down and read them with a microform machine. If you want your own copy, you use the microform machine with the built-in photocopier (which costs a dime or a quarter per page). A library with CD-ROM material will be able to provide you with more detailed instruction and help.

Don't get freaked out if you go into a college library and find call numbers like LB.138 instead of good old Dewey decimal numbers. Most academic and other large libraries use the Library of Congress cataloging system, which is just as easy to use once you're used to it. Basically, books are shelved in alphabetical order according to their call numbers. AR books come before ZT books. LB books come before LM books.

Courses

Find out what courses are available. Check: dance and martial arts studios, museums, art centers, community education listings, foreign language or culture centers, college and university catalogs, community colleges, and as many other sources as you can think of.

Also, see chapter 19, School as a Cultural Resource.

Local colleges and universities

A college or university provides not only courses and libraries, but also a continual array of lectures, concerts, and workshops open to the public. Find out about these events by reading college newspapers or checking college bulletin boards weekly.

Professors can also be wonderful resources. They are busy, which means they may not have time to sit around chatting with you. On the other hand, they might love to have your help--preparing microscope slides or running down articles in journals, and in connection with this help you may find yourself a mentor or guide. (If you learn to use the CD-ROM data bases, you can be a valuable research assistant.)

You can also study or hang out (and meet people) at the student union, or eat in the cafeterias (for social, not gastronomic, pleasure). You can join groups such as anti-apartheid organizations, dance troupes, and outdoor programs. No one advertises these as being open to the public, and technically sometimes they're not, but in truth the people who run these organizations often welcome participation from anyone who is interested. You just have to hang around a bit, look friendly and inquisitive, and ask if you can join in. Don't let one "no" keep you from finding a "yes."

You can often take courses at junior or community colleges through high school enrichment programs. If you go through these programs, present yourself as a home *school*, not a "dropout." *GWS* (*Growing Without Schooling* magazine) #49 tells about 13-year-old homeschooler Daniel Lewis, who took an ancient Greek course at Fort Wayne Bible College in Indiana, earning full college credit.

You may occasionally have use for a correspondence course. See chapter 11 and Appendix C.

Lessons
Vanessa Keith wrote in *GWS #32*:

I'm 14. I've never been to school (except one day with my cousin). I have been trading with neighbors for two years. I trade babysitting, washing dishes, and money for lessons. I have four lessons a week: sewing, weaving, botany, and piano. It works great if you have friendly neighbors.

Aside from courses, you can find private lessons informally--in Vanessa's style--or formally. Music teachers put up their cards in music stores. Sewing teachers put up their cards in sewing stores. Foreign language tutors hang fliers around college campuses. Also check the classified section of the paper.

TV and Radio
Relying on either too heavily will make you into a passive un-person, but do consider checking the TV guide and phoning your local public radio station to ask them to mail you a program guide. PBS presents informative programs on everything. Most don't treat subjects with the depth that good writing does, but the visual component often makes up for that. It's especially good for learning about dance, Shakespeare, opera, and other visual subjects. Radio programs are great for getting easy brainfood while you're making jam or sewing a tent. Public, college, or alternative stations often have interesting local shows and also provide the excellent programs of NPR (National Public Radio).

Also, there are a wide variety of programs called "instructional TV"--which are designed especially for teachers to use in school. They include "courses" on foreign language, science, math, and many other academic areas. These programs are sort of like super-teachers, because the people who put them together have much more time and money at their disposal than regular teachers. Regularly using one or two might be nice; regularly using four or five would probably feel like an impersonal hi-tech version of school. To find out what's available in your area, call the local PBS station and ask them to mail you an instructional TV guide.

Events and Resources for Schools
As a homeschooler, you are often just as welcome as school students to attend stuff like science fairs, young writers' workshops, spelling bees, and some athletic events.

For instance: the National Geography Bee is open to ages 8-15. Homeschoolers are welcome. You can get information by writing to National Geography Bee, National Geographic Society, Washington DC 20036.

Museums

Museums are more than exhibits, though when you're not in field-trip mode the exhibits themselves can blow your mind.

Museums also
-need volunteers
-have internship programs
-give demonstrations (like blacksmithing at a Colonial museum)
-give classes, workshops, and events which are open to the public
-have private libraries which they might let you use if they know you (maybe after you've volunteered for a while sorting dead butterflies into different trays)
-have staff who are experts in their fields.

Art Centers

Art museums or "centers" will have many of the same types of resources as museums. They offer high quality classes and a chance to meet talented artists.

Science or Technology Centers

also offer many of the things museums do. Also need help.

Bulletin Boards

Every community seems to have at least one place where people put up notices and fliers telling about events, lessons, used flutes for sale. Try natural foods stores or co-ops, laundromats, cafes where college students or granola-eaters eat, and bookstores. Also, when you want to get your own message or advertisement out, make a flier and hang it up.

Newspapers

Once a week, most newspapers list classes, cultural opportunities (auditions for a musical, for example), and events. In addition to these listings, they sometimes include more detailed information about "educational" opportunities. If your community has alternative newspapers or free newsletters published by various organizations, they will often list different *types* of opportunities.

Small, specialized retail stores

are a terrific place to start learning about a lot of things. The people who sell outdoor equipment, weaving supplies, garden tools, South American folk art, solar panels, or ballet shoes often have considerable expertise in their fields. You can also learn a lot by walking through such shops and glancing through any magazines or books they sell. When a particular store owner helps you, return some goodwill by buying your supplies from him or her. Sometimes small shops have higher prices than huge chain stores, because they have to pay higher prices for their goods in the first place. Just remember that when you spend your money, you vote for the kind of world you want to live in. Would you rather live in a world full of K-Marts or a world where Mike owns a friendly bike store down the street and knows what it's all about?

Your government

can do a lot for you, which makes sense considering that your parents give it a big chunk of their money. For instance, by reading *The Encyclopedia of U.S. Government Benefits*, edited by Roy Grisham (Avon, 1975), I found out that the U.S. Travel Service can arrange through its Visitor Services Division for travelers from overseas to visit your home. The government can also help you get small business loans, obtain aerial photographs, and find access to many other surprising things.

And don't forget

zoos, ports, workplaces, the YMCA, the phone book, churches, city governments, factories, arboretums and gardens, hobbyists, parks and pools, clubs and organizations, and travel agencies.

school as a cultural resource

This book has said a lot of nasty things about school. Now it's going to say something nice. Schools have darkrooms, weight rooms, computers, microscopes, balance beams, libraries. They have choirs, bands, track teams, maybe even a Spanish class you want to take. Many enterprising homeschoolers have found ways to use the school resources they want without having to endure everything else.

This chapter tells about a few of these ways schools can cooperate with homeschoolers, and gives examples of particular homeschoolers who have taken advantage of school resources. If the schools in your area have never tried anything like this, you can pass this information along to them, and assist them in setting up a program that helps both you and them. Yes, them.

How do you think schools get the money they need to pay teachers, buy chalkboards, and shop for new math books? The state tax people give it out, based on the number of students enrolled. If they have to take you off the rolls, they lose dollars--probably around 4,000 per year, but maybe more or less depending on where you live.

If someone works out a way to keep you on the rolls--full-time or part-time--then your school can keep some of that money. When the homeschooling movement comes of age and sweeps the nation in ten years or so, arrangements like this can help schools save face and keep giving salaries to people--a far better use for tax dollars than nukie bombs.

Some school districts already have elaborate homeschool programs which can help you by lending textbooks, allowing you to take certain classes, and/or paying a certified teacher to see you each week (to fulfill any state requirements about certified teachers).

In Port Townsend, Washington, Seth Raymond (chapter 41) participated in a program like this. To fulfill legal requirements, a group of unschoolers and a certified teacher, Marcie, spent two hours together each week, engaged in some type of class or activity. Also, Marcie was available to work with each homeschooler for a few hours at the beginning of each semester to set goals and figure out what to call their activities. If they wanted her advice or guidance during the semester, she gave it. At the end of each semester she looked at their completed log books and gave credits in various subjects. For the people who requested it, she gave grades based on whether they had fulfilled the goals they set for themselves.

Students' main official task was to keep track of their activities, using a daily log book. Seth's log book had places for math, reading, biking, Spanish, science, drawing, history, occupational education. Some of the entries went like this:

> Occupational Ed: "Stacked firewood, cooked breakfast, mowed lawn."
> Biking: "Edited music tapes for biking," "bike competition--placed 4th."
> Science: "Watched and identified birds"
> Reading: "Read Mice and Men."

Some families have convinced their districts to not only provide access to school buildings and textbooks, but also to give an allowance for supplies. You can likely negotiate a similar situation; after all, you have leverage. The school will make more money off of your enrollment than it will spend on you, even with a substantial allowance.

For instance, Susan Swecker of California wrote in *GWS* (*Growing Without Schooling* magazine) #76, August 1990, about what happened after an administrator approached her homeschooling group. It was his idea to set up some kind of partnership. Before the group met with him, they met together and decided what conditions they would agree on. They knew they could be assertive since they were five families strong, and for each of their kids the district would gain $3,000. They presented the following list of requirements to the administrator.

1. No testing unless someone [a homeschooler] requests it
2. Use of the school library and computers at specific times
3. Use of audio-visual materials, darkroom, and supplies
4. One field trip each month
5. Access to school psychologist, speech therapist, nurse, and other specialists
6. The right to research and order our own academic and art materials
7. $400 per child per year to purchase academic and art materials
8. The right to use the building housing the gym, home economics room and restrooms for bimonthly meetings and potlucks on Saturdays, especially during the winter
9. The right to attend summer school and other school functions and workshops
10. Home visits by the homeschool coordinator as needed

The administrator wisely agreed to the whole list, and as far as I know everyone lived happily ever after. With $400, you can buy a lot of good books and a tall stack of silk shirts to paint.

Other homeschoolers decide to attend school part time, and convince local officials to cooperate. In *GWS* #33, Pennsylvanian Janet Williams describes her "seventh grade" daughter Jenni's new schedule after previous years of pure homeschooling:

Her schedule is as follows:

Monday - 1st period Computers, then home.

Tuesday - 1st Industrial Arts, 4th Recess, 5th lunch, 6th Science, 7th Phys. Ed, 8th Art.

Wednesday - 1st Speed Reading, 4th Recess, 5th lunch, 8th Chorus.

Thursday - 1st Spanish, 4th Recess, 5th Lunch, 6th Science, 7th Phys. Ed, 8th Bi-weekly clubs.

Friday: home all day.

....Periods when she is not in a class, she works independently in the library or computer room.

In California, most districts have an independent study program, which can sometimes be adapted to fit homeschoolers' needs. Thirteen-year-old homeschooler Mylie Alrich told me that thanks to her participation in her district's independent study program, she belongs to a school gymnastics team and has a pass so she can go to school dances.

Even if you are not officially enrolled in school, schoolpeople will likely give you what they can, especially if you're sweet. Fourteen-year-old Pat Meehan of Florida wrote me, "The schools here are very helpful. We get a lot of our videotapes from the county teachers' professional resource center through the school I would attend if I were going to school. Everything is very cordial. Some of the teachers are watching how we do because they are thinking of home schooling their own children."

Sixteen-year-old future dentist Leonie Edwards, of Minnesota, quit school in seventh grade. She has access to the school library, and every fall she helps with the high school musical.

Many other unschoolers report on good relationships with schools-- they attend on special days or to give presentations. For instance, *GWS* #70 mentions a homeschooling puppet club in Vermont that performs for schools.

In 1985, the Michigan Supreme Court ruled that public schools had to "open their elective and supplemental classes to private school students [including homeschoolers] who get their basic education elsewhere..." The court said, "Public schools are open to all residents of the school district...This statutory right to public education is not conditioned upon full-time attendance." (See *GWS* #44.)

In Washington, homeschoolers have the legal right to enroll part time in school, and also to participate in school activities including interscholastic sports.

In Oregon and Vermont, districts have occasionally paid for homeschoolers' Calvert curriculums. (See *GWS* #6 and #25.)

See Chapter 27 for examples of unschoolers who participate in school athletic programs.

Finally, another way to get access to the school things you want is to skip the legalities and quietly go straight to the people who have what you need. The choir director just may be overjoyed to let you use a music practice room during lunch. Can't hurt to ask.

the
Glorious Generalist

What, Miss Llewellyn, is a glorious generalist?

A generalist, in general, is someone who knows about a lot of things. But a glorious generalist must be distinguished from the heap of ordinary generalists.

The cheap flash generalist merely knows a lot of trivia. If he is especially flashy he can also recite amusing quotes by famous people. Nothing wrong with that, but the glorious generalist goes way beyond.

The almost-but-no-cigar generalist knows about a lot of things. He may even know a lot about a lot of things. But it stops there.

If the glorious generalist has a lucky tricky verbal mind, he can also spew trivia and quotes. I often wish I could do that. Pretty likely, the glorious generalist knows a lot about a lot of things, but not until he has been in business for a while.

The glorious generalist sees the world whole.

Because he sees the world whole, the glorious generalist can communicate thoroughly with people of every profession, religion, or background. He can pick up any book or magazine and find in it a connection to his own interests. If he is an all-the-way-there glorious generalist, maybe he can do mystical/scientific things like read the meaning of the galaxies in a fistful of sand.

How does the glorious generalist operate?

He starts with faith that the universe has meaning. This faith comes in two varieties--he can trust that a God, or an otherwise entitled Ultimate Reality, exists and created all this or guided it into place. Or, he can trust himself and other humans enough to believe that he can *make sense* of it all, that even if there is no *actual* collaboration between the pattern of a spider's web and the lyrics to that Led Zeppelin song, he can still weave it together in his mind so that it has harmony and order, like a stained glass window in a French cathedral.

Also, he trusts language. He believes that with language he can bridge almost any chasm between himself and another person.

Once you trust enough, you are a glorious generalist. You are not afraid or bored to be trapped in a stalled elevator with a nuclear physicist, an Eskimo shaman, an opera singer, or a milk delivery person.

What if the universe looks like a complete junkyard, and you *don't* trust it to make sense? Don't misunderstand me. Chaos shapes reality too; nothing *real* is as uniform or predictable as the rows of offices in a tall office building. As long as your mind is honest, your understanding of the universe will be in flux, an ocean not a sidewalk. But you can't even ponder or acknowledge change or chaos until you have some order in your mind, a canvas for that wildness to burn its image into.

Anyway, if your universe is a junkyard, don't be afraid. A lot of that is just school-scars, so much flying at you so fast that any kind of basic understanding of anything seems completely elusive. Once you recognize your confusion, you can start to relax. It doesn't take a special I.Q. level to be a glorious generalist; *everyone* could be one. In fact, I think we all come into the world as glorious generalists. Most four-year-olds aren't bewildered, and it's not for lack of questions and wonder.

Confused or not, go ahead and initiate yourself into the society of glorious generality. The fear will wear away; the cosmos will take shape in your mind.

Some steps to take

--**Become a student and observer of a glorious generalist.** First, you'll have to find one. (A lot of full-time mothers, by the way, are closet g.g.'s, though they probably haven't noticed.) You can check your candidate out to see if she meets some of the following criteria established by the nonexistent Criteria Board of the Universal Committee of Glorious Generalists. But if she fails the test, that doesn't rule her out. I hope you have some intuition, because you'll need it for this and later in life also.

1) Does the suspect take you seriously? If she knows you, does she ask you questions that go beyond mere politeness? The glorious generalist wants to learn from *you*.

2) Does she exhibit a wide range of interests? This sometimes shows up in a tattered, diverse library, or in scrapbooks or menageries or cluttered projects.

3) Are her friends a motley crew? Are they a mixture of young and old, this profession and that, three religions and five philosophies, hippies, yuppies, and rednecks? (Not that the glorious generalist herself would describe them so slickly. She tends not to slap labels on people.)

4) Does she attend to the basic structure of her life--what she eats, how she cares for her body, how she treats her plants?

5) Is she unintimidated by specialists? Does she judge people on their capabilities rather than on their degrees? Is she brave enough to decorate her own house, raise her own kids, without worrying that she's not an "expert?"

6) Have you ever heard her laugh and say, "*Everything* is connected!"

7) Does she preach or repeat trivial doctrines? If a Christian, does she follow you around with a little booklet that reduces the Bible to "Four Spiritual Laws?"

This test is not as tricky as the ones in magazines where you have to add up various numbers of points for each yes or no answer. I always hated scoring those tests. A yes on any of the first six are clues as to some gloriousness, but a yes on number seven is a bad sign to the contrary. It is fine, however, for the g. generalist to be deeply religious. I'm sure you get the distinction.

Once you find this person, try to hang around and notice how they think, talk, and find out things. But don't worship. Glorious generalists are usually humble people who don't wish to be fussed over.

--Read the biography of a glorious generalist. Or read a book written by one. Here are a few of my votes. Yes, there is a cookbook in the list as well as a book about physics. Often, the glorious generalist has written one or more books that make an ordinary subject seem wonderful and infinite, or a complicated subject seem understandable and fascinating. The glorious generalist can zoom up and down on the scale of broad to specialized knowledge. A good way to find out about glorious generalists' books is to perk up your ears when someone says, "Well, it's a book about baking bread [or about political campaigns, or whatever] but it's really a book about life."

Christopher Alexander, *A Pattern Language* or *The Timeless Way of Building*
Gregory Bateson, *Steps Toward an Ecology of Mind*
Fritjof Capra, *The Tao of Physics*
Lewis Carroll, *Alice in Wonderland, Through the Looking Glass*
Annie Dillard, *Holy the Firm*
John Fire and Richard Erdoes, *Lame Deer, Seeker of Visions*
Joseph Campbell with Bill Moyers, *The Power of Myth*
Molly Katzen, *The Enchanted Broccoli Forest*
Barry Lopez, *Of Wolves and Men*
John Muir, *How to Keep Your Volkswagen Alive*
Michael Phillips, *The Seven Laws of Money*
Robert M. Pirsig, *Zen and the Art of Motorcycle Maintenance*
Tom Robbins, *Even Cowgirls Get the Blues* (don't read if you're offended by explicit sex)
Rudy Rucker, *Mind Tools: the five levels of mathematical reality*

--Get your hands on the best resources for Glorious Generalists. Subscribe to *Whole Earth Review* magazine. Buy a copy of *The Essential Whole Earth Catalog*, and the earlier out of print editions from a used bookstore. The people who put them out are the most glorious bunch of generalists at work in this country now. Their catalogs and magazines are the ultimate tool and text. Mostly, they review books on every imaginable subject. But you don't have to actually track down the books and other resources they recommend in order to have fun; just reading the reviews and excerpts is a vivid journey through the big universe. It is a glorious mind indeed that describes the *Tao Te Ching*--the classic book of ancient Chinese philosophy-- on the same page as a book about sewage treatment. The page heading is "Whole Systems: Water," and it all fits.

I used to read *The Next Whole Earth Catalog* every night before I went to bed, though it made sleep difficult. After about six months of that, I started finding and using books they suggested. This is not a paid advertisement.

Another important resource is the *Utne Reader*, a magazine which reprints "the best of the alternative press"--unusual articles on the cutting edge of just about anything. Also, each issue runs an advertising section called "Off the Newsstand," where you can find out about specialty magazines focusing on topics like anarchy, socially responsible travel, or Dan Quayle.

--Cultivate the habit of browsing. Make it a point of view and a way of life. If you deliberately sniff out the territory, you will have constant fun knowing new things, and every once in a while you will run into something unexpected that changes your perspective.

Browse in the realm of words: Sometimes when you are in a library, just wander into the shelves and look at what's there. Look at the piles people have left sitting around on tables. Notice the variety of magazines, investigate a couple. Do the same in bookstores, preferably strange and atmospheric bookstores rather than B. Dalton's. Look to see what books friends have on their shelves. Ask which are their favorites. Take a mental bubble bath in the children's library. Flip through the yellow pages at home and the college catalogs at the library. Read the newspaper now and then. Know what's on TV and radio, and tune in when the moon turns blue.

Browse in the material world: walk somewhere new every few days. Go into a different store, take a different trail, look in the pet food or cookware section of the supermarket, swim in a different stretch of the river. Literally and figuratively, that is.

--Ask big questions of people you meet. Find out what they do (even if they go to school--what else do they do?) and trust that they can explain their interests and work to you. See if you can grasp the essence, the ultimate point, of what they do. Some good questions to ask are:

What got you interested in what you do?

What were the first steps you took to get involved?

Why does your work matter? Where does it fit in the world?

What questions are you asking in your work? (Or, what problems are you trying to solve?) How are you trying to answer or solve them?

This last one, by the way, is my magic wand question, one I kind of learned from reading the 20th-anniversary issue of the *Whole Earth Review*. I don't always need it, but when someone refuses to believe that I am truly interested in his master's thesis on environmental economics or in her work as an electrical engineer, it opens doors. Clement, my friend the biology research assistant, kept saying, "Well, it's complicated" when I asked him exactly what he was up to. Finally, I said "What questions are you busy asking in that esoteric laboratory?" And he told me. He was asking what role a certain hormone played in the life of a certain caterpillar. He hoped that the answers would give a clue as to the role of other hormones in human epilepsy. Not only does conversation like this dissolve barriers between seemingly different people, but it also reveals the beauty and meaning of things we call "academics." In my rather unscientific approach to life, I learn more from conversations with people like Clement than I ever did in school. College included.

Sometimes you will run into people who really can't explain for you what they do. Put on your suspicious hat. If it can't make human sense, does it make any sense? Some people in government bureaucracies don't seem to know anymore where the ground is. That's the kind of out-of-touch mentality that's going to blow up the world, if anything is going to. The good (and strenuous) book to read on this subject is *Standing By Words*, by Wendell Berry, very glorious.

--Be ye not frenzied. (Teachers in school cannot easily be glorious generalists because they are frenzied. In this sense they are deplorable role models, although their frenzies are not their fault.) The idea is not to fill your mind up like a crowded refrigerator. The idea *is* to weave a prayer rug out of everything that comes your way.

--Pay attention to the details of your own life, such as what you eat, how you speak to your friends, how you walk down the street. The better you understand yourself, the better you understand everything else. You stand at the center of your prayer rug; you can't leave yourself out.

--Let yourself cross boundaries. Be prepared, while you are reading Blake's poetry, to come up with a physics question you want answered. Entertain yourself with treats that stir it all up, like the artwork of Escher--as Stewart Brand describes it, "Geometry set at its own throat via the images of dreams."

I suppose while we're here in the generalist chapter we might as well talk about cultural literacy. Sigh. The concept has gotten quite the media attention ever since E.D. Hirsch, Jr. wrote about it in several bestselling books. By the time you read this, school curricula will probably explicitly include "cultural literacy." The idea is that we don't get enough inside jokes.

When someone mentions the Wright brothers (who did quite nicely without much school in their teenage years, thank you) or the Sistine Chapel, you won't know what they're talking about if you're not culturally literate.

I have no argument with Hirsch's basic idea--even if we don't always need these terms to understand each other, we do need them to understand our past and a lot of the best reading. But please don't get all bent out of shape about it. First, whenever someone says something you don't "get," you can ask them what they're talking about or write it down and look it up when you go to the library. Second, if you keep your eyes open in a Glorious way, you'll be plenty culturally literate. I don't particularly recommend hyperventilating your way through Hirsch's books as if you were studying for the Ultimate Exam called Living in Western Culture. Living in Western Culture is *not* an exam. It's a feast.

Ultimately, education is about our connection to the universe, our place in it. The bigger that connection, the bigger our lives and dreams. Through what we undertake to know and understand, we can be as immense as the milky way--glorious indeed.

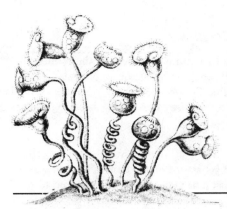

chapter 21

unschooling science

Science is one of the best reasons to quit school.

It took me a while to figure this out. Several college admissions directors told me that their unschooled applicants had weak science backgrounds. Among the teenagers who wrote me about their unschooled lives, a few said they felt like they skimped on science. Coming from an unscientific background myself, I felt as if I were encroaching on forbidden territory. In a bit of panic, I thought about changing my title to *The Artistic or Literary Teenagers' Liberation Handbook.* Instead, I researched extra hard and called extra loudly on the expertise of my scientific friends--and I ended up believing that a mass unschooling movement could inject new life, responsibility, and genius into the world of science.

No doubt, science presents special challenges to the unschooler. Lab equipment is expensive. Lab equipment is *intimidating.* This chapter tells you how to get around these difficulties, as well as how to make scientific use of the big wide world that schoolteenagers miss out on.

Why do unschooling and science go together? How should you approach science without school?

1. You have the whole universe, not just a grey room, for your laboratory. Use it. "Most people, most of the time, learn most of what they know about science and technology outside of school," says the National Science Foundation. [*]

2. School treats science all wrong. It usually allows no play and is afraid to ask you to do serious work. But real science is made out of play and very hard work, mixed together. It's too bad we think of sciences as the most austere and forbidding of the disciplines, because the only way you can start right is to mess around. Tease your mind with inspiring books and trips to beaches and roadcuts. Make questions: why are clouds shaped like billows of ice cream? Why are all the cottonwoods in the park dying?

My brother noticed people in his freshman class at Caltech whose actual knowledge base was scanty--perhaps they hadn't yet studied calculus or much physics--but something had inspired them strongly enough that they

---

* quoted by Roger L. Nichols, President and Director of the Boston Museum of Science, in a letter to the editor of *The Boston Globe,* 10/12/87

craved the scientific tools with which to continue exploring their universe. This "something" had varied--for one it was staring at the night galaxies, for another reading a rather poetic book called *The New Physics*. What they ended up holding in common was *questions* and *desire*, two of the best beginnings for anything.

Einstein's play went like this:

> Someone ... asked Einstein how he had got started on the train of thought that led to the theory of relativity. He said that it had begun with two questions that he had asked himself, and couldn't stop wondering about. One was, "What does it really mean to say that two things happen at the same time?" The other was, "If I were riding through space on the front of a beam of light, what would I see, how would things look?"*

The ultimate institutional scientific mental picnic, by the way, is the Exploratorium in San Francisco, a science museum of sorts. It gets you heaps of extra credit points in the play department.

Science also demands intense, serious work. Scientists have immense responsibility to handle information carefully and honestly, in order to tell the truth about their subjects. Without a school schedule, you can take all the time you need for careful scientific investigations. You can wait for the right weather; you can observe the growth of molds for years instead of one lonely Friday in the lab.

3. Outside of school you have the chance to get involved with real scientists and real scientific work.

My friend Heather, currently a Watson scholarship finalist and senior biology major at Reed college, suggests helping scientists with their research. Scientists always have more ideas than they have time to follow through on, she says. A biologist, for example, might need someone to catch aquatic invertebrates, record information from climate gauges, check traps, or collect water samples.

Phone up graduate students--who cannot afford to pay research assistants--and ask if you can help. Or put up neon pink notes in university science buildings. If you live near a college without any graduate programs, approach seniors, who often have a labor-intensive project to complete, or professors.

If you try this, expect to be inspected. Although you are offering to provide free labor, you could completely ruin someone's research by being irresponsible with data. Heather says it's a good idea to do an inventory of your past before you start to contact anyone. List all the experience you have which shows that you can be precise and systematic. This could be descriptions of scientific work you've done on your own or in school. It could include recommendations from previous teachers. Work as a surveyor's assistant is the

---

* *John Holt,* "Einstein's Questions," *GWS* #9, p.2

ideal background; certain kinds of cooking--candy making, for example--require precision too. So do woodworking and drafting. If you have little experience with anything of this nature, be ready to explain convincingly that you *know* you'll work carefully. If your scientist feels you aren't yet qualified, ask what you can do to become that way.

Similarly, Teri Jill Mullen writes in *GWS #78*,

> I am acquainted with a homeschooler who is interested in chemistry, and I have a good friend who is a chemist. I asked my friend if she would allow an 11-year-old boy to just hang around while she worked. She asked her boss, who was once a college professor. He was *very interested* and now this 11-year-old homeschooler has access not only to a chemistry lab, but to a very educated, friendly chemist. Certainly a boy his age in school would not find time for just hanging around and watching someone work.

Along the same line is an article in *GWS #29* which quotes liberally from a paper entitled "How Children Can Become Experts," by Dr. David Deutsch, theoretical physicist and founder and director of a small computer company. Deutsch writes about a hypothetical 12-year-old who has a keen interest in physics. School won't help much, he says. Books will, but only for so long:

> The point here is not that he will run out of facts to learn: he will not. The point is that factual knowledge from such sources actually constitutes only part of what a physicist needs to know. The more important part is a complex set of attitudes and ideas concerning, for example, the recognition of what constitutes a physics problem, how one goes about solving it, and what might be acceptable as a solution. One can learn such things in only one way: by participating in the physics culture. That is how graduate students learn physics when they are finally permitted to participate in real research. And this--research alongside real physicists--is what I think our hypothetical child should be doing.

Deutsch goes on to say that school is not the way to become a scientist, any more than it is the way to become a carpenter. The adult physicist would first benefit from having the apprentice do small problems--"sub-tasks" that did not require overall physics knowledge, but which nevertheless contributed to his work. The young apprentice would benefit from watching the physicist think, and from being able to ask questions. Eventually, however, the relationship would intensify:

> [The apprentice] would begin to "think like a physicist" as he unconsciously assimilated inexplicit knowledge simply by observing a physicist solving problems. He would begin to enjoy more and more the inner rewards of doing physics. At the same time he would become steadily more useful to me in an

ever wider range of sub-tasks. Factual knowledge would come to him without specific effort, as a side-effect of pursuing his interests. Later he would begin to grasp the details of specific problems which I was working on, and he would begin to find research topics of his own. I would find myself learning increasingly from him, both directly and because one always learns by explaining things to a willing listener. And because we would naturally have many problems and interests in common, he would be a particularly helpful colleague for me. Finally the apprentice would be such no longer, having overtaken his teacher-colleague in knowledge and skill. This is perhaps the greatest long term benefit which would accrue to both parties.

I must stress that I am not thinking of "child prodigies" in the above example. I am convinced that arrangements such as the one I describe can and ought to be the normal way of entering any profession...

For specific examples of unschoolers doing science-related "work" with veterinarians, museums, and zoos, see Chapters 34 and 35.

4. If you are artistic, or if the grey smelliness of most school science classrooms dismembers your enthusiasm, you can do lush colorful sketching unschooled science, particularly as a naturalist or geologist.

---

anti-propaganda note:
Don't be brainwashed by the Bush administration's misguided emphasis on science and math education. Their goal is that American schools will produce an average population that knows more science and math than any other country's average population. This goal is based on a dangerous, narrow sense of economic competition; it is much more likely to lead to an imbalanced, neurotic society than to any life-sustaining technological breakthroughs. I decided to bother to mention this because Your Government will be spending lots of money in the next few years to push schoolstudents to believe that science and math are gods that can fix anything. They're not. Furthermore, even if you *are* a bigtime science or math fan, school is not where it's at, for reasons stated all through this book and particularly in this chapter and the next one.

What is science, anyway?

Science is not, of course, planets and zygotes, but rather a methodical process of studying them, which mostly boils down to finding facts that can be proved again and again, in the same way. At normal atmospheric pressure, water always freezes at 0° Celsius. That's Science. It's predictable. It's been tested, but if you don't believe it you can test it for yourself. If your water freezes at 15°C, phone the newspaper.

An important early task, in doing any kind of science, is knowing what this scientific method business entails. Unfortunately, school courses don't necessarily impart this understanding to you. They didn't to me. However, you can read about it in almost any science textbook, in the first chapter or thereabouts. Or in any encyclopedia article on "science" or "scientific method."

While you're figuring out method, also think about the limits of science. Some things can't be understood with science, because they will never react the same twice. People are a good example. That boy you like, for instance. If you send him red roses tomorrow, he might reward you with a grin that puts you on a cloud. If you had sent him red roses last week, he might have fed them to his pet caterpillars.

Science has plenty of previously discovered "facts" for us to learn, but the heart of science is the process of *finding* facts through experimentation. Please recognize, therefore, the difference between reading the results of others' experimentation and conducting your own experimentation. Both are important, and some books are wonderfully inspiring, but to actually practice science, you must use the scientific method for yourself.

What sciences, and when?

One little side benefit of unschooling is that when you hear about intelligent research on education, you can put it to work for you *now*. Soviet, Chinese, and Japanese students generally do much better in science than Americans, and one likely reason for this is that they study all branches of science at once. In other words, they might study biology on Mondays and Wednesdays, physics on Tuesdays, and chemistry on Thursdays and Fridays, for four or five years, instead of one year of each all separated out. Absorbing it over a longer period of time, they remember it longer.[*]

Eventually, American schools will probably follow their example, but first, the Experts will have to argue about it in fourteen meetings, and then the textbook companies will have to develop new curricula, Ph.D.'s. will have to test the new curricula on nine school districts and write dissertations on the results, your school district will have to "allocate funds" (fork over money) for the new textbooks, and the science teachers will all have to go to workshops that tell them how to adapt to a new schedule. That's bureaucracy. Give it five years, at least.

In the meantime, consider approaching your own scientific work in a spaced-out way. Or not. As you like it. At any rate, biology, chemistry, and physics are standard preparation for science majoring in college. Geology and subcategories of the others, like field zoology, are optional.

---

[*] Sharon Begley, "Not Just For Nerds," *Newsweek*, April 9, 1990, p.61.

Finding Lab Equipment

If you look hard enough, you will find the lab equipment you need. Some ways unschoolers find access to microscopes and other toys:

-by making arrangements with a teacher or school to come in and use equipment. This might work especially well if you offered to grade quizzes or wash beakers in return. Also, if you find an inspired teacher-scientist, you might end up with a mentor too.

-by becoming involved as a volunteer, apprentice, student, or indefinable presence at a local museum or science center. Read about Seth Raymond's work at a marine science center in chapter 41.

Hostex News, 5/82, says,

An 11-year-old boy conducts regular research projects at the Museum of Natural History in New York. He is one of the few living "protozoologists" to observe the rare act of a paramecium forming a protective wall around itself as the surrounding water dries up.

-by using lab equipment at a parent's college or place of work.

-by buying equipment. Aside from a good compound microscope, most isn't expensive, unless you want to have better facilities than schools do. If you want to buy, you can decide *what* to buy by making a list of necessary equipment for the labs in your textbooks.

-by always mentioning their needs when they meet people. Gwen Meehan, mother of unschooler Patrick, wrote in *GWS #73*: "I happened upon a marine biologist with a Ph.D that included some education credits. He has invited Pat to come use his microscopes and ask questions any time he likes."

Do you really need lab equipment?

Yes, but maybe not as much as you think. Most lab experiments in high school textbooks don't demand much in the way of supplies. The most serious equipment any of them require is a compound microscope, Bunsen burner, and triple beam balance. In the dozen-or-so textbooks I investigated, however, the majority of labs required little more than beakers, test tubes, crucibles, petri dishes, medicine droppers, graduated cylinders, and for physics a lab cart, recording timer, pulley, connecting wires, and dry cell. My friend Clement-the-biology-research-assistant points out that you can make do, in many cases, with substitutions. Use a candle instead of a Bunsen burner, any sort of scale rather than the triple beam balance, random plastic containers instead of official petri dishes, etc.

Mail order science equipment:

-Carolina Biological Supply Company, 2700 York Road, Burlington, NC 27215, (919) 584-0381. This *fat* catalog costs $16.95, but is worth it if you want a huge selection of scientific supplies. In 1304 pages, you can shop for a real human skeleton (or the bones of dozens of other animals--a gorilla skull, a rattlesnake skeleton), chemicals, plant and animal tissue cultures, living things: amoebas, paramecium, centipedes, termites, silkworm eggs, salamanders, African clawed frogs, fertile quail eggs. Don't be misled by the name; Carolina also sells physics, chemistry, and other science supplies.

-Edmund Scientific Company, 101 E. Gloucester Pike Barrington, NJ 08007-1380. Ask for their *Annual Catalog for Technical Hobbyists*, which costs $3. Edmund provides everything from microscopes to dry ice makers to Geiger counters to telescopes to science fair guide books to a model kit of the human tooth, along with a lot of raucous fun like "moon blob," "magnetic marble magic," plastic spiders, and such.

-Jerryco, Inc., 601 Linden Place, Evanston, IL 60202 (708) 475-8440. A charming catalog for 50 cents, which will not only sell you all kinds of industrial and military surplus, but make you laugh too. Solar panels, pipets, and lots of unscientific weirdness like gold metallic jackets and a scratch 'n sniff book about three-course business lunches.

-Science/Math/Technology catalog from Learning Things, Inc. 68A Broadway, PO Box 436, Arlington, MA 02174. They sell an "Ultrascope," which is a very inexpensive (under $15) microscope. According to people who use it, its quality is excellent, although since it magnifies only up to 300X, it won't do for certain kinds of advanced work. Also a wide variety of supplies for biology, physics, laboratories, chemistry, technological projects, etc.

-Nasco Science catalog, from Nasco, 901 Janesville Ave., Fort Atkinson, WI 53538-0901, (414) 563-2446. One of the major school suppliers, with therefore a wide variety of school-type science equipment-- dissecting tools, lab books, model rockets, soil testing kits, microscopes, lab furniture, the works.

General science reference books:

-*Concise Science Dictionary* (Oxford University Press, 1987): useful if you want to do a lot in one science without studying the others. While you are reading about marine mammals and run into chemistry words, look them up fast here. If you have textbooks for all the sciences, you shouldn't need it.

-*The Art of Scientific Investigation*, by W.I.B. Beveridge (Random, 1960) is old but still in print and clear and wise. Written by a Cambridge professor and researcher of infectious diseases, it thoroughly explains how to go about scientific experimentation on a serious level. Also, it acknowledges all the way through that scientists are people, not machines, and that their personalities affect their work. If you are badly addicted to large print textbooks complete with color photos and textbook-speak, you may be put off at first by this book's quietness: no diagrams, no baby-talk. Stick with it, and you will be rewarded by clear, friendly language and very helpful teaching.

Other general resources and ideas

-Read **popular books** on science. I've recommended a few under each branch of science, but there are many others. If you've never read this sort of thing before (schools rarely assign the stuff), be prepared to get amazed and inspired.

-Check out some **children's experiment books** from the library, like *The Chemistry of a Lemon*, or *101 Physics Experiments for Children*. There's nothing wrong with simple experiments; without lots of complicated equipment and procedure, nothing distracts you from the strange beauty of scientific reality.

(If you want to seduce your reluctant self into science, try forgetting textbooks for a while and combining the previous two ideas--popular books and kiddie experiments.)

-There's no law against using **high school textbooks** and working through them at home, just don't let them rule your life. Try to choose them by looking through several, comparing the way they organize material and especially how clearly they describe laboratory experiments. (Unlike in math, there are few obvious "best" science textbooks, so I've recommended only two specific texts, one for physics and one for geology.) Advantages of textbooks: they cover all the basic territory and provide a good overview and broad understanding. Usually, they are easy to understand. They have glossaries and thorough indexes; they make great reference books when you have a question. Disadvantages: using them *slavishly* is unnecessary and usually boring. Also, textbooks are expensive, if you can't borrow them. One way to use them: skim through, read the instructions for all the labs, and carefully do a few labs that interest you. Save most of your scientific energy for better stuff, like playing with wires or hatching a crop of ant eggs.

-If you like textbooks, you can always use **college texts** too. Try your local university bookstore to see what current classes are using, and then save money by finding these texts at libraries, used book sales, or by posting notices saying what you're looking for.

-Write the **Exploratorium** Store for their **booklist**. It describes great books in all scientific departments, for all ages. You can order from them or use the recommendations to help you in the library. If you don't plan to order from them, be a pal and send a dollar for postage. Exploratorium Store, 3601 Lyon Street, San Francisco, CA 94123. (415) 561-0393.

-If you consider yourself an environmentalist, put your scientific efforts to work for a local or national **conservation organization**. The Audubon Society, for example, needs volunteers from time to time to do things like count salamanders and monitor acid rain. Local groups sometimes conduct restoration projects, such as rehabilitating a polluted stream. To become involved, watch the newspapers for stories of such projects, or phone up all the local conservation groups. Your library undoubtedly has a list. Alternatively, write the national offices of these groups and ask for addresses and phone numbers of local groups. Some addresses listed in Chapter 38. For lots of ideas and examples of environmentally healthy work going on in science and other fields, see the *Whole Earth Ecolog* (Harmony, 1990).

-Form a **science co-op** with other unschoolers or friends of any age. Buy equipment together, share ideas, discuss projects openly. As you become better scientists, eventually you may want to apply for grants together.

-Read **scientific magazines**. *Science News* is especially good: short, up-to-date (published weekly), clear. By subscription only: *Science News*, 231 West Center Street. P.O. Box 1925, Marion, OH 43306-4025. Look for other magazines at your library.

-The **Earthwatch Institute** is a bunch of scientists who conduct research all over the world--and let people pay to help them out. Spending the money to go along on one of their projects sounds like a better educational expense than tuition at an expensive school or college; however, they do also give scholarships. Some of their work relates to textiles, folklore, etc., but most is scientific. Projects last from two to three weeks.

Examples: studying moths in Papua New Guinea while staying in a "tribal guest house," training sea lions in California, doing lab work (which will contribute to a map of the Pacific Ocean) on a Soviet research ship. You must be at least 16. Information from Earthwatch Institute, 680 Mount Auburn Street, Box 403N, Watertown, MA 02272.

If you might major in a science in college

Do all the math you can. Get comfortable with the scientific method by conducting some experimentation and being as precise as possible. Read the work of other scientists, both popular and scholarly. The detailed advice of professors at the ends of the sections on biology, chemistry, and physics might interest you, but it essentially boils down to math, method, and inspiration.

In the long run, college itself is not necessary for the development of a great scientist, but graduate school is definitely valuable. (No law says you must have a B.S. to go to graduate school. You *will* need plenty of knowledge and solid, inspired scientific experience.) Going to graduate school, say my scientific friends, is the first really valuable level of education, more or less equivalent to an apprenticeship. Many of them--including my Caltech graduated brother--feel that with a few good books and lab equipment, they could have taught themselves all they learned in college.

Scientists without school:

William Lear, 1902-1978, founder of the Lear Jet Corporation, quit school after eighth grade to work as a mechanic. He studied radio in the navy during WWI, and went on to invent hundreds of electronic devices, mainly various navigational aids for private aircraft. Later, he developed the Lear Jet, as well as stereo tape systems for cars and the first lightweight automatic pilot for jet planes. *

---

* Information from *Current Biography Yearbook 1966*.

A 1980 UPI story from Eight Dollar Mountain, OR:

...You wouldn't expect to find a space-age scientist living with computers and telescopes atop a roadless hill on the edge of the Kalmiopsis Wilderness, 30 miles southwest of Grants Pass, Oregon.

But then, Paul Lutus is a man who's spent his 33 years doing things in different ways.

...As a bookwormish "extremely precocious and arrogant 12-year-old," he idolized Albert Einstein. Believing school would "lead to ruin," the seventh grader dropped out to study astronomy and electronics on his own.

When his parents didn't accept that decision, he moved out. Under the wing of a foster family, the 12-year-old became a television repairman. At 16 he qualified for a Federal Communications Commission radio-television license and later worked as a radio announcer in San Jose, California.

At 20 he launched a career as a "street person." He earned a panhandler's living in San Francisco by sketching portraits, singing folk songs, strumming his guitar, holding bubble-blowing classes.

He switched to a research associate position at Mt. Sinai Medical school in New York. Then he pedaled his bicycle from New York to Colorado where he took a job designing research equipment for the molecular biology department at the University of Colorado.

In 1974 Lutus began work as a NASA consultant in San Francisco. He moved to his hill at the base of Eight Dollar Mountain a year later. He designed computer programs that helped the Viking spacecraft fly to Mars, and he's the electronics engineer who invented a new kind of lighting for the space shuttle.

And the *Christian Science Monitor* describes Vincent J. Schaefer, one of the world's top atmospheric scientists, who left high school after two years. At seventeen, he and three other teenagers started their own small archaeology magazine. The New York State Department of Archaeology noticed it, and the state archaeologist invited Schaefer along on a month-long field trip.

In order to help his family earn money, he took an apprenticeship at General Electric. At GE, Schaefer found a mentor who encouraged him to conduct his own experiments in the laboratory. Eventually, without any college or university training, Schaefer discovered the first method of seeding clouds. In 1961, he founded the Atmospheric Sciences Research Center in New York. For the next 15 years, he directed it as the leading professor. The newspaper article passes along Schaefer's "secret of success":

- Work on your own.
- Learn by doing.
- Seek out worthwhile people and make them your friends.
- Read books.
- Take advantage of every good opportunity to learn something.
- Remember that mature people enjoy helping young people who are trying to find themselves and realize their potential.

Shaefer insists that anyone with the desire could do what he has done. "You have to have a sense of wonder," he says, "and be aware of everything that goes on. You have to develop what I call 'intelligent eyes'--be intrigued with the world and everything in it."[*]

Unschoolers doing science

Britt Barker, now in her early 20's, followed her interests in wildlife and classical music instead of going to school. Her music and writing get mentioned in chapter 39, but here and now you should know about a couple of the scientific things she did starting at age 16. For one, she traveled with naturalists in Canada, assisting them while they wrote a book on endangered species. For another, she received a grant to participate as a team member on an Earthwatch Institute expedition to study wolves in Italy. You can read about these experiences in her book, *Letters Home*.

After "high school" age, Britt kept up her independent style rather than attending college. She again volunteered for Earthwatch, this time at the Bodega Bay Marine Lab in California. At 19, she was offered a three month position for fall 1987 as an intern at Point Reyes Bird Observatory in California, working with a biologist and four graduate students. Next, she spent six weeks tagging elephant seals for the Farallones National Wildlife Refuge near San Francisco. By that time she had been offered a winter job in Arizona monitoring bald eagles from land and air, using radio equipment.[**]

Kathleen Hatley wrote in *GWS* #53 that her son Steve, 13, had

developed a strong interest in freshwater fish. Aside from actually going fishing, which is his very favorite thing to do, he managed to read every available book in the library, including five volumes of a fish encyclopedia. He worked out a deal with a friend who is a graduate student in fisheries, to supply him with worms and perch fillets for his specimens. In return, Steve received a large, fully-equipped aquarium, in which to keep his own specimens. A highlight of the year was when he got to "seine" a local river (drag the river

---

[*] From Emilie Tavel Livezev, "Self-Educated Scientist's Formula for Life-long Discovery," in *The Christian Science Monitor*, 12/20/1982.
[**] Britt Barker, *Letters Home*, details in bibliography

with huge nets to bring up small fish to study) with the curator of the University Life Sciences Museum. Next week, he starts an apprenticeship with the ranger at a nearby lake (who happens to be one of the most knowledgeable naturalists around). He will be learning, among other things, how to manage a camping and fishing facility. This interest in fish led into many other areas, as a real interest always does--climate, pond and stream ecology, life cycles of insects, etc.

My older children continually reinforce my belief that when a child has an interest in something, they have a real need to plunge much deeper into the subject than a normal school curriculum ever allows...

BIOLOGY

If you plan to give your brain to biology, even partially, think carefully about what kind of animal experimentation is okay with you, and for what purposes. Although you'll start small, it's a good idea to keep your ethics married to what you do. A biology student I know is fed up with most biological work. Too much of it, she says, reflects no purpose beyond feeding scientific egos, at the expense of (for instance) frogs who get genetically engineered to have mashed up faces, mashed up legs, mashed up brains. Also, think about *manipulation* versus *observation*. Often, you can find scientific knowledge by carefully recording your observations, rather than actually interfering with whatever you're studying.

Popular reading:
-Anything by Stephen Jay Gould or Lewis Thomas.

-Ernst Haeckel, *Art Forms in Nature* (Dover Publications, 1974). A psychedelic picture book to make you fall in love, even with tapeworms.

-James D. Watson, *The Double Helix*. Tells the story of the discovery of the structure of DNA. Reading it, you watch scientific method, minds, and friendships in action. In that respect, it is like a mini-apprenticeship. "As I hope this book will show," writes Watson, himself one of the scientists, "Science seldom proceeds in the straightforward, logical manner imagined by outsiders."

-Jane Goodall, *My Life With the Chimpanzees* (Pocket Books, 1985). I mention this book because you can read it in 45 minutes and it tells, briefly, how Goodall set up her project in Africa without benefit of college training. (Instead, she found herself a mentor.) You can also write the Jane Goodall Institute for Wildlife Research, Education and Conservation, PO Box 26846 Tucson, AZ 85726, to find out if you can help in their work.

Mail order:
-A skeleton construction kit--cardboard, anatomically correct--is available for $29.95 from National Teaching Aids, Inc., 1845 Highland Avenue, New Hyde Park, NY 11040. Their catalog also has posters and models of dissected frogs, worms, etc.--visual aids which could partly replace actual dissection.

-Beautiful anatomy charts available from the American Map Corporation, 46-35 54th Road, Maspeth, NY 11378, (718) 784-0055. Free catalog.

Be a naturalist
The naturalist is the one with a butterfly net, a carefully labeled collection of abalone shells, an aquarium, a miniature museum, two pet boa constrictors, a field diary full of sketches and notes, a worn pair of hiking boots, and quartz crystals from a trip to Wyoming instead of the corner New Age Shoppe. The naturalist makes science rich, beautiful, and personal, rather than dry and remote.

Natural history (the naturalist's path) is an ideal scientific avenue for an unschooler, since you have all the time you need outside in "the field," and it can be very inexpensive as well as rigorously, respectably scientific. Naturalists are usually well-rounded scientists--geologists and climatologists as well as biologists--but they deal mostly with botany and zoology.

"What really makes a naturalist?" asks Gerald Durrell, in *The Amateur Naturalist* (Knopf, 1983), "...A naturalist first of all has to have a very enquiring mind. He seeks to observe every little variation in nature and to try and discover its origin and function....A naturalist should also be an assiduous note-taker, recording every detail of his job with accuracy and neatness."

Durrell's book is all the book you'll need, for a while, though it covers only botany and zoology--no rocks and such. It is clear, beautifully illustrated, and comprehensive, organized around 17 different environments including your own house and local fields as well as coastal wetlands, coniferous woodlands, deserts, etc. There are sections on techniques, equipment, and setting up a workroom-- all you need to know to turn your love of nature into science. Also, Durrell constantly points out cheap or free ways to get the job done-- substituting a razor blade for a scalpel, for instance. Durrell, by the way, famously collects animals for zoos and conducts other naturalistic adventures. As a child, he rarely barely went to school.

If you want naturalistic help with rocks and minerals or climate study, Vinson Brown's book *The Amateur Naturalist's Handbook* is good. It's great for plants and animals, too, just not as lush as Durrell's book.

To help you draw beautiful pictures in your naturalist's diary, see *Nature Drawing: A Tool for Learning,* by Clare Walker Leslie. If you are hopeless like me, backtrack to *Drawing on the Right Side of the Brain*, by Betty Edwards (JP Tarcher, 1979).

You will eventually want field guides, such as the Peterson series, which will help you identify birds, animal tracks, mushrooms, etc. The *Sierra Club Naturalist's Guides* don't have lots of pictures, but each one gives a clear, thorough background to the geology, botany, and zoology of a particular region like the Pacific Northwest or Southern New England.

Popular reading:
-Aldo Leopold, *A Sand County Almanac*
-Annie Dillard, *A Pilgrim at Tinker Creek*
-Edward Abbey, *Desert Solitaire*
-Edwin Way Teale, *The Insect World of J. Henri Fabre*

Preparation for college biology

G.J.C. Hill, professor of biology at Carleton, says that laboratory experience in chemistry, physics, and biology is expected background for potential biology majors. He is frustrated with students

> that have had lecture/seminar/discussion group experience but lack involvement with the equipment and visual observations, data analysis, and understanding of experimental design. *Problem solving* in the biological disciplines is a necessity; biology is an empirical science not a theoretical one.

Professor Hill would also like (but not necessarily expect) freshmen to have

> a general familiarity with the major sub-disciplines of biology: genetics, physiology, organismic, anatomy/morphology, evolution and cell/molecular in both animals and plants. I am not suggesting Advanced Placement courses, just a one-term general survey at the high school level. One of the problems we face is that many high school teachers use their biology courses for single sub-discipline presentations (primarily genetics, for example) or as a platform for socio-biology (personal hygiene, AIDS, greenhouse effect, pollution, etc.) without providing the fundamentals of biology. This may give the student problems at the college level when he/she is expected to spend a full year in introductory courses learning a massive vocabulary of basic terms and concepts. The problems are not insurmountable but they do add to the burden of initial adjustment and may foster a sense of inadequate preparation.
>
> As to the "ideal student": someone with an enthusiastic curiosity about what makes nature "work" without the preconceptions or prejudices of "that's impossible" or "I don't believe in..." or "You can't do..." This must be

combined with the intelligence to know the difference between improbability and sheer fantasy. Biology is a discipline filled with many levels of discovery, all of which pertain directly or indirectly to how we live in the world and how we perceive it. Anyone who continues to experience a sense of awe about the natural world is the "ideal student" as far as I am concerned--*as long as it goes beyond the mere "gee whiz" stage....*

CHEMISTRY

Please refer back to the information on general science learning at the beginning of this chapter. Mail order suppliers offer plenty for chemists.

Popular reading: Chemistry seems to have fewer bards than other sciences. Maybe you will eventually write the book that does for sulfur dioxide what *Cosmos* did for the big bang theory. In the meantime, read the excellent but partly outdated *Asimov on Chemistry*, by Isaac Asimov (Doubleday, 1974).

Preparation for college chemistry
Marc S. Silver, Chairman of chemistry at Amherst, advises

I would suggest that a freshman *needs* to know very little chemistry to do well in beginning chemistry at Amherst. We *like* them to know some of course-- understand the implications of the Periodic Table, know the common ionic species, etc--but that is not essential for success. Those who do best have the ability to solve word problems and to do algebra. These are certainly the skills I should most emphasize. Of course, being smart helps too.

The chemistry chair at an ivy league university says,

Some of our freshmen place out of our general chemistry on the basis of their high school experience, which I suppose is my ideal for the way freshmen should be prepared. Based on what I am told by my students and my own experience, I have concluded (unhappily) that many high school chemistry courses are pretty thin....

In my experience, the troubles students have in general chemistry, if they have trouble, usually stem from mathematical problems, not from lack of prior knowledge of chemistry. Many students have difficulty converting ideas they "know" at a verbal level into algebraic expressions they can solve to get answers. This skill is essential for success in all the physical sciences.

The algebra needed for general chemistry is elementary. Students see it as high school sophomores. The crew we get undoubtedly passed the math courses in question with all A's. What many of them did not come away with, however, is facility at using the math they "know" to do useful things for them. They never really internalized it.

It follows that the preparation students need for college chemistry is any preparation that enables them to use algebra as a tool. They can get that skill in math courses, physics courses or chemistry courses, but just so long as they get it, I can teach them general chemistry successfully. It certainly makes it easier for me and for them if they had some chemistry before I see them, but it is not absolutely essential.

PHYSICS AND ASTRONOMY

"When Buckminster Fuller was in the navy, he asked himself why the bubbles in a boat's wake were round. This might sound like a "dumb" question, but it led him to geodesic domes and hundreds of other discoveries."
--Paul Hawken, *The Next Economy*

A dream was the best physics lesson I've ever had. It was the first day in a physics class. The professor said, "Your first assignment is to roll a ball. No writing, no reading. Roll your ball everywhere and always watch it. Roll it in the park, roll it in the street, and roll it in the kitchen."

Good textbook, etc:
-Particularly for people with weak math backgrounds: *Conceptual Physics*, by Paul G. Hewitt. You *do* need math for advanced physics, but you can get a surprisingly substantial start *without* math, thanks to this profound book. At the end of each chapter, rather than ask you to work equations, it gives you exercises to test your understanding, like: "Imagine a super-fast fish that is able to swim faster than the speed of sound in water. Would such a fish produce a 'sonic boom?'"
-*Exploratorium Cookbooks*, I, II, and III. These give detailed instructions for building replicas of the famous fun exhibits at the Exploratorium. Most of the "recipes" relate mainly to physics, and explain such delights as 3-D shadows, a harmonograph, a Bernoulli Blower, a person-sized kaleidoscope, and a pendulum table. Unfortunately, the books themselves are expensive, and some of the exhibits (but not all) cost a lot of money to build. Check your library or ask them to order the cookbooks. You may also be able to track down copies in high schools, university libraries, or museums. Catalogs I, II, and III are $70, $50, and $70, and include 82, 52, and 67 exhibit recipes, respectively. Or you can buy all three for $175. The Exploratorium will mail free tables of contents if you ask. Also, the Exploratorium offers a magazine called the *Exploratorium Quarterly*, $15 for four issues. Exploratorium Store, 3601 Lyon Street, San Francisco, CA 94123. (415) 561-0393.

Popular reading:

-David Macaulay, *The Way Things Work*. Explains the physics of cars, guitars, parachutes, stereos, spacecraft, etc. with fantastic drawings and a hairy mammoth sense of humor. Supposedly a children's book.

-Stephen Hawking, *A Brief History of Time: From the Big Bang to Black Holes*. A terrific and *understandable* book about the ultimate physics question: the origin of the universe and all the related orbiting big issues.

Preparation for college physics:

Alfonso M. Albano, chairman of Physics at Bryn Mawr, describes the background needed for his introductory physics courses:

> Minimum: a working knowledge of plane geometry, algebra and trigonometry. The student must be able to follow simple geometric arguments, to solve linear and quadratic equations, as well as coupled linear equations in two variables. She must be able to graph simple functions as well as infer information from simple graphs. She needs to have some familiarity with exponentials, logarithms and trigonometric functions, and be able to perform some rudimentary manipulations with them.

> Calculus is neither a prerequisite nor a corequisite for the introductory course, but the basic notions of calculus are introduced and used. The textbook is calculus-based. It is not essential for the student to have had previous exposure to calculus (or to physics, for that matter).

> Ideal: In addition to the basic mathematical skills listed above, some exposure to calculus would help. Beyond these, of far greater importance perhaps are curiosity and an open mind and a capacity to keep being surprised and awed by the realization that some aspects of the universe do seem to be understandable. And yes, we do get some of these students every now and then!

The chair of physics at another highly respected liberal arts college says,

> Apart from general things applicable to all disciplines, like the ability to think, write, and speak clearly, the main thing [a beginning physics college student] needs is a solid background in high school mathematics, up to but not necessarily including calculus.

> What else would I like such a freshman to know or have? Some prior exposure to physics at the high school level is probably useful, but we do not require it even in our introductory course for potential majors. The same goes for computer experience; the ability to use a word processor and to write simple programs in a language like Basic or Pascal can make things easier but is not necessary. Our most exciting students are often those who have read widely

and enthusiastically in the popular literature about physics and astronomy, though they may have little in the way of special or advanced preparation.

Gary Wegner, professor of physics and astronomy at Dartmouth, wrote me particularly about astronomy:

> A freshman interested in a career in astronomy at Dartmouth majors in physics. There are astronomy classes that one can take that satisfy the requirements for the major. All of these have the first two general physics courses as the minimum prerequisite. Thus in principle a student can take astronomy after arriving with little or no physics background.

> The ideal students, however, should have calculus, high school physics, and knowledge of computers. In general, I recommend that an undergraduate get as strong of a background as possible in these areas in order to go on to graduate school. Generally speaking, a Ph.D is required to do professional work in astronomy....

GEOLOGY

Geology challenges you to look at the earth, wherever you are, and ask how it got the way it is. As such, geology is a great science for detective-types.

Popular reading:
-Any of John McPhee's "geology" books: *Rising from the Plains, Basin and Range, In Suspect Terrain.*
-*Dance of the Continents: Adventures with Rocks and Time*, by John W. Harrington (J.P. Tarcher, 1983).

Good textbook: *Earth*, by Frank Press and Raymond Siever, fourth edition (W.H. Freeman, 1986). Easy to find, new or used, in the vicinity of any college. This clear, broad introductory college text is aimed at the beginning student without any specialized science background. Nevertheless, it contains lots of detailed information. It is not a lab book, but it describes landforms that you can go looking for in your own territory.

TECHNOLOGY AND COMPUTERS

People who work with technology are usually called "engineers." (William Lear, described early in this chapter, was an unschooled and uncolleged electrical engineer.) Another word for technology is "inventions," scientific knowledge put to work for people--whether in the form of space shuttles, wind-powered laundromats, or snowboards. Two terms which aren't mentioned often in school are "appropriate technology," or "sustainable technology," meaning the kind of machines and tools that use energy and other resources efficiently and wisely, things that run on solar, wind, or human power (like bicycles), and stuff like sewage recycling plants and organic agricultural methods.

We need all the innovation we can get in this department. A lot of it will come from people who find out how civilizations did things before the industrial revolution, and then adapt these old-style methods and tools to fit 21st-century needs. You can be one of these people; *The Essential Whole Earth Catalog* suggests plenty of excellent books and other resources to start with. A living history farm or museum is also a good way to become intimate with such technology; see the history section in chapter 23. Solar technology, by the way, is an area whose leaders have mostly learned all they know from independent experimentation and sharing ideas--not from college or other school programs.

If you are interested in working toward a sustainable, ecological future, you will want to know about the New Alchemy Institute, where they do technology that is inexpensive, human and beautiful rather than expensive, cold and sterile. The Institute researches food, energy, water and waste treatment systems on a twelve acre farm in Massachusetts. You can become a member for $15 (student rate) which includes a year's subscription to their magazine, free information sheets on topics like aquaculture and wind power, and free admission to the Institute. Or, you can send $3 (refundable with purchase) for their catalog which sells "resources for the ecologically minded." Better yet, see chapter 33 for a description of apprenticeship opportunities at the institute. Catalog requests and membership fees go to New Alchemy Institute, 237 Hatchville Road, East Falmouth, MA 02356.

Computers? Everyone already seems to know that there are a lot more self-taught 13-year-old computer whizzes than knowledgeable adult "computer teachers," so I won't bother preaching that computers can be your unschooling friends. Barb Parshley writes in *GWS #32,*

> I am presently apprenticing in the most positive sense of the word, under someone who designs computers....One day, as I expressed my regret to him for my not having gone to college for a degree in this field so I could work better for him, I asked him what his degree was in. He chuckled and said he didn't have one. Being sure he misunderstood my question, and also sure he must be progressing toward his doctorate, I restated my question. He said once again that he didn't have a degree, not even on a high school level. In fact, he never went past eighth grade. He is self-taught, and is designing computers for companies both here and abroad.

If you have a computer or access to one, consider learning to program. There are all kinds of realms to get into--creating games or other software, hacking, networking...but you will discover these and more for yourself.

chapter 22

unschooling math

"The world is colors and motion, feelings and thought...and what does math have to do with it? Not much, if 'math' means being bored in high school, but in truth math is the one universal science. Mathematics is the study of pure pattern, and everything in the cosmos is a kind of pattern."
--Rudy Rucker, *Mind Tools: The Five Levels of Mathematical Reality*

"Most people leave school as failures at math, or at least feeling like failures."
--Sheila Tobias, *Overcoming Math Anxiety*

First, basic math and math panic. Then, higher math. Also, please see the anti-propaganda note in the beginning of Chapter 21.

Basic math skills

are extremely helpful if you plan on keeping track of your finances, gas mileage, or calories. Of course, you can use a calculator for most of life's necessities.

If grade school didn't help you to adequately develop your basic math skills, you can practice them on your own in a relaxed way. To pick up where you left off, use Saxon's *Math 54, 65,* or *76*--see more information on Saxon books later in this chapter.

Here are a couple low-key ways you can enjoy math:

1) Read "Harper's Index," in every issue of *Harper's* magazine. The index is about the world in general--especially sociology--but it gets its points across with eloquent numbers. For example, the October 1990 "Index" included the following tidbits:

Percentage of Americans who believe in ghosts: 25.
Years it would take Jim Bakker to earn enough to pay his federal fine at his current job cleaning prison toilets: 2,331.
Average number of words in the written vocabulary of a 6- to 14-year-old in 1945: 25,000.
Average number today: 10,000.

2) Do logic problems--you can find them in some crossword puzzle-type books, or in logic problem books.

Math Panic

often goes hand in hand with low math skills. When we're scared of anything, it's impossible to learn. A book that can help you understand your fear and do something about it is *Overcoming Math Anxiety,* by Sheila Tobias (W.W. Norton, 1978). Also, Tobias has some excellent chapters that explain confusing math concepts, from fractions to calculus.

You might also like more contact with the homeschooling math community:

-*GWS* (*Growing Without Schooling* magazine) prints frequent suggestions on math learning which are honest, thoughtful, and devoid of silly educational terminology.

-You could subscribe to *The 4th R: Reasoning,* a newsletter published by Alpha Plus, who sells carefully chosen math books and software mainly for younger children--just what you need if you're an intimidated teenager. The newsletter, written by Jim and Janet Lathan (Janet has a Masters in Math and Computer Science) provides some creative perspectives on math. In the copy they sent me, there was an article about learning math through the sport of orienteering, for example. Alpha Plus, 418 Robinwood Drive, Hagerstown, MD 21740-4476, (301) 733-1456.

Higher math

That is to say, upper level algebra, geometry, trigonometry, and calculus. Why bother? If you want to do anything scientific or understand theories about the nature of the universe, or if you want to design structures or invent technologies, math is your necessary tool. It is also the way a lot of people search for beauty. The *Encyclopedia Americana* says math can "woo and charm the intellect," and that "the symbols can be employed neatly and suggestively, just as words are used in poetry."

Does everyone need higher math? Certainly not. Too many of us school-educated people end up with more math than we'll ever use in our lives, yet not enough to help us really *do* anything like build a bridge.

College? You may need math to get in. How much depends on how selective the college is and whether your other academic accomplishments are thick enough to balance out lack of math. Once you are in, you likely won't need to take any if you major in humanities or arts. If you major in a social science, you will probably take some statistics. Even in colleges that require a balanced diet of general courses, you can probably avoid math. For instance, at Carleton we were required to take any three courses in math and science, which meant you could take three science courses and skip math.

Books--mathematical philosophy

School doesn't encourage most of us to see the strong connections between math and reality. These books will start your brain blowing:

Mathematics: The Language of Science, by George O. Smith (G.P. Putnam's Sons, 1961). Out of print, but available in some libraries. You can read this wonderful kids' book in an hour. Like many simple explanations, it is quite profound. It zips through math history and the purposes and definitions of different branches of math, including strange events like the discovery of zero. It's not a textbook; it has no "exercises."

Carl E. Linderholm, *Mathematics Made Difficult* (World Publications, 1972). Hilarious and abstruse, this book takes simple things and makes them incredibly complex. It starts by challenging your idea that you know how to count. It reminds us that math has more questions than answers, and that whenever we add, subtract, even *count*--we operate on a heap of assumptions. With Linderholm, we get a chance to look underneath these assumptions into the labyrinth.

Mind Tools: The Five Levels of Mathematical Reality, by Rudy Rucker (Houghton Mifflin, 1988), will make you fall in love with math. *Mind Tools* will not likely confuse you, yet after you finish, the way you think about math--and the universe--will be changed forever.

Ludwig Wittgenstein, *Remarks on the Foundations of Mathematics* (MIT Press, 1983). "The mathematician is an inventor, not a discoverer," says Wittgenstein, a dead philosopher. This difficult book is heavy on logic and profundity. It will tease and prod your cortex.

In a Dewey decimal library, the 510.1 section is math philosophy.

Textbooks

In the past, many homeschoolers have had a difficult time with math. Textbooks didn't explain things well enough, or include enough review, to help most people learn on their own. Now that the Saxon books have arrived on the scene, however, those days are over.

Likely, you've already used the Saxon books in school. Everyone seems to agree that they are by far the best in-depth math textbooks. They have led to phenomenal increases in test scores and numbers of students who choose to take higher math. They make sense because they are based on the principle of review. Therefore, instead of learning something and forgetting it, you do it again and again throughout the book until it becomes second nature, a living language rather than a forgotten vocabulary list. The books also laugh sometimes and are clear without a teacher's help, although you can order teachers' books if you like. Or, you can buy homeschool packets which include the regular text plus an answer key.

Saxons can guide you through algebra, geometry, trigonometry, and calculus. You may be able to borrow the books through your school. Or for a catalog, write Saxon Publishers, 1300 McGee, Suite 100, Norman, OK 73072.

Where to start? If you've been confused in the past, start where you feel comfortable, even if that means in a book supposedly several years behind your grade level. I took math through calculus in high school. I got a C once in 8th grade, an F the last semester of 12th grade calculus, and the rest B's and A's. In other words, I supposedly learned something. But I couldn't have told you then, and I can barely tell you now, what any of that math was about. I never had any idea what the quadratic formula was for or how we got it. I don't remember how to find logarithms or do differentiation. If I ever decide to learn math again (and there's a good chance of that), I'll start with John Saxon's *Algebra 1*.

H. Steinhaus, *Mathematical Snapshots* (Oxford University Press, 1969). This innovative book uses visuals--photos and diagrams--to explain math concepts and equations. It is not light reading; take it slowly. It is good for people who prefer to learn visually and spatially rather than with words. It is also helpful training if you want to start thinking more visually and spatially. You need some experience with algebra and geometry to understand it.

Mathematics: A Human Endeavor (A Book for Those Who Think They Don't Like The Subject), by Harold R. Jacobs (W.H. Freeman, 1982), is the other great textbook. Although it is a serious textbook, it is good enough that most public libraries have a copy. People like it because it is fun and clear. I recommend it instead of the Saxons *if* you want to do some higher formal math and love it, but not in great depth. It includes (in just one volume) algebra, geometry, statistics, and trigonometry, getting its points across with generous use of jokes, games, puzzles, paradoxes, and magic tricks. The answers to most of the problems are in the back.

The chairmen say

The chair of a very selective liberal arts college math department says,

If the freshman wants to major in math or science he/she should be able to get a grade of 4 or 5 on the advanced placement BC-Calculus exam. The ideal preparation for a normal student includes math courses from some colleges. This should be easier for a "homeschooler" who does not worry about fitting college courses into a high school schedule.

Frank Morgan, chair of mathematics at Williams, simply informed me that algebra and trigonometry are necessary for freshman-level courses, and that the ideally-prepared student has also studied calculus.

An unmath student

Amelia Acheson shows a bit of what's possible when she writes about her son in *GWS #42*:

Alazel (16) loves math--he bought a set of accounting books from a local high school teacher and hurried through them. When he asked her for more, she was amazed at how far ahead of her classes he was. He also got a college supplementary text in trigonometry, and covered most of that between November and March. Then he set that aside and did no math for several months. About two weeks ago, he found his dad's analytic geometry book. It took him about three days to work through most of it, and demand a calculus course. In one and a half weeks, he has devoured about half of what college professors turn into a year's hard work for freshmen. His dad has promised to coach him through physics when he gets integration under his belt...

chapter 23

unschooling
social science

*"My grandmother wanted me to have an education, so she
kept me out of school."*
--Margaret Mead, anthropologist extraordinaire

This chapter describes ways to study "social sciences"--history, anthropology,
sociology, geography, political science, economics. Most of these fields are
quite related to each other. In writing this chapter, it was hard to decide
whether to stick some resources under geography or anthropology, under
political science or history. In the end, I decided to not get bent out of shape
over it. All these "separate" fields can grow more meaningful when they are
allowed to merge a bit, as you can tell from reading the following account.
Kathleen Hatley writes in *GWS* (*Growing Without Schooling* magazine) #45
about homeschooling her sons, including 12-year-old Steve:

> We have been very active this year in the peace movement, and this has
> provided the older boys with a very direct type of learning in the area of
> "social studies." We have constructed a section of the Peace Ribbon, regularly
> met with and written to our representatives (they were quite thrilled to get their
> first correspondence from their Congressmen), viewed numerous films and
> attended lectures on Central America, and met priests, nuns, and refugees for
> some first-hand information about U.S. involvement in Latin America. Because
> of these experiences, they follow the news and current events with great
> interest, enjoy reading about the geography and history of Central America,
> and even practice their Spanish...

HISTORY

History is not merely what happened in the human past, although school
doesn't usually point this out. It is rather the *study* of what happened in the
past, and it is full of opinions, arguments, and inconsistencies.

History goes far beyond dates, names of presidents, and wars.
Although that should be obvious, I mention it because it wasn't obvious to me
until after I'd endured high school and taken an enlightening college course.
History asks all kinds of questions about relationships and patterns: What role
did Christianity play in the rise of the medieval European medical profession?
How did art influence peasant life in eighteenth-century Russia? Why are there

wars? How did the experiences of early European explorers in America change European attitudes toward the natural world? How has the etiquette of warfare in Japan changed over the centuries? How did our current prison system develop? How did the structure of villages change during the industrial revolution? Where did compulsory schooling come from?

Understand the difference between primary and secondary sources: a primary source is a document (or sometimes a painting, etc.) produced by someone at the scene of the crime. A letter home from a soldier in the Civil War is a primary source. A secondary source is a historian's interpretation of a variety of primary sources, like a *textbook* about the civil war.

Since history is based mainly on written documents, it usually looks back only as far as a culture's written heritage goes. Archaeology--a branch of anthropology--looks further into the past, since its clues are found more in physical objects than in words.

Here is a long, though asymmetrical and incomplete, list of ideas and resources for unschooled history:

Primary Sources

A fascinating collection: *Eyewitness to History*, edited by John Carey (Harvard University Press, 1987). Truly a history book you can't put down, *Eyewitness* bulges with primary sources from all over the world and all throughout history. It's not always pretty, but it grips. A caliph of Baghdad describes a tenth-century Viking funeral, telling mostly about the girl who volunteers to be cremated along with the Viking and his ship. A soldier at Gallipoli (WWI) writes about burying his friends in the sides of the trench, and how parts would stick out:

> Hands were the worst; they would escape from the sand, pointing, begging, even waving! There was one which we all shook when we passed, saying, "Good morning," in a posh voice. Everybody did it....We couldn't stop shitting because we had caught dysentery. We wept, not because we were frightened but because we were so dirty.

Tales of death and destruction are thankfully interspersed with treats like an eighteenth-century English lady's description of a Turkish bath, and Neil Armstrong's description of his first moments on the moon.

Twentieth-century primary sources--a short list, not intended to be comprehensive, only to give a few good ideas:

-James Agee, *Let Us Now Praise Famous Men* (with photos by Walker Evans). Agee tells about sharecroppers in the South during the depression of the 1930's. People read it in English class too--it is a moving and beautiful piece of journalism. Skip the beginning. Start in the middle. Then go back.

-Anne Frank, *The Diary of a Young Girl*--Jewish life in hiding in Nazi Germany.

-John Hersey, *Hiroshima.* A journalist's detailed 1946 story of six survivors of Hiroshima, starting from just before the bomb dropped and following through with exactly what happened to each of them during and after the explosion.

-Anne Moody, *Coming of Age in Mississippi.* The firsthand account of a black woman who grew up during the Civil Rights movement and took part in sit-ins and other history-making events.

-Aranka Siegal, *Upon the Head of the Goat: A Childhood in Hungary 1939-1944.* Another Jewish tragedy--though at least she lives to tell the story from an adult perspective.

-Studs Terkel, *Hard Times: An Oral History of the Great Depression.* Studs Terkel is the nation's master at recording oral histories. In this book, all kinds of people tell of their experiences during the depression.

-Studs Terkel, *The Good War: an Oral History of World War Two.* A variety of Americans give their viewpoints--women at home waiting for news of their sons and husbands, 18- and 19-year-old soldiers in Europe.

-Elie Wiesel, *Night.* Just about as terrible as it gets. *Night* tells about Wiesel's boyhood in Nazi prison camps; his family dies, his faith dies. With anti-Semitism rearing its head once again all over the world, it is extremely important that people read books like this one.

Find autobiographies in the 921 section of your library, along with other biographies, in alphabetical order according to the subject's last name. Browse around in the section, and you'll find something good you didn't know you were looking for. I found *Blame Me On History*, the wonderfully written, fast-paced autobiography of Bloke Modisane, a black activist who fought for freedom and human rights in South Africa.

Secondary Sources

General information:

-*The Times Atlas of World History*, edited by Geoffrey Burraclough. If you want a solid overview of world history, this book will meet your needs. Try reading a two-page spread every day. Each of these spreads is a self-contained unit, with maps and illustrations, with titles like "From hunting to farming: the origins of agriculture," "The 9th and 10th century invasions of Europe," and "East Asia at the time of the Ch'ing Dynasty." You can also skim through the glossary, not memorizing, just finding what you like and thinking, "Oh! So that's who Alexander the Great was!"

-Any library will have interesting history reference books including atlases and dictionaries, such as *A Dictionary of Chivalry*, by Grant Uden.

-*The Concord Review* is a very high quality scholarly journal full of high school students' historical essays. It is both more scholarly and more entertaining than any middle school or high school level texts you are likely to read. Subscriptions are currently $25/year, from The Concord Review Business Office, PO Box 476, Canton, MA 02021. See the next section for more.

Specific information:
Biographies can bring it all alive. The 921 section in a Dewey decimal library is packed with them, alphabetized according to the subject's last name. Choose carefully.

Libraries also have heaps of books about particular historical problems or events. Many are dull or written in very academic language. Many are terrific, such as:

-Fernand Braudel, *Civilization and Capitalism*. This three volume set takes a long time to read but is fascinating, detailed, and not especially difficult if you start at the beginning and go slowly. It covers 15th- to 18th-century Europe--the rise of capitalism in the preindustrial world. By the way: one nice bonus is that it doesn't pretend to be a *comprehensive* European history; rather, it acknowledges its focus on economic themes. (Most school textbooks also focus on specific themes, such as wars, governments, and white men's exploits, but they pretend to be general history books. By pretending this, they say that other perspectives, and other stories, don't exist.)

-Dee Brown, *Bury my Heart at Wounded Knee: An Indian History of the American West* (Holt, Rhinehart, and Winston, 1971). The side of American history we don't often hear. Broken treaties, murders, other foul play.

-Susan Griffin, *Woman and Nature* (Harper and Row, 1978). Griffin gives us a strange, terrible, powerfully eye-opening account of the way that men have thought about women and nature over the past several thousand years. The book's style helps to get the message across, written in a combination of prose and poetry.

-Suzanne Massie, *The Land of the Firebird* (Simon and Schuster, 1980). A lavish, colorful history of Old Russia, focusing especially on the arts. Full of sensuous descriptions of feasts and parties and weddings and church services and palaces, and dramatic narrations of the lives of tsars and tsarinas.

-*Foxfire*--volumes 1 through 9, edited by Eliot Wigginton (Doubleday). The outstanding Foxfire series is based mostly on interviews with old people in the Appalachian hills. They include detailed information on fiddle making, burial customs, snake handling, ghost stories, and dozens of other "affairs of plain living." High school students in Georgia conducted the interviews.

Historical Novels
Some people think of historical fiction as being a skewed, subjective view of the past. They're right, of course. But the same is true of any other

source, primary or secondary. Historical novels can give you a greater feel for a time period than textbooks can. Usually, their authors are historians in their own right who do extensive research--reading all those textbooks and primary sources and visiting the setting of their work. Their novels often include notes in the front or back that tell about their research and other background information. Before you read a historical novel, you can increase your understanding of it by reading a brief description of the time and area in a good encyclopedia or atlas, such as *The Times'* described above.

If you want a variety of short pieces, look for an anthology of historical fiction, such as *The Undying Past*, edited by Orville Prescott (Doubleday, 1961).

For novels, the following authors and books are known both for historical accuracy based on careful research and for great entertainment:

-Marion Zimmer Bradley, *The Mists of Avalon*--based on the King Arthur Legends but also reflecting the early Celtic world and religious tradition.

-Pearl Buck, Asia. Especially *The Good Earth* (rural China before and after the Maoist revolution). Buck's parents were missionaries in China and, by the way, she didn't go to much school.

-Willa Cather, *My Antonia* (Bohemians on the midwestern frontier), *Death Comes for the Archbishop* (19th-century New Mexico).

-James Lincoln Collier and Christopher Collier, early American history, American revolution. *My Brother Sam is Dead*, etc. Collier's books were very popular with my students and are not difficult reading.

-Charles Dickens, *A Tale of Two Cities*. Paris and London at the time of the French Revolution, quite the tearjerker.

-Esther Forbes, the American Revolution--*Johnny Tremain*.

-Robert Graves, the Roman Empire and ancient Greece--*I, Claudius*, *Claudius the God*, *The Golden Fleece*, *King Jesus*.

-A.B. Guthrie, Cowboys and Indians and the American West. *The Way West*, etc.

-Morgan Lywelyn--novels set in the early Celtic world. *The Horse Goddess*, for example, takes place in the eighth century B.C. in what are now the Austrian Alps.

-James Michener, mostly U.S. history (*Chesapeake* is considered his best). Also other subjects such as Palestine and the Jews (*The Source*).

-Margaret Mitchell, *Gone with the Wind*--Georgia in the 1860's, during and after the Civil War.

-Naomi Mitchison, Ancient Greece and Roman Empire. Her best are supposedly *The Conquered*, *Cloud Cuckoo Land*, and especially *The Corn King and the Spring Queen*.

-Katherine Paterson, Japanese history, "young adult" novels: *The Sign of the Chrysanthemum*, *Of Nightingales That Weep*, *The Master Puppeteer*.

-Mary Renault--classical Greece. Especially *The King Must Die* and *Bull from the Sea*.

-Irving Stone, biographical novels--about the Lincolns, John and Abigail Adams, Michelangelo, and others.

-William Styron, *The Confessions of Nat Turner*. This story of the only major black slave revolt in America won the Pulitzer Prize.

-Gore Vidal, U.S. history--*Empire, Washington D.C., Burr, Lincoln, 1876*. Lots of people say Vidal is the very best historical novelist.

Movies can be historical fiction too.

Just don't be brainwashed. Recognize that any movie has an editorial perspective, no matter how objective it seems. As with historical novels, you can make more sense out of what you see by first checking an encyclopedia or historical atlas. A little background knowledge on the *Ballets Russes*, for instance, makes the movie *Nijinski* far more interesting.

You can find excellent documentaries (*The Atomic Cafe, Woodstock*) as well as hundreds of good movies based on actual events--*The Mission, The Ballad of Gregorio Cortez, Glory, The Last Emperor, Brother Sun, Sister Moon, The Killing Fields, All the President's Men, Silkwood...* Also, movies can give you a feel for another time and place even when they are not based on actual events. Filmmakers go to great lengths to recreate authentic settings, bringing us outstanding movies like *The Razor's Edge, The Seven Samurai, Good Morning Vietnam, The Color Purple, Jeremiah Johnson*, and *Dances With Wolves*.

Living History

I've decided that the living history movement is to unschooling social studies what the naturalist's domain is to unschooling science. (Did that sentence make sense? It's the sort of charmer you'll run into by the dozens on the SAT.)

In other words, living history projects are one more proof that learning-in-the-world is far thicker and richer than learning-in-school. All over the world, you can join groups of people who make a hobby, an education, or a vocation out of recreating a particular period of history, in lifestyle, costume, language, and skills.

In the Rocky Mountain states, "buckskinners" run rampant--mountain men with muzzle loading rifles and tipis. Last year, two of them invaded our social studies class for an afternoon, spinning yarns and wearing moccasins. Lots of eyes lit up, for a good two hours.

All over the country, you can find enclaves of medieval enthusiasts who belong to the Society for Creative Anachronism. They joust in authentically crafted suits of armor, embroider stunning 14th-century-style dresses, and teach each other to play music on ancient instruments.

Many living history projects revolve around farms, and that fact brings me to one of the little sermons I know you enjoy so much.

Living history goes way beyond mere academia. It even goes beyond being a creative way to have a raging good time. Living history projects could help fix this planet:

We now realize that many aspects of "progress," or "the industrial age," or whatever you want to call it, hurt the planet and our lives. For instance, most American agriculture now depends on petroleum-powered machinery and on incredible amounts of pesticides and chemical fertilizers. Organic farmers are leading the way back toward healthier food growing, but they don't yet know everything that farmers did in the Goodolddays.

When the world got "modern," few people thought that the "old ways" would ever be important again--and so much of this complex lore was forgotten. Historians recorded dates of wars and names of governors, but few people had the vision to write down the ways that people *did* things--herding cattle, growing vegetables, tanning leather. As the world grows once again less mechanized, less consumptive, more human, and healthier, it needs to recover this information.

When living history fans spend their time working with ox teams and water-powered wheat mills, they reclaim for all of us the knowledge of how such things work. From there, we can go on to adapt them to our 20th-century lives and beyond. Appropriate technology, some call it.

Access:
-Society for Creative Anachronism: call the information desk of a local college or university, ask around at a renaissance fair, or write SCA, P.O. Box 743, Milpitas, CA 95035.

-*The Book of Buckskinning*, several volumes, edited by William Scurlock. (Rebel Publishing Company, Route Five, Box 347-M, Texarcana, TX 75501). These books overflow with lore and give detailed instructions on making equipment, using muzzle loaders, and acquiring skills for the "black powder" movement. To contact other mountain men and women, write the National Muzzle Loading Rifle Association, P.O. Box 67, Friendship, IN 47021.

-Find out about hundreds of other fascinating living history farms, festivals, museums, magazines, suppliers, and organizations around the country in *The Living History Sourcebook*, by Jay Anderson (The American Association for State and Local History, Nashville: 1985). This book tells you everything you need to start participating in a group, or to simply find a museum or festival and watch other people make history out of themselves.

Seventeen-year-old unschooler Andy Endsley describes his involvement in a program called "Living History Units" in *GWS #77*:

We dress up in a costume or uniform from a period in history, and then spend time at historic sites, or do reenactments of battles, for the enjoyment of the public and also for our own enjoyment. A lot of work goes into the historical accuracy of the uniforms. Being involved with this now takes me all over the country....Since the unit I was in was known for its special attention to historical accuracy, we were asked to be part of the battle scenes in Glory...

-If there are no living history sites near you, consider starting your own--carefully, with the guidance of experts. If you can present your idea charmingly, you will find businesses or foundations to help pay for the project.

Other History Activities

-At the basic level, you might want to know a sort of timetable as to what "major" events happened when. I see no reason why you should memorize this information unless you want to--however, it can be so constantly thought-provoking that you might like to decorate your bathroom wall with it. You could make a timeline, based on one from a book or historical atlas.

-Visit places near you where the past is visible--sometimes this means an official historical monument, sometimes a restored house, sometimes a cousin's attic, sometimes a rusty ghost town. Often these places reek of tourism; you may need to spend several hours just sitting, slowly conjuring up images of what happened there, letting the tourists fade, almost slipping into a trance. It also helps to visit historical places when few people are present-- dawn, Monday mornings, maybe even if you're lucky when a museum is closed to the general public. Remember, you are not on a school field trip. Don't be in field trip mentality. Stay as long as you like. Be quiet and dream into the scented past.

-Submit your very best historical writing to *The Concord Review*. If your work is published, consider yourself greatly honored. (Editor Will Fitzhugh, former teacher, says, "I would welcome essays of around 4,000 words, typed, with endnotes, on any historical topic, from secondary students learning at home or on their own, or wherever.") More data a few pages back under secondary sources, general information.

-Conduct your own historical inquiries. There is plenty to be found, interpreted, and presented to the heap. You might record oral histories in the style of Studs Terkel, soliciting the stories of the elders in your community or city. A helpful short book is *The Tape Recorded Interview*, by Edward Ives (University of Tennessee Press, 1980), which clearly discusses equipment as well as subtleties like the dynamics of interviewing a husband and wife together versus separately.

-Your own family history would surely love to be investigated and written down by you. In turn, researching such personalized history can make *general* history more meaningful. In GWS #36, Virginia Schewe writes about her 14- and 13-year-old boys as well as her 9-year-old daughter:

> Quite by accident this summer, I opened the doors to genealogy and suddenly history became very interesting to the youngsters. After we discovered that a great-grandpa had been in the Army during the Civil War, did a little research in the service records, traced his path, and read about the battles he had taken part in, the Civil War wasn't just some old dumb scrap anymore...

The library has useful books, such as *Genealogy: Finding Your Roots: How Every American Can Trace His Ancestors at Home and Abroad*, by Jeanne Eddy (St. Martin's Press, 1977).

-To share your original research, start a publication like *Foxfire*. (See above under secondary sources, specific information.) If you want to start a similar project, you'll want companions (*get your friends out of school!*) and you may want to contact the Foxfire people. Since so many teachers have been inspired by the project, advisor Eliot Wigginton has printed some instructions and guidelines. (The Foxfire Project, Rabun Gap, Georgia 30568. Include a SASE if you write them.)

By the way, in my always-humble opinion, Foxfire-type projects are important partly for the same reason living history is: they can help us reclaim the wisdom that we need in order to live abundantly in an ecologically healthy way.

-If you become especially enamoured of a specific branch of history, you may want to travel to the appropriate setting to look at ruins, meet the locals, meet other scholars, and inspect special collections of documents and artifacts at libraries and museums.

-Combine history with something else you love. See chapter 33 to read what Anna-Lisa Cox did with her interest in costume. If you like cars, get involved with the local antique car collectors' clubs. Or collect old jewelry, knives, books, tools, horse tack, gramaphones, whatever. You can do this for free by keeping a scrapbook collection instead, cutting out pictures of such things in magazines, and labeling them with any notes you wish to add.

-If you become a serious collector, open a small museum. It need not compete with the Smithsonian. You could house it in a spare room or even in a corner of your bedroom. You could open it to the public occasionally or only to friends and fellow enthusiasts.

-Make a timeline for the subjects that interest you--team sports, the Protestant church, anything.

Preparation for College History

In general, colleges will expect that you have some general knowledge of U.S. history and Western history. For more specific guidance, here are the words of the experts:

Alice B. Robinson, Chair of History at Wellesley College, suggests,

A freshman needs to know how to read, reason, and think analytically. She needs to realize that just for something to appear in print does not necessarily mean it is true or useful. She has to have some idea about what constitutes evidence; of the relationships between fact, inference, and opinion; of why the historian selected certain facts to include and ignored others. If she does not have that minimal degree of sophistication, she at least needs to be open to learning about and appreciating it...In terms of knowledge, a student needs to have just plain general background information about this country and the world at large. For example, I've been floored to have students without a clue as to what a bishop is (i.e. not even know it has something to do with religion), or ignorant that there are "books" in the Bible, or with no geographical knowledge (i.e. mixing up Poland and Belgium).

Ideally, students who are well-read, who have had travel opportunities or other interaction with people different from themselves, and who are intellectually and socially at the more mature end of the 17- and 18-year-old spectrum make the best history students. Aptitude and attitude are probably more important than lots of specific knowledge. Self-discipline, intellectual curiosity, willingness to work, enjoyment of study, ability to accept and profit from constructive criticism all make for an ideal student. Probably the "unschoolers" are not as grade-conscious as many schooled are, which would be a great big plus, as far as I am concerned.

...For schooled students, success in Honors classes and A.P. classes allow them to by-pass introductory work and take courses with greater depth and more challenge. If homeschooled do something similar they should be well-prepared for college, too.

Clifford Clark, professor of history and American Studies at Carleton, shared the following advice:

Minimum expectations for a Carleton freshman's success in Carleton history courses: Carleton history professors expect their incoming students to have various kinds of preparation. First and most basic, they should have the reading and writing skills that are essential for survival not only in history courses but in college in general. On the reading side, they must be able to identify the argument in an essay and restate it briefly in their own words. They should be able to test the argument in terms of its logic, internal consistency, and reference to the sources. And every student of the historical record needs to be able to read quickly and to skim if necessary so that they can get the main arguments out of a two-hundred page book in three hours or less. On the writing side they need to be able to compose an expository essay that sets forth their question or thesis in the introductory paragraphs, develops an argument with reference to their source materials in the body of the paper, and draws their conclusions at the end.

In addition to these basic reading and writing skills, a good student should have a sense of the basic chronology in American history and some preparation in European history, Asian history, or some other major historical literature. They need to have taken at least two history courses, have read some interpretive books or articles beyond the basic textbook, and have been exposed to some primary sources, i.e., materials written in the time period being studied. They also need to have the minimal research skills that will enable them to look up material in the library using more sources than simply an encyclopedia.

Finally, the minimally prepared student should be able to recognize the complexity of studying the historical past and to frame his or her arguments about the past in such a way that they recognize and evaluate the merits of different interpretations before choosing the one they most favor.

The Ideal Preparation for a student: In addition to the background and skills mentioned above, the ideally trained incoming student would come to college with a burning fascination with the past and an intense desire to understand it. This frame of mind might, in some cases, be likened to a detective mentality. An inquiring mind, full of questions, is a rare commodity and is much prized by teachers.

The best students add to this quality of mind a greater degree of sophistication in reading and writing than his or her minimally prepared counterparts. The ideally prepared students will not only be able to identify and paraphrase an argument from an essay or book, but would also be able to decipher the assumptions upon which the argument rested. They will also have enough self-consciousness as writers to recognize the position of their audience and choose the writing strategy designed to make their arguments most effective. For most people, these will be skills acquired only through substantial contact with reading and writing historical studies of various kinds.

ANTHROPOLOGY AND SOCIOLOGY

"Anthropology is the study of human beings as creatures of society. It fastens its attention upon those physical characteristics and industrial techniques, those conventions and values, which

distinguish one community from all others that belong to a different tradition."--Ruth Benedict, *The Patterns of Culture.*

Sociology is the same thing, except a sociologist investigates her own culture. Thus, unlike the anthropologist, she can use introspection as a major tool.

In the unromantic opinion of my little brother Richard, a Reed anthropology-major dropout, anthropology means going out and looking at exotic people and writing down what you see so you can preserve them in libraries so that no one feels guilty for sending Progress in to destroy their traditions. However, Richard also acknowledges that some anthropologists use their knowledge to help restore cultures, like scientists who use their knowledge to heal devastated ecosystems. Such anthropologists sometimes work with the governments of developing nations to save as much of a threatened culture as possible, at least preventing their complete destruction. *Cultural Survival Quarterly*, described below, exemplifies this movement.

General resources

-For a fairly general beginning, try Ruth Benedict's *The Patterns of Culture*. Start with Chapter Two, which is full of stories. Then go back to Chapter One, which is more abstract. Pages 24-30 give a glimpse of strange powerful versions of adolescence.

-*Funk and Wagnall's Standard Dictionary of Folklore, Mythology and Legend*, edited by Maria Leach. Contains more than 8,000 short fascinating articles on topics like blues, Chinese folklore, eating the sacred animal, hanging, Robin Hood, wolf society, and zombi.

-*Cultural Survival Quarterly* is an anthropology magazine with a political agenda. In its own words, "Since 1976, *Cultural Survival Quarterly* has addressed issues of both immediate and long-term concern to indigenous peoples throughout the world. The *Quarterly* serves to inform the general public and policy makers in the U.S. and abroad to stimulate action on behalf of tribal people and ethnic minorities." This magazine covers topics like the impact of tourism on the Haida Indians of British Columbia. Find it in a college library or write Cultural Survival, Inc., 11 Divinity Avenue, Cambridge, MA 02138.

Popular reading

The books in the following list are profound and surprising, though most of them are less formal and analytic than textbooks or scholarly works:

-Carlos Casteneda, especially *The Teachings of Don Juan: a Yaqui Way of Knowledge* and *A Separate Reality: Further Conversations with Don Juan.*

-Robert Coles, M.D., *Children of Crisis*. In five compassionate volumes, Coles looks mostly at the lives of poor children in the United States.

-Jacob Holdt, *American Pictures* (American Pictures Foundation, P.O. Box 2123, New York, NY 10009, 1985). Holdt, from Denmark, hitchhiked through America for several years in the 70's, staying with very poor families and selling blood to earn money for film. The result is this book and a long slide show by the same name, phenomenal unflinching works of compassion. You need a strong stomach to take it--photos of dead bloody people on the street, families living in incredible poverty, black men eating from tin trays in prison...next to pictures of rich white girls in velvet bedrooms. For the slide show, keep your eye on local colleges' schedules of events, or contact the foundation for a schedule.

-Theodora Kroeber, *Ishi in Two Worlds* (University of California Press, 1962), insightfully describes the life of Ishi, the last survivor of a Californian Indian tribe who was "adopted" by anthropologists in the early 20th century.

-Barry Lopez, *Of Wolves and Men.* The mind-blowing difference between the way Eskimos and other native peoples relate to wolves and the way white America relate to them. All of Lopez's books are books about the whole universe.

-Richard Nelson, *Make Prayers to the Raven,* about the relationship between the Koyukon people of the Alaskan boreal forest and their non-human surroundings. From the book:

Koyukon people often comment on the physical similarity betweeen bears and humans, although to them this does not imply kinship. The resemblance is striking, and somewhat frightening, when a skinned bear is laid out on its back. Adult black bears usually weigh under two hundred pounds and are about five feet long from nose to tail, not much different from a stocky man. Bears can also look like people in the forest, especially when they stand erect to get a better look at something. I was told that they occasionally stand to peer across an open area, shading their eyes with one paw just as a person would.

These human characteristics make Koyukon people a bit uneasy--the solitary figure standing mysteriously at the edge of timber at dusk, the skinned carcass lying like a corpse in deep grass. Stalking, killing, and dismembering such a creature seems to have a faintly murderous and cannibalistic feeling about it, something not consciously felt with any other animal.

-Studs Terkel, *Working: people talk about what they do all day and how they feel about what they do.* Great stuff for a sociologist to interpret. Read the words of a prostitute, a farmer, a strip miner, a hotel switchboard operator, a bar pianist, a policeman, a lawyer, a gravedigger, and many more.

-Colin Turnbull, *The Forest People.* The BaMbuti pygmies of the Congo rainforest live in amazing harmony with their environment. As far as they are concerned, the forest is their father and their mother, and it likes them. When anything goes wrong, they figure the forest must be sleeping--so they wake it up with lots of music. This moving book turns a lot of people on to anthropology.

-*The Portable North American Indian Reader*, edited by Frederick Turner (Viking, 1977). Native American experience in their own words.

"Advanced" reading in anthropology and sociology:

-Read ethnographies, which are anthropologists' studies of particular cultures. Written mainly for other anthropologists, they're densely academic and not intended to be especially entertaining--but they *can* be fascinating. One of the most enjoyable is *Pigs For the Ancestors*, by Roy A. Rappaport, about the natives of New Guinea.

To find other ethnographies, look under "ethnology" in a college library catalog.

-Read anything by Claude Levi-Strauss--difficult and worth it. Especially *The Savage Mind*.

-Anything by Clifford Geertz. You might start with *The Interpretation of Cultures: Selected Essays* (Basic, 1973), especially "Deep Play: Notes on the Balinese Cockfight" and "Thick Description: Toward an Interpretation Theory of Culture."

Archaeology

is a branch of the anthropology tree, with lots of ripe fruit ready to be slurped up by unschoolers. There are two great possibilities: dig or do archaeology "living history" style. For lots of opportunities in both categories, subscribe to *Archaeology* magazine, Subscription Service, P.O. Box 928, Farmingdale, NY 11737.

To dig, you can also contact Earthwatch, whose expeditions unearth guns in Bermuda, excavate a prehistoric Asante site in Ghana, etc. (see chapter 21), or your state parks people, or the National Park Service: Office of Chief Archaeologist, Division of Archaeology and Anthropology, National Park Service, Department of the Interior, Washington, DC 20240.

To turn yourself into a part-time cavewoman or a Viking-style voyager:

-contact local natural history museums to see if they have any need for "interpreters."

-Find out about likeminded companions and organizations in *The Living History Sourcebook*, described above under "living history" in the history section of this chapter.

-You do not need an organization to learn the skills of another culture; you can experiment on your own. Early in his teens, my charming little brother Richard took to refining his archery skills and riding horseback into the hills with nothing to eat except what he could find. He learned about local edible plants; he grew one fingernail very long and sharpened it--a "digging" tool. None of this was intended to be especially academic, but it reflected and enhanced his intense fascination with cultures who live--and lived--closer to the land. (Several years later, he temporarily abandoned his AFS host family in Ecuador to sneak off into the Amazon and drink ayahuasca with the natives. That was anthropology too.)

National Geographic also covers archaeological discoveries, if you want to just read about them and look at pictures.

An unschooled and uncolleged sociologist

Eric Hoffer wrote *The True Believer*, an extremely influential book about fanaticism and mass movements. He had no formal education, but rather a "hunger for the printed word." He worked at various jobs--mainly as a longshoreman on the docks of San Francisco--and wrote several other highly acclaimed books.*

GEOGRAPHY

Finally, America falls in love with the rest of the world. The drumbeats we listen to in the nineties, the earrings we wear, the fruit we eat--it all reflects the richness of a thousand cultures' traditions and talents. Geography is one of the most fun and lavish thoughts you can immerse yourself in, especially when you are out beyond the limits of school.

General knowledge:

-*National Geographic* magazine. You can buy back issues very cheaply at thrift stores. There's nothing like it, though it conveys a strange subtle arrogance and sexism.

-*Gaia: An Atlas of Planet Management*, edited by Dr. Norman Myers. One of the better tools for saving the world, this book investigates global crises involving land (ocean pollution, rainforest destruction) and people (illiteracy, poverty). Lots of photos and charts and illustrations--an enticing book.

-Choosing an atlas is an education in itself. Inspect all the choices in your library's reference section. Especially look for a local atlas.

-*Man in Nature*, by renowned historical geographer Carl Sauer, is an easy book about Native Americans living with the land. Rather than rave about Sauer's detailed yet simple information, I will merely say that Native American nations themselves have chosen this book for their schools, and that poet Gary Snyder thinks it's great. That should be plenty of recommendation.

---

* Information from *Current Biography Yearbook, 1965*

Specific knowledge:

-In the 900 shelves of your library, you can find dozens if not hundreds of books about specific parts of the world and people who live there. Especially watch for unpretentious stories told by the natives themselves. A terrific example is *The Land I Lost: Adventures of a Boy in Vietnam*, by Huynh Quang Nhuong (Harper, 1982).

-See the *Insight* Travel Guides series (APA Productions). With photos and fascinating cultural and historical information, they make great geography books as well as travel guides with depth. Countries and regions range from Bali to Alaska to Israel to the American Southwest.

-Check back in the anthropology section for information on ethnographies. Ethnographies overlap from anthropology into geography.

-Watch movies set in cultures different from yours, fiction and non-fiction. Outstanding examples: *The Emerald Forest, Salaam Bombay, The Milagro Beanfield War, The Gods Must Be Crazy, Local Hero, El Norte, Wedding in Galilee*.

Activities:

-Keep a scrapbook. Focus on pictures of worldwide dwellings, farming practices, celebrations, whatever. Those cheap *National Geographic* back issues come in handy.

-Find out what music from other cultures you like. Most libraries have some international music. The *Explorer Series* by Nonesuch Records is especially good for instrumental music, including Japanese flutes, African drums, and Indian sitars.

Also check the "worldbeat" or ethnic sections of alternative record stores. Some great international "pop" artists whose music strongly reflects their ethnic heritage are Ofra Haza (Yemen), Clannad (Ireland), King Sunny Ade (Nigeria), Queen Ida (Cajun territory U.S.A.) and Sheila Chandra (India). Dynamic traditional music includes Sweet Honey in the Rock (African-American spirituals), Jean Redpath (Scottish folksongs), The Chieftains (Irish), Miriam Makeba (South Africa), and The Bulgarian State Radio and Television Female Vocal Choir, which will stop your heart or break it.

Notice that a lot of your favorite music probably has strong ethnic influences. Peter Gabriel, for example, has been especially innovative in weaving global sounds into his work.

Finally, if you are a musician, enrich your work by soaking up some faraway sounds.

-Learn to cook and eat the foods of a new culture. You'll find a smorgasbord of ethnic cookbooks in the 641.5 shelves of the library.

-Put a map of the world or your state up on the wall. Look at it.

-Throw a party, combining several elements of a culture that interests you. You could recreate an entire traditional celebration, such as a Russian New Years' festival, complete with an ice slide, costume workshop and authentic games. Or you could simply serve the right food and play the appropriate funky music.

-Have a pen pal. A nice big established organization is International Youth Service. They provide pen pal names and addresses for people between 10 and 20 years old. They currently charge $1.10 per name, and you must request at least four names at once, from your choice of over 100 countries worldwide. International Youth Service, PB 125, SF-20101 Turku 10, Finland. Include a SASE when you write them for information.

-Go international folkdancing. I can't imagine a more interdisciplinary thing to do, since you'll end up not only whipping your feet through incredibly complex patterns, but also learning about geography, international music, and costuming. More importantly, I can't imagine many things that are more *fun*.

-And obviously, travel if you can. But that's chapter 29.

Map resources

-If you live around mountains, order a raised relief (three dimensional) map of your region from Hubbard Maps, P.O. Box 104, Northbrook, IL 60065.

-Road maps and atlases for all over the world are available from the American Map Corporation. They also sell a wide variety of bilingual dictionaries, guidebooks, and beautiful wall maps of the U.S. and the world. Free catalog from American Map Corporation, 46-35 54th Road, Maspeth, NY 11378, (718) 784-0055.

Local Geography: Bioregionalism

means living *where* you live, which is surely as important as living *when* you live. Bioregionalism means knowing and caring about the landscape and the people near you. It means cultivating the perspective that where you live is the most beautiful place on earth, even while you realize that every other place is also the most beautiful place on earth--for other people. If anything saves this planet, it will be people who love where they are--ceasing to live in abstract fantasies, plugging in and talking to their neighbors, noticing the first leafing out of trees in spring, climbing the nearest butte to get a look at the lay of the land, going out dancing to local bands instead of being seduced only by the faraway stuff on MTV, reading poetry by local authors, snacking on hometown blueberry muffins instead of on Ripples potato chips.

The best *national* magazine for bioregionalists is probably *Raise the Stakes*, published by Planet Drum Foundation ($15/year, P.O. Box 31251, San Francisco, CA 94131). Through this magazine you will also find news of bioregional events like the annual North American Bioregional Congress. Every so often one of their magazines includes a directory of bioregional groups; you may order the latest directory separately for $4.00. Also have a look at *Home! A Bioregional Reader*, edited by Van Andruss and others (New Society Publishers, Philadelphia, 1990). Another excellent resource is the *Essential Whole Earth Catalog* (look up "bioregions" and "reinhabitation" in the index). And see issue #32 of *CoEvolution Quarterly* (in many libraries). Other important spokespeople are Gary Snyder and Wendell Berry.

A bioregionalist perspective will influence everything you do, from eating to reading to making friends to deciding whether and where to go to college. In your library, look up books on various aspects of your particular area--its history, the lifestyles of Indians who lived there first, its geological background and agricultural products. More importantly, go for walks in your neighborhood, eat in a cafe that is not a McDonald's or other import, bicycle around the outskirts of town, get to know the pigeons or the bums in the park.

ECONOMICS

"Always remember that the economy is the relationship between living beings and the earth--another living 'being.'" --Paul Hawken, *The Next Economy*

Unfortunately, too many economists are narrowly entrenched in their field, interested only in money and stocks and such. They fail to see that the workings of money itself are abstract, taking their meaning only from the reality beneath them: land, food, water, soil, air, sunlight, and human creativity, diligence, and wisdom.

From that perspective, I recommend the following books, whose authors see the big picture and give a sense of the connections and movements in economics:

-Paul Hawken, *The Next Economy* (Holt, Rinehart, and Winston, 1983). Hawken describes our current transition from a Mass economy to an Information economy.

-In *The Next Economy*, Hawken himself says, "If I could recommend a single book on the economy that might lift the veil of our economic crises, it would be Fernand Braudel's *Structures of Everyday Life*." The human activity which has the greatest effect on economics, says Hawken, is the everyday tasks that make our lives move--baking bread, doing laundry, catching fish.

-*Home Economics*, by Wendell Berry (North Point Press, 1987). No statistics here. This collection of essays focuses on the way that the health of individual households and farms makes up the economic health of the whole planet. It also discusses the relationship between the industrial economy and the greater global economy--the economy that goes beyond money.

If you want to read about economics in the more ordinary, narrow sense of the word, try the 330 section of your library, or these:

-Henry Hazlitt, *Economics in One Lesson* (Arlington House Publishers, 1979).

-Richard Maybury, *Whatever Happened to Penny Candy?* Simple, fun, much-praised explanation of economics, available from Bluestocking Press (see appendix C).

-The children's library, of course. *How to Turn Lemons into Money: A Child's Guide to Economics*, by Louise Armstrong, is fun.

-Read *Forbes*, or *Money*, or other gold-watch fast-car magazines about money. It will probably take some time before you understand all the jargon.

POLITICAL SCIENCE

When I wrote this section, it was January 1991, and the U.S. had just gone to war against Iraq. The world felt dark and small; there was talk of a draft. If the worst continued, I thought, some of my readers would be sent to fight. In a letter to a former student, I wrote:

> If teenagers had more say in the world, the world would be a much cleaner, more peaceful place. The people who wage war and destruction have so little to lose, it seems...they're no longer young, they won't be around to see garbage dumps and nuclear waste blot out the face of the earth, they're not the ones who have to meet the "enemy" face to face and shoot, they spend far more time with their documents and diplomats than with their grandchildren. It seems tragic and unthinkable that you are so alienated from the actions of your government.

Now, as I make last minute changes to this book, it is March 1991. The war is over; a cherry tree blossoms outside my window. We all breathe easier, though across the world a country is in ruins. My sense of urgency about all this has diminished, but the political structure of the world has not changed or improved. It *still* seems tragic and unthinkable that you are so alienated from the actions of your government.

How can you begin to make sense of it? I suggest 1) getting involved, and 2) getting informed.

By getting involved, you can start to build a bridge between you and what happens in the world. You can't vote, but you can go out in the streets with a sign or a flag, or play your guitar at a rally, or organize a vigil. You can work to get a city ordinance or a statewide or nationwide bill passed. Plugging yourself in will empower you and give you an unbeatable education. For a bit more on activism, turn to chapter 38.

By getting informed, you can share the thoughts of the world's greatest political philosophers, and build your own 1990's thoughts on top of their wisdom. You can then keep this thinking quietly inside yourself, or else begin to talk about it or take action on it. By staying in touch with current events, you are better able to decide what changes need to be made in the world. Knowledge is power.

Current events

Read a local paper--not necessarily every day, but perhaps once a week. Pay special attention to local news and politics, because locally your voice can easily make a difference. Read the editorial page especially, to find out how your community feels about things, and to clarify your own opinions. For national and world news, read the *New York Times* or the *Christian Science Monitor*. Your library probably subscribes. Or, you could read a weekly like *Time* or *Newsweek*.

National Public Radio has excellent news programs and thoughtful in-depth interviews and commentaries. NPR can usually be heard on college, "alternative," or public radio stations.

Know who your local and state representatives are; keep their names, addresses and phone numbers handy in case you should want to tell them your opinion or ask them for information. If you contact them frequently and thoughtfully, they will start remembering you and taking you more seriously as time goes by. Politicians need this sort of regular contact with a few people so they don't start living in a dream world where all their constituents are barely real.

Political theory

These are the works which have most influenced and/or thoughtfully criticized Western political systems:

Plato, *The Republic*
Aristotle, *Politics*
Thomas Hobbes, *Leviathan*
John Locke, *Second Treatise of Government*,
John Stuart Mill, *On Liberty*
Karl Marx and Friedrich Engels, *The Communist Manifesto*
Niccolo Machiavelli, *The Prince*
George Orwell, *Animal Farm, 1984*
Alexis de Tocqueville, *Democracy in America*
Henry David Thoreau, *On the Duty of Civil Disobedience*

By the way, most of these are described invitingly in Clifton Fadiman's *The Lifetime Reading Plan*.

Also read the *U.S. Declaration of Independence* and especially the *U.S. Constitution*. The constitution itself and books about it can be found in the 342.73 section of your library.

You could also look for a collection of short bits of important political writing, such as *Great Political Thinkers*, edited by William Ebenstein (Holt, Rhinehart and Winston, 1969, 4th edition). "The purpose of this book," says Ebenstein's introduction, "is to present the major turning points of western political thought from Plato to the present..."

If Thoreau's idea of non-violent civil disobedience interests you, you might research further into the practice. See the writings of Martin Luther King, Jr.; watch the movie *Ghandi*. Your library may have a related anthology, like *The Quiet Battle: Writings on the Theory and Practice of Non-Violent Resistance*, edited by Mulford Q. Sibley (Quadrangle Books, 1963). See chapter 38 to find out how to get training in non-violent action.

Also, there are important new political theories and models springing up. Many of them come out of the peace movement, the women's movement, and new religious traditions. One of the most important and visionary new political writers is Starhawk, whose books *Dreaming the Dark* and *Truth or Dare* present a radically fresh, empowering way of looking at politics.

Finally, see the excellent section on politics in *Whole Earth Review* No.70 (Spring 1991).

Miscellaneous activities and organizations:

-To better understand the judicial system, attend trials.

-Youth Ambassadors International holds youth summits for "youth ambassadors" from the Soviet Union and the U.S. and Canada. Also, it conducts an annual summer camp in the USSR. YAI is a non-profit foundation "whose goals and purposes encompass providing the youth of the world forums and mediums of expression for their own ideas and visions of a safe, sane and friendly world in which to live." Youth Ambassadors International, P.O. Box 5273, Bellingham, WA 98227.

-The World Game Institute, inspired by the work of Buckminster Fuller, conducts powerful workshops for high schools, universities, and organizations--including United Nations Representatives. In their World Game Workshop, one hundred participants play a game on a huge map, trying to solve the world's problems. Find out their schedule and your chance to get involved by writing World Game Institute, University City Science Center, 3508 Market Street, Philadelphia, PA 19104.

-Amnesty International is one of the few organizations that is at least as interested in your labor as in your money. Also, it draws support from people of all political persuasions--you don't have to be right wing, left wing, or center wing to believe in what they do. Their work consists mainly of writing letters to governments worldwide--Turkey, Malaysia, South America-- on behalf of prisoners who are being tortured. Usually, it focuses on "prisoners of conscience"--people who are imprisoned for their beliefs. Amnesty International, 322 Eighth Avenue, New York, NY 10001.

-See chapter 38 for related ideas and information.

chapter 24

unschooling "English"

The best English teacher in the world would hardly say a word, especially to the whole class at once. She would stay out of your way, let you read all you wanted, and not try to organize any cute conversation about the motivations of the characters or the relationship between the setting and the theme. She would not keep you from writing by "making" you write. She would sit peacefully at her desk, reading *Pride and Prejudice*. If you went to her, she would put her book down, smile, and consider your questions.

Unfortunately, if this teacher ever existed, she is surely fired by now, because every time the principal came in to check on her, she was not busy asking you the difference between Metaphor and Simile. She was violating the first law of teaching, which is Thou Shalt Be Busy.

Fortunately, since you are out of school, her nasty luck need not distress you. Instead, you can go sit under the persimmon tree with your literary treasures. If you want conversation about setting and theme, or more intricate matters, you can go find it in the company of other people who want it too.

*

"English," as they call it, means reading and criticizing literature, and also writing--expository and "creative" writing. This chapter covers these territories and also touches on mythology.

LITERATURE

Literature is words telling us our lives. Our lives are funny, profound, and tangled. So are the good stories about them.

The study of literature happens two ways. The first and most wonderful way is simple--reading something because you like it. If you don't read for enjoyment, you lose.

The second way, which is also wonderful as long as it stays honest, is literary criticism. That's when you first read something, and then talk (or write) about it. Unfortunately, dull and insensitive approaches to criticism ruin a lot of people's love of reading, let alone their potential enjoyment of criticism. Too many college English majors end up hating their former favorite books, after nailing them into caskets made of words like "deneoument," "flat character," and "narrative voice."

Sometimes literary criticism seems utterly ridiculous, a way to make insecure English professors feel as scientific as scientists, even though they're not and shouldn't be. At its best, however, criticism can deepen your relationship with literature, enabling you to be twice as moved.

Criticism, by the way, does not mean saying *bad* things about literature. It means saying analytical, thoughtful things about literature, after asking questions: What does Shakespeare's use of the word "nature" reveal about the relationships among Lear and his daughters? Can a feminist appreciate Edward Abbey? What does the barometer in *Surfacing* show about the relationships between the men and women in the story? What effect does the concept of royalty have on Hamlet's fate? What does the film version of *The French Lieutenant's Woman* show about the relationship between reality and fiction? How do Anne Beattie's stories successfully combine self-reflexivity and the study of human movement and relationship? How do "The Miller's Tale" and "The Franklin's Tale" complement each other? What is implied by the differences in Mrs. and Mr. Ramsey's language, in *To the Lighthouse*?

Some people--could be you--can love this. Others can only laugh or run. There is no shame in feeling either way. It *is* a shame to turn against reading stories just because you don't like to publicly dissect them afterward. It is a worse shame to perform literary criticism if you can't also simply enjoy reading for the fun of it.

Do you *need* to analyze the books you read? No, no, no, a thousand no's! You don't need calculus to use long division and basic algebra, or to get along marvellously in the world. And neither do you need to get into heavy criticism in order to love and be changed by great books.

How can people who hate to read study literature?

They can watch movies.

Movies, like books, can be "classics" or cheap laughs. You can criticize a good film just as academically as you can criticize *The Tempest*. Richard Skorman's *Off Hollywood Movies* (Harmony, 1989) is a good field guide to the video store.

Always watch a movie for pure enjoyment the first time. (Watching for enjoyment doesn't mean you won't notice things like symbolism and plot structure, just that you shouldn't force yourself to think this way.) If you plan on deeply understanding any movie, the second and thereafter watchings can be as analytic as you like.

Of course, it is a sorry state to hate to read, but that's beside the point.

Which of the millions of books should you read?

There is no single answer to this question. Nobody except a vampire has the time to read all the great stuff. That's good news for you, since it means your answer to the question "What have you been reading, young man?" is potentially as good as anyone else's.

Of course, there are a lot of books that count as classics, and a lot more that don't. What counts? Why is *Sweet Valley High* out and *Romeo and Juliet* in? No one quite agrees, but we have several generally accepted definitions: good literature is made up of written works that have endured the test of time and offer something of value to our present culture. It is made up of stories that take us beyond mere entertainment, raising questions about the way we live and die. Ezra Pound wrote, "A classic is classic not because it conforms to certain structural rules, or fits certain definitions (of which its author had quite probably never heard). It is classic because of a certain eternal and irrepressible freshness."

Why bother to read the stuff? Mainly for enjoyment, as I said already. To be lifted out of yourself, to fly, to cry. To broaden your perspective and to learn about human nature. We can look to literature when we face a dilemma or crisis, because literary works show different ways of handling all our situations--birth, falling in love, losing love, failure, success, betrayal, loneliness, watching parents age and die, wanting money, getting money, hating money, losing money, enduring war, facing death.

Introductions

-Be aware that most of the "classics" you usually hear about have been written by white men in England or America. Don't *avoid* books by white men in England and America--after all, they are the people who have had the most opportunity and encouragement to write during the last few hundred years. Therefore, they have written a lot of the greatest stuff. But also make an effort to find some of the other greatest stuff--literature by women, literature from all cultures and colors. Most newer literary anthologies are pretty well balanced. If you get an older (cheap, used) anthology--pre-1982 or so--at least look in a newer one to notice what you're missing.

-If you might want to read a lot of English literature, especially the delicious magical old stuff from *Sir Gawain and the Green Knight* through Malory, Chaucer, Spenser, Milton, Shakespeare, and Blake, you'd best prepare yourself to get their inside jokes by reading the *Bible*, some Greek mythology, *The Odyssey*, and *The Iliad*. If you don't want to read the whole *Bible*, read the first five books of the Old Testament, *Job,* The *Song of Songs*, *Isaiah*, the four Gospels, First and Second *Corinthians*, and *Revelations*.

-If you're learning a foreign language, don't miss out on reading its best literature. One of the peak experiences in my short-life-so-far was sitting in the late afternoon sunshine of the winter solstice at Macchu Picchu's stone solar dial reading *The Heights of Macchu Picchu*, by Pablo Neruda, in Spanish.

--For companionship, join or start a book discussion club.

Bibliographies

A bibliography is a list of books. It helps when you're confused and lost in the literary universe. You've heard of Shakespeare, of course, but then you've also probably heard of Danielle Steele. Why should you read Shakespeare? And how do you know what else you should read, if you don't have an English teacher? (Once you've been out of school a while, you will not feel insecure without teachers. At first you might. Therefore, the bibliography.) You can ask your librarian for a list of books, or you can try my favorite:

The Lifetime Reading Plan, by Clifton Fadiman (Harper and Row, 1988), gives a list of "classics" by 103 authors, including plays, novels, essays, poetry, and biographies. For each, it gives a one or two page description of the author, the piece itself, and its social and historical context. Also, in the back of the book is a list of critical works you can read if you want to take anything deeper. To actually read the literature he recommends, you'll need to go to the library. By the way, Fadiman also recommends a few other books on history, math, art, etc. If you are one of the nervous college-bound, know that reading some of the books described by Fadiman will make any college admissions department happy.

Miss Llewellyn's miniature teenage bibliography:

This list reflects my conviction that the teenage years are a time of powerful personal transformation and vision. As a teacher, I noticed that most teenagers seemed to especially enjoy literature which put them in contact with the bizarre and visionary, the wild, the edges, the unexplained sides of human nature. Through literature, they sought assurance that no matter how saran-wrapped the adults tried to make things seem, reality is big and weird. My friend Keith said he liked being around his friend Mary because she made him feel like he had a place in the universe. I didn't ask him what he meant, but I translated his comment into my relationship with literature. No matter how strange my thoughts or hopes, I can always count on literature to mirror them, and to assure me that I am not alone.

Most literature can do this for you, but here is a short list especially tailored for searching teenagers:

Novels
Maya Angelou, *I Know Why the Caged Bird Sings*
Hal Borland, *When the Legends Die*
Ray Bradbury, *Dandelion Wine*
Rita Mae Brown, *Rubyfruit Jungle* (sexually explicit, offends a lot of people)
Lewis Carroll, *Alice in Wonderland*
Dante, *The Inferno* (not really a novel, but a very long poem)

William Golding, *Lord of the Flies* (I vehemently disagree with his pessimistic view of human nature, but this is a compelling, provocative psychological novel.)

John Knowles, *A Separate Peace*

Everything by Madeleine L'Engle, starting with *A Wrinkle in Time*

C.S. Lewis, *The Chronicles of Narnia, Out of the Silent Planet, Perelandra, That Hideous Strength*

Carson McCullers, *The Heart is a Lonely Hunter*

Tom Robbins, *Even Cowgirls Get the Blues* (rated R--some sex, some drugs)

Ignazio Silone, *Bread and Wine*

J.R.R. Tolkien, *The Lord of the Rings* trilogy

Alice Walker, *The Color Purple*

Richard Wright, *Native Son*

Short Stories

Sherwood Anderson, *Winesburg, Ohio*

Shirley Jackson, "The Lottery"

D.H. Lawrence, "The Rocking Horse Winner"

Ursula LeGuin, "The Ones who Walk Away from Omelas"

Barry Lopez, *River Notes, Desert Notes, Winter Count*

Edgar Allen Poe, anything--especially "The Masque of the Red Death"

Essays and non-fiction

Edward Abbey, *Desert Solitaire* (skim until you find what you like--a wild start is "The Dead Man at Grandview Point")

Annie Dillard, *Holy the Firm*

Kahlil Gibran, *The Prophet*

John Fire Lame Deer and Richard Erdoes, *Lame Deer, Seeker of Visions*

Peter Matthiessen, *The Snow Leopard*

Henry David Thoreau, *Walden*, also "On the Duty of Civil Disobedience"

Revelations (in the *Bible*, preferably New International Version or other easy to read translation)

Plays

Arthur Miller, *The Crucible*

Shakespeare, *Hamlet*

Sophocles, *Oedipus Tyrannus*

Movies

Dead Poets' Society

Harold and Maude

Jesus of Montreal

One Flew Over the Cuckoo's Nest

Equus

The Last Wave

Picnic at Hanging Rock

Poetry
-William Blake, anything--*Songs of Innocence and Experience* (not as innocent as they seem), *The Book of Thel, America: A Prophecy, The Marriage of Heaven and Hell*
-Allen Ginsberg, *Howl*
-The lyrics to your favorite songs, such as those by Pink Floyd, U2, or Led Zeppelin.

Also, here is a short list of great **love literature**, in case you should need it:
-*The Song of Songs,* out of the *Bible*
-Emily Bronte, *Wuthering Heights*
-Any poetry by Robert Herrick, especially "Corinna's Gone a-Maying"
-Edgar Allen Poe, *Annabel Lee*
-poetry by Sappho
-Shakespeare's sonnets
-Various dusty old books in any college library--track them down by typing "love literature" or "love poetry" into the computer. At the University of Oregon, I found old leather-bound collections of Chinese and Arabian love poetry.
-There's a terrific new anthology of short bits of love literature, but you may puke when you see the cover and the title. It's *Wedding Readings: Centuries of Writing and Rituals for Love and Marriage*, edited by Eleanor Munro (Viking, 1989). The edition I saw had pink bells on the cover, which almost stopped me cold. But inside I found a very imaginative eclectic grouping of poems and other readings, relating not only to marriage but also to romance and love in a broader sense. Munro included Aztec love songs, poetry by Shelley, Keats, and Wendell Berry, parts of a speech by Chief Seattle, and many other unexpected passages.

Resources: anthologies
An anthology is a collection of literature--a lot of stuff in one book. Cheap and handy.

If you want to own one general anthology, own *The Norton Introduction to Literature,* any edition. If you want to begin to learn about criticism--how to "read" in the academic way--read the commentary in between the selections. If you want guidance in writing about literature, read the section in the back. Otherwise, just read the stories, poems, and plays.

If you want to own two or more anthologies, own some Norton Anthologies, like *The Norton Anthology of American Literature.* These are fat books with fine print, wrinkly thin paper, and tons of treats. They are cheaper, more fun, more serious, and less censored than high school literature textbooks. Also, you can buy them very inexpensively at university used book sales, or by posting a notice that says what you want on a college campus.

Your choices include anthologies of English literature, American literature, world literature, women's literature, poetry, short stories, and essays--just to name the ones I've used and loved.

Technicians of the Sacred and *Shaking the Pumpkin*, edited by Jerome Rothenburg, are my favorite translations of poetry (mostly traditional poetry) from primal ("primitive") cultures. *Technicians* covers the whole world, *Pumpkin* just Native North America. The poems here are real; they sting and caress.

Eye of the Heart, edited by Barbara Howes (Avon, 1990), is a rich collection of Latin American short stories, which will leave you with new favorite authors.

Words in the Blood, edited by Jamake Highwater (New American Library, 1984), is a collection of contemporary Indian writing from North and South America.

Resources for critics

(Remember, you can get a gentle start in criticism by reading the commentary throughout *The Norton Introduction to Literature* or another good text.)

-*A Glossary of Literary Terms*, by M.H. Abrams (Holt, Rhinehart, and Winston, 1981), gives you all the language you need, along with lots of examples, to talk like an English professor. It explains terms like elegy, irony, and Russian Formalism. Required in many college English classes.

-If you want to be hardcore, start reading criticism and writing your own. If you like C.S. Lewis and medieval English literature, start with C.S. Lewis' criticism--it is as clear and wise as his fiction.

-Hit the scholarly journals. Read a few to get an idea of whether you want to major in English or another literary field in college--the dense difficult papers in them are just the type of thing you'll be writing, again and again, in any English department. If you do like these journals, read them and become a precocious expert. Write your own criticism in the same vein. Eventually, send in an essay and see if they'll publish it.

College?

The possible majors are usually English, Classics, or comparitive literature. Also, if you major in a foreign language often you can "concentrate" on reading literature in the original. The best departments, especially for a traditional English or Classics major, are mostly at small liberal arts schools. The best preparation is reading the *Bible* and Greek mythology, developing strong writing skills, getting your heart broken at least once, and coming prepared to learn to read all over again.

MYTHOLOGY

Mythology is a lot bigger than they tell you in school. It is not just a bunch of cute stories about why the moon changes shape. It has to do with the deepest dreams, hardest questions, and ultimate destinies of the human race.

Resources

-*The Power of Myth,* by Joseph Campbell with Bill Moyers. You can watch it on videotape (interviews) or read the book. Afterwards, anything else by Campbell.

-The children's library, for gloriously illustrated versions of the myths themselves.

-*Funk and Wagnall's Standard Dictionary of Folklore, Mythology, and Legend,* described under Anthropology in chapter 23.

-*Parabola: the Magazine of Myth and Tradition.* Published quarterly, $20/year or find it in college libraries. Each issue centers on one topic, like ceremonies, guilt, mirrors, or the tree of life. This wonderful magazine proves that scholarly work can stay meaningfully connected to life. Parabola, 656 Broadway, New York, NY 10012.

-Edith Hamilton, *Mythology. The* standard, though it focuses mostly on Greek myths and leaves others out.

What you can do:

-Try to write for journals like *Parabola.*

-Incorporate myths into your artistic work--poetry, art, music. Make up your own mythology--that's what William Blake, J.R.R. Tolkien, Ursula LeGuin, and other authors have done in their writing.

-If the myths of a particular culture fascinate you, find out more about that culture's history, geography, etc. Consider learning the language.

-Write your own retellings of myths, adding details, personal interpretation, and perhaps illustrations. Two outstanding examples are *Till We Have Faces*, by C.S. Lewis, and *Prince of Anwyn*, by Evangeline Walton.

YOU THE WRITER

First, the acquisition of basic writing skills. Second, the development of literary talent--setting about projects such as journalism, essays, poetry, plays, short stories, novels.

Basic writing skills:

We learn by example. Therefore, the best writing teacher for most people is lots of reading.

Common sense, too, will take you a very long way. I've had several students who spoke articulately, but who panicked and fell apart when they had to write, because school had coached them to believe writing was difficult and mysterious. Together we found that all they needed to do was slow down and imagine themselves talking, and then write what they heard themselves saying in their heads. Simple? Yes. Silly? No. School doesn't often advocate common sense solutions, because if everybody trusted their common sense, they'd stop feeling they needed school "professionals" to learn.

Be sure not to expect anything to come out perfectly the first time. At first, brainstorm, jot down your thoughts, and just spill everything out freely. Don't bother about spelling, perfect word choices, punctuation, etc. You can organize and reword things the second time around. On the third pass, you can finesse it up, use a thesaurus, get rid of passive voices, check spelling, worry about commas. Writing is a *process*; for almost everyone, it requires several steps. If you try to get it all right in one step, you'll set yourself up for failure.

The basic idea is that you can't both create and censor at the same time. So first you write and create, then you censor and structure and limit. You've probably already learned to write this way; most schools now are pretty good about teaching it, though it's a relatively new approach.

Three excellent books on learning to write expressively through this process are Gabrielle Rico's *Writing the Natural Way* (J.P. Tarcher, 1983), and Natalie Goldberg's *Wild Mind* (Bantam, 1990) and *Writing Down the Bones* (Shambhala, 1986). *Wild Mind* seems mainly aimed at people who want to be "serious" writers, but can free writers of any level.

If you want criticism on your writing, ask your friends and family. Ask what confuses them or repeats itself. Also invite them to give you any other feedback they think of. What some of your readers may lack in "professional" expertise, they will more than make up for in the amount of time and energy they can devote to critiquing your work. Even in my tiny 26-student school I was too swamped with my students' writing to give enough response to any of them.

If writing skills--especially punctuation, usage, mechanics, etc.--don't come naturally, then arm yourself with a few helps: Strunk and White's *The Elements of Style*, and possibly a good general textbook. I recommend Warriner's *English Grammar and Composition*, by John E. Warriner *et al* (American Printing House, 1977).

If you want to work on grammar--for foreign language study or whatever--Warriner's texts are excellent for that too.

Beyond basics: developing literary talent:

Of course, to be a writer, all you really have to do is write. Frills like writers' conferences are unnecessary. And if you *don't* write, no amount of writing instruction will pull a novel out of your navel. Once you are writing, however, outside stuff can help:

-There are lots of books about how to write in any library. Most are abominable. Several are outstanding:

For non-fiction, William Zinsser's *On Writing Well* (HarperCollins, 1990).

For more creative writing--mainly fiction and poetry: *Wild Mind*, by Natalie Goldberg (Bantam, 1990).

For word choice, fun, the writers' lifestyle, and fiction writing-- especially novels and screenplays: *Starting From Scratch: A Different Kind of Writer's Manual*, by Rita Mae Brown (Bantam, 1988).

-Apprentice yourself via mail or in person to a writer you admire. Send him something short you've written. Enclose a SASE. Ask for his feedback, *if* he has time. Make sure to point out that you'll understand if he doesn't have time. If he's extremely famous (which means busy), or if your work is sloppy, he'll likely not respond in great detail. Try someone else. Several teenagers, including Tabitha Mountjoy, 14, and Kim Kopel, 16, do writing apprenticeships through the mail with Susannah Sheffer, editor of *Growing Without Schooling*. (Her book on the subject of homeschooled writers will be published in early 1992 by Heinemann-Boynton/Cook.)

-Apprentice yourself to a great writer by studying her work carefully. Some techniques: copy passages of her writing into a notebook (to help yourself understand her style). Try writing in her style. Read her best works again and again. Memorize parts of her works. Read her biographies, letters, anything you can find that tells *how* she wrote. Eventually, try the same process with a different writer.

-Start or join a local writers' guild or support group. C.S. Lewis, J.R.R. Tolkien, and other friends met to share and discuss their writing in a group they called The Inklings.

-Attend writers' conferences. There are real ones mainly for adults (but without age requirements) and sometimes okay ones for school teenagers, which you can get in on too.

-Take a course in writing--*if* you trust the teacher. It only makes sense to be taught by real writers. What right most secondary school English teachers (like yours truly) have to pretend to teach "creative writing" is beyond me. Teachers need not be *professional* writers, as long as they are willing to share their work and you think it is good. A lot of writers do teach, particularly in occasional college courses. Examples of teaching writers are Ken Kesey, Allen Ginsberg, and Natalie Goldberg. If you don't find a writer-teacher, skip it.

If you are interested in a course, you might consider looking for one in writing *creativity*, or journal writing, or something along that right-brain line. While I sit at my computer endlessly day after day, my housemate Caroline is taking a wonderful weekly class called "women's journal writing workshop." They start with guided meditations, like imagining wandering through a big house and meeting a wise old woman. Then they spend half an hour or so writing poems or prose--or drawing--based on the meditation. They finish class by sharing their work with each other in a supportive atmosphere.

-If you want to try to get your writing published, use *The Writer's Market* and *Poet's Market*, published annually by Writer's Digest Books, and *Market Guide for Young Writers*, edited by Kathy Henderson (Shoe Tree Press, 1988--updated frequently). By the way, Jud Jerome--poet, essayist, and editor of *Poet's Market*--unschooled his daughter ahead of the crowd--see Chapter 39.

-If you have the initiative, consider producing your own magazine--one way to get your writing published as often as you like. The world needs a sort of *Growing Without Schooling* magazine specifically for teenagers, written and produced by teenagers.

-See your writing as a way to make a difference in the world--join Amnesty International and write letters on behalf of tortured prisoners, write your senators thoughtful letters about injustices that steal your sleep, write the utilities company outlining your ideas about ways they could encourage energy conservation.

Journalism: the neighborhood newspaper

Living fully at home is as important--and sometimes as difficult--as living fully in the present. Just as many people imagine that their lives will begin in the future--after they graduate, get promoted, marry, or retire--many also act as if events downtown, or in New York, or in Paris or South Africa, are more important than what happens in their own neighborhood.

If more people cared about where they lived, we'd all have less to worry about and more to celebrate.

And that's one place where your writing talents can step in and make life fuller for everybody who lives within a few square miles of you. Every neighborhood would be made happier and healthier by a small, sincere, well-written newspaper that celebrates local people and events. Give the behind-the-scenes story of the bed and breakfast inn down the street, or a profile of the old lady who adopts stray cats, or an explanation of where your neighborhood's sewer goes after it leaves each house.

Think of your newspaper as a kind of *magazine*. Focus on the interesting personalities and details behind your stories; merely printing what-why-where-who-and-how won't satisfy people's desire to understand their neighbors. Better to publish one significant issue each month than a poor-quality, rushed weekly. For examples, read profiles and feature articles in all kinds of magazines and newspapers. You could also encourage letters to the editor, and include an editorial page.

Don't think of your paper as a "kid-produced" newspaper, or it will probably end up matching people's expectations of kid-produced things--dumb and cute. Just think of it as an important way to bring your neighborhood closer together.

A typewriter and paper is all you really need. If you are lucky enough to have a computer, you can work with any word-processing program or go high tech with a desktop publishing program. Black and white photographs can add interest, but they won't copy well unless you have them halftoned by a graphic design or newspaper company. For other graphics, use your best friend's artistic talent or check into Dover's pictorial archives for all the free illustrations you can possibly use. (The illustrations in this book are mostly from Dover books, which are available in art supply stores, libraries, or through the mail--see chapter 26.) Photocopy your finished newspapers, preferably on recycled paper, and distribute them. You might give your first issue away for free, but from there on out give people the chance to subscribe for money. If you write decently, neighbors will gladly pay for your paper. In fact, you can also likely get local businesses to pay for advertising space.

Of course, your paper could have a focus other than your community, such as city-wide teenagers' lives and activities outside of school, or news of your extended family.

Do be sure you don't invade anyone's privacy by publishing embarrassing facts about their lives. And be careful that what you write about other people is true. Generally, however, as long as the focus of your paper is positive, and as long as you write it yourself or with friends, you'll have no need to worry about legal issues. Investigative reporting, or a paper that questions local issues, can be important also, but that's a whole different ballgame. If you might make anyone angry, you'll have to be certain not to make any legal mistakes; research carefully before starting anything controversial or "political." An excellent start is *Author Law and Strategies*, by Brad Bunnin and Peter Beren (Nolo, 1983).

You probably won't need any books to tell you how to make your newspaper; mistakes and experiments (i.e. *experience*) will guide you. But you can always have a look in the 070.5's or check the card catalog. One excellent help is *Editing Your Newsletter: How to produce an effective publication using traditional tools and computers*, by Mark Beach (Writer's Digest, 1988).

Craig Conley, a 15-year-old former homeschooler attending Louisiana State University, wrote about his newspaper in *GWS* (*Growing Without Schooling* magazine) #30:

I first got interested in writing newspapers five years ago when I was present at the collapse of an historic old hotel in Joplin, Missouri. I wrote an article about the history of the hotel and how it collapsed, trapping four men under the rubble. I added other articles about what my family was doing, and what was going on in town. Soon I had a whole newspaper.

....Now my paper is read by 40 families, in 15 different states. It is called Craig's Quarterly *and each issue ranges from 12 to 30 pages. It contains book reviews, news articles, art work and stories. Subscribers send in articles they have written....*

Reporting on activities...is good training for life. It makes me more observant and analytical. I try to look at people I know and new people I meet as possible subjects for an interview and sometimes this leads me to ask questions I might never ask otherwise. The most fascinating people are really in your own backyard...

Unschoolers in English Unclass

In *GWS* #40, Evelyn Tate said that her teenaged daughter Amy had several younger pen pals. She illustrated her letters to them, and planned to start writing stories for them in response to their letters.

Janey Smith wrote about her daughter in *GWS* #43:

Lindsey (almost 13) decided to enter an essay contest for a women's fair at the University. She was to pick a contemporary woman who she thought would find a place in future history. She chose Margaret Thatcher, read a difficult biography of her, had to figure out lots of stuff about British government, wrote the essay, and won first prize. This consumed her interest for a couple of weeks.

Katherine Houk describes her 15-year-old daughter Tahra's literary endeavors in *GWS* #43:

...She worked with some film-makers as production assistant on a HUD film about housing discrimination.

The rest of her time was devoted to reading a tremendous variety of books, writing her poetry (five volumes!), and working on her music (guitar and bamboo flutes).

In November of this year, Tahra's poetry brought her a paid job! She was one of 60 New York State poets who read their work at the State Museum in Albany. We went to hear her and listened to some of the other poets as well. From what we could see she was the only "child" reading....She...met some interesting people....She puts in countless hours on her writing because she loves it.

English In-Spite-Of-School:

Katherine McAlpine is a successful freelance writer who mostly does commercial work. In *GWS* #66, she writes:

Two things made those [high school] years bearable. First, literature. I'd play sick every chance I could so I could stay home and read. Or I'd play hooky and hide out all day in the county library. (Bless those librarians. They never reported me, though they must have realized that I was truant from school.) I read widely and wildly, whatever captured my interest, without direction or guidance. When I happened upon "The Waste Land," there was nobody to tell me what it was supposed to be about, how I was supposed to evaluate it, or that it was supposed to be very difficult. So I read all of T.S. Eliot's notes on the poem, then half a dozen critical studies, then a bunch of stuff on the Grail legend, and drew my own conclusions.

Unschooled writers:

Ernest Hemingway said that Beryl Markham, author of *West With the Night*, "can write rings around all of us who consider ourselves as writers." The book describes Markham's experiences as a pilot in Africa, as well as her childhood and teenage years on a remote farm in Kenya. There are occasional allusions to "lessons" to be done--apparently Beryl was more or less "homeschooled" by her father. However, her youth was dominated by more exciting things--hunting boar with spears, being attacked by lions, listening to Murani legends, watching Kikuyu dances, apprenticing with her father as a horse breeder and trainer. At 17, when her father moved to Peru, she stayed in Kenya and trained race-horses. Later, she learned to fly. Her writing is graceful and direct, and full of good stories.

Jack London, author of *White Fang*, *Call of the Wild*, and lots of great outdoor stories like "To Build a Fire," quit school at 14 to seek adventure.

chapter 25

unschooling foreign language

Foreign language is not really a discipline of the same intensity as the study of molecules or epic poems until you are far past fluency. As a beginner, you are not studying the language from an academic perspective; you are merely trying to speak and understand it, to use it as a tool. But as you learn, you may wish to flirt with interesting academic questions, like: how does a language reveal or shape the culture it belongs to? For instance, in Russian, the verb "to get married" is different for men and women. For women, the term literally translates, "to go behind a man." In Cantonese, the symbol for "angry" breaks down into symbols for two men and a woman. (If this sort of inquiry interests you, you might as well get yourself a good etymological dictionary and investigate your mother tongue. Also, you should read things by Mary Daly, which may infuriate you.)

Why study a language? 1. In order to be able to communicate when you travel, 2. In order to read (for example: science in German or Russian, literature in Greek or French), 3. Because you like words, or 4. To get into a selective college.

How we learn languages

There may be a lot of mystery about how we learn languages, but we don't necessarily need to figure out this mystery any more than we need to figure out why we like chocolate. By thinking for a few minutes about how children learn to talk, you will understand all you really need to know about learning a new language.

Any natural language learning starts with lots and lots of listening. Before most people can actually learn a language they need to hear it constantly for days or months. If you decide to start by working with a textbook, fine, but at the same time expose yourself to the sound of the language, through foreign movies, subway rides, college language clubs, whatever. That's the way babies do it. Don't worry that you can't understand what you hear. Don't try too hard. Relax. Don't worry, be happy.

Along the same lines, many people find it much easier to converse in a strange tongue after a little wine. Under a bit of influence, the conscious mind gives up some of its control; intuition and the subconscious mind rise to the surface. Sentences filter in as a whole rather than as a set of separate words. That's why I thought Russian dinners, soaked in vodka, were so much fun in college.

Of course, I would never advocate Breaking The Law so you absolutely mustn't drink any alcohol ever until you're twenty-one unless you visit a barbaric nation that doesn't monitor teenagers' morality in this way. I *do* advocate finding other ways to attain the same relaxed, soft brainscape that alcohol can induce. Deep breathing can help. Trance can too, if you know how to do that. Or you can try simply listening to music or dancing rhythmically or staring at a candle flame. In general, you want the linear, logical left brain to recede, so the fuzzy, intuitive right brain can rise. Once you're in that frame of mind, go ahead and talk.

Keep these ideas in mind as you decide how to learn your language.

Language for travel

If travel is your reason for learning, you don't need to learn until you actually arrive in a new country--if you have plenty of time, that is. Certainly the most exciting and vivid way to learn a language is to use it because you need it. If you like this idea, you can try several approaches:

-Find out about language schools in the country you will visit, and plan to enroll as soon as you arrive. Often these schools will arrange for you to live with a family, if you wish. You can find out about trustworthy schools by checking travel guides in the library. Some areas are famous for their language schools. For instance, many people begin a journey through Latin America by spending a month in one of the many Spanish schools in Antigua, Guatemala.

-Learn how the basic sentence structure works and how verbs are conjugated. Memorize a few key phrases like "thank you" and "Where's the bathroom?" (This should take a few hours, using a book, tutor, tape course, and/or video cassette.) Then take a dictionary with you and go. Panic on the plane and do some more last minute studying. Make a complete idiot of yourself for a while. Don't hang around with other English speaking people. From personal experience, I highly recommend this method. In third world countries, it's cheap. It's fun. It's life. It works.

-Spend a year or more learning a language through books or other resources (as described below). Once you feel comfortable with your skills, plan a short trip. This method demands self discipline, and is definitely less romantic and effective than the previous two ways. But hey, it's safe. Your school board will approve.

-Enroll in a foreign exchange program. The obvious trouble is that you may have to go to school, which won't be any more fun, after the first few weeks, than school in the U.S. of America. But you can always try a *summer* program so you don't have to go to school. Write CIEE (address below under "activities") for their "Advisory List of International Educational Travel and Exchange Programs," $5, or find it in a library.

-Use the innovative, common sense method described in *Language Acquisition Made Practical*, by E. Thomas Brewster and Elizabeth S. Brewster

(Lingua House, 1976), which shows you how to learn from a native "helper," *using* the language rather than getting bogged down learning *about* it.

-See related information in Chapter 29, which is all about travel.

Language for other uses

If you decide to learn a language for college, "the future," or another abstract reason, choose carefully. This can be one of the more important choices you make in life, since it can strongly influence what you are capable of doing, where you travel, and what you can read. Consider these factors: Are there countries you eventually hope to visit? What languages are most widely used? (Spanish is an excellent choice for that reason.) What are your interests and possible future plans? (If you know you want to conduct research in the jungles of Ecuador and Indonesia, you may want to learn Quechua and Penan.) What languages are easiest? Do you want to learn the language of your ancestors? Will you need to read in a specific language? (For example, German is nearly necessary for many scientists. Russian, French, and Latin are great for literary scholars.) What cultures fascinate you?

Resources:

I hope you don't rely solely on books or other programs to learn a language; removed from actual human communication, it's no fun and a little bit insane. But in combination with a native tutor or a foreign friend, programs can help you organize and practice your learning. In bookstores and record stores, you can find a variety of cassette programs that help you to learn a language through listening and repetition. Instructional TV runs video programs like España Viva. Bookstores and college bookstores also have various texts for learning languages. You might check to see what books local colleges are using and then look for a used copy.

A cheap way to get an introduction to almost any language, from *Growing Without Schooling #70*: Contact the American Bible Society in New York and get a Bible from them in the language you want. The reader who sent the idea in to *GWS* liked using Bibles because they were inexpensive and full of good stories. If you are familiar with Bible stories already, that will help. If not, find an English Bible (try Revised Standard Version or New International Version) and read them both together. Go for the story parts, like in *Genesis*, *Ruth*, or *Matthew*.

Here are two cassette programs widely recommended by unschoolers and others:

-*The Learnables* cassette program, developed by the International Linguistics Corporation. This program, now available through John Holt's Music and Book Store (see Appendix C), has received rave reviews in *GWS* magazine. It teaches languages (French, German, Mandarin Chinese, Russian, Spanish, English, and Czech) by having you listen to words and phrases again and again, following along in a *picture* book. After ten lessons, you begin speaking gradually. The program never asks you to read or write, trusting that these skills can be learned easily after you absorb the spoken language. Many young children use the program successfully, which is a good sign that it makes sense--after all, young children are the experts on natural language learning.

-Audio-Forum Courses, based on listening, understanding, and repeating. Mostly developed by the U.S. State Department's Foreign Service Institute, these courses come in three lengths depending on how much time and energy you want to invest. Fifty-six(!) languages are currently available. Audio-Forum also sells foreign language games, books, musical records, and videos-- language instruction courses, foreign movies, French operas, T'ai Chi instruction. Audio-Forum, 96 Broad Street, Guilford, CT 06437, 1-800-243-1234.

Activities:

-Host a foreign exchange student for a year--homeschooling families *can* do this, though the exchange student will go to school. For a list of most programs, see the "Advisory List of International Educational Travel and Exchange Programs" published by the Council on International Educational Exchange. If it's not in your library or available through a school, you can send $5 to CIEE, 205 East 42nd Street, New York, NY 10017. If it seems a bit odd to live with a student when you are not one, try to set up an unschooling exchange by writing to *Growing Without Schooling*. Although subscribers are mostly American, some are foreign.

-Another possibility is to house a foreign college student. Contact the foreign student support services at local colleges to see if they can help with arrangements.

-Or just befriend an exchange student.

-Find out if your city has a foreign language center. Some of these centers not only offer classes, but also host regular lunches where people--both fluent and stumbling--talk informally.

-Find out when a local college or university has language tables. This means that during lunch or dinner in the cafeteria people who want to speak Japanese (or whatever) sit together and try to make sense. Again, some may be native speakers and professors, others will be beginners or merely curious. If you're like me, you think you'd feel way too stupid waltzing into unfamiliar territory populated by people older and smarter than you. Ignore this feeling. All the other students probably feel just as self-conscious as you do, regardless of their age.

-Go to foreign films, with or without subtitles. Better yet, rent a foreign video and watch it many times.

-In *Homeschooling for Excellence*, David and Micki Colfax report that their son Reed (now at Harvard) "joined the local Spanish soccer team, developed an ear for the language, and has had the easiest time of [their three sons]."*

-As you approach fluency, you can read literature in the original language. You can listen to exotic radio stations on a shortwave radio. You can begin to make linguistical forays into the structure of the language itself, if you so desire. You can work as a tutor or translator (maybe as a volunteer at first). You can work as an American representative on a Soviet fishing boat, like my friend Laurachka. But as you approach fluency, you will think up plenty of your own ideas for ways to use and improve your language skills.

The professors say:

In general, they say that *if you want to learn a language in an academic setting, you have to know English grammar.* If yours needs help, use a good text like Warriner's *English Grammar and Composition.* (For most people there's no reason to bother learning English grammar *unless* they want to learn a foreign language in a methodical, academic way.)

Nancy Saporta Sternbach, Assistant Professor of Spanish at Smith College, writes,

> What we like best in our first-year students is the ability to think, the motivation to study and the desire to learn Spanish. Generally we find that a student who writes well, and is well-read, in English has less trouble translating those skills to a foreign language than the ones who also have trouble writing in English or whose grammar background in English is weak.

> Of course, we teach many levels of Spanish, even to our first-year students, depending on how much Spanish they've had before and how well they do on the placement exam (which consists of a grammar section, a listening comprehension and a composition) they take when they arrive. Some, who have studied many years of Spanish, go directly into a literature class. Others find a review of grammar useful. Still others will want to perfect speaking and writing skills in a conversation class. But, for beginners in the language we recommend a good grasp of the concepts of grammar (i.e. knowing what verb tenses and the parts of speech are, and how to use them correctly) in their own language, and the willingness to study in order to learn.

Richard Sheldon, of Dartmouth's Russian department, advises:

> I would say that the most important thing for success in our Russian classes is a knowledge of English grammar. I'll never forget the day I was talking blithely about direct objects only to have a student raise his hand and ask what one

---

*David and Micki Colfax, *Homeschooling for Excellence* (Warner, 1988), p.93

is....We have noticed over the years that students who have studied Latin in high school have a minimum of difficulties. Getting used to a language with cases and inflected verbs is a big help.

chapter 26

unschooling the arts

On Halloween I wanted to be Max from Maurice Sendak's *Where the Wild Things Are*. I got sidetracked and sat down marvelling at *The Art of Maurice Sendak*. On page 22, I ran into the commentary on My Subject:

> "I hate, loathe, and despise schools," [says Sendak] ....To this day, he tends to look on all formal education as the sworn enemy of the imagination and its free, creative play...."School is bad for you if you have any talent. You should be cultivating that talent in your own particular way."*

This chapter can't teach you to draw gnarly monsters or sing like the wind. Instead, it aims to help you decide how to start cultivating that talent of yours in your own particular way, and to inspire you with descriptions of other unschoolers' artistic work. It can't give in-depth help with everything; it can't even *mention* everything. The arts are endless, especially because artists are always making up new kinds of art. I'll briefly discuss studio and fine arts, film and video production, architecture, crafts, and performing arts. But first:

General advice:
-Find out what your city offers. Call your city council or chamber of commerce and ask them to mail you information on local arts. If you have a center for the performing arts, put your name on their mailing list.

-Don't divorce art from the rest of your life. Remember that decorating your bedroom, planting a garden, playing your harmonica at sunset, making cards for your friends, painting a mural on the garage, singing a lullaby to your sister, making up dances in your basement, and arranging vegetables on a plate are all worthy of your most impassioned artistic efforts. If art does not serve to make life more meaningful, it is empty.

-If you have talent, dedication, and a unique approach, you may want to consider going into business as an artist--a photographer or drummer or whatever. Most of this book's relevant information is in chapter 36, but if you want to look for nationwide jobs or contracts, you may also want to use one of the market guides published by Writer's Digest. They include *Photographer's Market, Artist's Market, Songwriter's Market*, etc. Each is updated annually and lists thousands of publishers, magazines, movie makers, poster companies,

---

* *The Art of Maurice Sendak*, by Selma G. Lanes (Abrams, 1980).

and others who buy art. Also, these guides give valuable advice on marketing (selling) your work.

-The *Essential Whole Earth Catalog*, which I can't help but mention every hundred pages or so, does an exceptional job of pointing out excellent books and magazines for artists and craftspeople. My own book recommendations are scanty; I see no reason to repeat their work.

-Write Dover for their free art catalogs. Dover publishes dozens of cheap copyright-free books of design which you can use to inspire your pottery, quilts, greeting cards, etc. A couple that I use and love are *Ancient Egyptian Designs for Artists and Craftspeople* and *Traditional Japanese Crest Designs*. Dover Publications, Inc., 31 East 2nd Street, Mineola, NY 11501.

STUDIO AND FINE ARTS

Check out any local art museums or art centers. Art supply stores are good places to find out about classes and lessons. Art supply stores are also good places to wander and get inspired by the colors and textures of paints and pens.

Art History
"For every reader of books on art, 1000 people go to LOOK at the paintings. Thank heaven!"--Ezra Pound

Art history means studying other people's art, not doing it yourself. The two activities go hand in hand, of course. Take a cue from Ezra, and look more than you read. Go to museums. If you don't have any museums in Dinkytown, go to the library and look at the oversize books in the 700's section, like *2,000 years of Japanese Art, The Early Comic Strip, The Art of Jewelry, Italian Painting, Turkish Carpets,* and *Picasso: The Artist of the Century.* At a poster store, buy yourself a couple nice prints to hang above your baseball card collection.

Drawing
Realistic drawing skills are necessary for many forms of art, from architecture to sculpture to fashion design as well as making portraits.

For starters, try *Drawing on the Right Side of the Brain* by Betty Edwards (JP Tarcher, 1979), which can turn any patient artistic failure into a modest artistic success.

If you want a class, find one with a live model, preferably nude. Artists need this training to develop a clear sense of the human form.

In *GWS #45* there is an amazing ink drawing of a leopard, the work of 12-year-old Jess Perna. Judy Perna, his mother, writes,

Jess is 12 (seventh grade) and Mark is 10 (fifth). They are excellent students, but hated school since second grade. School did not leave Jess much time to draw (he needs about 50 hours weekly)...Jess has grown very social since leaving school. Before he would hardly converse with anyone outside the family...He has drawn six commissioned pictures since November and is having his first art show in a few months.

Unschooler Carey Newman's experience in selling her artwork is described in Chapter 36.

And *The Tale of Beatrix Potter*, a biography by Margaret Lane (Penguin, 1986), quotes Potter:

"Thank goodness, my education was neglected...I was never sent to school...The reason I am glad I did not go to school--it would have rubbed off some of the originality (if I had not died of shyness or been killed with over-pressure)."

Instead, Potter spent her time writing, drawing, and studying nature.

Photography

If you're serious, find access to a darkroom. Start your search by visiting local photo shops and telling them what you're looking for. If you can't find one, consider setting up your own and renting time to other photographers, or else forming a co-op.

Aside from reading good books and magazines, you'll want to look carefully at the work of other photographers. Every once in a while an outstanding photographer writes a book explaining exactly how he or she made certain photographs. One such book is Ansel Adams' *Examples: The Making of Forty Photographs* (Bulfinch, 1989).

Ansel Adams, by the way, wrote in his autobiography about the end of his school career at age 12:

Each day was a severe test for me, sitting in a dreadful classroom while the sun and fog played outside. Most of the information received meant absolutely nothing to me. For example, I was chastised for not being able to remember what states border Nebraska and what are the states of the Gulf Coast. It was simply a matter of memorizing the names, nothing about the *process* of memorizing or any *reason* to memorize. Education without either meaning or excitement is impossible. I longed for the outdoors, leaving only a small part of my conscious self to pay attention to schoolwork.

One day as I sat fidgeting in class the whole situation suddenly appeared very ridiculous to me. I burst into raucous peals of uncontrolled laughter; I could not stop. The class was first amused, then scared. I stood up, pointed at the teacher, and shrieked my scorn, hardly taking breath in between my howling paroxysms.*

At this point, the Authorities invited Adams to leave school. His completely excellent father bought him a year's pass to the 1915 Panama-Pacific International Exposition. Ansel went every day, enchanted by an organist, paintings, sculpture, and science and machinery exhibits.

His first photos--about a year later--disappointed him, so at 14 he persuaded the owner of a photofinishing plant to take him on as an apprentice. He went on to become perhaps the world's greatest photographer, as well as an expert mountaineer and avid conservationist.**

Also see Chapter 41 for a description of unschooler Seth Raymond's photographic work.

Pottery, sculpture, and painting:
Again, try to find a way to share the equipment and space you need, through an artist's co-op or through city art programs. Art supply stores are a good place to start asking questions. If you're just starting out in a field, consider taking a class--especially one that lets you come in to use studio space during non-class hours. Once you know what you're doing, consider an apprenticeship.

Filmmaking and video production:
An apprenticeship, as usual, is a great way to learn. Of course, so is experimenting on your own and analyzing other people's films and videos.

In *GWS #25*, Eileen Trombly writes about her unschooled daughter:

Lori had taken a video course at Connecticut College at the age of 11. Her intense interest in this area caused her to volunteer her services in the filming of several political campaigns in New London, and also for the annual March of Dimes Telerama. She has continued this volunteer work for the last seven years and is now number-one camera person and assistant director for the Telerama. The director from New York phones to be assured of her participation each year. As a result, Lori received a job offer at the Eugene O'Neill Theatre here in Waterford, via the theater director in New York...

A year and a half later, Lori is in college and Eileen writes again *(GWS #33)*:

Lori has already been offered a position at O'Neill for next summer and was given her *own studio* this summer. Even though we're 15 minutes from the

* From Ansel Adams and Mary S. Alinder, *Ansel Adams: An Autobiography* (New York Graphic Society Books, 1990).
** Information from *Current Biography*, 1977

theater she sleeps nights at the mansion provided for the convenience of the N.Y. critics, etc. She often works late hours and is completely immersed in what she does.

Unschooler Andy Endsley writes in *GWS #77* that his work as an extra in *Glory* and *Dances With Wolves* (see chapter 23) led to a greater interest and involvement in film:

I like behind the scenes work, and I'd like to continue working on the technical aspects of film....You meet people who remember you, and they give you a call when they need you on another project. A week ago I got a call from our contact out in Montana. He wants me to work for three and a half months as a production assistant.

A trio of filmmakers who dropped out of high school:

Claude Berri, responsible for over a dozen films including *Jean de Florette, Manon of the Spring*, and *Tess*. Because he was Jewish, he spent WWI in hiding, an experience which later inspired his first film. Afterward, he had to go back to school, but says, "I was literally allergic." He dropped out at 15 and worked as a furrier while he took an acting class. At 17 he got his first bit part in a movie.

John Boorman, maker of T*he Emerald Forest, Deliverance, Hope and Glory*, and *Excalibur*, dropped out at 16 and went into the laundry business. After a year he started writing for women's magazines.

David Puttnam, producer of *Chariots of Fire, Local Hero, The Killing Fields*, and *The Mission*, dropped out at 16 and began working at an advertising agency.*

Architecture

Serious learning comes not only from reading and looking at pictures, but also from walking through the streets of your city and as many other cities and towns as you can get to. Apprenticeships, too, can be invaluable. (See Chapter 33 for a description of one unschooler's architecture apprenticeship with her father.)

In Arizona, you can visit Paolo Soleri's Arcosanti, a visionary, futuristic-looking energy efficient town built on the concept of "arcology," which combines architecture and ecology. People from all over the world pay to take workshops and help with the work there. You can sign up for an introductory seminar; to continue in a longer workshop your parent must participate also unless you are 18. For information, Arcosanti Workshops, HC 74 Box 4136, Mayer, AZ 86333, (602) 632-7135 or 254-5309.

If you're interested in architecture, you'll naturally find out about the work of famous architects and about cathedrals and Greek temples and such

---

* Information on Berri, Boorman, and Puttnam from *Current Biography 1989*.

(architecture books live in the 720's at the library). But don't miss out on the beauty and wisdom of "vernacular architecture"--more humble buildings like yurts, log cabins, and English cottages. An outstanding book for starters is *Shelter* (Shelter Publications/Ten Speed Press, 1990).

Also, for a unique, beautiful, human approach to architecture, see the works of Christopher Alexander, especially *A Pattern Language*.

Finally, don't miss the "children's books" of David Macaulay-- *Cathedral*, *Castle*, *Pyramid*, etc. Each shows, in fascinatingly detailed drawings, the designing and building processes that went into these monuments.

In his autobiography, Frank Lloyd Wright writes (about himself), "What he was taught in school made not the slightest impression that can be remembered as of any consequence." Wright dropped out of high school to take a drafting job with a professor of civil engineering, and went on to become one of the world's most innovative and admired architects.[*]

Crafts

The thousands of possibilities include decorating eggs Ukrainian style, knitting sweaters, carving wooden boxes, marbling paper, making jewelry, weaving a rug or Scottish kilt, making a patchwork quilt.

You can often find free classes through yarn supply shops, bead stores, etc.--you buy their stuff and they gladly show you how to use it. Be inspired by looking at local craftspeople's work at fairs, and if someone's work moves you, ask if you can take lessons from or apprentice with them.

The library, Dover catalogs, and *The Essential Whole Earth Catalog* can give you all the bookish support you need to start any project. If you're into funky jewelry or arty clothing, look for the magazine *Ornament*.

Craftspeople often find inspiration in collections of folk art. Some museums have good collections. If you're ever in Santa Fe, New Mexico, don't miss the chance to feast for a few days in the overwhelming Girard Wing of the Museum of International Folk Art.

Aside from the visual art forms I've mentioned, there are many other applications of artistic skills I don't have room or expertise to discuss. For instance, you can design clothes, do graphic art, design wallpaper or fabric, create animated films, or decorate hotels.

Liz Claiborne, fashion designer and founder of Liz Claiborne, Inc., escaped school because her father considered formal education unimportant. Instead, she studied fine arts in Belgium and France. She entered the world of fashion at age 21, when after winning a design contest sponsored by Harper's Bazaar, she began doing assorted jobs in New York's garment district.[**]

---

[*] From Frank Lloyd Wright, *Frank Lloyd Wright: An   Autobiography* (Duell, Sloan and Pearce, 1943).

[**] Information from *Current Biography Yearbook*, 1989.

PERFORMING ARTS

Good performing arts opportunities in school are the exception, not the rule. However, if your school has one of the exceptions, I know better than to tell you it doesn't matter. My school had one of the exceptions, and despite the rest of the drudgery I endured, I am still thankful for having belonged to the Capital High School Concert Choir and the Capital Singers. When I think much about it, though, I get angry anyway. Music wasn't my first love; dance was. Because I didn't like my school's trendy-girl-boofy-hair dance program, I sang instead. It was a terrific music program--but I wonder how my life might have gone differently if I had quit school and danced my heart out.

If your school does have programs you want to participate in, see if you can swing it through Chapter 19 tactics.

Alternatively, find a program elsewhere--a city youth symphony, a good dance school, a little theater, community musicals, a church choir. Or, you could run away and join the circus. And don't rule out college groups. One of my college's modern dance troupes included two local high school students. No one made a fuss out of their age or the fact that they weren't Carleton students; they were welcome because of their seriousness and talent.

And, of course, you can study or perform by yourself--break dancing on street corners, giving a violin recital, performing stand-up comedy, playing piano in a restaurant.

Or you can team up with friends--as a chamber orchestra, reggae band, tap dance troupe, theater company, or circus.

Music

Learn by practicing, experimenting, taking lessons, joining a band, playing your viola with your favorite songs on the radio, composing, being in the church choir or a big brass band.

Your library probably has books of Beatles songs, Beethoven's piano concertos, and 17th-century English folk songs, as well as a wide variety of CD's, tapes, etc.

Don't be stuck thinking the only instruments to play are the ones in school bands and orchestras. There are also pan pipes, organs, dumbeks, harmonicas, marimbas, okarinas, ouds, mizmars, lyres, sitars, and hundreds of other implements of bliss.

Stretch your ears by listening to different kinds of music. Try a classical music radio station on Sunday mornings. Public radio stations often offer a wide variety of programs, from traditional Celtic music to Brazilian rock. Phone them and ask for a program guide in your mailbox. Go to concerts. Look around in an "alternative" music store.

If you get serious, learn about music theory and composition, through books or tutors or classes. The unschooling Wallace family found creative ways to study music in addition to taking lessons from local teachers. Nancy Wallace, the mother, wrote in *GWS #30*,

> Ishmael...is studying music composition with a recent composition graduate from Cornell. Ishmael adores him, although I have grave reservations because he gives Ishmael so much homework that he has hardly any time to compose. In any case they are analyzing music from Gregorian chants to Debussy to Ravi Shankar, and Ishmael is getting a full scale graduate course in melody and harmony. Mostly, I have no idea what they are doing, with their sequences, modulations and chordal structures, but Ishmael seems extremely happy during lessons. He also takes music theory lessons from a woman up the street and she is teaching him "solfege," among other things...

At last report, Ishmael was 19 and living in Philadelphia, studying music while earning money by working as an accompanist and stage manager. His sister Vita, 15, has taught younger children to play violin in order to earn money for art supplies. Ishmael endured school until part way through second grade, when his parents couldn't stand any more to watch him suffer. Vita never went to school. As the two grew up, both developed a strong love of music. During the year that they were 14 and 11, they earned over $1,000 for playing recitals and winning competitions. At ten, Ishmael wrote a musical play, *Love's Path is Lumpy, or, Eat Your Spaghetti*, which was produced by the First Street Playhouse in Ithaca, New York. (Ishmael was the piano accompanist, of course.) Music is not all they do with their lives; you will find them mentioned in other parts of this book also.[*]

For more on the Wallaces, see Nancy Wallace's two excellent, insightful books, *Better Than School* (Larson Publications, 1983) and *Child's Work* (Holt Associates, 1990).

At age 14, artist Carey Newman (also see chapter 36) wrote in *GWS #68*:

> I have taken piano and theory lessons for ten years. While I don't plan to become a professional musician, I have reached a level such that I could work at it if I decided to. My mom has encouraged me to write piano and theory exams before quitting lessons for the purpose of using these certificates as stepping stones to get into the field of music if I were to choose to do so at some future date.

GWS #37 ran a reprint of a newspaper article about an unschooled musician, Gunther Schuller, head of the New England Conservatory of Music. Schuller had quit high school, and commented, "I have the feeling I would not

---

[*] See *GWS* #17, 28, 56, 64, and 70.

have been a very good music student in, for example, the rigid programs which allow for almost no electives, which some of our schools demand."

Irving Berlin, composer of over 1500 popular songs including "God Bless America" and "White Christmas," went to school for two years and then quit school at the age of eight and took various jobs to help support his family. Some of the jobs had nothing to do with music, but he also sang for tips, sang in shows, and worked as a singing waiter.*

Bo Diddley, legendary blues guitarist, dropped out at 15 and began playing guitar on the streets for tips.

Keith Richards, lead guitarist for the Rolling Stones, was expelled at 15 for habitual truancy, but went on to an art college where he was introduced to blues music.

Randy Travis, country singer and songwriter with three Platinum records, two Grammies and numerous other music awards, passionately hated school. He dropped out in ninth grade, worked at various jobs and began singing in bars, often with his parents chaperoning from the audience.**

Acting

The book is Constantin Stanislavski's *An Actor Prepares*, designed "to prepare the actor to present the externals of life and their inner repercussions with convincing psychical truthfulness."

Get involved in local theater, of course, but also think about staging your own play. Libraries have books that explain all the necessary aspects, including directing, set design, lighting, costume design, and business aspects. One such book is *Practical Theater: How to Stage Your Own Production*, ed. Trevor R. Griffiths (Chartwell Books, 1982).

If you're seriously interested in stand-up comedy, try to visit Chicago. Supposedly the world's most innovative comedy clubs reside there, and one of the best--Second City--teaches courses which are open to teenagers.

Unschooler Emma Roberts wrote in *GWS #68*:

I act a lot in our local community theatre....This past March I was in *Brighton Beach Memoirs*. I was the only kid under 16 in the cast. Being with all those adults really gave me a professional feeling. The adults were so serious and 50 kids weren't running around making noise. I felt that the play was more realistic than a bunch of kids on stage standing around waiting to say their lines. When I am in a play with other kids I want to hang around and play with the other kids and not really watch the play and pay attention. That is nice too, but I don't feel professional.

---

*   Information from *Current Biography* 1963.

For more on Emma's work in theater, and also for a description of another unschooler's theater apprenticeship, see Chapter 33. Read about an unschooler's clowning business in Chapter 36.

A few allies:

Eddie Murphy, according to *Current Biography* 1983, was an "indifferent student," and said school was "a never-ending party, just a place to get laughs."

Roseanne Barr, comedian and star of the TV series *Roseanne*, dropped out of high school at sixteen. She worked as a dishwasher and eventually started performing in comedy clubs.*

And Mel Gibson told journalist Roy Sekoff, "School bored me. I graduated, but just barely."**

Dance

Almost half of the teenaged girls who responded to my questionnaire were involved in dance to some degree, and many of them took three or more classes a week. Aside from taking dance lessons, you can audition as a dancer in musicals, start your own troupe, or move to New York to chase the dream of the ballerina.

For ballet students, an excellent new book has arrived: *Classical Ballet Technique*, by Gretchen Ward Warren (University of Southern Florida Press, 1989). With clear photos, this book explains all of the major ballet steps for men and women. To actually learn most kinds of dance you need a teacher, but a book like this can help you get much more out of dance class.

GWS #30 reprinted part of a newspaper article about Cathy Bergman, former unschooler and president of the National Association of Home Educators:

> Bergman said that as a teenager her goal in life was to be a ballerina. "I had to practice six hours a day in order to be a ballerina, which I couldn't do if I was in school. In a home school I could put all my energies into dance. That doesn't mean I didn't do anything else. You are inspired when you have so much free time to learn and grow. Your interest will lead to another interest. My ballet led to reading about ballet, and that reading gave me history. Reading that history led me to study great figures in art."

Of course, there is more to dance than ballet, tap, modern, and jazz. You can also learn flamenco (fiery controlled passion), international folk dance (lots of intricate footwork), Capoeira (Brazilian martial art/dance combination, very macho in case you care), Tai Chi (not strictly dance--graceful oriental movement focusing on the flow of energy throughout your body), belly dancing (sinuous undulation and intricate hip isolations), classical Indian

---

* Information on Diddley, Richards, Travis and Barr from Current Biography 1989.
** "Mel-o-drama," by Roy Sekoff, *Seventeen*, January 1991.

dance (complex everywhere, especially hands and face), square dancing, ballroom dancing, and hula--just to mention a few.

See Chapter 15 for a description of an unschooler and her dance teacher/mentor.

sports teams
and Otherwise Athletics

Unschool that body! What you can do with it in school is nothing compared to what you can with it on an icy hill or a surfboard or a green field or a horse or a bike or a dance floor. Plus, your muscle tone will automatically improve now that you're not spending all your daylight hours on a chair.

Move your body by yourself or with friends.

If you are serious about an individual sport (as opposed to a team sport), you will improve more outside of school, unless you have a truly outstanding school coach who has plenty of time for you. *GWS* (*Growing Without Schooling* magazine) #17 reports that tennis player Bjorn Borg taught himself to play in his childhood, stubbornly (and wisely) refusing advice that he didn't agree with.

If it makes you feel more real, attend competitions or other events. Can't get in? Organize your own. Don't be shy.

Need a team?

Alternatives to staying in school in order to be on a team:

1. Don't go to school but do play on the team. If yours is an individual sport, like tennis, train on your own but join them for tournaments. See chapter 19.

GWS #69 tells about an unschooled 16-year-old in Vermont who participated in his district's cross country meets. At one point, he ran up against a legal technicality which prohibited his involvement, claiming private schools (including home schools) had an unfair advantage (they could have an intensive training program). The coaches, who liked the kid and thought the rule stupid, started working to change it.

He skied too. Since the ski coaches also liked having him around, they let him participate through another technicality in the rules--a special guest category.

In GWS #78, Gretchen Spicer writes about her daughter Jessie's involvement in a high school gymnastics team. In ninth grade, Jessie decided to go to school for the first time, in order to be on the team. (She had taken gymnastics lessons since she was five.) She did well in school, but decided not to return for tenth grade--among other things, she felt alienated from her family, and had to drop piano lessons and some of her ballet lessons in order to make time for school.

The Wisconsin Interscholastic Athletic Association refused to let her participate as a homeschooler, but they finally worked out a compromise. Gretchen explains:

> They are willing to consider her a transfer student. She can transfer to the school one week before the first meet, take twenty hours of electives, and thereby be there for the time needed to be allowed to play on the team. She doesn't have to take core subjects, and she can arrange it any way she wants-- three full days a week, or four hours a day, five days a week. She'll continue this through the gymnastics season and then leave, and for now, she can go to practices without going to school at all.

> At first we were angry about this. It seemed ridiculous for her to have to spend all that time there doing things that have nothing to do with being on the gymnastics team. But she feels OK about it for now, because it's better than going full-time, and she'll take some things she wants, like an art class and driver's ed, and she can take study halls. We're not finished fighting this, but for the time being we can live with this compromise.

2. Join another team--through a community league, community college, private school, or church league.

3. Start your own team of unschoolers and dropouts. If there are enough of you, start a league. Experiment with coaching yourselves and each other--an excellent experiment in self-directed learning.

4. Change sports.

If you are looking for a new activity, don't think that your only choices are the things you used to do in P.E. Consider walking or biking to work, feisty teenage sports like skateboarding, snowboarding, or freestyle biking, yoga, gardening, hiking, climbing, skiing, kayaking, dancing, tai chi, horseback riding, martial arts, trapeze swinging.

A handy resource for a huge variety of sports is *The Sports Address Book: How to Contact Anyone in the Sports World*, edited by Scott Callis (Pocket Books, 1988). It gives addresses not only of famous athletes but also of sports camps, leagues, and organizations. By contacting a national organization such as the U.S. Hang Gliding Association, you can find out if there are clubs in your area.

Your library has books on fitness (aerobics, yoga, etc.) in the 613 section. The 796 vicinity is sports territory.

Some unschoolers in P.E.:

In *GWS* #43, Janey Smith writes about her teenaged son:

Seth did an interesting thing recently. He became interested in cycling and joined a bike club last spring. He's the youngest member by far. He trained for a race and did well last spring, goes on long rides with them (25-70 miles, 100 this Sunday), bought some needed equipment...This was getting expensive for him, so he made a deal with the owner of a local bike shop to work out purchase of things at cost. He won a summer race and came in third out of 50 (some experienced racers) a week ago. He reads biking magazines and books and plans his training and strategy...

Jesse Schwerin, 15, runs on a school cross country team in Massachusetts. His mother Virginia writes in *GWS #77*,

I ended up writing to the school and telling them what we were going to do--I didn't ask permission. I just wrote the athletic director of the school and said, "My son is a home-study student in the Lenox School District, and he's qualified for sporting events, and he will be joining the cross-country team." The people in the athletic department were encouraging--there was no problem at all.

Erin Roberts, 14, has played on an AYSO (American Youth Soccer Organization) team for the past few years. In the spring of 1990 she became a youth referee and a co-coach for a team of four- and five-year-olds. "This fall," she wrote me, "I will be playing for Boonesboro's Junior Varsity High School team. Everyone involved was very helpful about giving me the opportunity to play on this team even though I don't go to the school."

In 1979, a 14-year-old unschooled boy lived at a ski resort over the winter ski season alone in his father's camper, technically under the guardianship of other adults but actually on his own. He was able to ski as often as he wished, and his father commented in *GWS #12* that he "spent an interesting, difficult, exciting, productive winter there."

chapter 28

the call
of the wild

*Oh yes, I went to the white man's schools. I learned to read from
school books, newspapers, and the Bible. But in time I found that
these were not enough. Civilized people depend too much on man-
made printed pages. I turn to the Great Spirit's book which is the
whole of his creation. You can read a big part of that book if you
study nature. You know, if you take all your books, lay them out
under the sun, and let the snow and rain and insects work on them
for a while, there will be nothing left. But the Great Spirit has
provided you and me with an opportunity for study in nature's
university, the forests, the rivers, the mountains, and the animals
which include us.*

--Tatanga Mani, Stoney Indian[*]

I have always been grateful for the trust my parents have given to me and my
siblings. My younger brothers started backpacking, hunting, and camping
without adults in junior high. I first backpacked without adults at 16--me and
the two little brothers in the Sawtooth range. Richard dropped a big rock on
his foot so Ned and I took turns carrying his pack. We all drank the water
without purifying it; we spilled propane on our shortbread cookies; we brought
enough gorp to feed the world. We had a great time.

The freedom and encouragement my parents gave us led us all further
into the wild. I took a mountaineering course in the North Cascades and I
backpacked alone in a remote corner of Peru. Ned and Richard spent weeks
kayaking through the Sea of Cortez in Mexico. Richard sneaked around in the
Amazon when his AFS host family thought he was in Guayaquil. He took two
NOLS courses and now considers teaching for them. Ned kayaked around
Greece and biked through Turkey. My mom worries a lot, but she always
gives her blessing.

Most people associate outdoor activities with the heat of summer. In
summer school's out anyway, of course, so people who want to walk
boulderfields can do that and also be a Star Pupil. There are already good

* From *Tatanga Mani, Walking Buffalo of the Stonies*, by Grant MacEwan (Edmonton:
M.J. Hurtig, Ltd., 1969).

books that tell about these sorts of opportunities, because most teenagers (and college students) can already have access to them.

However, the summer wildernesses get more crowded every year. You may as well take advantage of September, October, and the other seven best reasons to quit school. If you live in a northern climate, it helps to have a big mind like John Ruskin, who said, "There is really no such thing as bad weather, only different kinds of good weather." Even if you don't want to camp in a snow cave because you're a cold-wimp like me, you will find that spring and fall are enchanting backdrops for outdoor activities, with their slanted light, mating elk, colored leaves, wet flowery meadows. Of course, if you have the money you can always head south.

If you are lucky enough to have parents as trusting as mine were, there's no limit to what you can do. I do have a couple words of encouragement and warning.

First, encouragement:

Generally, young people growing up now seem far more sophisticated in some ways than my peers and I were ten short years ago. For instance, they know and care much more about the world, the environment, and people who starve.

On the other hand, I see distressing signals that young people are increasingly *softer*, more cautious, overprotected by parents and other adults who don't know them well enough to trust them. I suppose it's also a reflection of our society in general, which at the moment reeks of a squeamish "better safe than sorry" mentality, with mandatory seatbelt laws, with lawsuits and sanitary codes and endless restrictions. Gumption and bravery are not especially in fashion.

Ignore fashion. Think for yourself. The wilderness does *not* come in a Styrofoam package, and you may never make "sense" of it, but so what? If you proceed with care, you are not going to die or get hurt outside. Well, you *might*, of course--but it's far more likely you'll die or get hurt in somebody's Chevrolet. Anyway, neither dying nor getting hurt are anywhere near as unhealthy as avoiding life.

Now, a warning:

Do it, but don't make trouble for yourself by going unprepared. If you don't already have outdoor skills, learn them in the company of people who know what they're doing. Take a first aid course. Choose equipment and clothing carefully, so you don't get hypothermia in wet cotton jeans. Don't confuse stupidity with bravery.

Companions and guides

You don't have to take a "course" to learn outdoor skills any more than you have to go to school to learn history. You can simply tag along with experienced outdoorspeople. If you don't know any yet, you can find them by posting a note on bulletin boards of outdoor equipment stores, or by contacting local mountaineering clubs. You can meet them more indirectly by attending local Sierra Club meetings or participating in other conservation organizations. For trips in other states or regions, put notices on the "outdoor" or "backcountry" bulletin boards of computer networks.

Don't rely completely on your companions' knowledge; read up a bit on your own also. The best, most thorough start is *The National Outdoor Leadership School's Wilderness Guide*, by Peter Simer and John Sullivan (Simon and Schuster, 1983).

Organizations

If you have difficulty finding informal guides, consider going on a trip with an organization. There are two excellent national schools, as well as hundreds of local ones all over the country. These programs vary from very cheap to very expensive. Some teach beginners; others organize experienced climbers for an "assault" on Acongagua or Annapurna.

Nationally speaking, the two old-timers are still considered the best. They are not cheap but sometimes have scholarship money:

-NOLS (the National Outdoor Leadership School) is probably the best *national* organization that teaches wilderness skills. Through courses that last approximately a month or a semester, you can learn to backpack, cross country ski, ice climb, kayak, etc. The courses themselves are usually extended wilderness trips through stunning areas like the North Cascades, Alaska, or the canyons of the Southwest. You have to be 16 for most courses, but there's also a course especially for 14- to 16-year-olds. Write for a catalog: NOLS, Box AA, Lander, WY 82520.

-Outward Bound is also a good place to learn skills; it is equally known for emphasizing "personal growth"--deliberately pushing the limits of your endurance and courage. Again, opportunities range all over the place, from backpacking and climbing to rafting. Outward Bound, National Office, 384 Field Point Road, Greenwich, CT 06830.

NOLS and OB are terrific, and their instructors have finely tuned skills and charisma. However, you can spend far less money by taking a course close to home, through the outdoor program of a university, the YMCA or YWCA, your community parks and recreation department, or local mountaineering (etc.) clubs. Also look for fliers in outdoor equipment stores. The Sierra Club runs outings both nationally and through local chapters--for local contact people, get information from The Sierra Club, 730 Polk Street, San Francisco, CA 94109.

-There are hundreds of good camps and outdoor environmental education centers in this country, but I mention the Hulbert Outdoor Center because it runs camps specifically for homeschoolers aged 10 to 15, and a 7 day wilderness adventure trip (backpacking or canoeing) for homeschoolers aged 11 to 15, as well as year-round programs for school students. The camp gets rave reviews from homeschooling participants, and includes journal writing, lots of natural history stuff focusing on forest and pond communities, new games, trust and team building activities, and a ropes course. For information, The Hulbert Center, RR 1, Box 91A, Fairlee, VT 05045. Cost is currently $130 per person, for five days at the camp, or about $360 for the 7 day wilderness trip.

-For outdoor volunteer opportunities, see *Helping Out in the Outdoors: A Directory of Volunteer Work and Internships on America's Public Lands*, published every February and August. You do have to be 18 for some opportunities, and 16 for others. They list opportunities in tree planting, trail maintenance, living history farms, and more. For your copy, mail $3 to The American Hiking Society, 1015 31st St NW, Washington, DC 20007.

THE ACADEMIC WILDERNESS

You can combine your love of the outdoors with "academic" study, so that you could spend a whole year strolling the Appalachian trail with Spot and give the school board nothing to complain about. Here are some ideas, but first:

Beware

I have this horrible vision of wandering through the Chiracahua mountains and stumbling on some teenager who read my book. All around him are strange towers of volcanic rock. The sun going down splashes eternity everywhere. He sits hunched under a tree, reading a geology textbook, memorizing terms. Then he gets out his *Appreciating Art* book and dutifully studies the paintings of Monet and Van Gogh. Please don't be him.

Remember that a lot of the beauty of spending time outside is the beauty of simplicity--stripping your life of miscellaneous distractions and conveniences so your soul lays naked, ready to be *touched*. If you are a receptive enough adventurer, you will learn far more from quiet observation than from any contrived academia. Please keep these things in mind as you read through the following ideas. If you try to incorporate one or two of them into a trip, you may enhance your adventure. If you try to do it all, you might as well just stay home and nail a poster of Yosemite on your door.

Ideas

-Conduct field research; be a zoologist, ornithologist, botanist, or geologist. Collect, observe, experiment. Ask questions: what does the blackbird do if you come closer than 15 feet to its nest? Closer than ten feet? (But don't harass.) Record your findings in a notebook. See the section on being a naturalist in Chapter 21.

-Read background information on the area you're in. The Sierra Club Wilderness Guides are excellent companions, since they tell all about the plants, animals, and geology of one region. There are many other good books too, of course. Ask a local ranger station for ideas, or check the bookshelves in a local mountaineering store.

-If you are an artist, your possibilities are obvious. You can paint or sketch what you see, or you can work on another project. I always bring embroidery, because it is small and provides a nice meditative thing to do while I'm sitting on a rock.

-The same goes for writers. Of course, you don't have to write about "nature" just because that's where you are. You can just as easily work on your science fiction novel. However, there are some great role models out there for inspiration--people who write based on their outdoor experiences. Many of the more contemplative "nature" writers, such as Barry Lopez, Annie Dillard, Ed Abbey, and Peter Matthiessen, successfully combine tales of high adventure with profound commentary on life, the universe, and everything.

These people who write based on their wilderness experiences do not necessarily do the actual writing while they're out there, but they do need to at least take notes or keep detailed journals. Otherwise, memory fails.

-Which brings us to reading. "Nature writing" like that mentioned above is an obvious choice. But you can stick anything in your backpack: Thoreau, Emerson, Blake, Gary Snyder, the *Tao T'e Ching*. Anything Native American--*Lame Deer: Seeker of Visions*, *The Portable North American Indian Reader*, Jerome Rothenburg's poetry anthologies--is particularly appropriate companionship in the wild. In general, go for profundity. Jane Austen's world of social etiquette, delightful as it is, may seem petty in contrast to the mountains surrounding your tent.

-If you are interested in the relationship between people and wilderness, maybe you want to conduct a bit of sociology during your trips. When you meet someone on the trail, introduce yourself and get their permission to ask questions. Carry out a survey on whatever interests you-- why are they there? Do wilderness experiences make them Nicer to their Kids? When they are in an empty canyon is their belief in a God strengthened or diminished? How is their attitude toward wilderness different from their attitude toward their own backyard? Don't ask questions that don't interest you. Write up your results and look for a place to have them published.

Along this line, you may wish to first check into other people's wilderness sociology. For instance, Joseph L. Sax's *Mountains Without Handrails* questions the notion that wilderness vacations are a privilege of the elite.

Finally, don't shut yourself off to other ways of "learning"--quiet meditation, fasting, prayer...*stillness*.

Helpful Reading

-Don't miss the *NOLS Wilderness Guide*, mentioned above. For any outdoor activity, it gives important information on safety, technique, and equipment. Also, it has a timely section on minimum-impact camping--how to not hurt the wilderness while you enjoy it.

-*Outside* magazine covers a wide range of outdoor activity. Its yuppified, slightly sexist attitude always irritates me a bit, but information is high quality, inspiring, and usable. Also, you can locate all kinds of outdoor schools, expeditions, and equipment through its advertisements.

-*Backcountry Bikecamping*, by Mike Sanders (Stackpole Books, 1982).

-*Mountaineering: The Freedom of the Hills*, edited by Ed Peters (The Mountaineers, 1982).

-*River Camping: Touring by Canoe, Raft, Kayak, and Dory*, by Verne Huser (Dial Press, 1981).

-*Ski Camping*, by Ron Watters (Great Rift, 1989), includes the obvious, plus information on building and inhabiting snow caves.

Also, there are many excellent books that tell about other people's wilderness adventures. They explain in enough detail that you could base your own trips on theirs. Two good ones:

-Richard Bangs and Christian Kallen, *Rivergods: Exploring the World's Great Rivers* (Sierra Club Books, 1986). Exciting descriptions of ten river trips all over the world. Stunning photos.

-Barbara Savage, *Miles From Nowhere: A Round the world Bicycle Adventure* (Mountaineers, 1983). Young married couple bikes around the world.

In libraries: hiking, backpacking, climbing, 796.5. Biking, 796.6. Boating (including rafting, kayaking, and canoeing), 797.1.

See related books in Chapter 29.

The example

British unschooler Shawn Hargreaves, 13, joined with five other teenagers to organize a sailing trip. At last report they were sailing with the boat's two adult owners, but they themselves were sharing responsibilities for planning expeditions. He wrote, "The experience of sailing 1300 miles and taking responsibility for the ship and its crew has changed me a lot. I am much more confident and self-reliant, and can work better with other people."[*]

---

[*] Information from British magazine *Education Otherwise,* reprinted in *GWS* #72.

chapter 29

worldschooling

"Something hidden. Go and find it. Go and look
behind the Ranges--
Something lost behind the Ranges. Lost and waiting
for you. Go. "

--Kipling, "The Explorer"

Unfortunately, the world is not a classroom. It is difficult to find *An Introduction to Geography* and other marvelous books like that when you are changing trains in Bolivia or setting up camp in the Canyonlands. Without a chance to do lots of homework assignments on latitude and longitude, unschooled teenagers are surely handicapped and will be uninformed throughout their lives. Some of them bravely try to make their way through the world anyway. It's a wonder they're not all drowned or lost.

One of the more outrageous unschooling stories is that of Robin Lee Graham, who quit school in 1965 at age 16 and sailed around the world alone. It took five years and the whole world paid attention. His book, *Dove*, tells of all kinds of things no teenager should be allowed to face--battling loneliness and storms, losing a mast, falling in love in the Fiji Islands, feasting on shellfish in the Yasawa Islands and on roast pig and papaya with Savo Islanders, traveling with dolphins and cats, motorcycling through South Africa. "Was I different just because history didn't turn me on and boats did?" he asks.

At the age of 13, he had spent a year sailing in the South Seas with his parents. Then,

At fifteen I was back in a California classroom, my spelling still lousy, but I was almost as useful with a sextant as a veteran sailor. On our 11,000-mile voyage I had seen lands of unbelievable enchantment.

It is hard to believe that my parents, having allowed me to sail the South Seas at a most impressionable age, could ever have expected me to be a typical American schoolkid, to go on to college and graduate to a walnut office desk, a home on Acacia Avenue and membership in the local golf club.

I am sure Corona del Mar's high school is a good one. For me it was a return to prison. Beyond its asphalt playground and wired fences there were sunsplashed, palm-fringed shores waiting for my shadow.

Later that year, while making secret plans to sail away with friends, Robin says,

School became almost unbearable. It wasn't so much that I disliked learning--for I realized the need to be at least partially civilized and my grades were average--but that I detested the routine of school days, the unchanging pattern from the brushing of my teeth to learning English grammar. I came to hate the sound of the bell that summoned me to class, the smell of tennis shoes and sweat in the gym, the drone of history lessons, the threat of tests and exams.

Down at Ala Wai harbor it was all so different. I loved the smell of rope and resin, even of diesel oil. I loved the sound of water slapping hulls, the whip of halyards against tall masts. These were the scents and sounds of liberty and life.

When he actually sets sail for his global voyage a year later, he reports on the first day at sea:

At nine o'clock I forced myself to eat a can of stew and then tuned the radio to my favorite Los Angeles rock music station. It was interesting to hear the news announcer report that I was on my way--"the first schoolboy ever to attempt to sail the world alone." The announcer audaciously guessed a lot too, and guessed wrong when he added, "The most important piece of Robin's luggage is a shelf of schoolbooks."

"Like hell," I told the cats.

When Robin completed his voyage, Stanford invited him to enroll. He tried it, but quit after a semester (see chapter 31) to start a life of homesteading in Montana. (You can read about that in his second book, *Home is the Sailor*).

In case this story hooks you, *National Geographic* ran stories on the voyage in October 1968, April 1969, and October 1970. Also, you might check out the movie, surprisingly entitled *Dove*. (*Dove* was Robin's boat.)

I know people are not used to the idea of teenagers roaming on their own, despite the examples of occasional Robin Grahams. If you totally panic at the thought of exploring strange territory without your mother, independent travel is probably not for you. But if some excitement surges with the panic, maybe you should start fantasizing with maps. No significant legal barriers prevent teenage travel, and if you think you're ready, you are. Yes, tragedy could strike, but no more likely to you than to an adult, and far less likely than

if you walked through the halls of most inner city high schools in the U.S. of
A.

What does she mean by travel?

She means something in between going to the airport to pick up Aunt
Matilda and stowing away on a space shuttle, that's what she means. A drive
to Oklahoma or a train/bus/pickup truck/walking trip through South America
is exactly the sort of thing she has in mind.

She does not mean hiking the Pacific Crest Trail, because she talks
specifically about wilderness tripping in chapter 28. But you could use both
this chapter and that one to help plan a foreign-country-wilderness-excursion.

She does not mean going to Kathmandu on a week-long package tour
during which you stay at the Sheraton, because she is not enthusiastic about
such sorts of travel, and she has read lots of advice which warns her against
writing about topics which fail to enthuse her. She figures, anyway, that the
travel agents in your yellow pages are quite enthused about this topic, and that
you can ask them.

Why to travel and why not to travel

Why to travel: It's cheaper than private school and far more
educational. If you stay in the U.S. or Mexico or South America, it can be no
more expensive than public school plus the food and electricity you consume at
home. In *The Next Whole Earth Catalog*, Kevin Kelly wrote, "The drifters of
Europe in the '60's invented a contemporary form of education: extended
world travel. At about $3,000 per year, all adventures included, it is still the
cheapest college there is."

I will spare you a big gushy sermon about the joys of travel, since
you can make one up for yourself while gazing at any poster of a market in
Marrakesh. I *will* say that international travelling is an especially timely thing
to do as we shift into a more global economy and awareness. The U.S. is no
longer The World Power. We have no excuse for arrogance. We need to learn
from and about the rest of the world.

Why not to travel: because I said to, or only in order to learn about
people in other countries because the United States is no longer The World
Power. Don't travel if the idea doesn't intoxicate you.

Organizations that coordinate teenage travel:

-The Center for Interim Programs and Time Out, both described in
detail in chapter 33.

-The major helpful organization is the Council on International
Educational Exchange, which publishes the *Teenager's Guide to Study, Travel,
and Adventure Abroad* described below and also runs various programs and
publishes other literature. If you plan to travel abroad, be sure to send for their
free publications list and their free *Student Travel Catalog*: CIEE, 205 East
42nd Street, New York, NY 10017. Among their publications are *Volunteer!*

The Comprehensive Guide to Voluntary Service in the U.S. and Abroad, and various brochures--on scholarship programs, work abroad, educational programs in the third world, workcamps, etc. They also have a scholarship fund which awards money for transportation costs of selected young people who write a project proposal. (Ask for their brochure on The International Student Identity Card Scholarship Fund.) The CIEE exists "...to develop, serve and support international educational exchange as a means to build understanding and peaceful cooperation between nations..."

-American Youth Hostels, Inc. Through AYH membership you can stay in worldwide hostels very cheaply, though you are supposed to be at least 15 to use hostels on your own. Also, they sponsor trips, especially bicycle trips. Write for their catalog, *World of Adventure*, and membership information. American Youth Hostels, P.O. Box 37613, Washington, DC 20013-7613.

-If you are at least 16, you can go on a seminar with the Center for Global Education. This organization runs travel programs completely unlike others; its goals include "introducing participants to the reality of poverty and injustice, examining the root causes of those conditions, and reflecting on the role and responsibility of North American citizens to enter into public debate on foreign policy concerns." Seminars go to Latin America, the Philippines, the Middle East, South Africa, and Hawaii. If you are younger than 16 and especially mature, you *may* be able to go on a seminar if a parent goes too. Center for Global Education, 731-21st Avenue South, Minneapolis, MN 55454, (612) 330-1159.

-Volunteers for Peace "International Workcamps." You must be 16 or over to participate in a workcamp, which could involve construction, restoration, agricultural or environmental work. You also work cooperatively with other members (10 to 20 from four or more countries) to prepare meals. The registration cost includes food and a place to sleep. Average age of participants is 22. Camps run year-round, but most are in the summer. You don't have to speak any particular language to go. In the words of VFP,

> Workcamps are an inexpensive way to travel and a very effective way people can promote international goodwill. For a U.S. [$100] registration fee, your readers can live and work in one or several of 33 foreign or American communities for two to three weeks at each site. Our focus is primarily all of Western and Eastern Europe. We offer additional programs in Ghana, Tunisia, Morocco, India and Turkey in the "third world." Most people volunteer with VFP by registering for a number of consecutive workcamps in the same or different countries and thereby spend several months abroad...Through tangible work projects, and the challenges of group living, you can create a more positive and hopeful vision for the world and our future. In short, workcamps are places where the power of love and friendship can transform prejudice.

For a free copy of their newsletter, call or write Volunteers for Peace, Tiffany Road, Belmont, Vermont 05730, (802) 259-2759. Or, send $10 for the complete workcamp directory, and register early to get the camps of your choice.

-To find out about more organizations that sponsor volunteer programs around the world, see Bill McMillon's *Volunteer Vacations* (Chicago Review Press, 1989). You'll find opportunities for world wide archaeology and science as well as chances to help handicapped people vacation in Britain, and a whole range of other choices. Some, in the way of the world, may be restricted by age.

Travel companions and other informal arrangements

-In the travel department, like any other department, *GWS* (*Growing Without Schooling* magazine) can be most helpful. You could advertise for unschooling travel partners; you could make arrangements to stay with people in the directory who list themselves as hosts; you could read the magazine and stumble across occasional opportunities. For instance, in *GWS #35*, sailboat owners wrote in seeking a crew member on a long sailboat cruise through the Caribbean islands, Panama, Seattle, and Hawaii.

-Use computer bulletin boards to find traveling companions.

-If you have pen pals, arrange to visit them. See "geography," in chapter 23.

-If you're up for it, you can always start traveling on your own, staying in hostels, and then link up with other travelers. If you're female, think carefully about the hazards of being female and alone. However, know that in many third world countries you will likely be verbally harassed but not physically harmed.

-If you're heading to South America, be sure to join the South American Explorers' Club. The club not only helps people find travel partners, but also produces an excellent magazine, answers detailed questions, and provides maps. Also, they keep a cozy office in Lima, Peru, where members can hang out and go through files on tropical butterflies or recommended local guides for remote areas. South American Explorers' Club, 2239 East Colfax Ave. #205, Denver, CO 80206.

Mixing travel and academics:

First of all, get it through your head that traveling is certainly enough education all by itself. You don't need to cram scholastic stuff in in order to make it meaningful. But a few deliberately added cerebral endeavors *could* intensify your pleasure. Some ideas:

-Go to museums, wherever you are. Art museums, cultural museums, science museums, history museums. Take your time and remember to forget school-field-trip mode.

-While you travel, read about the history, natural history, culture, politics, art, or anthropology of the country or state you're visiting. Buy a few books before you leave home, while you're in planning and organizing mode. But also be ready to find more specific good books once you're in a particular area.

-Keep a record of your trip in a journal. Consider sharing the journal or adapting it for letters or essays. While unschooler Britt Barker travelled, she described her adventures for her weekly newspaper column back home in Ohio (see chapters 21 and 39). These columns eventually became a book.

-Keep a naturalist's journal of the plants, animals, weather, and geology of the areas you visit. See chapter 21. Make collections of rocks, feathers, etc.--if it's legal to do so.

-Take photographs. Be an *artiste* and pay attention to composition and other beyond-snapshot concerns. Be an eye-opener and capture scenes that most people wouldn't think of recording. Or sketch people, buildings, etc. *Always ask for permission before photographing or sketching people.* Timbuktu is not a zoo.

-Bring a tape recorder, and conduct oral history interviews. See chapter 23, "history." Or, simply use your tape recorder to record the sounds of your trip--a train ride shared with goats and farmers, an evening in the town square with kids and music playing.

-If in a foreign country, speak the language of course. Avoid English and speakers thereof. See chapter 25 for support and access.

Travel books and other resources:

First, books that tell you about how to travel:

-*The Teenager's Guide to Study, Travel, and Adventure Abroad,* by the Council on International Educational Exchange (revised yearly). This book focuses on international *programs* that you can participate in. However, it also talks briefly about travelling independently, and it gives excellent details on the logistical headaches of traveling--flights, passports, international student i.d. cards, etc.

-*Work Your Way Around the World,* by Susan Griffith. Covers the regulations for working in various countries, and includes information on volunteer positions too.

-Mountain Travel, *The Adventurous Traveler's Guide: Treks, Outings, and Expeditions.* Actually, this is just the expensive catalog of a trekking company, but it gives detailed itineraries and photos so you could use it to plan your own treks and remote adventures--through Mongolia or around Mt. Kenya. We are talking hardcore inspiration.

-*Classic Walks of the World,* edited by Walt Unsworth, gives "directions" for walking hut to hut in Italy, circling Annapurna in Nepal, etc. Details and photos.

Guidebooks:

A guidebook tells detailed information about a particular country or area. There are several series; these are excellent:

-Lonely Planet Guidebooks help with adventurous off-the-beaten-track travel, though the off-the-beaten-tracks are getting rather well-beaten lately. No Europe books. Titles range from *Bushwalking in Australia* to *West Asia on a Shoestring*. (The "Shoestring Guides" help low budget travelers.) With a nice sort of hippie mentality, the Lonely Planet people view travel as a vehicle for positive social change and learning. At bookstores and libraries, or information and newsletter direct from Lonely Planet Publications, Embarcadero West, 112 Linden Street, Oakland, CA 94607.

-The *Insight* Guides have lots of photos and substantial cultural and historical background, as well as detailed practical advice.

-*South American Handbook*, John Brooks, et al, editors (revised annually). Fine print, fat, an *incredible* amount of information.

Other People's Trips

-Tania Aebi, *Maiden Voyage*. At 18, sailing instead of going to college, Aebi was the first American woman to sail the world alone.

-Peter Jenkins, *A Walk Across America*. Sort of a Jesus-hippie perspective. Jenkins did just what the title says.

-Peter Jenkins, *Across China*. Then he walked across China.

-William Least Heat Moon, *Blue Highways: A Journey into America*. Moon went in a car. The literary critics loved his book.

-National Geographic Society, *Secret Corners of the World*, describes actual trips to out of the way places such as northern Afghanistan and Tierra Del Fuego. Stunning photos in the usual National Geographic style.

-Brian M. Schwartz, *A World of Villages*. Six years through back roads of Africa and Asia, emphasizing encounters with village people. No photos, doesn't need them. The words say plenty.

-Eric Newby, editor, *A Book of Traveller's Tales*. There are lots of anthologies of travel writing, and many are good. This one seems to have the widest variety. For instance, in the section on Africa, you find the words of 15th-century Portuguese explorer Vasco da Gama as well as English writer Cecil Beaton describing his 1967 encounter with the Rolling Stones in Morocco.

-John Krich, *Music in every Room: Around the World in a Bad Mood*. Not as pessimistic as it sounds. Funny and articulate. Focuses on Asia.

Miscellaneous resources

-*Homeschooler's Travel Directory*, available for $3.75 from the National Homeschool Association (see Appendix B). Lists, describes, and gives ages of homeschoolers all over the country and in some other countries who welcome homeschooling visitors.

-American Map Corporation offers road maps and atlases for everywhere, as well as a wide variety of bilingual dictionaries, guidebooks, and other products. Free catalog: American Map Corporation, 46-35 54th Road, Maspeth, NY 11378, (718) 784-0055.

-*The National Audubon Society Expedition Institute Program Catalog.* Personally, I would not want to be in their high school program, which, like any form of compulsory school, reeks a bit too much of arbitrary authority. Also, I've heard, they get on people's cases when their attitudes aren't cheerful or cooperative enough--as if you could or should change an attitude because your teacher tells you to.

However, someday you may want to take part in their alternative college program, and in the meantime, take some inspiration from their work. This is what they do in "school:" drive a bus all over the country, visiting migrant farm workers in Florida, working on the Green Island restoration project in Texas, talking with Lakota Indians about their political activities, hiking in Yosemite, etc. For a descriptive catalog, contact The National Audubon Society Expedition Institute Program, P.O. Box 67, Mt. Vernon, ME, 04352, (207) 685-3111. If you have no intention of enrolling, send them a dollar to be fair.

-Write CIEE (address above) for their "Advisory List of International Educational Travel and Exchange Programs," $5, or find it in a library. You can always try a *summer* exchange program so you don't have to go to school.

-The 917.3 section of your library has an incredible variety of books with American trip ideas. You get all manner of books about American exploration--stories of people who've done it and advice on how to do it, general and specific--*Great American Mansions, National Park Guide, Discovering Historic America, Cavers, Caves, and Caving.* In fact, all through the 910's and 930's--990's you will find books about worldwide travel and geography.

Unschoolers at large:

In *GWS #52* Dick Gallien writes:

Just got a call from Linda Salwen of New York....Her homeschooled 14-year-old son found the money, which included $500 from the local paper, to fly with his bike to California where he has started biking *alone* back to New York to raise money for either peace or world hunger....Next year he is planning on biking in Russia.

Unschooler Anita Giesy, of Virginia, spent her "senior" year working in a grocery store to make money for the next stage of her education, a year-long trip driving around the country. In planning the trip, she writes

When all my friends were trying to decide what they were going to do after high school, I started doing the same thing. Among my friends, there seemed to be three choices going around: go to college, get a job, or join the military. I decided that the military wasn't for me. I thought about college, but decided that this wasn't the right time for me. Looking at where I wanted to go and what kind of career I might want, and thinking of all the people I've heard about who changed their jobs halfway through their lives to do what they always wanted to do, I decided that if I want to do something that takes a college degree, I can get one later.

So I looked at what I wanted to do with my life now and I decided the answer was travel. That is when I conceived my plan to see America....Different lifestyles, cultures, and ways of doing things interest me.

I have a good friend in Massachusetts who I met through *GWS*. In the summer of 1987 I went up to her farm for a week and became a part of her family. She taught me about taking care of her horses and I helped out, including cooking, and I went with her to various community activities. After that visit I went up two more times. Five days after I got my driver's license, I started on a two-week driving trip to Massachusetts and back. That's the kind of thing I'd like to do with other families across the country, to come in and live as a useful member of the family.*

After this letter appeared in *GWS*, about 40 families wrote to invite Anita to stay with them. Midway through her journey, she stayed with me. She told me about other unschooled families and teenagers she'd met--Michael, 19, now in college to become a Greenpeace-style lawyer, paying his way through by working in a camera shop and doing photography on the side...Matt, 16, a computer hacker and programmer who entertains fantasies of breaking into NASA. And she told me about the structure of her trip. She takes time every evening to write in her trip journal, with the idea of possibly writing a book about her experience. The pace of her journey has worked well--five or six days with each family gives enough time to get to know them. To other young travelers, she advises that the most important thing is to be adaptable, to consider it all an opportunity to learn. "As long as you don't have any particular expectations," she said, "Everything that happens is a bonus." Anita gave me an article she'd written for another homeschooling newsletter. Part of it says,

So I planned it all out and on September 8, 1990 I set off on my great journey. From Virginia, I went criss-crossing the south out to California, staying with homeschooling families all the way. I've been as far south as Florida and New Orleans. Before I'm done, I'll go as far north as Vancouver, Canada. The families have been wonderful and I've been able to live, work and play with them. The first family I stayed with, the father was a potter. The day after I

---

* *Growing Without Schooling*, #74

arrived was clay mixing day and I helped mix one ton of clay. I stayed with a midwife and got to go along on a birth. I stayed with a college art teacher and got to model for his art class. Every family is a new learning experience and a new friend. And I guess you could say, I've gone from a homeschooler to a worldschooler.

chapter 30

other school stuff turned unschool stuff

What about the rest? Health, typing, drivers' education, home economics, woodshop, and of course graduation? Information to help you with all of it is waiting patiently at the library and in your community. This chapter is just a quick road map. Like the rest of the book, it doesn't try to show *all* of the roads--an impossible task.

Health and sex education

If you have ovaries, look at *The New Our Bodies, Ourselves*, by The Boston Women's Health Book Collective (Simon and Schuster, 1984), an empowering, detailed, easy-to-understand book written by women for women. Although its information is not quite the latest available, it is nevertheless the best book to turn to for overall information on the female reproductive system, sexually transmitted diseases, pregnancy, childbirth, abortion, birth control, etc.

If you have testicles, I'm sorry no one has yet written a book like this for you. But...

Changing Bodies, Changing Lives, edited by Ruth Bell (Random, 1988) (also put together by the same group of people who did *Our Bodies...*), is a good sex ed book for all teenagers, full of straightforward quotes from teenagers as well as very sound no-nonsense medical information.

For a general understanding of the human body there are some terrific kids' books, like *The Magic School Bus: Inside the Human Body*, by Joana Cole, or *Blood and Guts*, by Linda Allison.

If you want to look at hundreds of detailed colored drawings of every human body part and system (skeleton, blood vessels, etc.), see *Gray's Anatomy* (various editions, a good cheap one is Crown's paperback, 1977). And Dover publishes an excellent *Human Anatomy Coloring Book*, by Margaret Matt and Joe Zeimian.

For more, the 616 section of your library has books on drugs, AIDS, skin care, alcoholism, and dozens of other health topics.

Drivers' Education

Try to take a course through public school. Many homeschoolers contact a local school and arrange to do this. Most school districts offer summer drivers' ed classes which should not be difficult for you to sign up for. You can also learn on your own (with an adult present) by getting a permit and then passing a test. Or, you could take private lessons.

Autoshop, Woodshop, etc.

I'm not lumping these together because I think they're not important; I'm lumping them together because they never fit in school in the first place. Far better to get out and apprentice yourself to a mechanic or a cabinetmaker. Also, there are heaps of books, and classes offered through various community programs. In *GWS* (*Growing Without Schooling* magazine) #38, a mother wrote:

> My son (12) and I are taking a small engines repair class two nights a week, through adult education. This is the same class taught to the junior high kids, but in the evening. We bring our own engines to repair. It is attended mainly by retired gentlemen, but this time my 72-year-old mother-in-law and my son and I add a little variety to the class. We've really learned a lot in spite of all the help we got from these very nice old men who couldn't believe we were capable. So far we have repaired three lawn-mowers and a go-cart. This includes grinding valves and installing new piston rings and gaskets...

John Boston wrote in *GWS* #42 about his son Sean, 15:

> When the high school would not let him take Auto Shop without signing up as a full-time student, he enrolled in a Regional Occupational Program auto course, even though he was below age 16. He now attends a weekly class session, with hands-on training on our old truck and car, and spends three mornings a week at a local auto parts house.

Business classes

Again, far better to learn by doing it. Start your own business or work for someone else's. Good books described in chapter 36. Plenty more in the library. Good courses on bookkeeping and such through community colleges.

Typing

Typing how-to books in any library--652.3--also various computer programs available. It doesn't matter whether you learn on a typewriter or a computer, except that since a computer is easier most people like it better. It *does* matter that you learn the standard finger positions, since you can never get fast with the two-finger hunt-as-you-go method. Yes, it's annoying and slow at first. So was learning to talk, and aren't you glad you didn't settle for a ten-word vocabulary?

Once you can type, learn to use a good word processor.

Home Economics

Home economics, in my ever-humble opinion, suffers unforgivably in school, which ought to keep its dirty hands off. Home economics is about as basic and important as anything gets; it deals with the fundamental workings of our lives: the way we spend our money, what we eat, how we heat our homes, what clothes we wear, the skills we have to help us take care of these things.

Your library has plenty of how-to books to help you learn all the skills of home economics, from bread baking to making your own leather jeans. For instruction, look not only to the community education people but also to the bulletin boards of fabric (etc.) shops and to 4-H groups.

Furthermore, two thirds of the counties in the United States have an official county home economist, paid by the government to help people solve homemaking and community problems. Call your county administration office (in the government pages of the phone book) to find out if you have an economist, and what services he or she offers.

Home economics really is *economics*, in the deepest sense. Which is to say, home economics is about the way your life, food, garbage, and consumption fit into the world. All those popular new books about thousands of ways you can help save the earth are really home economics books--when you decide to recycle your newspapers, buy locally grown fruits, and eat less beef, you are making home economics decisions that help the greater economy--the economy that is bigger than your home and far bigger than money.

Graduation

Graduation is one of the closest things our culture has to a rite of initiation. In public school, it's often impersonal and boring, but nevertheless an important ceremony. As an unschooler, don't neglect to find some way of celebrating your passage into adulthood. Of course, your options are endless and potentially far more meaningful than an ordinary "commencement exercise." You could create an elaborate ritual, or plant a tree, or you could simply let your family and friends take you out for dinner and make a toast in your honor.

In inventing your event, you might wish to research the rites of passages of other cultures, such as vision quests and potlatch feasts. Don't neglect to look into your own ethnic or religious heritage for ideas. You can find ideas in anthropological books; also see *The Book of the Vision Quest: Personal Transformation in the Wilderness*, by Steven Foster (Island Press, 1980).

Alternatively, you could ask a trusted adult or friend to put together a ceremony or ritual *for* you.

Of course, you could "graduate" at 16 or 19--there's no reason it has to happen at 18. You might plan the timing around a natural transition, such as completing some major project, or starting to apply to colleges, or choosing to move into your own apartment.

In *GWS #77*, Dawn Bowden describes her ceremony:

It was just my best friends and my relatives and neighbors. Manfred and Barbara [of The Learning Community, a private school that helps homeschoolers] stood up and talked, and presented me with a diploma, and they each gave me presents.

It was so nice, because it was even more recognition than you get when you graduate from a normal high school. They both said something to me; they didn't just say something in general to a class of 500.

By the way, there is probably no reason you can't go to a local senior prom, if you are a prom going type. But there is also no reason you can't organize your *own* elegant romantic dance--an unschoolers' ball.

chapter 31

college without high school

I imagine that Grant, Drew, and Reed Colfax are tired of being invoked as proof that you don't need grade school, middle school, or high school to get into Harvard. So I won't mention them, or Grant's post-Harvard Fulbright fellowship, or the list of other colleges such as Yale, Princeton, Amherst, and Haverford which also admitted them.

Yes, unschoolers can go to college.

We don't hear about them when they go to the University of Montana, and they no longer make a media splash when Harvard welcomes them. Lots of people saw the Colfaxes on TV, but few know of, for example, unschooled Elye Alexander who was accepted both to Harvard and Middlebury College for the fall of 1990. (His interests included writing poetry and studying insects and birds. Also, he was a state medalist and a black belt in Tae Kwon Do.)[*]

Unschooled teenagers themselves are unworried about their collegiate futures; the majority I heard from said they were college bound, with likely futures including librarian, veterinarian, gym teacher, dentist, ice skating instructor, airline pilot, lawyer, engineer, pediatrician, botanist, psychologist, and nurse midwife. They had done their research and knew that college was open to them. Unschooler Jeff Richardson told me that Oklahoma State University sends a recruiter specifically to interview homeschoolers.

In fact, I didn't hear from any teenagers who were planning definitely *not* to attend college. A lot said college was a possibility, but only if they were specifically interested in an area they felt they could learn best in college. They made an explicit point that they would not attend college to learn in a general sense, because they already knew how to do that no matter where they were. If they wanted to write, act, farm, or run a business, they knew they didn't need to necessarily go to college.

If you want to go to a very selective college or university, and the Harvard examples above aren't enough reassurance for you, I hope the next few pages will ease your mind.

I put the following question to the admissions directors of lots of those famous schools--the "small and superb" national liberal arts colleges and

---

* See *GWS* #75.

the "best" national universities listed in the October 1989 *US News and World Report*. (I also mailed the letter to two schools not listed there--The College of William and Mary and St. John's College.)

> ...If an applicant to (Barnard, etc.) had completed little or no formal schooling, would you still consider her? I am not talking here about the stereotypical teenage dropout, but rather a creative, enterprising individual who has done one or several interesting things with her time, such as started a business, played in a jazz band, traveled, written comic books, volunteered in a Sierra Club office, or raised boa constrictors. I also mean someone who has taken care to meet your admissions requirements other than attending school--studied English, math, foreign language, science, and social science on her own or with a tutor, and taken AP or achievement tests as well as SAT's demonstrating that she performs as well as your successful applicants...

Of the 27 admissions directors and officers who responded, none said no, although three were skeptical. Most said they would be completely open to such applicants, but that they didn't want their openness to be misinterpreted as welcoming people who had merely "done their own thing" for several years and not bothered to learn math or strong writing skills. Some were already accustomed to the idea and warmly positive. But all agreed, with varying levels of enthusiasm, that they'd willingly consider such an applicant.

Worst first. One rather pessimistic response came from Grinnell. The admissions officer pointed out that he was open to reviewing any candidate, but that the homeschoolers he had previously considered had been poorly prepared. On a similar note, John A. Blackburn, Dean of Admissions at the University of Virginia, said:

> ...We will consider students who have not completed a high school diploma in a traditional setting. The burden of proof that one has become educated in the areas we consider important is on the student, and it is a difficult task to accomplish. To be quite frank, the students who have been home schooled are often well versed and well read in a few areas, but there often are blank spots in their education. In the cases we have seen, the students usually are well prepared in terms of literary criticism, the use of a foreign language, the study of government or history, but in most cases, their background in science and math is quite lacking.

> As we both know, there are not many examples of self educated people in history; Benjamin Franklin is the person who jumps to my mind first, and in his case, I would say that it was because of his strong intellect, intelligence and perseverance that he was able to accomplish what he did. I doubt that the average person in this world could do the same. For that reason, I believe that public schools are essential, for the association with fellow students and teachers and the stimulation that comes from that experience is extremely

beneficial for most people. But, there certainly are cases in which home schooling can work and work well....

What shall we do with these responses?

First, avoid the mistakes that the previous unprepared applicants made. If you want to go to a selective college, know what it takes. Just being unschooled or homeschooled doesn't make you Harvard material. It's not that you might not be *good* enough, just that you may not have chosen to fulfill their kind of college requirements, or that you may not be ready or willing to submit to a structured learning environment. Also, even if you *are* Harvard (or Princeton, or Pomona...) material, you may not get in. At Harvard, only about one out of every eight applicants gets in, and most of the *applicants* (let alone *accepted* applicants) have quite the list of accomplishments, despite the time drain of school. It may be safe to say that being unschooled makes your application stand out, but it will *not* make up for what they consider a weak academic background.

Second, be ready to educate confused or hesitant admissions people. Tell them explicitly what you have been up to, and take the initiative to politely correct misconceptions. Benjamin Franklin, for instance, is only one of *many* self-taught successes in recent history. Furthermore, most people experienced with unschooling stress that they (or their children) are mentally way ahead of their peers not because of their "strong intellects," but because they have room to grow. Remember that the homeschooling movement is still in its infancy, so college people haven't yet had the chance to see much of what it's about.

And on behalf of these few nervous admissions directors, let me feed you some words of caution. Notice what kind of person I described in my letter. I did not merely say someone who didn't like school and quit. Having been to one of these colleges myself, I knew better.

Most admissions people were quite positive. Robert E. Gardner, Dean of Admissions and Financial Aid at Davidson College, said

> Like most institutions, we have rules for the masses, and we break rules when it seems just and proper to do so. It really depends more on the individual than anything else; we would consider, and probably admit, a strong person and refuse to consider a weak one....Let me add that if a student had been "schooled" at home by one or both parents, presumably in a way that resembled a formal education, although not in a typical "school setting," we would be very interested, indeed. Such individuals are often the yeast that leavens the bread and would be a welcome addition to any educational environment.

> ....Good kids are wherever you find them, and it is really too bad so many colleges look in the same places. Given the general state of many schools

today, it is not at all clear that all of the bright, highly qualified kids are found within the halls of accredited institutions. For an adolescent to pursue knowledge on his/her own, outside school, speaks very highly for his/her motivation, genuine interest in learning, and willingness to take risks in a good cause. Seems to make sense to me.

Larry Clendenin, Director of Admissions at St. John's College in Santa Fe, wrote

It just so happens that St. John's has admitted students such as you describe and will continue doing so given certain essential reassurances that they are capable of succeeding in our rigorous program.

Bates College Director of Admissions William C. Hiss says

Bates, like most colleges, has a set of printed admissions requirements that include a high school transcript and a number of recommendations....But the faculty gives to the Dean of Admission the right in any particular instance to forgive requirements, including that of a high school diploma if we are convinced the student has proved themselves ready for Bates in other ways.

The Senior Admissions Officer at an ivy league university responded

Candidates who have, as you describe, "taken care to meet your (our) admissions requirements other than attending school" and who are presenting compelling admissions cases, in their own right do very well in our admissions process and throughout their undergraduate careers at [our college].

....For the majority of admitted students there must be something else [beyond academics] that sets the student apart from the rest. It certainly can and often does fall within the nonacademic realm--a musician, an actor, an athlete, an artist, a community worker, an employee (to name only a few) who puts forth distinguishing credentials within the context of our applicant pool. None of these activities must be school sponsored at all; thus, I do not see the candidate who is not trained within the school setting to be placed at a disadvantage in our process.

The director of admissions at one of the nation's most prestigious technological institutes cautioned that he wouldn't want to mislead anyone, and didn't want the school's name mentioned directly. Nevertheless, he said,

The hypothetical candidate you have described in your letter...would be a viable candidate here...Whereas the prerequisites for candidacy expressed in our literature include a year of chemistry and physics at the high school level, and so on, the Admissions Committee will review the credentials of anyone proposing to study here. That is, a diploma is not a requirement and, given adequate basis, other formal requirements could be waived.

Some admissions officers were downright enthusiastic, like Thomas S. Anthony, Dean of Admissions at Colgate University:

I have little doubt that I would be delighted to admit a person [like that] described [in] your letter. Besides, I would like to see a large number of them in any class. In addition to the normal skills required for success in college, people like this would have a degree of initiative, independence, self knowledge and philosophical perspective that would make them desirable college students indeed. I suspect they would also have a degree of maturity not often encountered in typical college first-year students....

It may interest you to know that we have had students who bore some of these characteristics over the years. I recall particularly one young man who did attend high school, but he might as well not have been there. After leaving school, he spent three years working on a tug boat in the Gulf of Mexico where he wrote a book *a la' Pascal's Pensees* and went into business selling Mexican food with a member of the Dallas Cowboys. He enrolled at Colgate and after some initial struggles ended up doing very well.

Duke University's Senior Associate Director of Admissions, Harold M. Wingood, says

Our experience with students educated in this fashion has been very positive. In many cases, they are among the strongest students in our applicant pool. They are usually very well read with eclectic tastes and unusual sensibilities. Because they have been out of the academic mainstream they usually have a different perspective, and can be a positive influence in the classroom. While I was working at another institution, we enrolled a student who had been entirely educated at home. She managed a highly competitive academic setting with aplomb and graduated with high honors. We have admitted to Duke students who have been educated at home, but in the last four years, we have not been able to enroll any of those students.

...There is no inherent bias against students whose academic profile or educational environment do not conform to the norm in our evaluation system. We welcome diversity in every form. Our goal is to enroll those students who have the greatest potential to contribute positively to the university.

Mark F. Silver, Associate Director of Undergraduate Admissions at Washington University, writes

My first response to reading your letter was: "Where is this student? Does he or she exist? How can we get him or her to apply to Washington University?" I am being somewhat facetious; however, the short answer to your question is that we would most definitely be interested in hearing from a student such as you describe in your letter. We have never stood on standard, traditional preparation as the sole criterion for admission. As a matter of fact, a number of [such] students, many from home-schooled situations, have been evaluated and admitted....

There are many factors that indicate success in college for prospective students, and academic achievement in a traditional setting is but one. Leadership skills, ability to cope with new and different situations, the ability to synthesize information in creative ways, and a person's intense interest in a specific field all add to the likelihood of their success in college. I often encourage students with whom I speak during my recruiting activities to consider taking a year off between high school graduation and beginning college to enhance just those skills.

Boston University has recently begun initiating contact with unschoolers. *GWS* #79 prints a letter written by the undergraduate admissions office, part of which reads:

Boston University welcomes applications from homeschooled students. We believe students educated at home possess the passion for knowledge, the independence, and the self-reliance that enable them to excel in our intellectually challenging programs of study.

Two homeschooled students currently attend Boston University. One is a sophomore in the College of Liberal Arts, the other a freshman in the College of Engineering. Both students are doing very well. Their educational and personal transitions from homeschooling to the University are a proven success.

If you are a homeschooled student interested in attending college or simply concerned to know more about your options in higher education, we would be pleased to talk with you....

Will unschooling affect your ability to get into college? Probably not. If you were on the path to the Ivy League when you were in school, you can stay on it out of school. If you were planning to go to a state university or community college, those doors remain open also. What may change: you will likely become a more interesting, skilled, and knowledgeable person outside of school, one whom selective colleges will find more enticing. Or, your values may change, and you may decide to work toward something besides college. The worst danger is that your values change and you can't forgive yourself.

You may become immersed in new directions and loves which consume your time, but remain tied to the idea that you "should" prepare for college. If your interests and loves are compatible with college, you will have no trouble. But if they are irrelevant to college--say, you spend all your time carving cabinets but you believe you want to go to college and get a degree in chemistry--good luck. You have some serious stuff to solve.

College *now*

An interesting tangent of the unschooling/college issue is the possibility of beginning college at an early age. If you plan to go to college eventually, maybe you would like to go to college *now.* Many unschoolers find that while high school is indeed a waste of time, college skips the busywork and has time to get to the point and beyond it. In fact, this was a recurring pattern among the teenagers who described their lives to me. They frequently led very unstructured, unpressured lives without school, which gave them freedom in which to develop one or several intense interests. Thus, by the time they were 14, 15, 16, or 17, many wanted to be in a challenging, meaningful (not high school) academic environment.

Homeschooler John Waldowski of Maryland, for one, took the GED at 16 because "he felt it was a waste of time to continue with his high school curriculum if he was capable of doing college level work, especially since his goal is to become a clinical psychologist, which will require several years of school."*

Some unschoolers begin their college careers by taking one or two courses through universities or community colleges, while otherwise continuing their unstructured, teenage lives. Leonie Edwards, who began working as a dental assistant at age 14, also began earning college credits through correspondence courses which will apply toward her pre-dental coursework.

Others enroll as full time students in state universities. Mark Edwards enrolled as a freshman at California State University, Hayward, at the age of 16 in 1976, after being homeschooled since eighth grade. His younger brother Cliff entered Chabot college at 15, and his brother Matthew was a freshman at Holy Names College in Oakland at 14, simultaneously working as a pianist and organist.**

Homeschooler Amy Hovenden enrolled at Brigham Young University at 14 in 1984. A newspaper clipping from the *Provo Utah Herald* says,

> She feels no major qualms about starting college at an age younger than most.
> "I feel excited and a little nervous," she said. "But I don't see any problems
> with it. The other students are just people, too."....Amy had to undergo nearly
> three months of intense scrutiny by college entrance boards to determine her

---

*   See *GWS* #71.
** See *GWS* #8.

social readiness as well as her scholastic ability. She was thoroughly checked for emotional stability, and was found to be very "balanced." *

M. Coleman Miller, who had been homeschooled until he was ten, graduated at 15 from Hillsdale College in Michigan with degrees in math and physics. "One of the most sought-after graduate students in the nation," he was also "adept at basketball and karate." **

GWS (*Growing Without Schooling* magazine) #50 reports on homeschooler Alexandra Swann, who completed her bachelors' degree from BYU at age 14 in 1985 through independent study. She had started at age 12 and worked for about three hours each day. After graduating, she began work on her masters' degree.

If you want to be at college with people your own age, you could try this: get about two years of college under your belt while you still live at home and hang out with your old friends. Do this however you want--through a community college, correspondence courses, whatever. Then, when you are 18, go off to college along with your peers--but as a junior, rather than as a freshman.

How your mature, unschooled perspective will influence your college experience:

First of all, it will help you get into college. Maturity always does. But it will also help immeasurably once you're there. Colleges increasingly encourage freshmen to take a year off for work or travel after high school and before college, as Mark F. Silver points out above. They feel that such a break gives the student a much wiser perspective and greater self-knowledge, as well as a better understanding of why they want to go to school. Also, several admissions officers pointed out to me that their "non-traditional" students almost always do very well. These are older students who have been working or otherwise living normal adult lives for several or many years after high school, and then decide that they want a degree. In these cases, their high school background has almost no relevance to either getting admitted OR doing well once they're in.

By leaving school ahead of the crowd, especially if you take yourself out into the world, you give yourself a most valuable clear head, a feeling for truth and reality that just doesn't happen until you're away from the world of intellectual guidance for a while. Coming from that perspective, all your decisions will be wiser--including the major decisions whether to attend college, where to attend college, and what to study.

But do you really want to go to college?

---

* See *GWS* #37.

**See *GWS* #40.

I wish someone had asked me this question, in a serious tone of voice. At our house it was assumed that one goes to college, and Not Just Any College, but a Reputable and Highly Esteemed one. Had I noticed that I didn't have to go, maybe I wouldn't have. Maybe I would have, but with clearer expectations.

This is how Native Americans answered the question, after Maryland and Virginia colonists offered to educate six of them for free at Williamsburg College in 1774:

> We know that you highly esteem the kind of learning taught in those Colleges, and that the Maintenance of our young Men, while with you, would be very expensive to you. We are convinced, therefore, that you mean to do us Good by your Proposal; and we thank you heartily. But you, who are wise, must know that different Nations have different Conceptions of things; and you will therefore not take it amiss, if our Ideas of this kind of Education happen not to be the same with yours. We have had some Experience of it. Several of our young People were formerly brought up at the Colleges of the Northern Provinces; they were instructed in all your Sciences; but, when they came back to us, they were bad Runners, ignorant of every means of living in the woods, ...neither fit for Hunters, Warriors, nor Counsellors, they were totally good for *nothing*. We are, however, not the less oblig'd by your kind Offer, tho' we decline accepting it; and, to show our grateful Sense of it, if the Gentlemen of Virginia will send us a Dozen of their Sons, we will take Care of their Education, instruct them in all we know, and make Men of them.*

Why do you want to attend college? Will college give you what you want? Are there other ways to get what you want? There are certainly excellent things about college, and most uglinesses of high school have no twins in college. Nevertheless, if you go to college without ever thinking about the possibility of not going to college, it takes on many of the same negative qualities as "compulsory" junior high or high school. *Don't enroll just because it's expected of you.*

Before you decide, I highly recommend reading *The Question is College*, by Herbert Kohl (Random House, 1989). Though it is directed toward parents, it discusses teenagers' futures--collegiate or otherwise--with respect and originality. I wish my parents and I had read it nine years ago.

Here are a few other perspectives to encourage you to think about whether you want a degree. Thirteen-year-old Anne Brosnan wrote me,

> I really don't know if I'm going to college or not. I might win a scholarship somewhere. I might be busy. I might be canoeing in Canada, or selling hammocks in Hawaii. It all depends. My plans for the future are to maybe be a pianist (therefore I might go to a music college) or a writer/poet (therefore I

---

* from *Touch the Earth*, edited by T.C. McLuhan (Simon and Schuster, 1971), p. 57.

don't really need to go to college). I could do a lot of things. I'd also want to have a farm. That's easily accomplished without a college education, especially if you can teach yourself through college just like you did high school and grade school.

Also see Kim Kopel's thoughtful exploration of the college question in chapter 42.

In *Dove* (see chapter 29), Robin Graham tells about being invited to enroll at Stanford after he completes his voyage. He and his wife Patti stick it out for a semester, but then can't take anymore:

What surprised us most was how little we had in common with our peer group because most of them had grown up in a different world. I had had the advantage of experiences that most people don't gain in a lifetime and I'd seen horizons far beyond the local ball park and movie theater. It was sad to see how some students straight from high school were ready to believe anything and were so easily duped by cynical professors, especially by one Maoist who was passionate about his bloody revolution. The students who applauded this professor loudest were the ones who owned the Porsches and the Jags.

We made some good friends among the faculty and the students. Most of the students genuinely wanted to see society changed for the better. Like Patti and me, they wanted to expose hypocrisy and they despised the brainwashing attempts to persuade my generation that the dollar buys the only important things in life.

It certainly wasn't Stanford's fault that Patti and I couldn't fit into the campus life. It's a great school and we knew how lucky we were to be there. But right from the start we had a feeling of claustrophobia. The walls of the classroom boxed me in so that I could hardly breathe. I began to fear that even if I saw through my years at the university I would be sucked into a life style which Patti and I were determined to avoid--the nine-to-five routine, membership in the country club and that sort of thing. That first semester at Stanford seemed as long as two years at sea.*

Anne Herbert writes in her "The Rising Sun Neighborhood Newsletter" in *The Next Whole Earth Catalog*:

I've noticed that when I meet people my own age who seem to have had a truly incredible number of adventures, they turn out to have not gone to college, so instead of doing one thing for four years they started doing two or three things a year as soon as they left high school.

---

* Robin Graham, *Dove*, pp. 194-195.

Realize that while a college degree definitely makes many *jobs* easier to get, unschooling all the way through your life probably makes it easier for you to make a living out of the things you love. Almost anything can become an independent business, whether in environmental consultation or in teaching and performing with steel drums. If you open up your head you can open up your life. Rather than go to college and graduate school to become a marine biologist, for instance, you could go straight to the coast of British Columbia at the age of 18, begin conducting your own research on salmon spawning (investing far less money than you would in college), and by the time you were 22 or 23, you'd probably look far more appealing than laboratory rat-people to the powers who hire marine biologists. Of course, by that time you might have come up with ways of making your research pay you without having an employer. You might even be hiring your own laboratory rat-people.

A degree-crazed society like ours, in fact, is a big cop-out. It discourages true expertise. People are unlikely to ask, "What makes him a knowledgeable person? What is he good at? How is he good at it?" Instead, they ask, "What's his degree? Where did he get it?" That's all they think they need to know. As an unschooled and/or uncolleged person, you will frequently butt up against the assumption that you know nothing. I figure you can nobly accept these situations as opportunities to clarify muddy minds. And after enough of you refuse to play the degree-crazed game, the rules will change.

Instead of college, you could just get on with life--or you could design your own course of study, unschooling your way through college. Kendall Hailey did just that, and wrote a book called *The Day I Became An Autodidact* (Dell, 1989). If you want to unschool on a high academic level, I strongly recommend using *The Independent Scholar's Handbook*, by Ronald Gross (Addison-Wesley, 1982), a thorough guide to conducting intellectual projects without being a student, professor, or research assistant.

If you are interested in the humanities, the most intense college learning usually happens when you write papers. You might want to take a course or two to get a feel for writing papers, and then keep it up on your own, using scholarly journals as a gauge of your own work, sending your papers to scholars you admire or to journals, for possible publication. Also, you could ask a professor for guidance in designing a college substitute program.

Of course, saying yes to college is perfectly fine too, as long as you *think* about it first. Anna-Lisa Cox, whose activities are described in chapter 33, wrote in *GWS #74*,

The last time I wrote I was still undecided about going to college. I knew it wasn't my only alternative. I could keep on giving the historic fashion shows I've been giving, or take an internship in a museum leading to a job. But in the end I decided that college would give me a chance to do more exploring, and I knew that's what I wanted to do. So I went through the rigors of college applications and got accepted at the college of my choice. An interesting note: I found that my homeschooling, far from being a hindrance, was an asset. With colleges looking at clone high school students, a homeschooler really stands out and gets noticed. It is true that applying as a homeschooler takes extra work, and just being a homeschooler doesn't mean you'll get into Harvard, but it can give you a valuable edge.

Finally, just as there are lists of people who accomplish all manner of wonders without going to school, there are even longer lists of people who succeed spectacularly without college. As you'd expect, many of them are artists and writers, but they also include scientists such as Jane Goodall, who had no university degree, nor any formal training in ethology, when she began in her work with chimpanzees in Tanzania. (After she'd been at it for five years, however, she wrote a thesis and Cambridge awarded her a doctorate.) Steve Jobs and Stephen Wozniak, founders of Apple Computers, dropped out of college. Physicist/architect/generalist extraordinaire Buckminster Fuller was expelled from Harvard. A few other people on the uncolleged list include Ernest Hemingway, Paul Gauguin, Amelia Earhart, Eleanor Roosevelt, Harry S. Truman, Lewis Mumford, Ralph Lauren, Robert Frost, Walt Disney, Charles Schultz, and Roger Tory Peterson.[*]

Some collegiate options

Even if you are certain you want a degree, you need not earn it in the standard expensive age-18-to- 22 method. Here are a few alternative paths you might consider:

-Investigate the tricky underground ways to get a degree with far less time and money than most colleges require. You can replace from one to four years of normal college with independent study--correspondence courses, colleges that give credit for life experience, and passing tests that earn you credits. If you want to look into these alleyways, you definitely need *Bear's Guide to Non-Traditional College Degrees*, by John Bear (Ten Speed Press), which is updated annually and probably waits this very moment in the reference section of your library. *GWS* #18 tells about Emil Berendt, a 16-year-old who finished his B.S. before he graduated from high school, by studying at home and passing exams.

-If you have no idea where you want your life to go, consider putting college on hold. In the meantime, you could travel, work, continue to learn on your own. You might want to use the help of Cornelius Bull, whose Center for Interim Programs is described in chapter 33.

-Make a point of knowing about all kinds of colleges. Coming from your unschooling perspective, you may want to look into "alternative" schools such as Evergreen, Prescott, Antioch, St John's, Naropa, Deep Springs, or The Audubon Society Expedition Institute. (None of these, by the way, have much in common with each other.) Also, look into specialized colleges like

---

[*] Sources: *Current Biography, 1979 Book of Lists*, GWS #17, GWS #59.

technological institutes (Caltech, Harvey Mudd, MIT), art schools (San Francisco Art Institute), music schools (Juilliard, Oberlin), universities that focus on agricultural programs (Colorado State University), unique opportunities like the outstanding international folk music and dance group at Dusquesne University in Pittsburgh.

In choosing the type of college you attend, think about this statement, written by the dean of admissions of a very competitive liberal arts college:

We have admitted two [unschooled] students, and we may admit another this year. ...We are a rather traditional college of Liberal Arts and Science with an enrollment of 2,000, all undergraduate and all in residence. I mention this because I do not believe we represent a good choice for these kids. We have found that they are accustomed to doing what they want to do and only what they want to do. They have not had to make many of the daily adjustments that kids in public schools have been forced to make, so they have no experience in adjusting to rules, regulations and procedures with which they are not sympathetic. One of these students is leaving to try out a larger university and we will be surprised if she returns. The second student seems to be having similar problems but the jury is still out as to whether he will stay or leave. We are admitting another such student for next September and he appears to be so bright that they are hardly able to measure him! We do not yet know if he will attend, but we suspect that he will not.

So the bottom line here is that while we are very high on these kids, we tend to doubt that we are a good choice for them.

Getting in, part 1: State Universities and Community Colleges

Admission to most state universities and community colleges is a fairly cut and dried process. You will probably have to take the GED and pass it. If that worries you, coach yourself with Barron's *How to Prepare for the GED*--your library should have the latest edition.

Each state has a minimum age requirement for the GED, often 18. Homeschoolers are working to abolish this minimum age requirement, but in the meantime you can often get special permission from a schoolboard to take it sooner. Ask local homeschoolers whether they know of anyone who has been able to take it at an early age.

GWS #27 offers this story:

Last February, our daughter (16) became impatient at having to wait till she was 18 to take her GED test and start her course at the Technical Institute (she has decided she wants to be an astronaut!) So she talked me into appealing to the school superintendent for permission to take the GED before reaching the required age....As soon as he understood our request he said he would be happy to oblige, and that was that.

For information on taking the GED in your area, contact a library, high school, or community college. You can also write for general information directly to General Educational Development, GED Testing Service of the American Council on Education, One Dupont Circle, Washington, DC 20036.

You may not even need to take the GED. Most big universities do have some kind of clause in their admissions requirements that leaves room for admitting students with "special circumstances." Of course, if an epidemic of unschooling breaks out (Go team!), your circumstances will no longer be special. I figure having to take the GED is painless compared to having to take six years' worth of school, including a few too many unimaginative exams.

If there's a specific university you hope to attend, write their admissions department and ask whether they have any specific guidelines for homeschoolers.

Getting in, part 2: How to prepare for admission into and success in a traditional liberal arts college

Traditional colleges want their incoming freshmen to have a broad, thorough education. Normally, they measure this education mainly by looking at high school transcripts. Their verdict also depends heavily on recommendations from teachers or other adults, on an application essay, on the strength of one's "extracurricular" interests and achievements, on standardized test scores, and sometimes on an interview.

Do your best to see the admissions process through the eyes of admissions officers. When an admissions officer looks at your unschoolish application, her job will instantly grow both more interesting and more confusing. Without the standard transcript of courses and grades, she will need assurance of some other variety that you are a strong candidate. The more clearly you show what you know, what you can do, and how you've spent your time, the sweeter her job will be. As Carleton Dean of Admission Paul Thiboutot points out, he prefers students with traditional backgrounds because "The simple matter is that this background gives us the easiest means for evaluating readiness to pursue college study." Admissions people have incredible paperwork, and if tons of you descend on them all at once, it will be difficult for them to be happy about it. Don't be their logistical nightmare.

Nevertheless, colleges are increasingly prepared to deal with nonstandard applications. The admissions director at Washington University says

Our only concern in evaluating such individuals has been: Are they prepared to meet the academic demands of Washington University? So, assuming your hypothetical person to exist, we would rely on standardized testing, AP or

Achievement tests to evaluate their academic preparation. On those rare occasions that students approaching your description have applied to us, we have often requested a formal interview on campus.

Of course, despite the headaches you will cause, you can also delight admissions people. Set yourself apart from the masses who are only applying to college because it's the next step in a routine they've never thought about. Make the people who read your application feel honored that you *want* to be at their institution--even though you know from experience that you could choose to learn independently instead.

And make their fears go away. Unless they have had some positive experience in the unschooling department, admissions people may be full of all the worst stereotypes about homeschoolers. They may suspect you of not having any social skills, or of never having heard of Darwin, or of not knowing much math.

More reasonably, they may be concerned that you will have a difficult time adjusting to a structured learning environment. Delsie Z. Phillips, Director of Admissions at Haverford, speaks for many when she says,

> The academic program at Haverford is structured, and the faculty give grades. There are not other options. It would be important to us to know that the student understands this and is truly seeking the kind of educational framework we provide.

If you don't want to be in college, you *will* have a difficult time making peace with structure. Or an impossible time. Don't be mistaken as to why these colleges exist. Don't feel that they owe you places in their freshman classes. They don't. Don't think they should accept you because you're an interesting person and then let you do whatever you feel like doing. By enrolling, you are agreeing to play their game. Their game is a good one. But there are other good games.

There are books devoted to each of the following aspects of college admissions. A good all around guide is *Getting In! The First Comprehensive Step-by-Step Guide to Acceptance at the College of Your Choice,* by Paulo De Oliveira and Steve Cohen (Workman Publishing, 1983). My purpose here is only to point out the *difference* unschooling will make in each of these areas.

Testing

The more confused an admissions committee feels about your day to day academic preparation, the more it will be forced to rely on standardized test scores to decide how smart you are and what you know. Your test scores will definitely be more important than the average school-student's. One dean of admissions writes about unschoolers' tests, "the stronger the better, and the more the merrier." John Blackburn, Dean of Admissions at the University of Virginia, recommends the following:

My advice to [unschooled] students is to take as many different achievement tests as they can. The normal number is to take three in one sitting, but I would suggest that the student take English Composition, Math (preferably Math Level II), a foreign language, American History, at least one of the sciences and literature. AP tests would be helpful, but since most students take them in the spring before they enroll in college, the scores are not usually available for evaluation. If a student can take a sizeable number of AP tests in the spring sixteen months prior to matriculation, then the admissions office would have the AP scores available for the normal period of evaluation.

You might as well establish a friendly relationship with tests at your earliest convenience, by taking them more than once. Consult books on SAT's, ACT's, and Achievements at any library--you will find sample questions as well as basic information about the tests. There are many books on studying for these tests. One with a creative, effective approach is *Cracking the System*, by Adam Robinson and John Katzman (Villard Books, 1986), which helps you to understand the brains of the people who write these tests.

Some people swear that test preparation courses improve your scores. I wouldn't bother, but then I've always thought standardized tests are fun. It probably boils down to whether they scare you or not. If they do, by all means take all the courses and practice tests you desire.

If you want to be automatically considered in the National Merit Scholarship program, be sure to take the PSAT in October of your "Junior" year.

In any case, be certain you register for the tests you need in plenty of time--by April of your "Junior" year for the SAT, May for the ACT. You can get registration forms through any local high school.

References
You will need at least two letters from adults who know you and believe in you. If you were in school, these people would probably be teachers. If you're not, they won't be. Instead, employers or mentors do nicely. Probably, no one in your family will qualify, although many colleges will *also* want to hear from your parents regarding their role in your education. (If your parents have mainly supported you in your own decisions and activities, they shouldn't lie and say they've been teaching you at home. That only preserves the dangerous misconception that people can't teach themselves.) Harvard-Radcliffe sometimes asks for a detailed autobiography in lieu of teacher recommendations.

Interview
Some colleges don't require interviews for everyone, but they may require an interview of you. Again, you'll have to give them a full, convincing picture of yourself and your strengths to compensate for your missing transcript. Also,

you may have to get it out of their heads that people who don't go to school are social misfits. Don't cry for your mother, even as a joke.

Interviews don't necessarily have to take place on campus. Colleges who want students from all over the country send admissions officers to travel all over the country and recruit students. During this time, they also conduct interviews. You can ask any local high school counselor for a schedule of college recruiters. Or, if you know which colleges you want to apply to, you could write them directly and ask about their recruitment schedules.

The application essay

will not be much different for you than for schooled people, except that it will count more. Since you can't show them A's in English, they will want to see for themselves how well you write. Unless you spend your unschooled life writing articulate things that get published, that is. Be sure to write about something that matters.

Outside interests

Colleges want to know what you do with your time besides textbook academics. (Part of the reason for this is they consider their student body part of their curriculum. They figure if you're an interesting bunch, you'll learn neato things from each other and more people will want to go to school there.) If they see that you know how to love something and chase it and do it and be it, great. Harvard is especially explicit about wanting students who not only fulfill standard academic requirements, but also demonstrate expertise in an additional area of almost any kind. This is your showcase, since unschooling is all about doing what you love.

In lieu of the high school transcript: college coursework

After hearing from both admissions officers and unschooled teenagers, I strongly advise: before you apply to a selective college, take at least one course through a local university or community college. This way, you both prove that you can handle college-level, structured coursework *and* find out cheaply whether you *like* doing it. Certainly, success in a college class shows your readiness for college better than success in high school can. You may be able to do this through a high school enrichment program (homeschoolers can have access to many "school" programs), or you may have to first get your GED and then enroll. Phone them up, explain yourself politely ("I would like to take your course in Beginning Japanese"), and ask how to go about it. You don't *have* to do this, of course, but it will reassure nervous admissions officers tremendously. Bowdoin Director of Admissions, William R. Mason, commented:

> We have two entering freshmen this year...who were completely home schooled. Each of them did take local college courses and the support from

teachers was exceptional enough to convince us that both these students possess superior academic ability.

If your application is especially scanty, a selective college may even *ask* you to start by enrolling elsewhere full time. For instance, Delsie Phillips of Haverford says, "In some cases we have asked students who lack formal education and testing to enroll in an open admission college to prove their ability to excel in a structured situation. When they have presented appropriate grades, we admit them."

Your daily bread

The main part of getting ready for college is becoming a well read glorious generalist with knowledge of literature, history, political structures, math, science, and foreign language. (This doesn't mean you need to get it from textbooks or lectures.) The more selective the college, the more of all this you need. Also, admissions people expect that you have strong reading, writing, and math reasoning skills, and some degree of comfort with scientific process and laboratory equipment.

You will most likely end up writing, in detail, exactly how you have approached your academic studies. Therefore, you need to keep careful records with dates. List the books you read and the textbooks you use, the lectures you attend, the specialists or professors with whom you converse, the letters you write to senators or scientists, the trips you take, the experiments you conduct. Hold onto any writing you do.

To be a strong candidate, you'll probably need to be reading, writing, conducting scientific experiments, and working math problems for two to four hours, five days a week, eight months of the year. If I'm sounding grim and you're grossing out, just remember that to do college prep the school way, you'd spend at least six hours daily in school, plus homework, and not learn as much. More importantly, remember that it should be fun, and needn't orbit around textbooks or worksheets. If you hate it no matter how you approach it, put your life on a different path and get happy.

Actually, this is a key to your happy future. If you enjoy *preparing* for whatever kind of college you want to attend, you'll probably enjoy college itself and the kind of life it pushes you towards. On the other hand, if you have to force yourself to work trigonometry problems and read heavy books, you can also expect major frustration during college. Don't sacrifice your present for your future, because your present mirrors your future. All times, say the mystics and the physicists, are now.

Therefore: throughout your years of college preparation, stay in close touch with yourself. Don't get knocked off balance, don't forget who you are, and don't get frenzied or unhappy. Michael Phillips, in *The Seven Laws of Money*, talks about wanting to be rich: "Say you've got the $100,000 that you desired. You are now the process that it took you to get there. If you had to sell dope, you're a dope dealer with $100,000."

Translate that right into the world of college preparation. You want to get into Dartmouth. You do get into Dartmouth. You are now the process that it took you to get there. You could be a narrow, harried geek with cramped muscles, or you could be a perceptive, questing, lively human being. Test your motives every few months. If the U.S. of North America sent you off to war on your 18th birthday and all the colleges shut down before you came back--*if* you came back--would you bitterly regret all that time you'd "wasted" studying for it? Or would you rejoice over what you'd already learned? As they say, life is not a destination but a journey.

Part Four

touching the world:
finding good work

chapter 32

beyond fast food

Of course, working in the world is nowhere near as educational as a good career unit in social studies complete with worksheets. Nevertheless, we'll do our best in the next few chapters.

Academically equipping yourself, as described in Part Three, won't take all of your time unless you want to go *far* beyond your schooled peers. Part Four exists because most people, including teenagers, crave the chance to do real work--something that makes a difference in the world--instead of sitting and taking notes all day. Some work brings money, some doesn't. I talk about the kind that doesn't as much as the kind that does.

Chapters 33 through 38 tell you about specific organizations and resources for doing different kinds of work. Chapter 29 also lists a few helpful resources in case you want to work while you're traveling. This chapter is more general. It asks you to think about work as something that matters--not just a way to sell your time, body, and soul in return for cash. John Holt came up with a healthy definition in *Teach Your Own*: "By 'work' I ...mean...what people used to call a 'vocation' or 'calling'--something which seemed so worth doing for its own sake that they would gladly choose to do it even if they didn't need money and the work didn't pay."

Now versus later

When I was a teenager I hated the nonsense question adults asked: "And what do you want to do with your life?" Like the other standard, "Do you like school," it made no sense to me. It referred to some abstract future instead of my present. I always had answers, but my heart wasn't in them. At the time, all I really knew was that I had to go to school, supposedly so that I could later apply my school knowledge to whatever I did. Unfortunately, it didn't occur to me that I could also have begun doing the things that I dreamed about doing "someday."

In your unschooled life, the question of good work is a question about your here and now, not just a speculation about your future. In ten years, you may change your mind completely about everything, including what work you want. If that happens, you can get the skills and knowledge you need then.

Your task now is to use your time beautifully *now*. Your life isn't something that's going to start happening when you're twenty-one. It's happening today.

In fact, one of the great things about unschooling is that it makes healthy future work much more likely. It allows your present to blend with your future, with no forced split. Many unschooled teenagers wrote me with a clear sense of this connection between their present activity and their future work. Michael and Christin Severini, for instance: At fifteen, Michael takes flying lessons. He envisions later work as an airline pilot. Christin, thirteen, now dances with a ballet company and belongs to PETA, and she says, "My future plans are to become a professional dancer and to help animals in some way." The Severinis' plans ring with truth because their everyday lives are consistent with their future fantasies.

How to be psyched for Monday

Do work you love. You *can* do work you love.

This topic needs a couple hundred pages to itself. Fortunately, an entertaining, wise, and extremely knowledgeable woman named Barbara Sher has taken care of that, by writing a book called *Wishcraft* (Viking, 1979). Read it, and you will see clearly what it is you most dream of doing, and furthermore, how to make it happen. Probably, without the clarity her book brought to my life, this book wouldn't be happening, I wouldn't be teaching and performing Middle Eastern dance, and I might even still be teaching *school*. She'll get you out of ruts, pronto.

But I shall also add a few comments on the relationship between unschooling, money, and good work.

On poverty: no matter who you are and how much money you don't have, if you are an unschooler you can do work (now and all your life) that both fulfills your spirit and also pays your way.

One huge reason many "working class" people have so little chance to get out of the "working class" is lack of time. Generally, creative, fun work pays better wages than mindless minimum wage or "unskilled" stuff. However, before you can make a living by making earrings, coordinating advertising for the community performing arts center, or producing seminars on ecological restoration, you need time to develop expertise. Once many "working class" people are out of high school, their parents can't afford to support them through college or any other kind of transition. They have to scuttle right from high school into full time unskilled jobs, with no time to gradually become involved (without pay) in something they really *love*.

By unschooling, however, many people from poor families could break out of poverty. Instead of squandering their teenage years in school drudgery, they could invest that time in learning skills that will later provide interesting work, or in gradually building up a business or getting started in a field through volunteer experience. While they are teenagers, they can *afford* to volunteer or start a slow-growing business, even if they also have to bag groceries twenty hours a week at Spaceway.

In this regard, whether you are poor or not, enjoy your distinct advantage over adults. Unless your parents are the vindictive kind who say "go to school or get a job and pay your way," you aren't yet pressured to be financially independent. (If your parents do hint in that direction, remind them that the whole idea of education, in school or elsewhere, depends on children not being forced to earn money. You need time to explore, which is why you quit school in the first place.) In other words, part of your education can be doing terrific work even if it doesn't pay for your meals. Adults who have to buy the tofu don't have that luxury.

Of course, you might start a silkscreening business at 15 which succeeds spectacularly. Or you might begin volunteer work which directly leads to happy employment a year from now. But you can also do work that might *never* bring dollar bills--spending Tuesday mornings at a battered women's shelter, organizing a talent show, writing letters to senators, planting trees or a garden, teaching your mother how to use a computer.

Doing it

The possibilities, of course, are exhilaratingly endless, but to help you begin thinking I've grouped many of them into categories in the following chapters: apprenticeships, internships, volunteering, jobs, businesses, farm-related work, and activism.

There are several good books on each of these topics. One that covers many types of teenage work is Ruth Lembeck's *Teenage Jobs* (David McKay Co., 1971). Old but not outdated, it gives hundreds of good ideas *and* real-life examples.

Remember: You don't have to model your working pattern after typical adult working patterns. You can combine several jobs or activities. You needn't do anything for 40 hours a week. You can stir up a mix instead. The next chapters are crammed with stories, but here are just a few that help to show the variety that's possible in one life:

Lavonne Bennett writes in *GWS* (*Growing Without Schooling* magazine) #18 about her son, a "mechanical and electronics genius" described as a "stupid dummy" by a high school teacher:

We took him out of high school in the middle of his junior year...He's 17 now and has managed two stores for an electronics-product firm, parlayed a $150 clunker car up to a classic sports car, has bought equipment for his recording studio, has been a mentor for an eight-year-old boy, helping him to organize model-train layouts, and has given guitar lessons.

Ann Martin of England tells about her son, Nicholas, 14, in *GWS* #21:

He spends one afternoon [each week] in a shoe workshop where he helps out in exchange for tuition and will bring home his own hand-made shoes next week! He has been on a residential sports course, goes on trips with a local theater company, and he helps in a shop owned by a friend of mine, who is teaching him the basic skills of running a business.

Kandy Light wrote about her children in *GWS #47*,

Dawn (16) is in New York right now helping some friends while they have their third baby. They live and work at a health reconditioning center. Dawn has been helping in their various programs, learning massage, hydrotherapy, etc. She has also worked in their vegetarian restaurants. They want her to come live and work there....She also met some doctors while there, who have invited her to come work and learn with them at their health center in the South. Last year she was a full-time babysitter for a local school dean. The dean recently moved and called this week to ask if Dawn could come to live with them and teach *their* children at home (in California).

When here at home she is hired as a secretary for a local businessman, besides apprenticing with the Barkers at their Country School [see chapter 37]...She has also been asked to learn lay midwifery, train as a colporteur, gardener, etc. ...

Our 15-year-old twin boys, Tim and Dave, are apprenticing with an Amish man learning engine repair. They are learning first-hand how to repair tractors, lawn mowers, chain saws, etc. A neighbor has bartered two calves with them in exchange for them helping him do hay, plant corn, and occasionally milk his cows. Every day they work for another neighbor for four hours, landscaping his picture-perfect lawns and gardens and doing maintenance work. When our local principal moved, he hired them....They've earned $75 a day helping to move people. They, too, are apprenticing with the Barkers in Millersburg.

So welcome.

This world needs your contribution. We are starved for people who work with not just their hands and their minds, but also with their hearts.

chapter 33

apprenticeships and internships

If you know what kind of work you want to do, move toward it in the most direct way possible. If you want someday to build boats, go where people are building boats, find out as much as you can. When you've learned all they know, or will tell you, move on. Before long, even in the highly technical field of yacht design, you may find you know as much as anyone, enough to do whatever you want to do.
--John Holt, *Teach Your Own*

A great many of the people who are doing serious work in the world (as opposed to just making money) are very overworked, and short of help. If a person, young or not so young, came to them and said, "I believe in the work you are doing and want to help you do it in any and every way I can, will do any kind of work you ask me to do or that I can find to do, for very little pay or even none at all," I suspect that many or most of them would say, "Sure, come right ahead." Working with them, the newcomer would gradually learn more and more about what they were doing, would find or be given more interesting and important things to do, might before long become so valuable that they would find a way to pay her/him. In any case, s/he would learn far more from working with them and being around them than s/he could have learned in any school or college.

--John Holt, *GWS* (*Growing Without Schooling* magazine) #6

The situations Holt describes above are usually called apprenticeships or internships. They can take place in any field, from chemistry research to interior decorating. This chapter's jobs are to 1) tell about organizations that offer positions, and other organizations that can set them up for you, 2) tell you how to design and set them up on your own, and 3) give you a few examples of unschoolers' apprenticeships and internships.

But first, time out for definitions:

Both apprenticeships and internships are based on the concept of mutual benefit. The apprentice or intern gives labor in exchange for the chance to learn about a certain kind of work. The labor itself may seem repetitive or boring to someone experienced in the field, but should be interesting and educational for a newcomer. By the same token, the "master" or supervisor should not have to take a lot of time to stop and explain how to do things, because the apprentice will learn mainly by watching and doing. Sometimes the apprentice or intern is also paid in money, sometimes not.

What's the difference between internships and apprenticeships? Internships often involve office or administrative work, while apprenticeships usually focus on learning specific skills in a craft or trade. But many people use the terms interchangeably.

Organizations that offer apprenticeships or internships

There's nothing wrong with trying to get one of these already-established positions. Do keep in mind: 1) some of them may be somewhat rigid, although others will be flexible enough that you can adapt them to fit your particular interests. 2) They are all over the country and the world. Are you ready to pack up and move? 3) Some will be difficult to get, as you will compete with other people, most older than you. Many internships will be officially off-limits until you are 18 or so.

Hundreds of organizations offer internships. I will mention one I find especially tempting, and then tell you where to find out about others.

The New Alchemy Institute is a highly-acclaimed organization which carries out research on food, energy, water and waste treatment systems in Cape Cod, Massachusetts. Its aims include finding and sharing "knowledge that empowers individuals, recognizes and uses traditional knowledge, [and] minimizes reliance on expensive outside inputs." The site itself is a 12-acre farm--not a grey laboratory--and includes a compost greenhouse, a solar greenhouse, various theme gardens (herbs, native plants, wildlife-attracting species, etc.), a "pillow dome" greenhouse including ponds for raising fish and storing heat, research fields of cover crops, organic market gardens, a children's garden, and an auditorium full of demonstrations on insulation, low flow toilets, etc.

The Institute offers internships in market and community gardening, maintenance, construction, research, and other areas. Internships last two to six months and require twenty hours of work per week. Each intern works with a staff member on a specific project, but can also become involved in other aspects of the Institute. The Institute cannot pay interns, although it will offer a monthly stipend when it can afford to. It says, "The internship arrangement is viewed as an exchange of the intern's skills and energy for access to the institute's knowledge and resources." Interns must provide their own room and board, but the institute can help you find a place to live, and there are rooms available in a nearby house called "The Alchemage."

Because the New Alchemy Institute is so highly respected and quite well known, you may face some difficult competition for the internships. However, there are many other less formalized volunteer opportunities there; they "value help with gardening, research and other tasks. Together, staff, interns and volunteers work towards the common goal of building an ecological future." For more information, write the Intern Program, New Alchemy Institute, 237 Hatchville Road, East Falmouth, MA 02536.

Internships: on-the-job training opportunities for college students and adults (Writer's Digest Books, updated annually), describes thousands of other organizations' internships. It is divided into sections--Communications, Creative Arts, Human Services, International Opportunities, Public Affairs, Science and Industry. Some of the positions described offer stipends. Many provide room and board, free classes, college credit, and help with finding employment after you finish the internship. The majority say that their established internship positions are open only to college students. However, many are open to high school and even junior high age people. Furthermore, almost all the organizations say they are open to "independent" inquiries. In other words, they will consider ignoring normal requirements, possibly creating special positions for people who wouldn't fit into their usual internships.

Some of the positions *not* restricted by age or college status include working on costume and scene construction with a ballet company, conducting a research project for the Peace Corps, doing camera work or lighting for TV stations, writing and conducting surveys for a newspaper, and doing office work for a publisher.

If you use this book or a similar one, remember that the less famous organizations will be easier to break into. A small town newspaper, for instance, won't have as many applicants as The Washington Post.

Your library may also have more specialized internship guides, like Ronald W. Fry's *Internships: Newspaper, Magazine, and Book Publishing.*

Organizations that help to arrange apprenticeships and internships:

Don't waste your time with a mediocre organization, because you can probably do as well on your own, and save some money. However, a really excellent one can open up opportunities you never dreamed of, and turn out to be well worth the expense. In this really excellent department, there appear so far to be two people, Cornelius Bull and David Denman.

Cornelius Bull runs the Center for Interim Programs, P.O. Box 2347, Cambridge, MA 02238, (617) 547-0980. He has a list of around 3,000 opportunities all over the world, and is expert at matching clients with situations that reflect their interests. Not all of them are technically "apprenticeships" or "internships," but most involve some kind of interesting work. Many are inexpensive, providing room and board or even pay; others cost more due to travel and other expenses. Currently, he charges $800 for two years' worth of unlimited help. Most clients are college students looking for a way to take creative time off, or high school graduates wanting to do something meaningful for a year before they go to college. However, Bull is willing to work with teenaged unschoolers as well. In a talk at Choate, a highbrow prep school in Connecticut, he told the following story about one of his clients:

> I have a young kid who was totally allergic to school. He got through his sophomore year of high school, and he said, "Forget it, I can't do any more." He went off to Nepal. This kid is a magical climber. He is a human fly. They didn't care about that in high school. Why should they? That doesn't matter. It's irrelevant. So, he had never gotten any good strokes....Mountain Travel, the foremost trekking company in Nepal, watched this guy and was so impressed that they offered him a job and then discovered he was 16. They said, "Hey, go home and come back when you're 18 and work with us...."

Bull enjoys working with clients in person, but often does all the arranging during long phone conversations and through the mail. Some of the programs in his files are those of other organizations like the National Outdoor Leadership School, but some are unusual, out of the way opportunities he's personally tracked down through his huge network of friends, former classmates (Princeton), and former students (he taught and was headmaster of private schools for thirty years). Possibilities include working on organic farms in Spain, interning in wildlife rehabilitation in New York, doing whale research in Maui, and learning to conduct tea ceremonies in a Japanese castle.

David Denman offers similar opportunities through his somewhat smaller program called Time Out--619 E. Blithedale Avenue, Suite C, Mill Valley, CA 94941, (415) 383-1834. A former teacher, headmaster, director of admissions, etc., Denman has worked successfully not only with college students, but also with teenaged unschoolers and "dropouts." Like The Center for Interim Programs, Time Out arranges a wide variety of experiences, not just apprenticeships and internships.

When you hit 18, many more opportunities will open up. For instance, you can find an apprenticeship through Apprentice Alliance, an outstanding network of carefully screened professionals in a wide variety of fields such as architecture, fabric and fashion design, video and film, and writing. Contact Apprentice Alliance, 151 Potrero Avenue, San Francisco, CA 94103, (415) 863-8661. A different sort of organization which sets up apprenticeships for people over 18 is the Maine Organic Farmers and Gardeners Association, Box 2176, Augusta, ME 04338-2176 (207) 622-3118.

BAT Apprenticeships

A government agency, the Bureau of Apprenticeships, oversees formal apprenticeships in dozens of fields including bookbinding, bread baking, plumbing and carpentry. You have to be at least 16, 18 in some cases. If you undertake one of these apprenticeships, you will not have much free time for other pursuits. Also, you may not particularly like the way you are trained: my friend Rick wanted to be a carpenter, but not the sort of "construction worker" who pounds nails on future skyscrapers. He was more interested in doing small scale work like renovating houses, so learned by working for a small, non-union contractor rather than through a BAT apprenticeship. If you do want information on BAT apprenticeships, contact your state department of labor.

How you can arrange and design your own apprenticeship or internship:

Nothing prevents you from planning and setting up a position by yourself. You may need perseverance, but all you really have to *do* is decide what kind of a position you want, and then talk to everyone in your area who works in that field until you find someone you like who will take you on. A *very* helpful book is *The Question is College,* by Herbert Kohl (Random House, 1989). It discusses apprenticeships as an alternative to *college,* but most of the information in it is perfectly usable for people of any age.

You'll have it easiest if you already have adult friends you might like to apprentice yourself to, or if your parents know someone who might work out. But of course you can approach strangers too. After all, apprenticeships and internships help everyone involved. You learn by watching people who know what they're doing and by actually doing many of the same things they do. They get free or inexpensive help, as well as the joy and pride that comes from sharing what they love with an excited newcomer. Chances are, if you phone all the dog trainers in the yellow pages, at least one will welcome your company. Don't give up after one no-thank-you.

If you do arrange an apprenticeship or internship on your own, be sure to talk about your ideas and goals thoroughly enough that both parties have similar expectations. Write them down. If you envision three hours on weekday mornings of laying out newspaper copy, but Mr. Mendoza sees you sweeping floors and running errands, it won't work. Discover that *before* you commit yourself.

If you are interested in setting up a position away from home, various homeschooling magazines and organizations can probably help. The National Homeschool Association maintains a list of apprenticeship possibilities. *GWS* sometimes runs notices or want ads from people willing to offer work situations, apprenticeships, and internships, and similar notices from people *looking* for such positions. For example, someone wrote in *GWS #27,* "Wanted: apprentice to learn microcomputer programming. My ideal would be an unschooler, 10-15, who can commute to my small software company. I envision the apprentice spending about one day a week at first, later maybe about three days a week..." And a midwife wrote in *GWS #25*,

> If there were a young person who wanted to learn about the body, birth, and babies, I'd be glad to have them spend time here with me going on home births, and being present for the pre-natals, etc. I won't put any age limit on it, because I've learned from Wendy [her eight-year-old daughter] that if there's an interest, anyone can learn it. My daughter often knows more about what's happening than some of the mothers I work with!

Furthermore, homeschooling organizations themselves may offer positions. *GWS* sometimes has internship and apprenticeship openings, which could be a valuable start for someone interested in magazine production or general business management.

Also: You can use a sourcebook like *Internships* (described above) as an important source of information even without actually applying for an internship it describes. Find a position that sounds ideal, except for its location or age requirements, or whatever. Write the sponsoring institution for more information. Then find a similar institution closer to home. Write up a thoughtful but flexible proposal, and approach them with it. Be sure to point out that you have based your ideas on an organization similar to theirs--this will help reduce any reluctance they might have.

For information and ideas on farm-related apprenticeships, see Chapter 37.

Apprenticeships can happen in academic fields too. See Chapter 21 for a description of Vincent J. Schaefer, who became a scientist mainly as a result of an apprenticeship at General Electric. Also in Chapter 21, see the bits of Dr. David Deutsch's paper, "How Children Can Become Experts."

And by the way, reading books can be a bit like an apprenticeship, if you choose carefully and approach it that way. Some books really invite you inside to observe a person's work. For instance, *The Double Helix*, by James D. Watson (also described in chapter 21), brings you behind the scenes to watch the process of the scientific discovery of DNA.

Some examples:

Anna-Lisa Cox wrote about the process of developing an interest in historical costume and finding a related internship. First, in *GWS #68* she says:

> I am 17, and until I became a part-time student at the local college a couple of years ago, I had been schooled at home all my life.
>
> My main passion in life right now is, and has been for the last three years, social anthropology and history. Antique clothing has been the context which

brought these subjects alive for me. I became interested in antique clothing when I was living in England for a year with my family. I stumbled upon the Victoria and Albert Museum in London, which has one of the best costume collections in Europe. I was instantly fascinated by it, and I determined to find out more about the subject.

Now, three years later, I have a large costume collection of my own (acquired through hours of rummaging through charity shops, garage sales, and local estate sales), which I use in historical fashion presentations for local clubs, churches, and businesses. I am also the costume collection consultant for the local historical society. I find what I do very exciting. It's wonderful to be able to help friends date their grandmother's dress, or to teach them how to clean and preserve it....

A year later, she writes in *GWS #74*,

....My true love is museum work, tied to an intense interest in antique clothing. Luckily, my parents have been an incredible help and encouragement, patiently supporting me in my exploration and decision-making....

With the help of friends I was able to find [a museum internship], which I will be going to in April. Some friends arranged for me to get together with the curators of a costume museum near them. I was a little hesitant about even trying, as I had been disappointed so many times, but I decided to go ahead, and I'm so glad I did. The curators are three young women, all as excited and interested in costume as I am. When I first met them we talked for two hours straight. Around the end of our conversation, the head museum curator asked what museum I was in charge of! I decided to tell her the truth, that I had no museum experience, but she said she was very impressed with my expertise and would still love to have me come and work with them.

It all sounds so easy as I write about it, but getting to this point has taken enormous amounts of time and energy. In fact, last summer, when I was in England with my family, I went through an intensive search for an internship. I wrote and called museums. I even had a friend who used to be a costume curator helping me, writing letters of recommendation to old colleagues. But even so, not one internship came out of it. So I guess all I can recommend is to keep trying. There's an internship out there just waiting for you, if you have patience.

Elaine Mahoney writes about her daughter in *GWS #23*:

Kendra, 13 years old now, is an apprentice in a sewing machine repair shop. A family friend owns a repair shop and has been graciously sharing her knowledge and skill. Kendra enjoys spending time at the shop and is learning by doing. She answers the phone, waits on customers, makes bank deposits, and is learning the general maintenance and repair of sewing machines.

The next year, she adds in *GWS* #28:

> [Kendra] is in Tennessee at present [with 4-H], attending the World's Fair. ...One of the exciting parts about the trip is that they also plan to go to Kentucky to go to a sewing machine convention, which ties in nicely with her apprenticeship.

> In the fall, Kendra plans to take a correspondence course in sewing machine repair to acquire a certificate...

Lisa Asher writes in *GWS* #45:

> I am a 12-year-old homeschooler presently living in Barnstable, Massachusetts. My father is an architect, and I am, too. I am his apprentice.

> I first became interested in architecture a year ago, when I began homeschooling. I made floor plans (the overhead view of a house without a roof). My plans were not very good, not even buildable, but they were a start.

> About two months ago I got serious. I began to design buildable plans that took weeks instead of days to complete, and included sections and elevations.

> My father looks at all my designs and shows me where I need to fix something. When I have a good plan, my father blueprints it.

> I also help my father. When he has a completed design, he pays me to trace it. He also asks my advice sometimes. I even help design.

> Right now, I just design contemporary houses, because that is what my father designs, but I would like to design rustic houses also someday...

Gretchen Spicer writes in *GWS* #53,

> Jacob (15) and Tom, my husband, are working at an outdoor Shakespeare Theater. Jacob started as an intern at $100 a week, but within two weeks was filling the position of two interns and is now getting $200 a week....We get to see lots of plays and now the kids are quoting Shakespeare constantly. Our house has become a very dramatic place recently...

Judy Garvey and Jim Bergin write about their 13-year-old son Matthew Bergin in *GWS* #76:

Shortly after leaving school two years ago, Matthew began working with a man who has a landscaping business. He loves the work and because of his energy and enthusiasm he has now become a real asset. This summer he will begin earning a wage for his labors. What he has already received from this apprenticeship--new self-esteem, real skills, and an awareness of how the world works outside of school or his family--could never be measured by salary....

In *GWS #76*, 14-year-old Emma Roberts writes about the process of choosing and setting up a theater apprenticeship:

I don't remember how I got the idea to have a theater apprenticeship. The whole idea really appealed to me. I love theater, and spending a few days every week working on it sounded great. It would solve my problems about wanting to go somewhere every day, and it would be fun. So I began thinking about what would be the ideal situation for me. I concluded that, say, three days a week working backstage, in the box office, anything to do with theater would be great. I was sending out some headshots and resumes for auditions for myself, so I sent along a cover letter saying that I was interested in volunteering in their theater, explaining I was a homeschooler and very flexible. At first I felt kind of strange asking to be an exception, but I got used to the idea.

I hadn't heard from the places I had written to in Boston when one day my Mom and I were talking to the scenic designer at Mount Wachusett Community College, Patrick Mahoney. I do a lot of theater at The Mount.... so I know everyone pretty well. Mom happened to mention that I was looking for an apprenticeship in Boston, and she asked him if he knew of any places I could write to. Patrick said yes, he thought he did. Then he asked if we had considered The Mount as a possibility. We hadn't, because it hadn't occurred to us as being a real theater, but of course it is. I had recently had a chance to have a tour of two professional theaters in Boston and Worcester, and afterwards I realized how really professional the theater at The Mount is. Patrick said he would mention it to Gail Steele, the head of the theater department. I called Gail after about a week and we set up a meeting.

When I went to the meeting, Gail and Pat asked me what I would be interested in doing. I told them two or three days a week helping where I was needed would be great. They were really excited. Then Gail said she had talked to the head of the humanities department and he suggested I might like to take a few courses at the college. I couldn't believe it!

We set up for me to take two classes, The Fundamentals of Acting and Scene Tech, and get college credit. Going through the process of being admitted was a riot. You could tell they'd never heard of such a thing: a 14-year-old-girl who doesn't go to school wanting to come to their college and take classes. I finally got accepted, and I'm going to begin the whole thing in the fall. They offered for me to start the apprenticeship this summer, but I am so busy with a theater in Wilton, NH that I told them the fall would be better.

So I finally got a change, and if I ever want to go on to Boston to do an apprenticeship there, I can say, look, I've already had experience!

chapter 34

volunteering

"Volunteer work is a tremendous use of time," 17-year-old former unschooler Anthony Hermans told me, "It accomplishes a useful task, allows one to get away from the norm and provides many longlasting friendships. I have volunteered in community service clubs, at the local library, our wildlife sanctuary, and a local history reenactment park. My sister has helped at a local homeless shelter for women and children."

Two big thrills come with volunteer work: 1) the knowledge that you are helping something you believe in, and 2) a huge realm of possibilities. Volunteering can be *anything*, a free ticket into any world you want to explore.

Also, you can set your own schedule, working as much or as little as you wish. Few groups will turn you away because of your age. Volunteer experience looks great on a resume, and furthermore, volunteer jobs often turn into paid jobs.

In Colorado Springs, I can think of a wide variety of organizations largely staffed by volunteers: the senior citizens' support system, the soup kitchen, the Humane Society, a non-profit Latin American import shop. Every city has its own counterparts to these, and there are also chapters of environmental, social, and political action groups--Greenpeace, the Sierra Club, Amnesty International, the Greens, the Republicans, the Democrats, SADD.

But you're not restricted to the groups that actively search for volunteers. You can always go to an organization, person, or business you like and speak your piece--"I'd like to get involved with what you're doing--is there something I can do to help, for free?" or "I'm a mime; I'd like to teach a free weekly class at the Immigrant Center."

A few unschoolers have, ironically enough, decided to volunteer in schools. Though strange, the idea makes sense. First, a volunteer, being *voluntary*, is far more empowered than a compulsory-school-student. Second, part of the unpleasantness of many schools ties to overcrowded classrooms and overworked teachers; therefore, a willing helper can make some difference. By participating in school in a new role, you the unschooler can gain a new perspective on your own childhood and the whole issue of School and Society. Finally, children can only benefit from being exposed to the calm, fresh perspective of an unschooler, a person who isn't going to harass them about the usual things. *GWS #26* tells about a 14-year-old who spends two and a half hours every afternoon in an elementary school, and a 13-year-old who takes an hour each Thursday to read to elementary schoolkids and correct papers.

If you'd like more advice getting started, see Sara Gilbert's *Lend a Hand: The How, Where, and Why of Volunteering* (Morrow Junior Books, 1988). Written especially for teenagers, it describes over one hundred organizations and gives general information and advice.

Also, you can find resources for volunteering outdoors in chapter 28, and for volunteering around the world in chapter 29.

Unschoolers who volunteer

A parent writes in *GWS #36*:

Since spring, our 13-year-old daughter has been volunteering at a science museum two days a week. To say that she loves it is an understatement! She's been doing a great deal of work in the museum's "mount room," cataloging their collections and learning names (in scientific as well as laymen's terms) of many birds and mammals in the process....She's becoming quite the birder. Occasionally she gets to go on a field trip with the museum's naturalist. And we all got to go (at special staff rates) on a whale watch sponsored by the museum....

The naturalist, by the way, has been very impressed by both of our children's obvious love of and knowledge of nature. He said that he'd be more than happy to take them out into the field any time. All the museum staff thinks that it's wonderful that our daughter had the chance to be doing this and have been very supportive, giving her a range of things to do to broaden her experiences there. Occasionally she will take over for the receptionist, and the accountant wants to teach her some of that. She can use the cash register and she helps get out mailings at times. Everyone has found out what a good worker she is and the demand has become high! Her major focus is and will be, at her request, the natural history work.

At 13, Alison McCutchen began volunteering at a library and in a vet's office. Her mother Ruth writes in *GWS #32*, "She enjoys both but favors the vet. During her first week she saw a dog spayed and our two ten-month-old kittens neutered. She described it to us in *glorious* detail and we all found it fascinating. She wasn't fazed by any of it."

A year and a half later, Ruth McCutchen sent this update to *GWS #41*: "Alison's (15) latest volunteer job is at the local legal aide office where she is filing and summarizing social workers' case notes. .."

Alison's sister Deborah was 16 when her mother wrote in *GWS #46*, "Deborah's latest volunteer jobs have been at the zoo: one in the Metazoo, an indoor exhibit with small animals, reptiles and microscopes, the other in the commissary where the diets are prepared..."

Theo Giesy writes in *GWS #26*:

Darrin (14) and Susie (12) volunteer three days a week at the Cousteau Society. They do all sorts of things, like work in membership. Darrin works mostly in the warehouse, packing things members have ordered (books, T-shirts, etc). He also drives the fork-lift.

Since they work there so much they were invited to the $50-a-ticket reception the night before the Calypso sailed. Darrin couldn't go so I got to go in his place. I met Jacques and Jean-Michele Cousteau. Darrin has made friends with Jean-Michele's son Fabien--they are about the same age and have many common interests.

I like the Cousteau's attitude toward their employees and volunteers. They appreciate Darrin and Susie very much. They were worried about the lack of work permits and the number of hours spent, so I wrote a letter on Brook School letterhead saying that they were working there as part of the Brook School Curriculum and under the responsibility of Brook School. That satisfied everyone; it looks official.

Darrin runs the spotlight for Tidewater Dinner Theater, $40 per week (six shows). That is why he couldn't go to the Cousteau reception. He hopes to be able to run the light board soon, $115/week. He enjoys doing spotlight and is treated as an adult around the theater.

12-year-old Frank Conley writes in *GWS #30*:

I am presently taking a veterinary medicine course at Louisiana State University. (This course is being given for "gifted and talented" junior high and high school students--I had no trouble registering as a homeschooler.) I became interested in learning more about it and decided to ask a local veterinarian if I could help out at his clinic in return for the experience of watching them work.

It has been very worthwhile. The three vets who work there have been very kind and helpful to me. They explain everything they do and not only allow me to watch but actually let me perform certain duties. They say I'm "indispensable."

So far some of the most interesting things I've done are: watch an autopsy on a cat, learn to draw blood from animals and prepare slides, take temperatures and fecals, watch surgery performed, and go along on emergency calls.

I go to the clinic nearly every day now, for several hours a day. I plan to take an animal science course next.

I recommend this way of learning to everyone. At first I was afraid no one would want my help, since I'm only 12, but the people I talked to were happy to have free help....

A mother wrote in *GWS #35*:

My oldest decided she would like to do volunteer work at a nursing home so we found one nearby that would take her at age 14. She works two days a week from 10 AM until 3 PM. The residents adore her and the feeling is mutual. The nurses have only praise for how well she has fit right in and all think she must be 18. She talks to residents, takes them for walks, holds hands, feeds them. The residents look forward to her coming. Most of all, Lauren loves to hear their stories of the old days. (We also like to talk about the criticism I heard that if my children don't learn to get up to go to school every day, they'll *never* be disciplined to get up and go to a job when they are older! Balderdash.)

Karen Franklin of Florida wrote in *GWS #72*:

Adam, our 12-year-old, spends a lot of time at the Science Museum ...Adam's big interest is marine biology, especially sharks. The director of the museum is an expert on this, has worked with the top people in the field. The main exhibit this summer was about sharks, so Adam, already quite an expert, led many tours and answered many questions.

chapter 35

jobs

I was like many other fullbloods. I didn't want a steady job in an office or factory. I thought myself too good for that, not because I was stuck up but simply because any human being is too good for that kind of no-life, even white people....
--John Fire (Lame Deer), in *Lame Deer, Seeker of Visions*, p.39.

Points

1. Don't be limited by the stereotypes that tell us what kinds of jobs teenagers can do. They are wrong. Teenagers can do more than babysit, flip pancakes, and wash cars. Ruth Lembeck's *Teenage Jobs* (David McKay Co., 1971), is old but it's a terrific brainstorm, with hundreds of perfectly good ideas and real-life examples. *Jobs for Teenagers*, by Ilene Jones (Ballantine, 1983) is less imaginative but great on technical details. Actually, both of these books do not limit themselves to *jobs*, but also suggest businesses and other ways of working.

2. Jobs in specialty retail stores are one of the best ways to get involved in a field that you love. Consider comic book stores, pet stores, book stores, jewelry stores, imported clothing stores, antique stores, feed stores, bike shops, cheese stores, bakeries, natural foods stores, piano stores, record stores. The people who work in these places are often very knowledgeable, and you will learn from being around them and the "stuff" itself. Also, retail stores frequently hire teenagers.

3. Know about your state's child labor statutes so you can figure out how to work around them, and when you need to be low key. Generally, you have to be 14 to get a work permit; employers are supposed to keep these permits on file for any employees under 18. You may have to get a permit through the counseling office of your ex-school. Some homeschoolers' employers, however, have only requested written permission from parents.

In general, both state and federal laws influence your situation. For more information, contact your state labor department (look in the phone book), or call local representatives and ask them to mail you copies of the statutes.

4. Consider looking for work through your parents' network of friends or through the homeschool community. *GWS* (*Growing Without Schooling* magazine) often runs advertisements or announcements of homeschooling families who want a teenaged live-in nanny, for example.

5. If you are especially young or have difficulty getting a job, consider offering to work for very low wages--but only at first. Once you're good at your job, don't feel embarrassed to ask to be paid more; if you work as well as an adult does, you deserve an adult wage. If you are legal and have a work permit, then in most cases you are entitled to minimum wage, no matter how old you are. If you feel you're being taken advantage of, discuss it with your boss. If that doesn't work, contact your state department of labor for information and help.

Another alternative, which need not be demeaning or unfair, is to work for trade. If you are quite young, this could make the whole situation easier on your employer, who could call you an apprentice or a volunteer and thus avoid trouble with tax people and labor department people.

6. You-the-unschooler have an edge on the best **summer jobs,** including jobs at camps, resorts, and National Parks, because such places prefer people who can work the whole season--often May through September, not just June through August. Check the library for books on summer jobs for teenagers and college students.

Stories
Rosalie Megli writes in *GWS* #20:

New opportunities are opening up for Lora, our 13-year-old daughter. She has made arrangements to begin part-time work at the local veterinary clinic, feeding animals and cleaning cages. She has also been made welcome to accompany the vets on farm runs and with office work. Since Lora loves animals and may be interested in veterinary science as a vocation, we are delighted with her arrangements. Lora got her work permit from the superintendent of schools with *no* stipulations regarding working hours...

Lora also has a small craft business (she makes herb-filled potholder mitts) and is going to buy a microscope with proceeds from pre-Christmas sales.

Eileen Trombly writes in *GWS* #24:

Amy was interviewed and accepted and jumped into the Avon world with both feet...She has done a good deal of baby-sitting and house cleaning at the rate of $1.00 and $1.50 in recent months. She has been in great demand due to her reliability and dependable qualities. Her duties as sitter expanded over the years and she was called upon by parents of newborns as' well as older children. During the summer months she even went on family sailboat cruises to Block Island, Newport, etc...Alas, burnout at age 15 set in and wages became insufficient for an ambitious ballerina who went through toe shoes faster than she could pay for them.

...Her first five days as an Avon representative were highly successful and she grossed a personal income of $100 within that time. Additional calculating indicates that she is working approximately two hours daily (at her convenience) and earning $7.50 an hour. Not bad for a 15-year-old. If she chooses to work more hours, she'll make more--it's her choice....Most of her customers are older people and are impressed by her confidence. In figuring out her finances even further she finds she is able to take additional ballet lessons, as well as save...

Pam Robinson writes about her 12-year-old son in *GWS #25*:

Jared has overhauled a lawn motor mower, truck rear-end, and transmission. He works summers for a neighbor driving a tractor that pulls a hay chopper and large hay wagon. He is paid very well because he is one of the most responsible, dependable employees in the area. This year at 12 he had the job of training and breaking in all the new help, 17- and 18-year-old young men. He is not required by us to work, yet he often chooses to work long hours, Sundays, and holidays.

He is completely in charge of his own education. He went through several interest periods. He was avid on American biographies at age seven; later studied astronomy and went through ancient history, especially the Roman emperors; lately he's been interested in architecture. He does not do much math. He can add, subtract, multiply, and divide. He works with fractions and percentages but is probably not up to grade level, and is definitely slower than those who have memorized math tables. He reads avidly, however; spends very little time writing, and probably falls down in spelling, grammar, etc...

John Melbourne was out of school at 13 due to severe migraines. He studied with a tutor about 30 minutes a week and read a lot. His mother, Shari, wrote in *GWS #28* that he was "working as a library page on Monday mornings, and was just appointed library artist (he does all of their posters for movies, library events, etc)...He's now taking a course in genealogy at the library--four weeks, twelve hours per week..."

Erin Roberts, 14, wrote me about her work with horses. She has worked part time at a riding stable for four years, guiding trail rides and otherwise helping out. She also works at an Arabian farm, Windsor Arabians, as an assistant trainer. "I especially help break their three- and four-year olds," she explains, "but I also help out with halter breaking the young ones as well as miscellaneous tasks around the farm." She recently bought a three-year-old halter broken Arabian gelding and trained him to ride. When I heard from her, they had just entered their first show and Erin said, "We didn't win any ribbons, but we had a great time."

In *GWS #34*: "This past week Jon (13) began working in a paint and auto body shop with his father, earning $115 a week..."

Scott Maher, 13, writes in *GWS #37*,

In September I went down to the Wakefield Pet Shop and asked the owner Steve, whom I already had known, if there would be any way I could come down and help. I told him how I was a home schooler and that I could come down in the mornings. Steve said we could try it out for a while and see what we think.

I went down on a Monday at 10:30 and first he showed me around and showed me how things are done...I started off feeding the birds and cleaning their cages. Next I swept the floor and fed the fish. Then I fed and watered the small animals, lizards, rabbits, guinea pigs, and cats. Some days I clean filters in the fish tanks and test the Ph of the water; other days I clean the cages and clean the glass. I have helped unload shipments and put stock away.

I have been working there almost four months now. I have waited on customers, given them advice, taken inventory, and I even take care of the shop if Steve has to leave. Soon I will be learning how to use the cash register.

There are two other boys my age who come down and help after school is out. The way we get paid is: $2 in trade for every hour we work, or $1 in money.

I think the best part of it is learning about all of the different animals, fish and birds and learning how to take care of them. I have been put in charge of lizards and small animals. It is a lot of fun to help out customers.

A year later, Mary Maher, Scott's mom, sent an update to *GWS #43*:

There have been many times when Steve, the owner, has called Scott at home and asked him to please come down for the day because he very much needed his help. On several occasions, Steve has had to leave the store for several hours and he has left Scott alone, in charge. When Steve opened a second pet shop in a nearby city, he often took Scott with him at night to get things unpacked or to set up displays or even to have Scott help put up paneling and install ceilings. Once in a while, Scott travels with Steve in the evenings to service or set up very large fish tanks for restaurants or private residences.

Customers don't seem to mind that Scott is so young. They will engage him in lengthy conversations on how to take care of a particular pet or how to go about properly setting up a fish tank. One fellow, an older man, took all Scott's advice on what fish were compatible for his new tank.

Recently, Steve has decided that he would like to sell pet supplies at a Sunday flea market in another town, and Scott will be in charge of the whole operation.

Eleadari Acheson, 15, writes in *GWS #76* about her work at a used bookstore and as a coach at a gymnastics club:

During the past two years the store moved to a larger location and my hours have increased to three five-hour days per week. My income and responsibilities have increased as well. I now buy and price books, clean, organize displays, make business calls, write business letters, conduct book searches, answer questions, and restock shelves. In addition, when the owners are on vacation I handle mail and banking.

At first I was the only employee, but a few months ago three more employees were hired....As senior employee, I am paid more per hour than the rest even though I am the youngest. When the owners are unavailable, the other employees call me when they have questions...

About her gymnastics work:

When I started I wasn't strong enough to spot even a front limber with the older kids. Now I'm spotting the older kids' back handsprings by myself. I also lead warm-ups and teach the less complicated tricks while the head coach teaches the harder stuff....

I consider my jobs the most important part of my homeschooling education.

Kristine Breck had been out of school six years by the time she wrote in *GWS #70*:

My main interest is animals. I recently had the opportunity to go from my home in Alaska to an exotic animal breeding compound in Florida, where lions, tigers, leopards, and other rare animals are raised. It was a dream come true for me because I had always admired the big cats and now I was going to live with them.

No doubt, I had worked for it, and it has been work I have loved doing. I trained several winning obedience dogs and a performing sheep, raised a musk ox, tamed a fox, trained and raced the World Champion racing reindeer, and taught my best friend, a horse, to do 35 circus tricks (so far).

Last summer when the Florida big cat people brought their educational exhibit to our small town in Alaska, I gave them a copy of my resume/portfolio. They said I had talent, and they came to our farm to give me an audition.

In February, I boarded the airplane for Florida....Since I was working with very special animals, some endangered species, the owners trusted me a whole lot to take good care of the young baboon, the llama, the lion cubs, and the baby leopard. I tried very hard and used all my knowledge to be worthy of their trust. And I must have been a good "nanny," because I never had any problems, and they invited me and my mom to come back and live and work on the compound permanently.

People I met were very surprised at my adventure. They usually guessed, "And you're only 16 or 17, right?" Actually, I'm 14, but under my circumstances, age was not important. Qualities such as knowledge, interest, and desire to learn were what mattered. It was a wonderful experience, and I think homeschooling is excellent preparation for the real world, because we live and learn right in it.

A year later, she wrote in *GWS #79*,

...This last summer I spent five months on the road, working for the Big Cat Show. I'd had other jobs before, but this one was intense, and in it I learned and practiced responsibility, financial management, and taking care of myself away from my family. I really enjoy traveling, and a person can learn a lot from the many situations and environments encountered. It seems like adjusting and making changes comes more easily after you've traveled.

....My next job was through people who knew me and said I was a mature, hardworking, ambitious young person, which I have always tried to be...In this job I handled camels and Nativity animals in the Radio City Music Hall Christmas Spectacular. It was a very impressive place to work and required staying in New York City for two months, which is truly an enlightening experience for anyone from a small town...

Kristine now lives and works at an animal park in Maine, and says she's saving her money "to buy a vehicle and equipment to take my performing animal show on tour independently."

Randall Kern writes in *GWS #67*:

I am 12 and have been a homeschooler all my life. I have been programming computers for six years. A year ago I started going to an IBM computer club, even though I didn't have an IBM yet. When we got one, last June, I became the consultant for our group.

The last meeting I went to was held in a newspaper office, because the computer they use for their accounting needed to be set up. When we got there we found out that the program they had bought didn't do what they wanted. So they hired me to write an accounts receivable and account maintenance program for the newspaper....

GWS #43 tells about Jeff Gold, who at 16 had dropped out of high school and was earning $2000 a week helping companies safeguard their computer programs.

GWS #56 reports that in between her global travels (see chapter 21), Britt Barker played classical piano for $30 an hour at a local inn.

Leonie Edwards, 16, loves her full time job as a dental assistant, and plans to become a dentist. She began working at 14 as a sort of assistant-to-the-assistant. At that time, she wrote in *GWS* #64:

> I work mainly with the dental assistant. I started doing things like cleaning rooms, sterilizing instruments, setting up trays, preparing the rooms for the next patient, and watching how the dental assistant did things. After a while they gave me more to do, such as getting the patients in and putting a movie on for them, filing, preparing syringes, making sure the rooms are stocked, and developing x-rays. Then I started assisting the dentist with several patients. Now the dentist calls me, instead of the dental assistant, to help with fillings and sometimes root canals.

"Thanks to homeschooling," she writes me now, "I can put 'two and a half years of dental assisting experience' on my college application." At the same time, she's working on a correspondence course from the University of Kentucky on Human Biology. The credits will build towards her pre-dental bachelor's degree.

chapter 36

your own business

Business isn't necessarily an all-week event involving high heels and power lunches. By teaching Wednesday and Saturday dance classes, performing in Middle Eastern restaurants, and selling scarves and finger cymbals to my students, I am running a business. I like it.

Starting a business can mean freedom, creativity, and expression and fulfillment of your unique talents and interests. It can involve nearly anything: breeding and selling tropical fish, cleaning peoples' attics, running a bead store, mending old books or jeans, starting a decent mail-order book club for teenagers, training horses, recording language instruction cassette tapes if you have a native tongue other than English. Of course, you can try any kind of work as part of a job, too--working in someone *else's* bead store, for instance.

However, once you know a lot about something, consider going into business for yourself. In a business, you answer to yourself and your customers (or clients) instead of a boss. Naturally, running your own business means you have to stand on your own two feet, and that nonexistent boss can't give you a paycheck. If you act wisely and love what you do, you'll probably *eventually* make a profit. If worse comes to worst, you could lose your investment of money; if your business is something like childcare or petsitting, you could possibly even be sued if a court held you responsible for damages. However, if you take reasonable care with whatever you are doing and don't make any empty promises, you should have no trouble.

There are two reasons starting a business especially suits itself to teenagers. First, you don't yet need to support yourself financially. You needn't worry about making fast money, so you can enjoy a slow start, learning gradually from your mistakes.

Many adults cannot easily afford to go into business, because they can't take the time off their original jobs to get started--and they have to keep those jobs to support themselves. Many businesses make no profit or even lose money their first year or so. This is mainly because most businesses require an initial investment--large or small depending on the type of business, your standards, and your ingenuity. Generally, a retail business requires the greatest initial investment--renting a store and buying all the things you plan to sell. (You can creatively cut costs anywhere, of course. My retail business has almost no overhead; it consists mainly of toting a box of sequined veils with me every time I teach a class or workshop.) At the other end of the spectrum, a service business requires little capital. To be a tutor, freelance photographer, guitar teacher, or typist would require only advertising and transportation costs plus the tools of the trade--camera, guitar, typewriter or word processor.

I do not wish to imply that your business *can't* make a profit in its early stages. Especially if it's your major goal to make money, you can do it. My friend Laura made bread and cookies every day when she was a sophomore in high school, and by selling them to teachers and students, she paid for her trip to Scotland the following summer.

The second reason starting a business is a great idea for teenagers is that it's one of the few legal, exciting money-making opportunities for people under the age of 18. Many places can't hire you until you're 16, but no one can stop you from running most kinds of businesses. Even if you're 16, finding fun work isn't necessarily easy. There's always McDonald's, but a degrading job like that is for someone who's too tired out--by school, for instance--to do anything better. (My brother Ned didn't like my using the word "degrading" here, for excellent reasons. I'm not saying it's necessarily degrading to cook, sweep floors, or serve food. I do feel a large standardized corporation whose main motive is profit inevitably steals vivacity and meaning from the lives of its workers.)

There are many terrific books which both tell about the legal and paperwork side of a business and give a general overview of the possibilities. For the most part, any business run by an adult could also be a teenage business. Remember, though, not to be limited by anyone's list; just because you've never heard of anyone who made a business out of helping kids build treehouses and forts doesn't mean it can't be done.

A few outstanding books to get you started:

-Paul Hawken, *Growing a Business* (Simon and Schuster, 1987). Also a PBS series. Helps you design and start a business that reflects your own interests and skills. An original, conscientious economist and businessman, Hawken has no college degree or other "qualifications" to interfere with his common sense.

-Bernard Kamoroff, C.P.A., *Small Time Operator* (And Books, revised frequently), gives you all the information you need on record keeping, taxes, and other technical headaches. Kamoroff writes in a friendly, clear style. I consider his book indispensable.

-Sarah L. Riehm, *The Teenage Entrepeneur's Guide: 50 money-making business ideas* (Chicago: Surrey Books, 1990). Gives a clear introduction to setting up a business and taking care of paperwork, marketing, etc., and gives detailed plans for 50 kinds of businesses, ranging from auto detailing to bumper stickers to catering. My only hesitation regarding Riehm's book is that it might encourage you to fit yourself into one of these businesses, rather than *invent* a business that fits *you*.

-Barbara Sher, *Wishcraft* (Random House, 1979), helps you get *anything* together in your life, but it's especially terrific for a project like starting a business, which can be overwhelming if you don't know how to break it down and get the support you need.

Also, you might subscribe to *Kids Mean Business*, Homeland Publications, 1808 Capri Lane, Seabrook, TX 77586. Although it's not especially creative or thorough, this bi-monthly newsletter does tell about a lot of actual businesses run by kids, such as staging mock weddings, selling decorated sweatshirts, and selling homemade suckers. Also, you can order books through the newsletter, like *The Teenage Entrepeneur's Guide* and *Kid Biz*. $8 per year; free sample issue. *Kids Mean Business*, Homeland Publications, 1808 Capri Lane, Seabrook, TX 77586.

When are you ready to start?

It depends on what you want to do. You probably already have some skills that could lead to a business without further training. The people I taught in school, aged 11 to 14, already had the expertise necessary to operate dozens of types of businesses, such as:

-giving skateboard lessons
-decorating and painting skateboards
-teaching or tutoring Japanese or Hebrew
-writing newsletters covering various issues
-sewing and designing clothing
-forming a band
-giving figure skating lessons
-coaching hockey or tennis
-teaching sailing
-picking up neighborhood recyclables (with help of older friends with drivers' licenses)
-making tie-dyed and batiked clothing
-producing videos
-making and selling food--catering, cookies, etc.
-raising and breeding various animals

Or, perhaps you'd like to do something you're not yet skilled in--but could be with some practice, guidance, and/or good tools. A job related to your interests is valuable training for a later business, especially when you're fairly new to the field. Or you can design a more independent training ground. Maybe you're a good tap dancer and would like to start a small professional troupe, but first you want to spend a year or so taking more lessons, giving amateur recitals, and studying all the old Gene Kelly and Fred Astaire musicals you can get your hands on. Good. Do it.

Yes, it's best to hold out long enough to be sure you're offering your buyers a quality product or service, but don't wait too long just because you have stage fright. Sometimes there comes a point when your interest can't develop any further until you put yourself on the line and start sharing your skill with the world. That happened to me.

After I'd taken a year of Middle Eastern dance lessons, I set a goal of performing professionally in two years. I'd moved to a new city and had an impossible time linking up with other dancers for lessons, so I practiced on my own every day and studied videos of other dancers. Finally, I reached a plateau where I felt dead-ended and frustrated at the lack of contact. I took the big plunge and nervously phoned up a local Moroccan restaurant--a year and a half before I had planned to start my "career." To my surprise, they thought I was pretty good. In fact, after my first performance I was signed on for a standing Friday and Saturday night engagement. Furthermore, although the first two shows were pure panic, in my bones I knew that the timing was right. A live audience was exactly the challenge that my dancing needed in order to progress.

To make your business successful on the most ultimate terms, be sure it is not only something you love and that the public will buy, but also something *good* for people and for this battered planet. I mean not only the *type* of business, but also your approach to it. As a belly dancer, I bring joy, cultural awareness, affirmation of womanhood, and friendly entertainment to my audiences. I help them celebrate, and that is good work. If I perceived my art differently, I might instead bring silliness, mild pornography, gimmicks, and cheap flash.

Run your business under the scrutiny of your own moral code. Mainly, just *think* about what you're doing and take time to do it right. If you open a catering service, consider an alternative to polystyrene foam (Styrofoam, etc.) packaging. As a fabric painter, you can find dyes and paints that don't harm water systems after you dump them down the drain. When singing for a crowd, aim not just to impress your listeners, but also to warm them and make them feel good.

Also, a lot of situations that we think of as teenage "jobs" are really small businesses--when you're babysitting, shoveling snow, and raking yards there's a fine line between "clients" and "bosses." While this sort of work may not be as glamorous as designing rock gardens, you can make it more meaningful simply by *thinking* of it as a business, and becoming more creative in your approach to it.

Unschooling can give you an advantage even in these typical teenage "jobs." Unschooler Lora Risley mentions in *GWS* (*Growing Without Schooling* magazine) #76, "I was allowed to babysit at children's homes and I earned quite a bit of money because I was available when the other babysitters were at school."

Unschoolers' experiences with business:

At age 14, Carey Newman of British Columbia wrote in *GWS* #68:

Right now I am working towards becoming a full-time artist. My parents have played a big part in my progress up to now.

When I was 12 my Dad asked the Sooke Museum about me having a solo show of my wildlife sketches in their gallery. The museum approved and said that I could have a show during December 1987 and January 1988. A lot of my time during the months before the show was spent preparing for the opening night, which close to 90 people attended. Through the next two months over half my drawings sold. I thank my mom and dad for pushing me to get everything ready for that show.

In February of 1988, I started on Northwest Coast Indian art. My dad, an Indian artist himself, was very helpful in showing me the rules of Indian design. Soon after, my father received an application form for the Sooke Fine Arts Show, a juried show that takes place in Sooke every year. Jokingly, I said that I should enter my Indian designs and silk-screen-print them. My parents turned it from joke to matter and said that I should try. They supported me financially by lending me the money to enter the show, and to buy silkscreening material. An artist friend of mine helped me to do the silkscreening. Two of my designs were accepted and I went on to sell 59 prints over a period of ten days, bringing in just over $2,000, from which I paid back my parents and bought more equipment and supplies to continue with this art form.

My mom later found out about the Okanagan Summer School of the Arts, got the application form, helped me apply for a bursary to cover expenses, and assisted me in composing a letter with samples of my work so that I could get accepted into a course that didn't normally accept anyone under 16.

At 13, Vita Wallace began earning money giving violin lessons (see *GWS #64* and *#70*). *GWS #64* pointed out that young teachers are sometimes actually *better* than older teachers since they know freshly what it feels like to be taught.

Amelia Acheson writes in *GWS #42* about her 12-year-old daughter, also Amelia:

She picked up a clowning book at the library last summer. Her first decision was to duplicate one of the costumes and gags she saw there for a Halloween costume. It turned out so delightful that she was invited to bring it to a day-care center to "show-off" and entertain the little kids. Over the year, that has grown to a business, and now includes all three of our kids. They have been paid for their clowning--they have their own business cards--they brought home a huge first place trophy from a parade--and, mostly, they have a lot of fun at it. They ride unicycles, juggle, do gymnastics. Tia does magic tricks (one of her magic books says that magic is a trade like no other--you have to learn it yourself at home). They sometimes work in partnership with a 14-year-old clown from another town who makes balloon animals--as a result, he is learning to unicycle, and they are learning to make balloon animals.

In *GWS #24*, a mother tells about her family's unschooling. They'd spent the first year with the Calvert curriculum (a correspondence school), and not especially enjoyed it. So they changed:

Into the second year, we started the family business. We sell and repair bicycles. We also sell all accessories associated with bicycling. The kids and I manage the store while Dad works his full-time job as a carpenter. (Unless you are very rich, outside income is necessary the first years in business.) He has an active role in the store evenings and weekends. Our 15-year-old son, who has the bike knowledge (from books and other places) manages the repair department, doing all repairs (training dad), keeping stock of parts and working with customers. Our 16-year-old daughter is the family organizer, keeps us clean and orderly, manages the store, selling and keeping up with the accessory inventory. Mom's (that's me!) main job is to keep the office going, books, etc...Sounds simple? It's not. But somehow it all works!

See other examples in Chapter 24 (a newspaper) and Chapter 37 (farm-related business projects).

pigs
and honey:
farm-related
work

Why?

1. For your edification. Becoming involved with the lives of the plants and animals that we eat fills a big gap in our "educations," a gap the schools can't possibly fill. The field trip to look at cows doesn't cut it. Nor does the photograph of cornfields on page 361 of your *American Heritage* book, or chopping up rats in biology. I may overly romanticize this one, because I am not *yet* a small farmer. But no one ever argues convincingly against the goodness of contact with the fundamental building blocks of our lives.

Undertaking any sort of agricultural project will be good for your brain. The Colfaxes (mentioned also in chapter 31) found that

> At home, our efforts to restore the land, to plant gardens, and to improve our livestock, stimulated interest in biology, chemistry, and, eventually, embryology and genetics. Clearing the badly damaged land provided lessons in ecology, and the construction of a house and outbuildings showed the boys the relevance of seemingly arcane subjects such as geometry. Drew, at seven, understood that the Pythagorean theorem was invaluable in squaring up his sheep shed foundation. Grant, at nine, discovered a Pomo Indian campsite on the ridge and was inspired to delve into North American archaeology, an interest which later broadened into studies of Mayan and Aztec cultures.[*]

One of the most delightful unschooling families I heard from was the Fallicks, from a small community near Davenport, Washington. They live without any conventional utilities, generating most of their own electricity from solar panels. They grow much of their own food, use an outhouse, and get water from a creek. Jj, the mother, described the *family's* education in part as follows:

---

[*] David and Micki Colfax, *Homeschooling for Excellence* (Warner, 1988), p.5.

Our activities have a yearly sort of cycle, tied to the seasons and seasonal/climate factors. The kids spend more time during the winter in indoor activities and most of their time the rest of the year outdoors. Just living here is an education...about electricity (why do you disconnect the solar panels from the house/batteries during electrical storms?) and wildlife (the list of what lives here that Kate is compiling is over a page and includes a bear and cougar)....We play instruments (between us all piano, guitar, clarinet, recorder, mandolin, and percussion/washboard)...[We] read aloud,...sing, etc. The kids are involved in 4-H, mostly home ec projects and the arts, plus church, a gifted kids group and the homeschool community.

In *GWS* (*Growing Without Schooling* magazine) #28, Lynne Hoffman wrote, "I've drawn up a chart of common farm chores and checked off which academic subjects each suggests to me." Her chart included "plan garden," "plan pond," and "carpentry" under geometry, "make cheeses" and "freezing" under chemistry, etc.

Of course, no one in their right mind does anything wonderful merely in order to be academic. There is something rather unsavory about growing red hot chili peppers in order to learn agricultural science. On the other hand, there is something savory indeed about growing red hot chili peppers because you want to grow red hot chili peppers, and accidentally catching a lot of biology, sunshine, cooking skills, and agricultural science--whatever that means--along the way.

2. To Heal the World, or a small bit of it anyway. Agriculture is in a bad way. Your breakfast eggs were probably the work of a hen who's never been outside; she lives in a wire pen barely big enough to turn around in, and the lights in her factory stay on all night to stimulate faster egg production. The grapes your boyfriend brought on Sunday's picnic were dangerously dusted with chemical pesticides that threaten the lives of field workers. The steak sizzling in the pan oozes hormones.

The modern agricultural expert, unlike the old-fashioned farmer, has forgotten the health of the rivers and wildernesses and small towns and--above all--of the people who eat plums and spinach, milk and bacon. He sees only chemicals, yields, efficiency, and giant new tractors.

In order for everyone to keep eating, say wise farmers like Wendell Berry, many more people will need to start farming, organically and on a small scale. Yet, we are *losing*, not gaining, farmers. According to an article in *Harrowsmith*, "The average age of farmers is 52....There are now twice as many farmers who are over the age of 60 as there are under the age of 35. Over the next 10 years, farmers will be retiring in record numbers."* So, I

---

* Craig Canine, "A Farewell to Farms," in *Harrowsmith Country Life* May/June 1991, p. 31.

admit, I kind of hope you will check out farming and get hooked. I figure that would help save human life on planet earth.

3. I also figure you might just plain have fun drying herbs, milking goats, baking bread, and carrying chicken shit to the compost pile--not to mention having room to *move*. Anne Brosnan, 13, of New York, laments,

> We live in the suburbs and have so far for seven years, but before this we lived in Minnesota in a rural cabin. We don't like it here in New York and we're selling our house to move back to a farm in Minnesota or a farm in Kentucky. I think that for homeschoolers the ideal place to live is in the country, because if you have freedom all day you should have a nice place in which to vent it. It seems so closed in here and we walk off our property in about 15 short steps. The kids here go to school for most of the day and when they come home they just roam about on skateboards or talk on phones, because there aren't really opportunities for anything when people live close together like this. It seems like kids here know about a lot of things but they've never tried doing them.

So what do you do, buy yourself forty acres? Hassle your parents to quit their jobs and move to the sticks? Knock on the doors of all the farm houses in Lane County? Nah. Exercise some initiative instead. Your brain may storm up a plan. Here are ideas and resources to get you going:

Go away and stay on a farm.
-If you subscribe to *Growing Without Schooling* magazine, place a classified ad explaining what you're hoping for. Be willing to work, of course, in exchange for room and board. Given the warm, open nature of the people who read and write for *GWS*, I suspect that this tactic would land you with multiple invitations in no time at all. You could probably find a situation with other unschooled teenagers, or one with younger children (whom you might help to care for). You could probably find an organic apple farm or a cattle ranch.

Of course, you would want to communicate very clearly with the family ahead of time as to your and their expectations, especially if you plan to stay a while. Be sure they know how inexperienced you are. Be sure you know how cold it gets in the winter, and what time you will have to rise and shine. Be sure you can coexist with each other's religious choices. Be sure you know how much freedom they feel like giving you. Rural homeschooling families run the complete range, from fundamentalist Christians who will not appreciate the Rolling Stones raging in your bedroom, to extremely flexible people whose own teenagers live next door in a converted barn and completely control their own academic, personal, and social lives.

Discuss whether you will mainly help with preexisting chores, or whether you might be allowed to undertake a new project, such as designing and planting an herb garden or building an outdoor solar shower.

Every once in a while, a family writes in to *GWS* to make an offer along this line. In *GWS* #18, for example, one rural family was looking for a live-in babysitter who would work ten hours each week. They offered to pay $50 per month plus room and board. In *GWS* #20, a family offered a small wage plus room and board for help with haying and gardening on an organic cattle farm.

-The *Homeschooler's Travel Directory*, available for $3.75 from the National Homeschool Association (see appendix B), lists and describes many rural and farm families who welcome homeschooling visitors.

-You could also place a classified ad in *Mother Earth News, Whole Earth Review*, or another magazine that attracts rural subscribers.

-Alternatively, you could plug into a preexisting program, such as a living history farm, which you can locate through the *Living History Sourcebook* (details, chapter 23).

-See *Healthy Harvest III*, (Potomac Valley Press, 1989), a directory which lists over 600 organic farms, organizations, apprenticeships, courses, and related information. (If not in your library, available for $18.95 from Potomac Valley Press, 1424 16th St, NW #105, Washington, DC 20036.)

But Miss Llewellyn, I don't want to leave home. I'd miss my little sister.

Well, I didn't say you had go away for keeps. You could try it for a week and come back. Your little sister will be right where you left her, exploring the contents of your underwear drawer.

But, of course, you can also indulge in Earthly Pleasures right where you live.

Local farmy things to do:

-Rather than live on a faraway farm, you could find a local one to spend time on, by putting up notices in local feed stores, talking to the farmers at the farmers' market, or asking everyone if they know a farmer who might like an apprentice. Someone will know someone.

Tabitha Mountjoy wrote about her work as a farm apprentice in *GWS* #68:

I first met Ms. Chaffin, who owns the farm, by buying a horse from her. My new horse, Shari, is now boarding there, so I help out around the barn. I sometimes feed, which includes graining, haying, watering, and anything else that each horse needs. I might clean stalls or lead horses to pasture for their exercising. I am also learning to give the ill horses penicillin injections.

-Join a 4-H group. I am sorry to admit that when I was a teenager, some nasty terms like "hick" ran through my snooty little fashion-conscious brain when I heard that term 4-H. If you think that way too, get past your stereotypes and get big. You can wear purple hair and angry black boots and still shear a sheep.

According to the World Book Encyclopedia, 4-H is the "largest informal education program for young people in the United States." Funded by the government, it revolves around sponsoring projects--not only in agriculture but also in career investigations, science, technology, etc. You can do individual or group projects. Look it up in the county government section of your phone book, or write the 4-H Central Office, 7100 Connecticut Avenue, Chevy Chase, MD 20815.

Elaine Mahoney wrote in *GWS* #28 about her daughter:

Kendra is a 4-H teen this year....The 4-H teen boys and girls work on community projects, organize dances, go on trips together, and study animal care, health, nutrition, gardening, and energy....Kendra went to the State House with 4-H and is going to Washington D.C. with them in July. She also has a proposal application to request funding of a community awareness project that she has in mind, sponsored by Reader's Digest, through 4-H.

-If you have a big yard, try a project or two right there, on your own. Maybe your parents even already have a garden, but you consider it their thing, not yours, or maybe they dump lots of chemicals on it. Ask if you can make your own fun. Due to city codes and neighbors with noses, you probably can't have piglets. You probably *can* have rabbits, kiwi fruit, blue corn, and a greenhouse full of gourmet salad things in the winter. Entice yourself with books from the 630 to 640 region of your library: *Cultivating Carnivorous Plants*, *Raising Your Own Turkeys*, *A Horse in Your Life*, *Growing Food in Solar Greenhouses*...

For help with gardening pests, soil testing, or other local issues, contact your county agricultural extension agent. Another good use of your family's tax money, this agent is paid to help farmers, gardeners, and homemakers solve agricultural and family living problems. There's no guarantee he'll know about healthy, organic solutions for problems, but likely he will. Call your county information number listed in the phone book government pages.

-Wherever you are, you could start a small agricultural business--growing and selling organic strawberries, specialty vegetables (edible flowers, for instance, bring $28 and more a pound), raising chickens and selling eggs, selling honey, drying and arranging flowers, raising milk goats or exotic animals like miniature horses, growing basement mushrooms, raising sheep and dying their wool...the possibilities are endless.

-Or, you could rent a spot in a community garden. Ask those amazing librarians for information.

-You could organize an effort to convert your city into a healthier place, with more fruit trees, community gardens, even mini-farms amidst the shopping zones. One good help: *The Edible City Resource Manual*, by Richard Britz, et al (William Kaufman, Inc., Los Altos, CA, 1981).

The examples

GWS #15 reports on unschooler Grant Harrison, then 14 years old and living in rural England:

> He has a small business running 100 head of poultry, selling the eggs to callers who come to his egg-grading room. Surplus cocks, etc, he will calculate to the last pence for their rearing costs and add his percentage for his time, and these are sold to the house. He has ten different pure breeds. He experiments with cross breeding. He is in need of a metal turning lathe which we [his parents] will help him obtain. He wants to make parts for the clocks which he mends, make a steam engine, parts of spinning wheels, etc. Already he has shown that he has tremendous aptitude in wood turning.

In *GWS #45*, Donna Spruill wrote,

> We live on a working ranch in central New Mexico...Our children (16, 14, and 7) have been homeschooled their entire educational experience...Living on a livestock ranch, the girls have ample opportunity to practice some veterinary skills, drive tractors and trucks, and operate small machinery. There's also time for observing wildlife and plant life and learning something about their immediate environment. We often take "field trips" to various historical and interesting locations around our state...

In *GWS #35*, Virginia Schewe wrote:

> Since we are a farm family, quite a number of our science projects are closely tied to agriculture. The latest project is a fish farm--complete with ten-gallon-aquarium for the showy stuff and a five-gallon nursery tank....Both boys did a man's work in the fields this past farming season....We put them on the payroll and they did a swell job... Mark (14) learned how to operate the combine and he also drilled (planted) over 100 acres of wheat this fall. Bill (13) did most of the disking and field cultivating just ahead of the planter, plus hauling the harvested grain.

In *GWS #30*, Laurie Fishel-Lingemann wrote,

> The girls (Star, 13; Deva, almost 6) have been going visiting a woman who lives 20 miles from here. This woman invited two other girls of similar ages to share four days with her; she expects them to cook and care for themselves and help her with her gardening and other projects. She is a talented artist with

fabric and crochet and plans to share her skills with them. Star brought her wool, etc., and was very excited...

Star is working as a volunteer at the library one day a week. She loves books, so you can imagine that she is in ecstasy doing this...

Star was very involved with horses (more in imagery than reality, although she had her own pony for several years) and thought she would become more involved when we moved. But as she has grown she finds craft work, reading and gardening much more appealing to her than working with animals. She had a hard time letting go of her "images," even felt guilty that she didn't want to own a horse (as though she were betraying herself!). After much tearfulness, she gave away her six geese and their goslings when she realized the inefficient set-up she had and that she was not really that interested or attentive to them. She has been much relieved and happy now that they are gone and has put much energy into her garden, which is thriving.

chapter 38
fixing the world: social and political activism

Being less than 18 doesn't make you less than human. Nor does it deprive you of a voice in the world, unless you let it. *Growing Without Schooling (GWS)* #68 tells about 12-year-old Andrew Holleman, a Massachusetts school kid who saved a woodland in his community from turning into condominiums. Andrew researched zoning laws and other information, wrote letters to legislators and TV anchor people. He got his neighbors together and told them what was going on, won their support, and circulated a petition. The developers' permit was denied.

Activism: Political Science in Action

If you see that something's wrong in the world, you can try to help fix it by working through or "at" our political system.

As you know, you can write letters to congressmen.* As you probably know, you can distribute fliers for political campaigns, knock on doors to ask for Greenpeace donations, and help other people register to vote--though you yourself can't yet vote.

Here are two major ways you can become more deeply involved--one working through the legal system, the other working more or less outside of it. However, these can be combined--for example, you can use civil disobedience to help raise people's awareness which can then lead to changed laws:

1. Get a new law passed.

---

* How to contact your senators and representatives in Washington: write them c/o U.S. Senate, Washington DC 20510 or c/o U.S. House of Representatives, Washington DC 20515.

Most bills (potential laws) are supposedly begun by senators and representatives, but they can also be written by ordinary citizens. Even if you don't want to go through the headache of writing an actual bill, you can write a detailed proposal, get other people to support your efforts, and urge your representatives to develop a bill.

First, identify a particular law that needs changing--does your city have fair guidelines for skateboarders? Does your state need a better recycling law, or a law that allows people of any age to earn their G.E.D. diploma? Should 16-year-olds be able to vote in national elections? Should congresspeople face penalties for breaking promises to their constituents?

Then, with the help of likeminded people, write down what you think the law should say. Attend city council meetings, or contact your representative and senators until you find someone who will consider developing and sponsoring your bill. For practical information about working on legislation, contact the League of Women Voters, in the phone book. Also, see *How Federal Laws are Made* (WANT Publishing Co., 1982).

If your issue is a popular one, then undoubtedly other people are already working on it. Plug into their efforts rather than start from scratch. Likely, your local League of Women Voters can tell you who's working on what. Also, of course, contact relevant organizations--Sierra Club, etc., for environmental issues, Planned Parenthood, etc., for birth control issues, and so on.

2. Participate in non-violent direct action or civil disobedience-- otherwise known as sit-ins, blockades, marches, demonstrations, rallies, protests, and political street theater.

Non-violent "direct action" usually refers to a dramatic act done in public in order to call attention to a societal wrong. Direct action can be legal or illegal.

Civil disobedience is the illegal version of non-violent direct action, meaning deliberately breaking a law that you consider wrong. The tradition has thousands of years behind it--remember all those Hebrew boys in the Bible refusing to worship kings' idols? Thoreau gave it new life in the 1800's when he refused to pay taxes that supported slavery and the Mexican War, and then wrote about his convictions in the essay "On the Duty of Civil Disobedience." As the story goes, Emerson came to see Thoreau the night he was in jail. "Why are you here?" asked Emerson accusingly. "Why are you not here?" countered Thoreau.

Whether you want to go all the way and risk arrest or become more softly involved by chanting in a peace march, my activist friend Heiko strongly suggests that you take a free workshop in Non-Violence, offered frequently in almost every city by peace groups. How to find these groups? Check local alternative newspapers (usually available at organic food stores or co-ops) and various bulletin boards. Contact Unitarian and Quaker (Friends) churches, or college peace groups. If you find nothing, write the War Resisters League (address below--"organizations") to ask for local phone numbers.

Non-Violence workshops last about six hours. They cover 1) the history and philosophy of non-violent civil disobedience, 2) consensus process--how to reach agreements, not just majority-wins/everyone else loses, 3) what to actually *do* when you're involved in civil disobedience--how to deal with police, how to let your body go limp when they carry you off, what not to say, etc.

Heiko further advises: don't try to do tough political work on your own. Surround yourself with support, both practical and emotional. At times, all your efforts will seem a failure. Don't give up--your role is small but essential. Drop by drop, water makes an ocean.

Speak for yourselves

Overwhelming issues like the environment, world hunger, and world peace certainly deserve your attention, but *your* rights are important too. Consider: the voting age, driving ages, draft laws, school and homeschool statutes, birth control and abortion issues, legal drinking ages, and child labor laws. Regardless of your opinions, these issues matter because they affect you directly. I encourage you to speak up and let your voice be heard.

You, the world

Thanks to popular new books like *Fifty Simple Things You Can Do To Save the Earth* (Earthworks Press, 1989), you probably already know that your own actions count. In the big picture, it helps when you don't eat tuna caught in dolphin-killing nets, when you use your junk mail instead of new notebooks for scratch paper. The *Fifty...* book and many organizations and people can help you decide what changes to make in your own life. But I have a couple things to add. Some people acquire strange military pious personalities when they first start changing their lifestyles for political/environmental reasons, temporarily losing touch with the things they care about most in the first place. So:

As you work to make the world a better place, don't turn into a robot. Keep it personal. Clean up a roadside pond and then go fishing there. On your way to the recycling center, give your apple to a baglady. Gestures will not, in themselves, get the work done, but they feed the spirit and keep the motivation alive.

Also, now that you live so correctly and sacrifice your time to Good Causes, don't condemn less perfect people. Remain humble. Recognize that no matter how good your intentions are, as a 20th-century industrialized-nation human being, some of *your* activities harm the earth. If you wear cotton, you support cotton fields full of pesticides rather than habitat for diverse wildlife. If you wear polyester--a petroleum product--you support a petroleum-dependent economy and global warming. If you use electricity, you are part of the reason the power company plans to damn another river. Don't kick yourself for what you can't do, but don't kick other people either. Kicking, in fact, *prevents* other people from getting involved--just like when your mom used to nag you to do your homework it made you want *not* to do your homework.

In the company of your parents, remain *especially* humble. Recognize that not only did they invite you into this world at great cost to themselves, but they also exercised tremendous patience when you went through your shop-till-you-drop years (*real* good for the planet), your three-page-long Christmas wish-list years, your "But Jonnice's mom bought *her* a new TV" years. Exercise a little patience and acceptance in return. You can talk *with* them, of course, but don't preach *at* them.

You can also combine your political convictions with your other work. Make a business out of recycling or planting organic gardens for busy yuppies. Volunteer to do research for Greenpeace. Find an internship with a shelter for the homeless.

Books:
-*Fifty Simple Things You Can Do to Save the Earth*, by the Earth Works Group (Earthworks Press, 1989). In case you haven't heard of this bestseller, it tells exactly what the title says. Short and sweet.

-*How to Make the World a Better Place*, by Jeffrey Hollender (William Morrow, 1990), is similar to *Fifty Simple Things*--easy to use and read. However, it is more comprehensive and covers hunger, peace, and human rights issues as well as environmental topics. Also, it gives addresses for dozens of specialized organizations like National Student Campaign Against Hunger, National Coalition Against the Misuse of Pesticides, and Peace Brigades International.

Organizations
Band together. Working with others makes it all possible, not to mention fun. Working alone gets meaningless fast. To start your own organization, see the excellent short booklet written by and for teenagers, *Student Action Guide: how to have a successful environmental club*. Although it focuses on environmental issues, you could also use it to form other types of action-oriented groups. Among other things, it explains how to work around interfering school schedules and policies if you want to start a *school* club. (Even as an unschooler you might choose to get your club *started* through a school, in order to reach as many interested people as possible. Then, you could hold continuing meetings at someone's home or a coffeeshop--somewhere more joyful and comfortable than school.) The *Guide* is available for $3.95 from YES! 706 Frederick Street, Santa Cruz, CA 95062.

(By the way, YES! is a group of six dynamic people ages 16-20 who are currently in the midst of a year-long tour--which they planned and organized themselves--raising environmental awareness at more than 200 school assemblies nationwide. Needless to say, they are neglecting their own formal compulsory educations at the moment.)

Or, plug into somebody else's organization. Here are just a few of the hundreds:

-Amnesty International (works to end torture and free "prisoners of conscience"), Amnesty International USA, 322 Eighth Avenue, New York, NY 10001.

-Greenpeace USA, 1611 Connecticut Avenue NW, Washington, DC 20009.

-Oxfam America (deals with hunger and poverty by funding self-help and disaster-relief projects in third world countries), 115 Broadway, Boston, MA 02116.

-PETA (People for the Ethical Treatment of Animals), P.O. Box 42516, Washington, D.C., 20015.

-Rainforest Action Network, 300 Broadway, Suite 28, San Francisco, CA 94133.

-Sierra Club, 730 Polk Street, San Francisco, CA 94009.

-War Resisters League, 339 Lafayette Street, New York, NY 10012.

A couple of small organizations you've probably not heard of:

-Peace Links is an organization founded and run mainly by women, with the goal of increasing communication between Americans and Soviets, of preventing nuclear war, and reducing military spending. They have thousands of Russian and other Soviet pen pals (who write in English) waiting for American pen pals (could be you). Also, they provide packets which can help you organize a group of teenagers or people-in-general to work for peace. To be connected with a pen pal or to request more information, contact Peace Links, 747 8th Street S.E., Washington, DC 20003. If you might want to start a local group, contact Linda Talbott c/o this address.

-Community Regeneration, a service of the Rodale Institute, can help you work with others to turn your community into a more neighborly, empowered, healthy, and meaningful place to live. Membership includes a newsletter, free access to the Regeneration Network Database, and inexpensive information from the organization's research files. Student rate for individual memberships is currently $15. Membership or more information from Community Regeneration Solutions, 222 Main Street, Emmaus, PA, 18098, (215) 967-5171.

The following lists are based on a wonderful chart my friend Heiko made for me. Although they repeat some of the information in this chapter, they are organized differently and tightly packed with ideas. They can both help you brainstorm *and* see the way that big issues can be addressed through major goals which are broken down into smaller subtasks.

Here are examples of general issues that people can work on:
environment, peace, social justice, women's stuff, racism, labor, farm, homelessness, hunger, Central America, gay/lesbian, consumer protection, human rights, handicapped access, Afro-American, Latino, Asian American, or Native American awareness and rights, religious freedom, old people's rights, young people's rights....

Here are some major ways people can address any of these (or other) issues:
1) Change people's attitudes through education (not necessarily *school* education, of course--getting media attention is a big part of this one).
2) Change laws--which can include electing decent congresspeople, working to get certain laws passed, and making certain that laws are enforced...
3) Change structures *directly*--support labor strikes, force companies to divest their stock in South Africa, start recycling programs, support boycotts, create shelters for battered women, etc.

Here are some options people (and groups of people) have in their approach to accomplishing these goals:
-be straight or be controversial
-be egalitarian or be hierarchical
-vote or use consensus process
-hire staff or be volunteer-only
-work on a grassroots level and/or make friends in "establishment"
-work with a group that already exists or start your own group

Finally, here are some specific strategies people can use to accomplish their goals:
(Generally, choose a few that most reflect the talents of your group and that will use your energy most efficiently. Don't try to do all these or you'll do none of them well.)

Make phone calls to representatives, write letters to representatives, make leaflets, distribute leaflets, staff offices, work at information tables during fairs and events, organize fundraising events, do library research, do original research, write press releases, call newspapers, help put together alternative newspapers, organize meetings, write proposals, attend public hearings, attend rallies and marches, get arrested, design and make posters or banners, perform guerilla theater, help prepare mailings, talk to your friends, go door to door and talk to your neighborhood, do coalition building with similar groups, volunteer at soup kitchens or women's shelters, etc... ◆

Part Five

the lives of
unschoolers

chapter 39

the
guinea pig
chapter

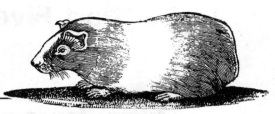

This chapter grew stubbornly out of my mailbox.

The book in your hands is spiked all through with stories of unschooled teenagers--where they work, what they think about learning, how they play soccer, which musical instruments they love. But I wanted to describe more of the people who wrote me about their lives, just to assure you they're real, just to give you a bigger idea of what's possible. In the next pages, therefore, I throw a party to introduce you to a few dozen of these teenagers, and toss in morsels of *Growing Without Schooling* (*GWS*) articles along the way. Each teenager herein deserves a whole celebratory chapter to herself or himself, but that's another book for another year.

Most of the people you're about to meet study a fairly traditional curriculum, including math, science, literature, history. I do not explain their academics in detail, but most use textbooks for math, and textbooks or library books for other subjects. Some also use PBS, tapes, computers, and museums. Many learn from adult friends. Some take courses through junior colleges, correspondence schools, or even public high school. Some have parents who are intimately involved with decision making and checking work; others work and make choices independently. Also, they don't necessarily study a lot of subjects at once--they might read biographies for a few weeks and then spend a month having a Relationship with a microscope.

However, some of the people here do not study *anything* formally. Even these completely "unstructured" teenagers usually find out about "academic" subjects in more depth than schooled teens do; they just don't do it on predetermined schedules. Most are avid readers, probably because nobody forces them to read.

Introductions will be made in alphabetical order. After they're finished and you've found someone to sit by, your author will make a few comments.

Tom Adams, 12, of Pennsylvania, pursues a variety of hobbies--collecting and cataloging stamps and football and baseball cards, collecting rocks, drawing, carving wood, reading mysteries, and playing baseball and football with friends. Eventually, he'd like to go to college and perhaps become a professional baseball player or a lawyer. He points out that living in a university town offers great advantages, since he has access to the university library, cultural events, and "knowledge bank" of professors.

Joseph Anderton, 15, of North Carolina, uses textbooks; he tests at two years above grade level. He spends much of his time working with his father, who is a heating and air-conditioning serviceman; he plans to earn a license in this field and maybe also go to college. Also, he plays football with friends and collects baseball cards.

Britt Barker, of Ohio, now a 22-year-old pianist and bush pilot, grew up passionately interested in wildlife and classical music. You can read more about her field biology and travel experience in chapter 21 (or in her own book), but I wanted to mention other aspects of her life here. Unschooled and surrounded by a close, warm farming family of seven, Britt began writing for publication at age 12 with an article for *Mother Earth News* on ponies. Two years later she began selling weekly word-search puzzles to a local newspaper, and wrote a second article for *Mother Earth News* (on dairy goats) at 15. An accomplished classical pianist and integral member of the family's farmsteading operation, she decided at age 16 to spend time away from home in search of new adventures, described in *Letters Home*. In 1986, she was chosen as one of *Teenage* magazine's "100 most interesting teenagers in the country."[*]

Britt's mother Penny sent me an update on her other kids. **Maggie**, 17, is a dedicated dog musher who keeps 30 dogs--Alaskan huskies and border collies. In Michigan, she conducts pack dog trekking and dogsledding workshops for people ages 11 and up. A newspaper clipping tells about a recent 50 mile race that she and her dogs won:

"You could see the joy in her face," Doty [a sheriff] said, describing the confident look of Maggie Barker. "She was smiling when she came over the hill and crossed the road."

Strait [another sheriff] noted that Barker always seemed to be about 10 minutes ahead of the next racer. She won by nearly 40 minutes.

Other unschooled Barkers are 16-year-old **Dan**, "the cellist," 14-year-old **Ben**, "the kayaker and boat builder," and 12-year-old **Jonah**, "the mechanic." "All so different," comments Penny, "It's great fun." All of the Barkers work together to run a summer program at their farmstead, where children visit for five days at a time, participating in farm activities.

Benjamin Israel Billings, 16, of Massachusetts, wrote,

I like to fish. I read a lot (Vietnam). I really like my music (progressive rock, classical, mens' choral, new age, folk and some Irish also). One of my favorite things is bike riding (I did 96 miles in an afternoon last summer). I play Dungeons and Dragons. Boy Scout activities are always favorites as well as

---

[*] See Britt Barker, *Letters Home* (in bibliography), and *GWS* #49.

church activities...I am receiving my Eagle Scout in April. I am currently serving as a Junior Assistant Scoutmaster...

Django Bohren, 13, of Louisiana, lives "on the road" with his family since his father, Spencer Bohren, is a musician. Between August and December of 1990, for instance, he's traveling through Louisiana, Yellowstone Park, Washington, Oregon, Montana, Wyoming, Colorado, Arizona, Michigan, Illinois, and Kentucky. He *did* attend school once for two and a half weeks and enjoyed it, but his unschooled life is full. Constant travel, obviously, exposes him to worlds most teenagers don't get the chance to see.

Anne Brosnan, 13, of New York, wrote a lot worth repeating. Her words read like poetry, and they send a strong pang through me. In them, I catch glimpses of the unschooler I might have been...

I learn by living and doing. At home we can do anything we want, anytime. Mom doesn't make us do any reading or schoolwork. Kids go to school to learn how to do things, but it wastes a lot of time and you can get by doing whatever it is and learning as you go along. I learned to play piano by playing it. I found out how to read music just from finding the note for middle C on the music and on the piano, and all notes followed. I learned how to read by reading, how to type by typing, etc. It goes on and on, and it's a very simple concept, really...

Anne lists her interests as

classical music, folk, ragtime, early American (classic) jazz, piano, banjo, harmonica and other instruments....I pursue the study of music by listening to it and playing it.

Mythology and folklore, legends and beliefs of all cultures, deep ecology, philosophy, the Gaia Hypothesis. (These following people I study and/or admire) Albert Einstein, John Muir, Robert Frost, Charles Dickens, Amos Bronson Alcott, Leonardo Da Vinci, Ludwig Beethoven, Wolfgang Amadeus Mozart, Johann C. Bach, Abraham Lincoln, the Tree as a Being.

Nature, ecology, wolves, etc. The Lives and Personalities of Wolves and Whales in Relation to Humans as a Study of Environmental Peace, archaeology, anthropology, genealogy, geography, lexicology, bibliophilism, auto-didactism. Books such as Charles Dickens', Shakespeare, Scott O'Dell, *Watership Down* (Richard Adams), *My Family and Other Animals* (Gerald Durrell). Fishnetting, knitting, cuckoo clocks, running, basketball, badminton, Famous Homeschoolers, poetry, calligraphy, philately, postcards, animal skeletons, geodes, owls, Carl Larsson, typing, Galapogos Islands, Sierra Club, newsletters, history, simple living, farming, treehouses (for permanent living), vegetarianism, African wildlife, composting, recycling, bicycles, Native Americans, canoeing, camping, and hats. I use no textbooks except one or two workbooks for occasional math, and no correspondence courses.

She explains what she does with her time:

I go to track and basketball practice for a total of about three days a week and games and meets on weekends. That's in the evenings. In the daytimes I practice piano for about 45% of the time (a lot, anyway), write letters, read, knit, practice basketball, track, tennis, etc., do some gardening or composting, make hammocks, clean house, sort books, knead bread, etc. I have a lot of projects going too such as writing articles and cleaning and stamp collecting.

Todd Brown, 15, of Virginia, says the greatest advantages of never having gone to school are "choices" and "freedom." From what his friends tell him, school sounds "hostile, barbaric, and monotonous." Todd approaches his many interests from a thoughtful, profound perspective. For instance, he says that *Star Trek* is "an extension of our dreams and a realization of our limitless capabilities." In addition to watching the show, he reads books and attends *Star Trek* conventions. His other major interests are entomology--"I love insects and arthropods of all kinds"--and making electronics devices--"I can't even begin to describe the joy of designing and testing a circuit." Also, he sails, uses a computer (no Nintendo), draws, uses a microscope, makes jewelry and models, and reads. Included in his academic work is Latin and philosophy. His father teaches him electronics. College? His sights are set on Virginia Tech. He enjoys his Boy Scout troupe and marine biology camp. He is curiously hard on himself for one gap in his "education": "I hate history although I firmly believe that history will repeat itself if not studied. This is a flaw I am *not* proud of."

Sharma Buell, 16, of Maine, uses no textbooks or tests. "We just sit on the rim of the big melting pot, stirring, throwing stuff in…tasting what looks good." A free spirit with a thoughtful outlook, she does "a lot of art," hitchhikes, and thinks constantly. "I've learned most things the hard way," she says, "from actual experience which, I suppose, does the trick--but nothing like a clean, safe textbook with a time limit to 'learn' controlled information."

Becky Cauthen, 14, of Georgia, spends her non-academic time playing piano twice a month for a homeschool group and three times weekly for church. A candy striper, girl scout, and member of her church youth group, she helps run a cattle and goat farm, sews some of her own clothes, bakes, and plays guitar. She says she would not consider returning to school: "I would be gone from home for seven hours or more and that's a lot of time wasted. Now I can take a break from a tough English assignment, go help doctor cows or walk in the woods, or play the piano and come back to my work refreshed."

Chelsea Chapman of Alaska is taught by her parents, though not school style. She explains in *GWS #74*:

> Let me try to describe our homeschooling. My mother teaches us culture, history, literature and things like that, while Dad teaches us math, chemistry, some history, and physics. We do schoolwork from about 8:00 a.m. to 12:00 or so. Often we don't do any at all, and we never do it in the afternoon. My Dad works one week and then has the next week off. When he is home, we talk about math and chemistry, and he gives us some problems to work out. Often he just draws us pictures of protons, neurons, etc. to look at and study. Today I wrote short essays on Pythagoras, Archimedes, and Avogadro. Knowing about their lives really helps me remember their respective theorems, principles, and laws.
>
> I love physics and things like that! I have always thought that I was just not a smart enough person to understand these things and that they were deadly dull anyway (something I got from school). But now I have discovered that they aren't hard or dull or stupid, and I am finally getting over the thought that "hard stuff" isn't for everyone.
>
> Now, I said my mother teaches us history and literature. We mainly read for history. In fact, we read all the time. My 11-year-old sister and I will read anything and everything. We are really allowed to study what we choose here. In fact, it reminds me of Summerhill school sometimes. I love poetry and read masses of Blake, my favorite. Shakespeare is all right; I like *The Tempest* best. In contrast, I have been reading DOS (Disk Operating Systems) and doing a lot on our computer. We really just work on what we are interested in. Often schoolwork is nonexistent, like when there are more important things to do like going to watch the start of the great "Yukon Quest" dog sled race!
>
> I'm going to be a naturalist/writer/artist/poet when I grow up. These all, I think, can be combined.

Alex Clemens was 13 when his mother wrote to *GWS* #16,

> Alex now programs the Apple II, works at the hardware store, helps our Supervisor at city hall, takes math from his former public school math teacher, writes journal and book reports for me, passed his karate green belt in June, and cooks his own meals.

Christopher DeRoos wrote to *GWS* #32 when he was 16,

> Two years ago...my mother started taking me to sit in on college courses. I am at Holy Names College in Oakland [California], where a friend also attends. He started there when he was 15...I am in computer sciences and economics.

I'm going to be taking an auto engineering class....I am serving on a Planning Commission--Sign Committee, reviewing the Alameda County sign ordinances...

My motto is from *Auntie Mame*, "Life's a banquet and most of you poor suckers are starving to death." Being home taught has been the best!

Jonas Diener, 13, of Virginia, studies nothing formally. Instead, he spends his time biking, reading what he wants to read, working on a computer, and playing around with electronic things--"lights and wires and stuff."

Katrina Fallick, 14, of Washington, is interested in "ecology action," fashion design and merchandising, and sociology. "Ecology action" means she plants trees and reads a lot to find out what else needs to be done. To pursue her interest in fashion, she investigates clothing stores and then designs and sews clothing which she predicts will fit the next trend. Also, she works on a steering committee which organizes a local homeschool fair (she helped to film a commercial for the fair), reads, hikes, writes to penpals and-- oh yes--studies academic things like math and history. She plans to take the GED at 16, so that she can take college classes. However, she emphasizes that she will go to college for "knowledge, not a diploma," and that she will "take whatever classes [she needs] at whatever college has the best program for what [she wants] to learn."

When this book was almost finished, Katrina's mom Jj sent me the following update:

She is in Spokane attending a high school level vocational program in fashion merchandising--living with friends and "home schooling" for her regular subjects. At 14, she is enrolled as a high school junior...it will give her entry-level job skills at 15 and she hopes to get a job at 16, take a few classes at the junior college and begin a career in fashion design...making her own designs.

More about Katrina and her family in Chapter 37.

Zachary Field, 15, Maine, plans to become a professional juggler soon, and practices for well over an hour each day. He says his academic studies are "very informal." Like many unschoolers, when he first quit school five years ago, he and his family attempted to set up a fairly rigid home program, which later grew very unstructured. His interests include extensive reading, riding his unicycle, and spending time with his friends, most of whom are fellow jugglers.

Benjamin Flagel, 12, Maryland, belongs to two 4-H clubs, reads a lot, plays baseball, basketball, and soccer, keeps a garden, and collects butterflies and baseball cards.

Nicole Flores, of California, wrote in *GWS #52*,

I dropped out of high school when I was 15 and in the ninth grade. My mom and her boyfriend made it legally possible by turning our home into a private school.

It's great. They've been providing me with resource materials and three years later I've become interested in subjects I would have shrieked about if I was still in high school. I'm writing science fiction stories, reading physics, and most importantly I've learned how to think for myself and make my own decisions. Basically, the freedom I lacked in school has enabled me to grow up...

Elise Foxton, 15, of Washington, is enrolled in both a general homeschooling correspondence program and also in an algebra course through the University of Nebraska. She echoes most of the homeschoolers I heard from: "You have more time to do things not related to school. I ride the horses I take care of while other kids are still in school." Last year she started successfully showing her two horses, and she takes weekly riding lessons.

Theo Giesy, of Virginia, was one of the first homeschooling *moms* in the 70's. Her grade-school-aged kids kept asking if they could stay home from school, pointing out that they got more of an education at home. Theo took them seriously and took them out, though at the time she had no assurance that it would work out legally. All four of her kids started taking ballet, and Theo recalls their experiences in *GWS #58*, ten years after they'd started. By that time, in 1987, her kids were 14, 18, 20, and 22. Theo writes:

Shortly after she started taking ballet, *Danile* [the eldest] began to be interested in a career in dance. When she was 13, she started performing with a small modern dance group that performed in schools. She has been performing with similar groups ever since. She got her own apartment before she was 18, since she was dancing with a group based in Williamsburg, 40 miles from our house. When she was 18 she told us that she didn't need our financial support any more and that she would tell us if she needed help. Besides dancing she teaches ballet and jazz classes. She has never felt the need for a diploma. When filling out the "school attended" slot in job applications she writes Brook school, grade completed: 12th.

Darrin also took ballet, and since he was not in school he could watch rehearsals and help by running the tape recorder. That led him into theater technical work. He kept taking ballet but was more interested in tech work as a career. He went to Antioch College for two years [beginning at 17], and during that time he began to think that he did want to dance. He left college and spent the past year studying at Boston Ballet. He recently signed a contract with Nevada Dance Theater for next year.

Susie enjoyed ballet but never planned to be a ballerina. She has considered musical theater and modeling. She has worked in the groups that Danile worked in, both as a dancer and as a tech person. Now she is dancing in a lounge. Next year she and Danile will both dance with a group that performs in schools and for other community groups. She doesn't know what she wants to do beyond that.

Anita is writing poems, a teenage romance, and moving notes to friends and family. She babysits for ten families, though she is cutting back to have time for other things. She makes beautiful earrings which she gives to special friends and occasionally sells. Had she been in school, I'm sure she would have been labeled "learning disabled" because she was a late reader....

It has been wonderful to watch all four children grow, learn and develop with no curriculum, no artificial schedules and no comparison with "the norm."

As I write, it is February 1991 and Anita is 18 years old, in the midst of a year-long road trip around the country (see chapter 29). When she came through Eugene and stayed with me, she told me more about the Giesys' lives. As a teenager, Anita developed a very strong interest in children, and held several long term daytime babysitting jobs with different families. Also, she was involved in 4-H, worked as a counselor for 4-H camps, taught workshops in earring making, did technical work for dance productions, and lobbied against a law requiring parental consent for minors' abortions.

Danile, 25, continues to dance with the company Ballet Tidewater and to teach ballet as well as some jazz and character dance. Also, she performs as a "heartbreak dancer," doing fifties style rock 'n roll dancing. Darrin, 23, is dancing as an apprentice with the Ballet Met of Columbus, Ohio, and considering auditioning for other dance companies or going back to college. He has also been a volunteer fireman and an EMT. Susie, 21, just returned from six months of traveling on her own in Europe. Before that, she danced with Ballet Tidewater, taught ballet to inner-city kids, and danced in a lounge.

Darlene Graham of Texas wrote in *GWS* #37 about her sons **Grant** and **Graham**,

Grant is 17 now and works as a carpenter while preparing to take his G.E.D. test. Graham, 14, has taken a breather from his violin lessons....He does quite a lot of auto repair with my husband, and is becoming very skilled and responsible. At his age, he loves anything to do with cars, and never complains about unloading livestock feed since it involves driving to the barn, backing up, etc., and maybe going once or twice up and down the driveway for good measure.

Ashia Gustafson, 13, of Washington, is extremely involved in dance, and is in fact considering a dance career. Currently, she studies ballet, jazz, tap, and modern dance. Also, she pursues a fairly "traditional" academic program through the Calvert School, a correspondence school described in chapter 11. She plans to attend college, and considers her academic knowledge and skills more well rounded, and generally higher, than that of her schooled peers.

Andrea Harrison, of England, became a member of Ludlow Orchestra at age 16. *GWS #15* reports:

> She plans to go on to Dartington to study music when she is 18. Until recently she has run a small business from one of the buildings [at home]. She obtained organic whole wheat from a neighbor friend, made bread and sold it from her little shop, but has now found that the demands were too great on her energy and time for her to do justice to her musical study. Some days this can be in the region of eight to ten hours of intensive study.

Gordon Hubbell, 15, of California, is a new unschooler studying Russian, English, and math. He spends as much time as possible skiing and mountain biking. He participates in ski races, reads books on ski technique, and skis "the Extreme" frequently. "With mountain biking," he explains, "I ride 18 miles everyday at a high cadence through varying terrain."

Jud Jerome, rather famous poet, essayist, playwright, etc., wrote way back in *GWS #1* about his daughter, from age 12 onward:

> To avoid the law [in the early 70's] we enrolled her in a 'free' school in Spokane, Washington, run by a friend who carried her on the rolls, though she has not yet, to date, seen that city or that school. She spent most of the first year here at the farm, pitching in as an adult, learning from experience as we were all learning. While she was still 13 we went to help another commune, in northern Vermont, with sugaring, and she loved that place--which was very primitive and used horse-drawn equipment--so asked to stay. This was an agreeable arrangement on all sides--and she has lived there now for over five years, except for one, when she was 16. That year she and her mate (ten years her senior) went to Iceland (Vermont was not rugged enough for them) to winter, working in a fish cannery. The next Spring they traveled, camping, to Scandinavia, hiked the Alps, then flew home--coming back with $3000 more than they left with after a year abroad. Last year, she wanted to apply for a government vocational program, for which she needed a high school diploma, so went to an adult education class for a few months, and took the test, passing in the top percentile (and being offered scholarships to various colleges). She "graduated" earlier than her classmates who stayed in school. I think her case illustrates especially dramatically the waste of time in schools. She is by no means a studious type, would never think of herself as an intellectual, has always been more interested in milking cows and hoeing vegetables and

driving teams of horses than in books, and in her years between 13 and 18 moved comfortably into womanhood and acquired a vast number of skills, had a vast range of experiences in the adult world, yet managed to qualify exceptionally by academic standards. By comparison, her classmates who stayed in school are in many ways stunted in mind, emotionally disturbed, without significant goals or sound values in their lives--in large part (in my judgment) specifically because of their schooling.

Clarissa Johnston, 14, of Georgia, who has been out of school for five and a half years, takes gymnastics four days a week. She studies most academic subjects using textbooks, but also attends a Spanish class at a high school and studies nature on her own. In addition to her fairly rigorous academic coursework and intense involvement with gymnastics, she appreciates the time she has (after chores) to be with friends, spend time outside, and read. She has already decided on a college, and hopes to become a botanist or P.E. teacher.

Vanessa Keith, now 21, of New Hampshire, never went to school. She never studied much, either, except algebra when she was 18, and some Montesorri-style reading, writing, and math around the ages of six and seven. Neighbors gave her occasional lessons in typing, French, math, and writing. Mostly, she followed her interests in crafts, weaving, and sewing. At eighteen she took the GED, her first test ever, without studying, and passed. Growing up, she spent four months of every year at work, picking apples and pruning apple trees with her parents.

John Keller, 19, of Minnesota, is currently a freshman at Carleton College. As a teenager, he learned under the guidance of his parents, who work with Wycliffe Bible Translators. He grew up living in Vietnam, Cambodia, and France as well as the U.S.; last year he spent five weeks traveling with his father in Europe. A potential French, English, or political science major, John is an Eagle Scout, a Boundary Waters canoe guide, and hockey player. He comments:

> In the 8th and 9th grades I used a prepared curriculum. Once we realized we could do a better job on our own, we bought texts and other materials, and planned grades 10 through 12 independently.

> Now that I am in college, I am more sure that I was prepared for it as well as anyone else. Also, I feel that I am a stronger individualist because of home schooling, and am less likely to just go with the flow of popular opinion on campus.

> Socialization was never a big worry for me, but all the same it is reassuring to see that I have made many good friends, that I feel comfortable participating in classes and discussions, and am involved in extra-curricular activities.

Suzanne Klemp, 15, of Wisconsin, has been out of school four years. "It was my idea," she writes, "because I didn't like the negative environment in public school, and because my teachers stifled my creativity." She studies algebra, English, biology, history, and other subjects using textbooks, but also focuses heavily on ballet; she takes classes *and* teaches classes at the YMCA. She has put together a youth group for teenagers within her local home-educators' group, and attends a church youth group. She plans to go to college and also hopes to get into a ballet company.

Hanna Lee, 13, of New York, rides her horse a lot and skates every Tuesday at an arena. She plans to go to Skidmore College to become a horse trainer.

Jason Lescalleet, 14, of Ohio, researches whatever seems interesting, programs his computer, reads a lot, and also uses textbooks and works problems. (For science, he uses the same texts his mother teaches with at Ohio State University.) He draws and reads "spacey, futuristic, high-tech things." He plays the violin, and advises beginning unschoolers, "If the school sends you a curriculum guide, ignore it." He plans to attend college and says, "I will definitely get into computers, maybe write video games that will make Nintendo turn as green as a John Deere Tractor."

Jessin Lui, 13, of Maryland, enjoys working closely with her mother in her studies of science, history, social studies, math, literature, and composition. Although she has never been to school, she is aware that without it, she has "extra time on [her] hands" for not only being with friends but also involving herself in interests like drama, singing, piano, ice and roller skating, and swimming. She plans to go to a university, and enjoys trips to the symphony, museums, and many different plays. Also, she says, "Sometimes we travel for long periods during the school year. We're usually not in a rush to come back."

Rebecca McGuire, 14, of Alaska, enjoys picking berries, making jam, gardening, cooking, sewing, biking, and boating. She appreciates the extra time no school gives her for being outdoors.

Rosemary McGuire, 13, also of Alaska, says that she is able to learn things like cooking, violin, piano, painting, and embroidery since "I have so much more spare time because I do not have to do any useless, boring, repetitive worksheets." She helps in the barn, garden, and house. Also, she enjoys drawing, swimming in the ocean, bird and animal watching, biking, skiing, canoeing, and hiking. She plans to go to college and to write.

Amanda McPherson, 16, of California, practices piano, cares for her rose bushes, reads her Bible, and arranges flowers. Her academic work includes all the "usual" plus music theory, and German and computer literacy at a junior college. (Last year she took algebra and biology through the junior college.)

Jesse McPherson, 14, of California, spends most of his time riding his bike, for which he belongs to a racing club/team. Also, he plays violin at least one hour every day, backpacks frequently in the Sierra, works part time, attends church, does chores, swims, and plays pool and basketball with his friends. (Part of his academic work includes Spanish and algebra at a junior college.)

Joel Maurer, 13, California, studies only math in a formal sense. Aside from that, he says, to learn, "first you have to be interested in something. The rest is easy. If you really like something you just track it down and soak it in like a sponge." In contrast, he recalls that in school he once "had a teacher that ran a classroom like a jail. Eventually I gave up and stopped turning in work." Skateboarding claims a big chunk of his time, and he insists emphatically that "homeschoolers have a better sense of humor than 'schooled' people."

Patrick Meehan, 14, of Florida, is thoroughly enthusiastic about this past year--his first out of school. Designated "profoundly gifted" by the school system, Patrick had desperately wanted to quit school since the fourth grade, and finally had a chance to do so this year. "I was frustrated," he writes, "by the poor attitude of the students toward learning/school, the low caliber of most of the teachers, the cruelty of the students toward each other, and intolerance of differences. Many teachers seemed to dislike students who asked questions." He reports that the greatest advantage of unschooling is "Time, time, time. I have my life back for my own use." What does he do with all that time? "I read a great deal," he says, "I draw, I create graphic art on my computer, I take time to *think*. This is the MOST important: thinking! We go to museums, art shows, travel...We watch a lot of documentaries....I help in the yard and sometimes in the house. I am learning to cook. I do sculpture. I take music lessons and practice."

Several months after I heard from Patrick, his mother Gwen sent an update:

> The projects he has undertaken have been very real, professional quality undertakings. He has just completed an amazing portfolio of his work which was mailed out to a video game company for consideration....

> The portfolio took great planning, hours and hours of drawing (there are over 63 individual drawings of varying complexity which took anywhere from an hour to three or more hours to design and execute). He then wrote all the descriptions of the games and the characters, a cover letter and the copyright paperwork. It took several months to complete and he worked so hard.

Gwen reports that Patrick, who began his first music lessons less than a year ago, is also learning to compose music, taking a class and using a keyboard synthesizer: "Pat puts in hours and hours a week practicing and composing. He could never have made such strides trying to fit lessons and back-up and creating into the few moments at his disposal were he being crushed under the traditional school burden! A whole, new level of accomplishment for him..."

Rebecca Merrion, 13, of Indiana, has never been to school. She says one of the greatest advantages of unschooling is the opportunity to travel "whenever you want;" she looks forward to a trip to Haiti during this "school" year. She does "academics" through reading and talking, and also works on her garden, takes two ballet lessons each week, and swims. She wants to become a photographer and travel to the outback of Australia.

Cathy Moellers, 17, of Iowa, has been taking gymnastics for eight years. She sews, hand-quilts, plays the piano, and works with cattle on her family's farm. She has been president of her 4-H club for the past two years and belongs to wildlife and gun safety clubs. Her goals for her adult life include living on a farm, having a sewing business, and raising a family.

Ariel Mortensen, 15, of Washington, has been out of school for four and a half years. After academics, she pursues a wide range of artistic interests. She "draws a lot," takes two two-hour ballet classes each week, and two piano lessons each month. A major focus of her life is costume design--she sews and designs costumes on her own and for a local theater. She plans to go to an art college in Seattle.

Tabitha Mountjoy, 14, of Missouri, writes,

> I have three horses, two that I am training. I also like to play hackeysack, swim and ballroom dance. I was on our town's swimteam last summer and plan to be a lifeguard this coming summer. With hackeysack and ballroom dance I go through the Communiversity. It is mainly for older people but they are usually very open minded toward young people.

Helen Payne, 13, Virginia, uses six textbooks and spends quite a bit of time on academics. She appreciates the extra time she has for taking six different dance classes, playing on a soccer team, babysitting, and reading. She feels that learning outside of school is more effective because she is not pressured to learn.

Janet Petsche, 13, Minnesota, also follows an extensive academic program overseen by her mother. With her extra time (after chores) she enjoys reading, embroidery, fishing, and canoeing.

Aurelia Rector, 12, Arizona, learns math, English, science, geography, and history "by example, by reading, paying attention, wanting to learn, being curious, working, and just living!" No textbooks, thank you. Very involved in the arts, she takes two ballet classes weekly, sings all over the country with a performing group called Kids Alive, and acts in a community theater. She considers her academic knowledge and skills higher than that of people in school, and admits to having a reputation of "being smart."

Kacey Reynolds, 16, of North Carolina, spent seventh through ninth grades out of school. She went back to public school for tenth grade to see if she was "keeping up," and was placed in several advanced classes and invited into the National Honor Society. She finished the year with a straight-A average and says, "I account this to my homeschool experience." Being out of school gave her time to focus on her main academic interest--history--and on her love of acting. She's taken several acting courses at a local theater, and has been in two plays and a promotional commercial for a TV station. She hopes to go to college for a BFA in Theater Arts, and also plays the violin.

Jean Rezac, 13, of Massachusetts, is one of the free spirits who informed me that she doesn't "study," although she considers her academic skills and knowledge as well rounded and otherwise equal to that of her schooled peers. She says she learns "by whatever I do during the course of the day." She is very interested in horses and works on a horse farm.

Jeff Richardson, 14, Oklahoma, draws and skateboards, with the goal of becoming a pro skater.

Debra Roberts, 15, of Oklahoma, takes pride in the variety of household skills she is comfortable with that "most schoolgoers do not learn until on their own." "I can sew and do household work," she says, "I know how to change a baby's diaper and rinse it out, and I know how to handle a houseful of kids." Also, her responsibilities include washing lots of dishes, and caring for 100 chickens, two turkeys, and nine goats. Her scores on the Iowa Achievement Test recently showed that she was working academically at the 11th grade level overall. She often goes to work with her father, where she is training to become an electrician. Some possibilities for college--if she decides to go--include library science, sign language, and veterinary science.

Erin Roberts, 14, Maryland, is focused in several directions. She uses textbooks some months and other months "just pick[s] up something here and there." She plans to go to college and despite her loose academic schedule, she figures she's a bit ahead of her schooled peers academically in everything except possibly math. An avid reader, she consumes mysteries, science fiction, animal stories, sports stories, classics, novels, "just plain anything." She lives on a farm and keeps busy with the animals. Chapters 37 and 27 describe her work on a horse farm and her involvement with sports.

Jennifer Ryan, 13, Minnesota, uses texts for math, computer, and history, and learns science, piano, and writing "by doing them." She loves to read and write, bake, play sports, act, sew and do crafts, and garden.

Michael Scott, 12, of Georgia, supplements his academic program by using and programming a computer, "building things," and biking. He says that his freedom to explore robotics and computers has led him to become greatly interested in these fields, enough that he wants to become an engineer or programmer. He is lucky to enjoy a variety of equipment at home, including tools, a computer, a lab quality microscope, a sewing machine, and lots of books.

Kevin Sellstrom, 14, California, volunteers at a school for the mentally impaired and takes piano lessons. His academic work includes math, history, English, and science. As a boy scout, he works as a den chief, assisting a group of first- through fourth-graders. In his own troop, he is a

Senior Patrol Leader responsible for planning activities. Mechanically inclined, he rides and repairs bikes. He writes:

> I am relatively experienced in repairing gasoline engines on cars, as well as bicycles, tractors, and other mechanical equipment. I learned these skills by watching my dad and other people when they repaired machinery. I like to build power supplies and other electronic and electrical devices that may or may not have particular uses.
>
> In earning my amateur radio license, I had to learn to send and receive Morse Code as well as electronic theory and on-the-air operating techniques. As an amateur, I participate in radio nets as well as talk to other amateurs in person. My dad earned his amateur radio license in the 1950's and still has it and has taught me much of the electrical and electronic theory that I know. He earned his license when he was 15 and I earned mine at the age of 13.

Christin Severini, 13, of North Carolina, says,

> I dance at a ballet school nearby. I am also in the company. I care for and help animals by not eating them or wearing them; being friendly, kind, and helpful to the animals I come across; and also by being a member of People for the Ethical Treatment of Animals. I also make a lot of different crafts at home. Some of them are: dolls, clothes for myself, friendship bracelets, baskets, and cards for special occasions--birthdays, holidays, anniversaries, etc. etc.

Michael Severini, 15, also of North Carolina, enjoys karate, woodworking, airplane flying, and ham radio. "I go to a karate school nearby six days a week," he writes, "and I sometimes compete in tournaments. I take flying lessons at a nearby airport and I do Ham Radio at home." Michael plans to earn a black belt and to become a commercial airline pilot.

Mae Rose Shell, 13, of Vermont, has never been to school and seems to be a particularly relaxed, healthy person with a wise outlook on life. She spends a great deal of time outdoors--swimming, biking, gardening, cross country skiing, ice skating. She loves to read because "it opens a whole world" to her. From books, parents, friends, and everyday situations, she learns math, geography, history, and spelling. Her "learning" is not structured; she is free to do as she likes all the time. "I ask questions," she says, "I read books." About her future, she says she'll probably take college courses in the event that there's a specific subject she wants to learn more about. She wants to be a mother and a writer, and considers herself very "in tune with nature."

Matt Snead, 12, of Georgia, plays on basketball, tennis, baseball, and soccer teams. Also, he plays the piano and sings in choirs. He wants to attend college and become a pediatrician.

Anthony Stabile-Knowles, 13, of California, learns by completely choosing his activities, books, and interests. "No coercion, rewards, or force are used, no set 'school' schedule." He has never used textbooks or "courses," but reads a lot, especially in the areas that interest him most: geography, US history, science, astronomy, art. He also likes aircraft, watching the news, discussing current affairs, drawing, and designing games. "I read a lot and study a little."

Colleen Stevens, 15, of California, was out of school from fifth to eighth grades, although she is now in school. She worked as a volunteer both at a "living history" historical site and at an animal museum.

Patricia Young wrote to *GWS #25* after 14 years of homeschooling her children,

> Our youngest is now in college in an honors program having received a scholarship from Interlochen Arts Academy for her last year of high school, graduating with honors. Three are currently doing honors work in college. Older ones have become: a lawyer, nurse, legal assistant, computer company executive, medical secretary. None had the least difficulty going on to the school of their choice.
>
> Our oldest daughter now teaches her four children at home.

And an anonymous teenager from California wrote in *GWS #20*,

> Almost four months ago, I took the California High School Proficiency test which is equivalent to being a high school graduate. I am now a 15-year-old high school graduate. I am going to Los Angeles Valley Junior College--I couldn't afford to go to a university. I go at night and work part-time in the mornings as a tutor for retarded teenagers...In the afternoon, I tutor first and second graders at the local elementary school. Each job pays $300 a month...I'm still living at home and probably will for a while....I'm still doing some writing, The Santa Monica *Evening Outlook* printed a short story I wrote, and another will be in my college's pamphlet on how to write, for which I am being paid $50...

What you can do with all the examples in this chapter

1. Be inspired and emboldened, but not limited. Pursue *your* dreams; don't try to duplicate someone else's life. If there's something you've dreamed of doing in "the future," dream of doing it now.

2. Don't you *dare* be intimidated.

Do some of the people I just described sound more mature than you? If they are, it's not programmed in their genes; it's just a side-effect of unschooling. It will happen to you too.

Do the people I just described sound more "gifted" than you?

One thing that unschooled teenagers and their parents have continually emphasized to me is that they do *not* consider themselves gifted or otherwise inherently different from other people. And they're not, except in one important sense--they're gifted with *time* and trust. If you are quitting school, these gifts can be yours too. With them, anyone can develop expertise and a wide range of happy interests. (Many unschoolers spent disastrous, unpromising years in school before they bloomed outside of school.)

Of all the points I want to make in this book, this is one of the most important. Let me quote a few people on the subject:

Bonnie Sellstrom, whose son Kevin is described above, wrote me, "I should emphasize that our boys are not gifted. They simply have a curiosity about life and living that we have not tried to squelch. When a question is asked we try to find an answer to meet their needs."

Chapter 26 admires Ishmael and Vita Wallace, talented young musicians. Their mother Nancy wrote a wonderful book called *Better Than School*. In a review of it, John Holt says:

> Many school people [say] that home schooling parents like the Wallaces, taking their talented children out of the schools, leave them [the schools] to struggle along with the less talented...The answer, as I said in the introduction to the book, is that it is as sure as anything can be that neither Ishmael nor Vita would have been stars in school. Not only would they have done very badly in most school subjects, but they would almost certainly have had all kinds of damaging psychological labels stuck on them--Learning Disabled, Psychologically Disturbed, the whole disgusting package. The school would have seen them not as assets, only as problems, and would probably have convinced them that they were nothing but problems...

Indeed, Nancy reports in *Better Than School* that before she took Ishmael out of school, his first grade teacher had this to say about him:

> Ishmael does seem to have a problem with listening skills...I've been playing a record that gives the children instructions on how to follow specific directions, and Ishmael invariably gets lost. His hearing appears to be normal, so I'm just not sure what to do. He also has a problem grasping "whole concepts." For example, if I read the class a paragraph, he can't tell me the main idea. He gets too involved with all the little details. I'm thinking that maybe we should have Ishmael tested, just in case we discover some kind of developmental problem. Then we can send him to the resource room for, say, ten minutes a day, so they can help him.

Maria Holt, whose wisdom can also be found in chapter 10, tells in *GWS* #35 about the time the education department officials came to visit her family's homeschooling operation. They were impressed, and Maria reports, "One of them said to me as they took their leave of us, 'You have unusual children.' I returned, 'That is where you make your worst mistake.' And I meant it. Our children are 'average.' There is not a genius among them..."

"What amazes me," writes Penny Barker in *GWS* about her kids,

Is that these are not "gifted" children--they spend most of their time doing what they want to do (after chores, that is). In the winter we do structured studies for a couple of hours each morning but that's about it. Most of their learning is completely spontaneous. As I write, Maggie and Britt stopped by the orchard (where I'm typing) to tell me they are going off to the woods to look for a doe Britt spotted this morning and to spot birds and record their calls on paper....I could go on and on about my average kids and their wonderful growth. It seems they have simply more time to grow and develop than other children I know who have probably more potential but so much less time to realize it because they are always stuck away in a school building.

3. On the other hand, don't underestimate.

Don't dismiss this list of multifaceted teenagers by saying, "Yeah, well, I take dance classes too, and I go to school." Naturally, just because you go to school doesn't mean you can't also do other things. But the question of time and energy is a big question. People who both go to school *and* want to focus on outside interests essentially have several choices:

1) Skimp on homework time, turning in work which does not reflect their full abilities. End up feeling guilty and humiliated.

2) Treat their personal interests as secondary, devoting only a few hours each week to them, or pushing them into weekends and vacations.

3) Sacrifice time they'd like to spend with friends.

4) Sacrifice time spent with their families.

5) Sacrifice sleep or relaxation time. Get stressed.

6) Take "easy" school classes which do not require homework (and which may be boring, and which will not impress admissions officers of selective colleges).

7) Be born genetically engineered to calculate differential equations in seconds and to carry on a meaningful conversation while rewriting a sonnet.

In other words: if you already live an amazing life with school, you can live an even more amazing and far more relaxed life without it.

Joshua, our last heroic guinea pig in this chapter

Joshua Smith, now busy in college, wrote me a most delightful letter about his experience with quitting school. It made me smile all day. If only I'd read it when I was 12! In part, it says:

It started about two and a half years ago...at the time I was attending what is known as a "magnet" school--a school designed for "advanced" students. During a period in late fall of my junior year, with upcoming exams I found myself stressed out beyond belief. It was not because of the subject content but because of the bulk amount of work assigned. There was essentially no time left for regular life outside of school. I would come home from school worn out and disgusted. Like any other student I would always look forward to Fridays as if they were a blessing from some divine being.

One particularly disgusting week essentially became the catalyst for the dramatic change over in educational methods. Arriving home one Friday I flopped down on the couch and after a few minutes announced my intentions to my mom. She had just recently pulled my sister, now ten, out of school...and so was supportive. It wasn't until she had removed my sister from school that I realized that there was an alternative.

Always being one not afraid to challenge the system I marched into school the following Monday and resigned. And oh did that cause a stink with the officials. My guidance counselor insisted that if I dropped out I essentially was through with my education. (School is not the only place we learn things; there is that small thing known as life.) No matter how much I explained the situation there was no recognition from her or from my ex principal. Oh well, no real big surprises there. The big surprise came when I explained it to my teachers--they were supportive of the idea. And my classmates? Most of them did not know what was happening until it was over for I literally breezed through school that day. The ones I call my friends all exhibited either acceptance, admiration, or envy....

I left school early that day and walked into the record of becoming the first official "drop out" of Hume Fogg Academic High School. That is a day I shan't forget in a long, long time.

Over the next week I got an offer from the school board of Nashville to return to the school system but to a different school (rather than the one that I went to and rather than the one I was zoned for, where violence [and teen pregnancy were] common). I was offered a school all the way across town with transportation. They were willing to break zoning restrictions just to keep me in the school system.

Needless to say I thumbed my nose at them and never regretted the decision. Hume Fogg had marked the eighth school I had been in and I was ready for a change.

Over the next year and a half I worked, studied, traveled. I went back to my home country, Canada, to visit a friend, went to Florida, East Tennessee, and Wisconsin. Over this time I developed an intense interest in photography and psychology. And something else, something more important. I discovered myself....I [had] never fit the mold they made for me at school completely. Oh sure, I got along okay with the teachers, but I got away with whatever I wanted to in school. For instance, I didn't like gym particularly so I showed up for roll count and then slipped out walking right past the principal in doing so. I assume they couldn't assume that I was quietly rebelling. So I smiled and stabbed them in the back. Leaving school gave me no one to rebel against so I had more time to self reflect and change subtly, to become someone I felt comfortable with.

To go to college I had to take two tests, the GED (for lack of a HS diploma) and the SAT. I have always done well on standardized tests no matter what I think of them, and these were no exception. The SAT scores put me in the [running for the] "highly competitive" range or colleges. But I chose to apply to two colleges that both had attendance of around 600 and where there was not an exceptional atmosphere of competitiveness. I had already had my fill of that scene and wanted no more. I was accepted to both colleges and am now pursuing two degrees in Psychology and conflict resolution. I go to Northland College which is in upper Wisconsin away from most major cities. I like it there; the weather suits me better...and there is a large percentage of foreign students, which provides a good way to get a multi-cultural experience....

Right now I exist as a quiet but highly influential individual in college. I helped found a chapter of the Green Political Party, worked on implementing environmentally and socially sound measures, such as increased recycling, G.E. boycott and stopping a low level radioactive waste dump in upper Michigan. When I work on campus it is as a photographer and as such my photos have gone around the world when they were included in the college directory which goes to several countries such as Japan, India, China, Canada, Korea, and many others.

Not bad for a drop out, eh?

chapter 40

your allies
among
the Rich
and Famous

I suppose it shouldn't have surprised me, but it did. I'd heard of a few "famous" people who hadn't gone to school, so I went to the library to check up on them. I steered into the reference section and sat down with a stack of *Current Biography Yearbooks*. I started by looking up the names on my list, but pretty soon I was just turning pages and laughing. Why?

1. On the average, one out of every five or six people featured had dropped out of school or else not attended much formal school. (The *Current Biography Yearbook*[*] is published every year. It contains hundreds of short biographies on people who are currently prominent in some field--worldwide government leaders, entertainers, scientists, writers, artists.)

2. In almost all of the biographies, it was clear that the forces which had shaped these brilliant lives had little or nothing to do with school. Instead, other experiences had inspired and nurtured them.

For instance, Luc Montagnier, French virologist famous for his research on the AIDS virus, was inspired to become a scientist mainly because 1) his father, a CPA, kept a laboratory in the garage, 2) he was allowed to have his own laboratory in the basement, and 3) at age 15, he watched his grandfather die of cancer.[**]

Also for instance, Steven Spielberg learned filmmaking by experimenting with his father's 8mm camera. In high school, he spent a lot of time making films in order to escape studying algebra and French. Later, he sneaked onto movie sets to watch (his high school grades were too low to get him into film school).[***]

3. Lots of famous people had to go to school--they'd probably never heard of "unschooling"--but had nasty commentary. Examples at the end of this chapter.

---

[*] *Current Biography Yearbook* (H.W. Wilson and Co., annual)
[**] Information from *Current Biography Yearbook 1988*.
[***] Information from *Current Biography Yearbook 1978*.

I am not bringing up the subject of rich famous people to suggest that it is necessarily fulfilling to be rich and famous. However, information like this is a good kick in the pants for all the unimaginative, illogical people who believe quitting school generates "failure."

Keep your ears open, and compile your own list of admirable independent learners. Here is part of mine, from various sources including encyclopedias and *Current Biography*. Some people on the list have more headroom in other chapters.

Some people who dropped out of high school or otherwise escaped much or all of the usual teenage schooling:

Ansel Adams, Joan of Arc, Roseanne Barr, Irving Berlin, Rosamond Bernier, Claude Berri, William Blake, Art Blakey, John Boorman, Pearl Buck, Liz Claiborne, Samuel Clemens (Mark Twain), Buffalo Bill Cody, Noel Coward, Charles Dickens, Bo Diddley, Thomas Edison, Benjamin Franklin, Henry Ford, George Gershwin, Whoopi Goldberg, Samuel Gompers, Maxim Gorki, Robin Graham, Patrick Henry, Eric Hoffer, John Houston, John Paul Jones, Cyndi Lauper, William Lear, Abraham Lincoln, Jack London, Beryl Markham, Liza Minnelli, Wolfgang Amadeus Mozart, Sean O'Casey, Florence Nightingale, Beatrix Potter, David Puttnam, Keith Richards, Clement W. Stone, Randy Travis, Frank Lloyd Wright, Orville and Wilbur Wright, Brigham Young.*

Also: one third of the men who signed the Declaration of Independence, the Articles of Confederation, and the Constitution of the United States had no more than a few months of schooling up their sleeves. Historian Harry G. Good describes several of them:

> Stephen Hopkins of Rhode Island, a farm boy, became a practical surveyor and learned politics as moderator of town meetings. Roger Sherman of Connecticut was apprenticed to a shoemaker and became successively a writer, publisher, and lawyer....Others read medical books and helped a doctor in his practice.**

For more, browse through any year's edition of *Current Biography*. Also, you might have a look at a booklet called *Famous Homeschoolers*, by Malcolm and Nancy Plent, available from John Holt's Book and Music Store (see Appendix C).

---

* Sources: *Current Biography*, *Famous Homeschoolers*, by Malcolm and Nancy Plent, *Dove*, by Robin Graham, various other biographies, *The Norton Anthology of English Literature, volume 2, School Days of the Famous*, by Gerhard Prause.

** Harry G. Good, *A History of American Education* (Macmillan, 1962), p.84

Wanna-be unschoolers

Brilliant people often got that way not because of school, but despite it.

Woody Allen said "I loathed every day and regret every day I spent in school. I like to be taught to read and write and add and then be left alone."[*]

Winston Churchill said "I was happy as a child with my toys in my nursery. I have been happier every year since I became a man. But this interlude of school makes a somber grey patch upon the chart of my journey. It was an unending spell of worries that did not then seem petty, and of toil uncheered by fruition; a time of discomfort, restriction and purposeless monotony."[**]

German novelist **Franz Kafka** said, "As far as I have seen, at school...they aimed at blotting out one's individuality." According to Gerhard Prause, Kafka

> not only hated the system and the increasing anxiety before examinations, but he was also convinced that school offered too little in relation to the amount of time he spent there. Above all he felt it did not offer enough that was practical and relevant. His greatest criticism was aimed at the fact that education in general attempted to make everyone equal and therefore ignored an individual's talents and abilities.[***]

Melina Mercouri is the Greek Minister of Culture, as well as a former member of parliament and an actress. "The one great affliction of Miss Mercouri's childhood," reads *Current Biography* 1988, "was formal schooling, which bored her to tears, but since she grew up in a household frequented by politicians, scholars, writers, and artists, she nonetheless received a good liberal education..."

Claude Monet, French impressionist painter, "grew up a lad of unembarrassed daring, rebellious and self-willed," says Charles Merrill Mount's biography *Monet* (Simon and Schuster, 1966). According to this biography, Monet said

> I was undisciplined by birth; never would I bend, even in my most tender youth, to a rule. It was at home I learned the little I knew. Schools always appeared to me like a prison, and never could I make up my mind to stay there, not even for four hours a day, when the sunshine was inviting, the sea

---

* *Current Biography Yearbook*, 1979

** Sir Winston Churchill, *Great Destiny* (Putnam, 1965)

*** Gerhard Prause, *School Days of the Famous*, translated by Susan Hecker Ray (Springer, 1978), p. 38.

smooth, and when it was a joy to run about the cliffs in the free air, or to paddle in the water.

Monet was especially rebellious in his art classes, where he made parodies and caricatures instead of the realistic drawings he was asked to do. Although his drawing teacher considered him untalented, by the time he turned 15 he was in demand as a professional caricaturist.

Pulitzer-prize winning historian **Edmund Morris** hated high school, and *Current Biography* 1989 says he "entertained himself by writing novels 'behind cover of an atlas at the rearmost possible desk of every class.'"

Charles Trenet, French singer, songwriter, and writer, went to a Catholic School--the "Free School of the Trinity," about which he said, "The school might have been free, but I was shut up inside."[*]

---

[*] *Current Biography Yearbook* 1989

chapter 41

the life freestyle: Seth Raymond

A newspaper clipping on the refrigerator catches my eye--a photo of a boy balancing on the handlebars of his bike, a few words underneath. It's cleverly written, but contains one small mistake.

> Seth Raymond, a 14-year-old Port Townsend High School student, spent part of last Friday studying physics, geometry, physical education, and possibly philosophy as well. The teacher was his bicycle; the classroom a slab of concrete near the beach at Fort Worden State Park. Raymond said he's getting ready for the February 4 Northwest Freestyle Association competition in Seattle. He's been studying his course only seven months, but by the looks of his twirls, hops, and balancing act, seems ready to graduate with honors.

Exactly. Except: Seth Raymond is not a Port Townsend High School student.

Instead, he is--as the clipping points out--a student of his bike, and also of a math textbook, some good novels, the marine science center on the beach, his parents, the Olympic mountains, and his Pentax camera. Seth Raymond is an unschooled student of life.

He is 15 now, in October 1990, and I am visiting. I am welcomed not only by Seth, but also by his sisters Vallie, 11, and Lydia, 4, and by his parents, Kath and Dan. They live in an elegant, simple, spacious wooden frame house. The honest beauty of wooden beams, ceilings, floors, and door frames mixes with the warmth of worn oriental carpets and pumpkins heaped in the windows. Right off, the Raymonds strike me as being a lot like their house: in their company, there is no pretense, nothing doctored up or faked. No wonder--it turns out they built this house themselves, together, over a span of three years.

Seth has never been to school, thanks to his parents' courage and independence. Kath recalls the decision. A cousin had begun teaching school and given up in disillusionment. "I'd never put my kids in public school," she had warned Kath and Dan. Hoping to hear some good advice about other choices--Montessori, maybe, or alternative schools--they'd gone to hear John Holt speak in St. Paul. But he didn't talk about Montessori; he talked about unschooling. Kath reminded me of my own first reaction to Holt's books when she said, "I'd never even heard of unschooling before, but as soon as he started talking, I felt like I'd always believed in it."

Over the years, sometimes they have been legal, sometimes perhaps not. As far as they are concerned, it doesn't much matter. If they should ever have to fight for their right to stay out of school, they'll fight. All the same, they are thankful they've never been harassed.

As Seth grew, the family lived in different areas. Wherever he was, Seth took advantage of local opportunities and followed his own changing interests. At eight and nine, for instance, he took ballet classes from a "tough guy" teacher at the Minnesota Dance Theater in Minneapolis. The high point was performing in *The Nutcracker*--six times on stage and once for the half-time of a Vikings football game.

One of Seth's largest memories is his work on the house. He recalls clearing and burning brush, cutting down trees, watching the excavation and laying of the foundation, helping with beams, pouring cement, running errands, nailing up sheet rock, helping install insulation under the house, sanding and gluing pipes, putting in windows, cutting siding, mudding, taping, painting, panelling. "It was a lot of fun," he says, "I learned a lot. It will be a lot easier if I ever decide to build a house myself."

Last year, he worked about 18 hours a week at The Shanghai, a Chinese restaurant where no one else spoke much English. He bussed tables and brought food out to customers. After a year, he wanted more time for other interests, so he quit.

Academics

The Raymonds belong to a homeschool group with the local school district's stamp of approval; the district pays a part time teacher, Marcie, who helps homeschoolers document their academic work, gives them credits for this work, and organizes a weekly educational activity, which takes two hours every Wednesday afternoon. In return, the school district gets to officially "enroll" the homeschoolers, which gives them more money.

Seth and Kath explain their mixed feelings about the program. "It isn't the best part of homeschooling," says Seth, "But it's only two hours a week. It's not like six hours a day, every day. And Marcie helps a lot with finding textbooks when we need them." He recalls one time the group set a goal for how many books they'd read in a month. "That was fun," he remembers, "because I did read more than usual." Furthermore, in exchange for the minor bother of keeping logbooks and going to the weekly activity, Seth and Vallie are unquestionably legal, legitimate, and even working toward high school diplomas--though none of this matters a whole lot to them.

Clearly, the Raymonds do not feel the least bit dependent on the program. If it wasn't there, they'd homeschool anyway. If homeschooling was illegal, they'd homeschool anyway--and they wouldn't hide it. In Minnesota they knew homeschoolers who lived in fear and hiding; every time their doorbell rang the kids ran and hid under a bed. The Raymonds don't want to live like that.

Seth enjoys the other teenagers in the group, who have their own "specialties" in dance, writing, and sports. His best friends, though, happen to go to school; they are his friends because they share his interests in biking and backpacking.

I flip through Seth's log book. Some days there are entries for science, history, Spanish. Sometimes it's just math, reading, and biking. There are brief notes under each category: "watched and identified birds," "bike comp, placed 4th," "edited music tapes for biking," "edited video for bike sponsor," "made poster for room," "bought used bike frame and started sanding it," "marine center," "read 'Berniece Bobs Her Hair.'"

In the back of the logbook are some pockets full of academic paraphernalia and things Seth has written. There are a handful of bulletins ("teacher's guides") to accompany the PBS series *Scientific American Frontiers*, with instructions for labs and notes. "Explain to students," says one of them, "That ordinarily, water freezes and ice melts at 0° Celsius."

*

I ask Seth about his work in various subjects.

Writing is not his favorite thing to do, although he sometimes likes creative writing. One of his stories won an honorable mention at Centralia College's writing contest (mostly school kids entered) last year. Also, he keeps a journal. No one else reads it.

Last year he worked through most of the Harcourt Brace Jovanovich textbook *Biology*, doing the labs and reading--although he was also involved with the local marine science center. He started in the middle of the textbook, with the chapters that interested him most, and later went back to the beginning. He wrote away for more information on ectobiology, because the idea of life on other planets especially intrigued him. Also, he enjoyed a "science champions" day in Seattle, a sort of science fair populated mainly by public school students.

History? "I've always liked history," he says, "but never used a textbook for it." Aside from reading books on specific historical events, Seth explores history in the field. With his backpacking friend Reg, Seth figures he's investigated every one of the thirty World War I bunkers at Fort Worden State Park.

Math, reading, Spanish, and physical education? I get to see these in action. While I am at the Raymonds, this is what happens after I get up on Monday morning:

Right off, I notice a conspicuous absence of the early morning frenzy that dominated when my siblings and I used to rush to get ready for school. People make their own pancakes, talk a bit, and at nine Seth and Vallie sit down at the dining room table to work math problems, with Kath occasionally answering questions. Seth uses the book *Math: A Human Endeavor*, which he likes much better than some previous math texts that "try to trick you." Math is okay, he says, but not his favorite thing to do. The clock ticks. Kath reads in the family room. I am overwhelmed by the calm, by the feeling of life *happening* instead of waiting to happen.

Vallie gets up a few minutes before ten and shuts her book. "How'd you do?" asks Kath. "Fine," says Vallie, "I got one wrong because I divided instead of multiplied." She gets a Shel Silverstein book off the shelf and curls up on the sofa.

At ten, Kath says to Seth, "Do you want to watch that star show?"

"It's been on a long time, hasn't it?"

"No, you just missed one."

"Okay."

But no one watches the star show. By the time it comes on at 10:30, Seth is upstairs on his bed, engrossed in his reading, *The Count of Monte Cristo*. It is his third novel since September. The others were *Of Mice and Men* and *To Kill a Mockingbird*. Since September, he has also read short stories by John Updike, Richard Wright, Ernest Hemingway, Willa Cather, and F. Scott Fitzgerald. He picks out his own novels, from the family's shelves, from booklists. He uses the public library heavily. "What if you started a book and didn't like it?" I ask. "I'd read something else," he says matter-of-factly, but points out that rarely happens. He loves to read, although he didn't start until he was about eight.

While he reads, Kath is next door at the neighbors'. Charming Lydia sings downstairs, "One of these things is not like the other," shaking the rattle she made last night out of two bowls and some beans. Dan is away doing construction work. Vallie works intently on a zigzagged friendship bracelet--today's mail brought instructions from DMC.

I look around in the quiet. C.S. Lewis and John Holt dominate the bookshelves. I also notice *Drawing on the Right Side of the Brain*, a jar of Play-doh, Steinbeck, Kipling, encyclopedias, A.A. Milne, Gibran's *The Prophet*, Bibles, *Black Elk Speaks*, *Othello*, *How to Stay Alive in the Woods*, *The Anatomy of an Illness*, a pile of *National Geographics*, *Pond Life*, *St. Francis of Assisi*, *Robert Frost's Poems*, *A Whale for the Killing*, *The Craftsman Builder*, *Woodstock Handmade Houses*. A globe sits on top of the shelves. Clearly, this is not one of those houses where they have a complete set of The Great Classics in order to appear intellectual in the upper-class way. Each book at the Raymonds' house makes sense, and each is worn and a bit creased.

On the walls in the family room, I find a map of the world and a glass encased poster commemorating Seth's dance debut. It has words: "20th Anniversary Loyce Houlton's Nutcracker Fantasy, Minnesota Dance Theater."

I visit Seth again. In his closet hangs a sleeping bag and a wetsuit. From behind a stack of sweatshirts on the dresser, I catch the golden glint of three trophies from freestyling bike competitions. A stack of bike magazines--

Go, BMX Plus--covers the desk. Seth sits on his bed, leaning comfortably against the wood panelling that he put up by himself. From a framed photograph across the room, a Seth original, the wide soft eyes of a deer gaze at him. In the window above his head sits his old Petri camera, gazing at *me*.

At noon Seth and I take sandwiches and sit down in the family room to watch *España Viva*, a Spanish instruction program on PBS. He has the accompanying workbooks, ordered through the mail, and completes one lesson a week to go along with the TV program.

After lunch, academics are sort of officially over, though Seth spends some more time with *The Count*. The rest of his day is dominated by biking, with a lot of conversation and a VCR movie on the side.

At dinner, we all hold hands and sing grace, and then Seth cuts a pineapple for dessert, far more elegantly than I ever could. Trained by The Shanghai.

*

With his calm schedule, Seth has had plenty of energy to pour into his major interests. At the moment, these are marine biology, biking, and photography.

The Marine Science Center

Last year, Seth's homeschool group organized a weekly "class" at the local Marine Science Center. Seth particularly enjoyed the center, discovering his love for marine biology, and he is now quite involved there, although the homeschool group has moved on to other activities. In the beginning, Seth recalls that they spent a lot of time just looking at the tanks full of starfish, crabs, anemones, fish, and octopi, and listening to the director. The director, Frank D'Amore, talked about the names of animals, the food chain--"who eats who," and the care of different species. The homeschoolers also used the Center's gauges to keep charts graphing the weather, precipitation, cloud patterns, and water temperature.

Although Seth has enjoyed all his time at the center, he did notice a sort of "teacher-class" feel in the beginning, "like they were the adults and we were the kids." Later, this feeling eased as the homeschoolers took responsibility for chopping meat, feeding animals, cleaning tanks, helping to collect plankton, using microscopes, and answering the questions of school kids on field trips. As time went by, Seth spent extra time there on his own, anywhere from two to four hours a week, and came to feel more involved on a serious level.

Last summer, Frank offered Seth a job at the center, but various other things got in the way. This year, however, Seth looks forward to continued working and learning at the center on an informal, individual basis. Last week, he helped during a fourth grade field trip, answering questions and setting up the microscope. Frank has talked about involving him in helping to set up a research project monitoring the ocean's temperature, collecting and studying plankton, or investigating the fragility of eelgrass. Next summer, Seth thinks he'll make working there a priority.

How will Seth's work at the center affect his future? He's not sure. He is grateful that it has awakened him to his love of marine biology. He'd like to combine this love someday with diving and snorkeling, preferably somewhere warmer than the Puget Sound. He does some skin diving now, but he explains that the Sound has low visibility, since algae grows thickly in cold climates.

Biking

Three things go whoosh. One is the crash of waves on the beach. Two is a seagull's wings. Three is Seth's bike making circles in the air. Not the whole bike, actually--one wheel stays on the ground. It's hard to describe where Seth is. Sometimes he's standing on a small lever at the hub of the front wheel. Sometimes he's kicking his legs over the crossbar as it pivots around. Always, his eyes are intent. This weekend, he will travel to Lewiston, Idaho, for a freestyle bike competition.

Seth has been freestyling for a year now. When his friend Mike gets out of school, they head down to Fort Worden State Park and practice for two or three hours. When the weather's good, Seth starts earlier.

A local shop, Aurora Cycle, sponsors Seth and Mike, meaning that it donates brake cables and "stuff like that." Mike's been biking for three years. Other local teenagers have been involved off and on, but Seth and Mike are the hardcores. Their practice is quiet, focused work, hushed except for the whooshing and an occasional comment. The sky is a bit damp. Soft coastal scrub surrounds their concrete arena. After a few hours, they take turns photographing each other.

Then they go to the Raymonds' house to look at a bike frame Seth is working on. After that, they go to Mike's and invent a strange unicycle with handlebars and a wheel but no pedals. To ride it, they stand on the fender or on the levers by the hubs of the wheel. For two hours they ride it up and down the street, experimenting with a rope tied onto the handlebars like reins. The rope provides tension, a bit more control. Neighbor kids come out to watch. When Dan gets home, he and Lydia come out too.

Though he enjoys his day to day biking experience more than competition, Seth competes well. At North American Freestyle Association competitions in Eugene, Vancouver, and Portland, he placed third in the novice category. In Spokane and at the regional finals in Kelso, Washington, he took first. (A few months after my visit, I learned that at the 1990 finals in Bremerton, Washington, Seth took first in his division, and also came in first in total points for the year.)

How serious is Seth about biking? "I don't think of it as a possible career or anything," he says, "but right now I like it a lot. Sometimes I think it could be fun to design bikes."

Kath tells me that the homeschool group invited Seth to teach a class on biking, for pay. He refused. "If anyone wants to learn," he told them, "they can come along and do it with us, anytime."

Photography

Seth smiles when I mention that Ansel Adams quit school at the age of twelve, because Adams' photographs have inspired a lot of Seth's own work. I can tell, as I admire the black and white print that took the "Best of Show" prize (including a $20 bill) at the 1990 Jefferson County Fair. A strangely angled view of a Victorian building, its hundred shades of grey give an almost 3-D quality.

Seth works with a Pentax he bought last year. Before that, he'd taken photos for two years with an old Petri he bought at a garage sale. It had no light meter, which forced Seth to think especially hard about what he was doing. He reads books on photography and experiments a lot. His interest in camping and the outdoors has intensified along with his photographic skills, and he sometimes dreams of a future in photojournalism. "I'm interested in outdoor work," he tells me, "Not in studio photography."

So far, Seth has put all of his focus into the first part of the photographic process--composing a picture, exposing the film. Now, he feels ready to get involved in developing his own prints, and is looking for access to a darkroom. There is talk in his homeschool group of setting up a darkroom this year. "That would be just great," says Seth, with a faraway look in his eyes.

One evening, we all nestle into Seth's bedroom. He shows slides taken during two Washington backpacking trips--one with his family in Neah Bay, the other with teenaged friends in the Olympics.

During the presentation, I gasp a lot. I find Seth's slides even more stunning than his black and white prints, dramatized by color as well as pattern and shape. One, taken at the Point of Arches in Neah Bay, depicts a soft grey landscape of mist, beach, and water, punctuated by sharp triangles of huge rocks in the water. Another vividly presents three boys' bare wet sun-tanned backs in front of a blue-white waterfall with a red flower in the corner.

Seth races through the slides, as if they don't deserve long appreciation. I plead with him to go slower. He obliges. We pause at a portrait of a spiralling plant. "What is it?" asks Dan. "Skunk cabbage," says Seth, "an alpine form."

There are a bunch of close shots of bald eagles. They had been eating a dead dog, so intent on their feast that they ignored Seth's artistic intrusion.

"For our national bird," comments Dan, "They sure are scavengers."

I pay special attention to a candid picture of Lydia minding her business about camp. "Seth doesn't usually do people pictures," laughs Kath,

"If we want people pictures of our backpacking trips, we have to do that ourselves."

"I like taking pictures of Lydia," he tells me later, "She doesn't *pose*. But I don't like to line people up in front of things. It looks so fake."

*

No doubt, Seth's unschooling works largely because his parents believe in it. There's not the least bit of "school" feeling in the house, even in the mornings when the math books are out.

Kath and Dan sparkle when they talk about unschooling. "Sometimes people use the Real World argument," says Dan, "You know--how are your kids going to survive in the real world if they don't go to school and learn how to live with adversity? John Holt said that was like putting your head in a vise since you know you're going to have a headache anyway. Also, part of the idea is that maybe instead of adjusting to the world as it is, you can help create a better one."

"And maybe," adds Kath, "people who watch homeschoolers will finally start to see that happy kids turn into happy adults."

We talk about the issue of unschooling with two-career families. With four-year-old Lydia, Kath feels some conflict over the idea of going to work, but she readily admits that Seth and Vallie would be fine without her. If they ran into problems with academics, they could ask her or Dan in the evenings, just like other kids ask their parents for help with homework.

"Yes," agrees Dan, "By the time kids are teenagers, parents don't need to be heavily involved anyway."

Kath points out that even though she's at home during the day now, she's not responsible for Seth's education. "I don't feel that I can, or should, keep up with everything he does," she says.

Kath went to college for one quarter. Dan never went. "We were schooled out," they tell me. "We probably went to the wrong end--we should have skipped all the early stuff and gone to college." They want Seth to be able to go to college, if he wants to. He does want to, unless a better idea turns up.

One of the biggest unschooling challenges for Kath and Dan has been a sense of inadequacy. For one thing, Seth was a late reader. He'd listen attentively to very long stories from the age of five, but didn't start reading until around eight. Kath read a lot of stories in *GWS* which told about kids reading at four and five. At times, she panicked, certain they must be doing something wrong. Fortunately, she restrained her impulses to push reading on Seth, and when he was ready, it happened.

For another thing, as they have heard about the glamorous activities of other unschoolers, they have sometimes felt lacking. "We'd read about homeschoolers in a big city, with museums and concerts and all, and we'd think, 'That's where we should be, in a city!' Then we'd hear about homeschoolers on a farm, raising goats and gardening, and we'd think, 'That's where we should be--on a farm! We'd hear about families who took long exotic trips, and we'd think, 'That's what we should be doing--traveling!"

"But we couldn't travel, because we were busy building a house," laughs Kath, "And of course in our moments of sanity we realized that if any of those city, farm, or traveling people heard about us, maybe they'd say 'That's what we should be doing--building a house!'"

I point out to them that Seth, with his expertise in biking and photography and his growing involvement in marine biology, is just as impressive as any other homeschooler. Then Dan speaks the truth: "And yet that's *not* the point, is it? Homeschooling isn't about competition. It's about living a meaningful life."

Update, March, 1991: 1) Seth has put together an inexpensive darkroom in part of the laundry room, 2) Seth and Mike can be seen biking on a Seattle TV public service announcement, "Be Oil Smart," 3) Seth and Mike also recently performed for an elementary school; they may soon do a show at a junior high, 4) Seth is attending drivers' ed classes twice weekly at Port Townsend High School, and 5) his latest project is restoring a two-person kayak.

bike class...Seth (left) and friend Mike Nash prepare for a competition.

Photography class...Seth's shot of Lydia and Kath won the youth
photography award at a contest sponsored by the Jefferson County Museum
for National Library Week, April 1991.

chapter 42

The journal, etc., of Ms. Kim Kopel, Autodidact

Kim Kopel is 16. She's never been to school. She lives in St. Louis, Missouri, she gives Irish dance lessons to two young girls, she's teaching herself to play a tin whistle, she weaves, writes, plays piano, and has from time to time been interested in physics, motors and machines. I am delighted to share with you a few bits of her journal, her explanation of the way she learns, and some of her thoughts on the future of her education and lifestyle. Keep watch in your bookstore, by the way; Kim hopes to get her whole journal published soon.

From the journal
When she was 14, Kim wrote:

Tuesday, September 6th, 1988 10:00 a.m.

Today is the first day of a new school year. So why am I sitting at home at the typewriter, instead of at a desk in a classroom? Because I'm self-educated. What I mean by that is that I'm in charge of my own education, of living my own life. For a long time I've called myself a "homeschooler," but I don't like to anymore because I don't think it's accurate in my case. I think of homeschooling as being just that--school at home.

For myself, I wouldn't choose any form of "school" as we know it-- not in a building designated as a "school," not at home, not on my neighbor's front yard. I don't want to have a teacher pour knowledge into my brain-- knowledge that someone else decided I should have. I don't want someone telling me what to think, when to think, when to read on what page out of what book, when to eat lunch, etc. I don't want to be "schooled" at all, and since I'm not, I don't want to *say* I'm "schooled." I've decided that "home-educated" isn't really any better than "homeschooled," because it sounds like I only learn things in one place--at home. That's such a foreign concept to me that it seems ridiculous.

So I've come up with the term "self-educated," even though people usually have no idea what I mean. I imagine it sounds like I teach myself

everything, which isn't much more accurate than saying I'm "homeschooled."
When I say I'm self-educated, what I mean is that I can decide what I want to
do, when, where and how I want to do it, and who, if anyone, I want to help
me. I can decide what kind of help I want, and find someone who will give me
that help, and won't start giving me help I haven't asked for.

Since I'm in charge of my education/life (I have the freedom to decide
how I spend my time), people often tend to assume that I just do whatever I
want; whatever feels good at the moment. That's not true. I'd rather not sweep
floors, wash dishes, do laundry, fix meals, mow lawns, but they're all things
that have to be done, and so even though they're not things I really like or
want to spend time on, I still do them. (For the obvious reasons that if I
didn't, I wouldn't have any clean clothes or dishes, and I wouldn't eat!)
Besides those things, there are also all the other requirements of daily life here-
-maybe we need to go shopping, or Mom needs me to watch my younger
sisters while she drops books off at the library, or we're having company, or
one of my siblings wants me to help them with something, etc. I'm not just off
in my own little world, floating around totally oblivious to what's going on
around me.

I don't think there's anything wrong with doing what I want--I don't
see any sense in spending my time doing things I hate! I guess it's just that
people think that if you don't have someone making you do things, you'll
never do anything that's hard for you, or take on any challenges, and that
you'll probably just sit around and watch TV, hang out with your friends,
party all the time--in short, "vegetate." In talking with people about self-
education, I've found that most of them find it very hard to believe that anyone
would actually do meaningful or hard or challenging things without being
forced to.

I guess that's because people look at the kids they know, and see that
a lot of them don't like school (which people translate as meaning that they
don't care about getting a "good" education, and are therefore irresponsible),
have to be reminded to do homework, won't do much around the house
without being made to, and would rather just sit and watch TV, etc. And so
they think, "Look; kids will hardly do anything worthwhile now, imagine
what would happen if they weren't being forced to do things!" If they imagine
that if kids were let out of school for good they'd probably just vegetate, I'd
say they guessed right. It seems to me that after you've spent a good part of
your life with someone else doing all the thinking and decision making for
you, you're going to need some time to get used to thinking for yourself, to
being responsible for your own life. There's a period of adjustment that kids
go through after they've been taken out of school, in which they have to
recover from whatever effects school is responsible for having caused--low self
esteem and self confidence, etc. etc.--before they can start focusing on what
they want to do in their lives.

But I've never been to school, so I haven't had to go through that process of undoing what school does. I've grown up thinking for myself, making decisions, being responsible for my life, so I'm at the point right now where I'm finding out what I want to do, and finding ways to do those things. Watching TV, hanging out, etc., are very empty and unsatisfying pursuits to me. I know that there's more to my life than that. I don't want to spend (waste) my time on those things; there are too many other important things to do (like watching the grass grow, for instance. That's how low those other things are on my list).

If I were saying this to someone in a conversation, I'm sure they'd want to know--as it seems everyone does--"Well, then, what *do* you do?"

I hope this journal will answer that question, and many others that I've been asked. I'm writing this journal for that reason, and also to try to create a picture of what my life is like, and to express my thoughts about a lot of things.

I'll tell you a bit about myself. I'm 14 years old. I love to write-- stories, letters, music, in my diary, and now in this journal. This is really the first non-fiction I've written--besides letters and my diary, of course.

I have a four harness, six treadle floor loom here at home which I weave on. I've liked weaving for a long time and had used a lap loom, but what I really wanted to do was learn to weave real things on a floor loom. In the fall of 1986, I went to an open house at a restored historic home where there was a weaving shop that gave lessons, so I signed up and took lessons for about a year, which I loved. And now I have my own loom. I'm trying right now to come up with a pattern for a Scotch tartan--the plaid the Scotch weave their kilts out of. I want to make a kilt or something out of the MacGallum tartan for myself, and Grandpa (Mom's dad) wants me to make some placemats or centerpieces out of it for him and some of our relatives (we have some Scotch ancestors on Grandpa's side of the family who we think were MacGallums).

I love music, too--I've taught myself, with some help from Mom (when I asked for it), to play the piano and keyboard (synthesizer), and I can play the guitar a little. I love to sing--when I play the keyboard, or any other instruments, when someone else is playing, when I'm listening to tapes or the radio, and any other time when I feel like it--which is pretty much all of the time! Even when I'm not singing or playing an instrument or listening to music, I think there's always a song running through my head!

I also like dancing. I've taken ballet lessons over the years, but I never seemed to get anywhere--I guess I got tired of all the barre work and of never really dancing. So now I'm going to start taking Irish step dancing lessons--I'm going to learn to do, among other dances, the Irish jig, which you've probably heard of. Sara [Kim's sister] and I are going to take lessons from Mary Mayer...at the Mary Mayer School of Irish Dance; our first lesson is September 16th. I can't wait; I've seen the dancing, and it looks really neat-- and I like Mary Mayer, so I think it's going to be fun.

Those are my main interests right now, although there are many other things I like to do.

Now I'm going to write down all the questions I'm asked most frequently about my education, and answer them as I wish I had when someone actually asked me! I don't know why it is that I can always think of a million better explanations after the conversation is over!

Q. What do you do?

A. That's the number one question I'm asked--unfortunately, because I hate answering it. It makes it seem as if the important thing is what I do, and not who I am, which is entirely backwards. I do lots of things, and I *could* do a lot of things that I don't. If I said I liked to draw, I don't think anyone could decide from hearing that whether they liked me or not. Now, I don't ask people what they do so I can decide whether they're weird or not; I ask them because I'm genuinely interested in hearing about the things that are important to me. I could be friends with someone who liked to do totally different things from me; just because they're not exactly like me doesn't mean they're weird or mentally ill. But I get the feeling that people ask me this question not because they're interested in hearing about what I like to do and in learning more about me, but because they want to know if I'm really getting an education "like everyone else." Well, I'm not! If I was, I might as well just go to school! Another reason why I dislike this question is that it makes me feel like I'm under investigation. From how strangely I get treated sometimes, when people ask me what I do, I feel like I should say, "Oh, I eat, drink, breathe, sleep, just like other humans!"

Q. How do you make friends?

A. By going places and doing things, like anyone else--just by being alive. I think people ask this question because they have the false notion that school is the only place where you can meet people and make friends. (Well, if it is, you'd better make some lifelong friends there, or else your social life will be nonexistent after you graduate!) I think you're very limited if you think that-- who you have for friends is left totally up to what kids happen to be in your grade or classes at the particular school you go to. And that's another thing about school--you don't get to have many friends older or younger than yourself, because you spend most of your day with people your age, give or take a year.

I have met most of my friends while pursuing my interests--for example, I count the teachers I had at weaving lessons as my good friends.

[In a later part of her journal, Kim commented, "I don't think it's how many friends you have that matters, but how good a friend each one is."]

Q. Do you have homework?

A. That sounds like I'm being asked if I have to do work around the house--like sweeping or dusting! But I guess what people really mean by "homework" is extra "schoolwork." Since I don't do *any* schoolwork, I definitely don't do "extra" schoolwork! But even if I did do "schoolwork" (working out of workbooks, textbooks, doing assignments, etc.), the question is still irrelevant, because I would be doing all my schoolwork at home, so it would all be "homework!" I wonder sometimes exactly what people expect me to answer--"No, Mom gives us assignments after our homeschool is out for the day, and we go to school to do them"?!

Q. How do you learn things your parents don't know about?

A. I don't think of Mom and Dad as being the ones responsible for educating me and living my life, so it has never occurred to me that I should only learn things they know about or that they deem important. I'm perfectly capable of and have always liked doing things and finding things out for myself; I don't need someone to tell me what I need to know or do and how to go about finding out and doing those things. When I decide I'd like someone to help me and ask them for help, I'm not asking them to step in and take over; I'm simply asking them to help me with a specific thing. Mom and Dad are just two of the many people I know who are willing to help me when I ask. If I don't already know anyone who can teach me something I want to know, then I find someone who can. I can either enlist other people's help in doing that, or I can do it myself--usually, I use a combination of both. A good example of this is when I became interested in Irish dancing and wanted to take lessons. I decided to ask Mom to help me get information on the different Irish dance schools in St. Louis, so I could decide which one I wanted to go to. Even though she couldn't teach me Irish dancing herself, Mom was able to help me find someone who could. The most helpful thing anyone can do for me is to listen and respond when I ask them to help me find ways to do the things I want to do.

Q. Is your mom a teacher?

A. No, although she had a minimal amount of teacher's training in college--and that training was part of what turned her off to schooling! (Her own school education also contributed to her decision to quit training to be a teacher, and to allow her children to educate themselves.)...

Q. How can your mom teach you if she's not a teacher?

A. Well, I'm not a "teacher" (in the sense that I don't teach at a school), and yet I'm perfectly capable of showing my four year old sister Katie how to make the letters of the alphabet. My brother Burt isn't a "teacher," but I've learned a lot of things from him by talking to him, about things he's read or heard about, and what he thinks about them. Besides, it would seem logical to assume that if a person understands something and/or can do it themselves, they ought to be able to explain it at least a little to someone else. (I've found that I learn a lot more about something I already know if I teach it to someone else--maybe because I notice things in teaching it to them that I hadn't before, or from a question they asked.)

And since Mom went to school, most people would assume that she learned there, and should therefore be able to pass what she learned onto us. How could anyone dispute that? By saying that you really need to be trained to teach, and not just know the subject you're teaching? Well, most of teachers' training (and actual work in school) is classroom management, and since Mom only has four (going on five) of us, she doesn't need to know how to manage a classroom of fifty. (I won't even get into the fact that many teachers in private schools aren't certified to teach.) Mom's qualified to be a parent, and she doesn't need to be anything else. Mom doesn't "teach" me anything--in the sense that she doesn't say, "OK, Kim, I'm going to teach you trigonometry now." I've learned many things from her, just by observing what she does, how she lives, and from talking with her. She always helps me if I ask her to-- but she only gives me the specific help I ask for, no more, no less. If she can't give me the help I need or want, I'll find someone else who can--and often times I'll ask Mom to help me find someone who can.

Reading, writing, and arithmetic
This is an excerpt from a longer essay about the way Kim has learned "the basics."

I have had very little formal "school" instruction; Mom has never planned out a curriculum for me, and has never instructed me in English, history, etc. I have learned things in my own way, my own time, at my own pace, while pursuing interests of my own choosing.

I learned to write when I was between the ages of three and four; I wanted to be able to write, so I asked people (Mom and Dad and other relatives and friends) how to make the letters of the alphabet. As soon as I could form the letters, I began writing letters to people; I would decide what I wanted to say, and then ask people how to spell the words. In this way, I learned correct spelling and grammar, and gained a knowledge of letters and words that later made it possible for me to learn to read. When I was about ten

I began keeping a diary, which I'm still writing in now, and at the same time I also began writing stories.

I learned to read pretty much the same way I learned to write, a few years later. I remember being read to a lot, which I really enjoyed, and wanting to be able to read. I learned to read from being read to, being answered when I asked, "What's that say?" (which was quite frequently), and writing, which helped me to recognize words. Most of all, I learned to read (and write--and do everything I know how to do) because I wanted to be able to. I never used any workbooks, flashcards, etc., when I was learning to read or write.

I learned math by using it--math is logical; you really don't need to have someone explain it all to you, because you learn it naturally while trying to count and figure things out. I learned to add, subtract, multiply and divide simply because I needed to do those things. I may not have always seen the fastest way to figure something out right away, but I knew what I was trying to find out, and what I needed to do in order to get the answer....

Unfortunately, when I was around 13 I took the CAT (my first test) and discovered I was below grade level in math--mainly because I didn't know the different processes by which they expected you to come up with the answers (although I was perfectly capable of finding them my own way). And being timed made me nervous, besides the fact that finding answers as quickly as possible had not been the focus of the math I had used before. Accuracy was the most important thing; speed comes from using math many times, and I really didn't need to do a whole lot of figuring at that time in my life. If I had had some real reason for being able to do math that fast, I know I would have been able to. But being able to figure quickly just so I could pass a test wasn't a good reason for learning something to me.

And yet, even after I'd finished the test, I felt nervous about not being at my grade level in math; I got it into my head that I needed to study math to "catch up"--merely for the reason of being at a certain place that some person who didn't know me at all had decided that I should be at simply because I was a certain age. So I got our workbooks and textbooks, and asked Mom to work with me on math, which she did.

That turned out to be a disaster--I ended up with a math block, because I'd worked myself into such a state over the test and trying to catch up that there was no way I could learn anything. I decided that math was stupid, because that was better than deciding that *I* was stupid because I couldn't understand it.

Also, I was unconsciously rebelling against doing something that had no real meaning or importance to me in my life. So I was making it impossible to learn math, because underneath, I really didn't want to learn it; I was just doing it because I felt I should. Finally I wore myself out with it so that I had a block toward it and was saying I hated it.

It's taken me nearly three years to get to the place where I can think about math again without panicking or feeling inferior--and I'm still not completely over the block. I'm trying now to regain the practical, applicable understanding of math that I once had.

Facing the future with integrity
In this recent piece, Kim reflects on issues that have confronted her in her late teens.

About two years ago I began to feel dissatisfied with my life the way it was. I was bored and restless; I wanted to be doing more things, but I didn't know what. I had a sense of standing on the threshold of a whole new world, of coming to a turning point in my life. I started asking myself a lot of questions about what purpose my life had, where I belonged, what I wanted to do; struggling to find myself.

In the midst of this, people began to question me more frequently about what plans I had for my life, and the tone with which they asked was noticeably more serious and intense than it had been a few years before. After all, I was high school age, and, "it was high time I knew what I was going to do with my life," they seemed to be saying. Needless to say, I started to feel pretty stupid for not knowing what I wanted to do with my life. I no longer felt comfortable saying, "I don't know," when people asked me if I was going to college, because, inevitably, they would be shocked, and start impressing upon me how impossible it is to get a "good job" (whatever *that* is) without a college degree, that one would never be able to live happily and be accepted by society if one did not attend college and pursue a career for the rest of one's natural life. So I couldn't *seriously* be considering anything but the "traditional" route of college and a career; that would be dangerous and immature. So I was told.

That made me angry--if I felt like ruining my life, it was no one's business but my own! And being expected to do something, anything, really irritated me--so much that at times I felt like going out and doing the exact opposite of what people said I was "supposed" to do.

I also resented having college, careers, decisions, etc., shoved in my face, because dealing with them distracted me from my search for a meaningful life. It was very frustrating to feel that I needed to be resolving the conflict and turmoil in my life, but not be able to because I had to deal with the confusions other people injected.

By continually pushing and pressuring me to go to college and do this and do that, people implied a complete lack of respect for and trust in me. I felt that they were saying, in effect, that I was incapable of taking care of myself, and would never "turn out all right" if they didn't hold my hand and steer me in the "right" direction. All in all, I was infuriated over the whole matter.

But at the same time, I was also scared. Suppose what they said was true? What if it really was impossible to get a job and support myself without a college degree? Hundreds--no, thousands--of nagging doubts, worries, and "what-ifs" crowded into my mind, and I began to feel that I should seriously consider attending college. I sent for information on several colleges and carefully read through it, feeling all the while that I was trying to wear a shoe that didn't fit. I spent a lot of time trying to decide where I wanted to go to college, what I wanted to major in, and what single thing I wanted to spend the rest of my life earning a living at. I bounced back and forth for a while--one minute I was definitely going to college, and the next wild horses couldn't drag me there.

I finally decided it was time to face all the pressures and fears, and find out if they were truly valid. I started to question the beliefs that had been presented to me as truths and facts. Like the idea that people should pick one thing to do (as a career) and then spend the rest of their lives doing it. How can you know and decide today what you'll be interested in doing ten or five or even two years down the road? Furthermore, should you be expected to know? And why isn't it considered normal to grow and change your priorities--what's wrong with moving onto something else when you've outgrown where you are right now?

I began to see that so much of this pressure to go to college, get a "good job," be successful, and so on, was based mainly on fear. "Do this, or this will happen to you." "Go to college, or you'll never be able to get a 'good job' and support yourself." And so forth. No one expected me to go to college because I thought I'd find a life worth living there, or that it'd be a place where I would mature as a person. They expected me to go because I'd end up a social reject and starve to death on the street if I didn't.

Something inside of me snapped at this realization. "That's it," I said to myself. "I'm not going to run my life on fear; what point is there in a life in which you do things because you're afraid of what will happen to you if you don't? How can you ever be happy if you live on fear--there will always be something else you have to do to keep something terrible from happening to you. I'd rather starve to death and be rejected than be afraid forever and never have a moment's peace!"

With that pressure off my shoulders, I was determined to get to the bottom of all the myths and fears. As I looked closer, I discovered a fear that was greater than all the others put together--the fear of not "measuring up" to society's standards, and therefore being unacceptable and rejected. You must go to college, because that's what every respectable person intent on "making something" of themselves is doing so they can get a "good job--one they can make a lot of money at, and that has prestige.

It became clear to me that schools exist for the purpose of instilling the "moral" that acceptance is the most important thing in life. I also realized that this "moral" is instilled so people can be controlled--if people believe that happiness is being accepted, they'll do whatever they're told they "have" to in order to be accepted, because they want to be happy.

After this revelation, I was able to see all the pressures and worries for what they really were--basically a lot of false fears and insecurities. It was sort of like turning on the light and finding that what had looked to be a terrible monster was just a shadow.

Now I had the time and space to focus on resolving the personal conflict and dissatisfaction with my life that I was feeling. I began to look closely at my life, and question many things about it. I asked myself, why had I always followed my interests day by day, letting them lead me? Why had I never planned my life out? Once I'd become interested in writing, why hadn't I immediately begun looking for places to have my writing published, or for people to read and criticize it? Why hadn't I said, "I'll write short stories for six months, then experiment with the essay format for two months, then delve into poetry for three months, try my hand at journalism for a month, revise my short stories and work on publishing them for the next six months after that," etc.? Why had I been content to live each day open to any new ideas for articles, or stories, or something entirely different to write; unafraid of the uncertainty that tomorrow held--actually, welcoming that very uncertainty as a possible exciting opportunity? And was there anything wrong with living that way? Did I need to abandon it, after it had served and suited me perfectly for so many years, because I felt the need for a change in my life?

After a lot of searching and questioning, I've come to the conclusion that I don't have to find one thing to do now and for the rest of my life. The whole world has opened up to me in a new sense since I've come to this revelation, and many important opportunities are becoming available to me now.

For example, last year I read an article about a children's choir here in St. Louis that sounded neat to me because I've always loved singing. Although I'd never had voice lessons, or been in a choir before, I decided to audition for the choir. I was accepted, and now, six months later, I've moved up into the highest levels of the choir, have ten two-hour rehearsals per month, and am planning to go on the choir tour to Atlanta this summer. Choir has become a very big part of my life.

As a result of being in the choir, another opportunity became available to me just recently. About a month ago I became interested in taking voice lessons, so I asked one of my choir directors if he knew any voice teachers he'd recommend. He told me that he wanted to start giving voice lessons, and asked if I'd like to take lessons from him. Because he's a really terrific person, and we get along very well, I told him I'd rather take lessons from him than anyone else. So I've been taking voice lessons from him for the past month, and I love it! And who knows what other opportunities will become available because I'm taking voice lessons--maybe chances to perform solo, etc.

Along with choir and voice lessons, writing is also very important to me. I've always loved to write--letters, stories, in my private diary, a journal of my education, and most recently, articles about homeschooling and related subjects. While I was trying to deal with the pressures and fears surrounding college, careers, etc., I spent a lot of time writing, in order to straighten my thoughts out. When I write, things that have been blurry become clear to me, and I see more and more of the picture, instead of just a tangled, confusing mess. Even when I'm not trying to describe and analyze beliefs, fears, philosophies, etc., it helps to write what I feel *without* trying to figure out why I feel the way I do. It's like I have to get it all off my chest first, and then I can start trying to work things out.

I'm almost always working on some article--whether it's one I've been asked to write, or one I've thought of myself. Even when I'm not working on anything specific (which is rare), I'm still writing; in my diary, and letters to people. I like to write a lot about learning, homeschooling, educational philosophies, and that kind of thing, because those issues are important to me. Right now I'm in the revising stages of an article about how I learned to read, write, etc., which I wrote not too long ago. I'm planning to submit it to a magazine, or several, once I'm finished with it. And I've got lots of ideas in the back of my mind for more articles I want to write.

My biggest project at this time is revising the journal of my education that I kept from September 1988 to 1989, and I'm hoping to have it published. The journal is full of descriptions and accounts of everything I did and read, people I met, etc., during that year. I poured out my thoughts, feelings and ideas about so many things into the journal as well; trying to understand myself and the rest of the world, trying to find out where I stood, and why. It's essentially my self portrait. I have so much material that revising it is a long, hard process. But it's worth all the time and work.

During the past four years or so I've established a writing apprenticeship with Susannah Sheffer, editor of *Growing Without Schooling*. Susannah always has helpful suggestions and comments on whatever I send her--for example, she'll say, "This part isn't very clear; is this what you mean?" "What you said here makes me curious to know more about such and such; maybe you'd want to expand on it," or, "You could change this sentence around like this to make it clearer," etc. Those kinds of suggestions really help me when I'm revising, because a lot of times I know that I've left something out somewhere, or that a paragraph needs to be rewritten, but I can't put my finger on exactly what's wrong, or how to fix it. I think that being able to have Susannah read and critique my writing is making me a better critic of my own work, because she makes me more aware of how my writing is going to sound to someone else.

Working on writing with Susannah has led to several trips to Boston to visit her, and the chance to volunteer in the Holt Associates office, to meet a lot of neat people, including one of my closest friends. Not to mention that Susannah has become one of my best friends as well.

I don't have all the answers to my questions yet, but as I continue to try to resolve and find the answers, things are falling into place and becoming clear to me. I've realized that it's okay to not have all the answers. I know now that all through my life I'll be growing, and that going through these periods of confusion and frustration is just part of the lifelong process of growing up. Instead of dreading these processes, I should welcome them, because each time I go through another one of them it means I'm moving onto the next stage of my life

2

appendices

Appendix A

bibliography: books and magazines to help you unschool

I put only 16 books and other resources in this bibliography, with fat excerpts, so you'd notice each of them. There are *many* books, magazines, and magazine articles on unschooling--you can find others on your own at the library. Also, John Holt's Book and Music Store catalog sells an imaginative variety of useful books. The resources here are the cream of the crop *and* the most relevant choices for teenagers. They deal with unschooling or learning in a *general* sense. Numerous resources for *particular* subjects are, of course, mentioned throughout parts 2, 3, and 4 of this book.

I. On unschooling and education (mostly by John Holt):

*John Holt, *Freedom and Beyond* (Dell, 1972). In this book, Holt started questioning whether we needed schools. Throughout, he writes mostly about freedom, choice, authority, discipline, and the relationship between schools and poverty.

> Not understanding freedom, we do not understand authority. We think in terms
> of organization charts, pecking orders, stars on the collar and stripes on the
> sleeve. If someone is above us on the chart, then ...he has a right to tell us to
> do what he wants, and we have a duty to do whatever he tells us, however
> absurd, destructive, or cruel. Naturally enough, some people, seeing around
> them the dreadful works of this kind of authority, reject it altogether. But with
> it they too often reject, naturally but unwisely, all notions of competence,
> inspiration, leadership. They cannot imagine that of their own free will they
> might ask someone else what he thought, or agree to do what he asked,
> because he clearly know or perhaps cared much more about what he was doing
> than they did. The only alternative they seem to see to coercive authority is
> none at all. I have therefore tried to explore a little further the nature of
> freedom, so that we may better understand how people of varying ages and
> skills may live together and be useful to each other without some of them
> always pushing the others around.

*John Holt, *Instead of Education: Ways to Help People Do Things Better* (Boston: Holt Associates, 1976). This book gives many ideas for ways to improve and change communities so people have more opportunities to learn outside of school. Also develops the idea that learning and doing are the same thing, and explains the difference between healthy teaching and school situations and unhealthy situations. (Basically, Holt says the difference is that healthy situations are not compulsory.)

> This is a book in favor of *doing*--self-directed, purposeful, meaningful life and work--and *against* "education"--learning cut off from active life and done under pressure of bribe or threat, greed and fear.

*John Holt, *Escape From Childhood* (Holt Associates, 1974). This book goes beyond the issue of school, covering many other ways that "minors" are prevented from living fully.

> For a long time it never occurred to me to question this institution [of childhood]. Only in recent years did I begin to wonder whether there might be other or better ways for young people to live. By now I have come to feel that the fact of being a "child," of being wholly subservient and dependent, of being seen by older people as a mixture of expensive nuisance, slave, and super-pet, does most young people more harm than good.

> I propose instead that the rights, privileges, duties, responsibilities of adult citizens be made *available* to any young person, of whatever age, who wants to make use of them.

*John Holt, *Teach Your Own* (Dell, 1981). This is the first and the most complete manual for parents who are thinking about taking their kids out of school. Some of the information won't apply to you, as it concentrates mostly on younger children and talks a lot about the way people learn basic math, reading, and writing skills. However, it also has solid thought and information on legal strategies, on good work situations for unschoolers, on the philosophy of unschooling, and other topics. This is an especially good book to have your parents read; a chapter called "Common Objections to Home Schooling" will help them clarify their own thoughts.

> Even in supposedly "free" or "alternative" schools, too many people still do what conventional schools have always done. They take children out of and away from the great richness and variety of the world, and in its place give them school subjects, the curriculum. They may jazz it up with chicken bones, Cuisenaire rods, and all sorts of other goodies. But the fact remains that instead of letting children have contact with more and more people, places, tools, and experiences, the schools are busily cutting the work up into little bits and

---

* Currently available through John Holt's Book and Music Store, 2269 Massachusetts Avenue, Cambridge, MA 02140. Write for free catalog.

giving it to the children according to some expert's theory about what they need or can stand.

What children need is not new and better curricula but *access* to more and more of the real world; plenty of time and space to think over their experiences, and to use fantasy and play to make meaning out of them; and advice, road maps, guidebooks, to make it easier for them to get where they want to go (not where we think they ought to go), and to find out what they want to find out. Finding ways to do all this is not easy. The modern world is dangerous, confusing, not meant for children, not generally kind or welcoming to them. We have much to learn about how to make the world more accessible to them, and how to give them more freedom and competence in exploring it. But this is a very different thing from designing nice little curricula.

John Taylor Gatto, "An Award-Winning Teacher Speaks Out," printed in *The Sun*, June 1990, and reprinted in *Utne Reader*, September/October 1990. The speech Gatto gave when accepting his designation as the New York City Teacher of the Year, 1990. (He was also Teacher of the Year 1989 and 1991, and NY State Teacher of the Year 1991.) Strong and direct:

It is absurd and anti-life to be part of a system that compels you to listen to a stranger reading poetry when you want to learn to construct buildings, or to sit with a stranger discussing the construction of buildings when you want to read poetry.

II. By or about particular unschooled teenagers
(Also see autobiographies or biographies of any of the people mentioned in Chapter 40):

*Britt Barker, *Letters Home* (Home Education Press, P.O. Box 1083, Tonasket, WA 98855, 1990). At 16, unschooled Britt Barker (now in her 20's) wrote about her experiences traveling and studying field biology in North America and Europe.

This excerpt is from Britt's trip through Canada, accompanying naturalists as they write a book on endangered species:

So much has happened in the past two weeks! After meeting the Schuelers, we started out by driving out of Boreal forest and into the prairies of Manitoba. It is quite interesting, this transition from one habitat to another. After leaving the rocky land of the Canadian shield, we drove into a forest of mostly spruces and some aspens. This changed as we went west, to being mostly aspens and only a few spruces. These gradually thinned out and became smaller until everything suddenly stopped in an almost perfect line and there we were, in open prairie. The spaciousness was wonderful and the land stretched out flat before us until it met the sky at a far horizon. The only trees to be seen were those planted by man. Prairies aren't always this flat--but this, the Red River Valley, is because it used to be a glacial lake. Therefore, the soil is so rich and fertile that it is all farmed, and is given no chance to grow the aspen trees that it might. While visiting this valley, we stayed at a 480 acre wheat farm. I had a chance to take a couple of rounds on the swather as it cut the wheat, leaving neat little rows behind it.

*David and Micki Colfax, *Homeschooling for Excellence* (Warner Books, 1988). After three homeschooled Colfax boys went to Harvard, their parents wrote this book and explained. It tells some of the books and other resources they used, points out vehemently that the boys' main "curricula" were their activities around the homestead, and answers the usual predictable questions about socialization, etc.

> Later that year Grant interviewed at nearly a dozen colleges and applied to two. We submitted a letter to each, describing his course work and evaluating his strengths and weaknesses as objectively as possible. In lieu of teacher and counselor recommendations, Grant provided letters from a half dozen people who could variously attest to his work in the community health center, his character and intellectual potential. He wrote a long essay that described his years on the ranch, his homeschooling experiences, and his hopes for the future. He was admitted to Yale and Harvard and entered the latter that fall.

Robin Lee Graham, *Dove* (Harper and Row, 1972), is Robin Graham's story of his 5-year sailing trip around the world, beginning at age 16. Here, at 18, he has just met his future wife Patti:

> We were children as we sailed the islands of the Yasawa group, kids reveling in sun and surf, knowing a glorious sense of freedom and timelessness. When the sun had risen high enough to warm our bodies and light the caverns and ledges in the coral reefs, we dived for shells and poured our treasure into *Dove*'s cockpit. We found violet conchs, zigzag and spotted cowries, grinning tuns (*Malea ringens*), quaint delphinia snails, pagoda periwinkles, murex, tiny moon snails, fashioned with a jeweler's skill, delicate striped bonnets, tritons, augers and olives.

> The cowries we loved best--some as large as a fist, skins silken smooth, dappled in warm browns. We swam together, Patti graceful as a dolphin.

Patricia Joudry, *And the Children Played* (Tundra Books, 1983). A Canadian playwright tells the hilarious story of keeping her kids out of school while

---

* Currently available through John Holt's Book and Music Store, 2269 Massachusetts Avenue, Cambridge, MA 02140. Write for free catalog.

living in the English countryside and being bankrupt. The narrative takes us from her daughters' infancy in the 50's through their teens and on into their adult lives as college student, secretary, and teacher.

"You what? You kept your children out of school!" People ask it with mingled horror and fascination. The fascination stems from remembered dislike of their own schooling; the horror is at the prospect of having kids home and underfoot.

But it wasn't all that much trouble. We didn't educate our children; we just gave them freedom to be. They educated themselves and each other. Nobody pushed them; nobody could have stopped them. There's only one way you can stop kids from wanting to learn, and that's send them to school.

*Nancy Wallace, *Child's Work: Taking Children's Choices Seriously* (Holt Associates, 1990). Nancy, whose two children are now in their late teens, watched them grow with sensitivity, insight, and trust. Both focused their lives around music, so this book will be especially (but not *only*) interesting to unschooling musicians.

Vita and Ishmael now spend most of each working day playing and composing music. Aside from the sheer glory of doing my own work to the melodic strains of Chopin ballades, Beethoven sonatas, and Bach preludes and fugues, living with Vita and Ishmael's music and being as involved as I am in their musical work has meant that of everything they do, it is the way they approach music that I understand and know most intimately. Often, I find myself using this understanding as a base or guidepost for looking at how they work on everything else in life. Watching the way Vita explores a new piece on the violin or piano, for example, teaches me about how she explores spelling or numerical relationships or art....

III. Unschooling magazines:

Growing Without Schooling magazine, bimonthly, currently $25/year from Growing Without Schooling, 2269 Massachusetts Avenue, Cambridge, MA 02140. In my opinion, the most important resource for an unschooler, written mainly by families who are busy doing what the title says. I won't quote from it here, since I've done so all through this book.

Home Education Magazine, bimonthly, currently $24/year from Home Education Magazine, PO Box 1083, Tonasket, WA 98855. A relatively new homeschooling magazine, with longer articles than *GWS* and regular columns.

---

* Currently available through John Holt's Book and Music Store, 2269 Massachusetts Avenue, Cambridge, MA 02140. Write for free catalog.

Legal information, lots of stuff about learning resources for younger kids, but news and ideas on teenagers too. Current issue $3. This excerpt from the November/December 1990 issue comes from an article called "A Homeschooling Day," by Maggie Barker, age 17:

> It is Monday. The usually quiet dog yard is suddenly a loud, barking frenzy as I push my dogsled out to where my 20 Alaskan Huskies are housed. They recognize the sled and harnesses and all want to run!
>
> My brother, Ben (13), lays the traces out and secures the end to the sled with a carabiner. I put the snowhook over a post and drive it into the snow. Next we select the six dogs we will take with us today as we mush 16 miles for the family's mail...

IV. Other very important general resources for life and learning:

The Essential Whole Earth Catalog (Doubleday, 1986). I've recommended *EWEC* and the related *Whole Earth Review* several places in this book, but I must mention it one more time here. The *EWEC* opens up more options than you ever knew existed, by describing and quoting from the best books (and other resources) in every imaginable category, from Exploring Space to Storytelling. It is also a graphic masterpiece, full of fascinating drawings and photographs charmingly splayed across the pages. Also see the earlier out of print (very useful) versions: *The Whole Earth Catalog, The Last Whole Earth Catalog, The Next Whole Earth Catalog*. These are available in libraries and used book stores. (Because of the nature of these books, to give you an honest feel for them I'd have to xerox a whole page. One short paragraph would be blasphemy.)

Whole Earth Review magazine, currently $20 for four issues or available in bookstores. The ongoing version of the *Whole Earth Catalog*, with exceptional articles on anything, from Japanese comic books to tropical reforestation. Mail your money to Whole Earth Review, P.O. Box 38, Sausalito, CA 94966, or (415) 332-1716.

Clifton Fadiman, *The Lifetime Reading Plan* (Harper, 1988), is described in chapter 24, but I wanted to mention it here also. This book invites you to read about 100 of the best pieces of writing that have come out of Western civilization--not just novels and poetry but also history, politics, philosophy, psychology, biography, and autobiography.

> The *Iliad* is probably the most magnificent story ever told about man's prime idiocy: warfare. The human center is Achilles. The main line of the narrative traces his anger, his sulkiness, his savagery, and the final assertion of his better

nature. He is the first hero in Western literature; and ever since, when we talk of heroic qualities, Achilles is somewhere in the back of our minds, even though we may think we have never heard of him.

Barbara Sher, *Wishcraft: How to Get What You Really Want* (Viking, 1979). The best book I know of to help you first set delicious goals you really care about, and then make these dreams come true. Here, she introduces a concept she calls the "Buddy System":

The Buddy System is a way of creating your "ideal family" in miniature. It's the most compact and efficient way I know to give yourself the kind of support system I've been describing throughout this book. Its principle is simple: you and a friend make it your shared goal to meet both your individual goals. It works because it's about a thousand times easier to have faith, courage, and good ideas for someone else than it is for yourself--and easier for someone else to have them for you. So you team up and trade those positive resources: your buddy provides them for you and you provide them for her or him.

How do you pick a buddy? She or he can be a close friend or roommate, but doesn't have to be. A new acquaintance or a neighbor can be just as good. This is an action-oriented arrangement first and an intimate friendship only if you want it to be. Your buddy will be giving you emotional and moral support, yes, but for a purpose: to keep you in motion. In fact, if you are close friends, you're going to have to keep the long, rambling heart-to-heart talks out of the business part of your relationship and save them for after hours.

Homeschooling
Organizations

The following lists are taken from *Growing Without Schooling*'s annual directory. As this book goes to press, they are already partially out of date. However, *GWS* publishes frequent updates. Write and ask about their *Homeschooling Resource List*, which currently sells for $2.50. It lists not only homeschooling support groups and organizations, but also correspondence schools, curriculum suppliers, helpful private schools, homeschooling magazines, and related organizations. (Growing Without Schooling, 2269 Massachusetts Avenue, Cambridge, MA 02140, phone 617-864-3100.)

If you write to any of these groups, please include a SASE (self-addressed, stamped envelope).

If you don't see a group listed in your own city or area, contact the closest one, or a statewide organization. These people will likely be able to put you in touch with another group in your own community. *By no means are all the homeschooling groups in the country named on this list.*

Also, many (not necessarily all) Christian homeschooling groups welcome non-Christian participants.

National or General Homeschool Groups and Magazines:

(These are only a few of the national groups listed in *GWS' Homeschooling Resource List.*)

Growing Without Schooling, 2269 Massachusetts Ave., Cambridge, MA 02140
Home Education Press, P.O. Box 1083, Tonasket, WA 98855; (509) 486-1351
Home Educators Single Parent Network, NHA, P.O. Box 58746, Seattle, WA 98138-1746; (206) 432-1544
Home School Legal Defense Association, Paeonian Springs, VA 22129; (703) 882-3838
Home School Researcher, 25 W Cremona, Seattle, WA 98119; (206) 281-2210
Homeschoolers for Peace, P.O. Box 74, Midpines, CA 95345
Homeschoolers Travel Network, PO Box 58746, Seattle, WA 98138-1746; (206) 432-1544
National Homeschool Association, P.O. Box 58746, Seattle, WA 98138-1746; (206) 432-1544

Homeschooling Organizations, listed in alphabetical order by state:

Alabama:

-Alabama Home Educators, P.O. Box 16091, Mobile, AL 36116

-Alabama Home Educators--Tuscaloosa Area, Rt 3 Box 633, Cottondale, AL 35453

-The Voice (Newsletter), P.O. Box 742, Tallassee, AL 36078; (205) 283-5018

Alaska:

-Alaska Homeschool Association, P.O. Box 874075, Wasilla, AK 99687; (907) 373-7404

Arizona:

-Arizona Families for Home Education, 639 E Kino Drive, Mesa, AZ 85203; 964-7435

-Home School Supplies, 1125 E Quick Draw Place, Tucson, AZ 85749

-Parents Association of Christian Home Schools, 6166 W Highland, Phoenix, AZ 85033

-Tucson Home Education Network, P.O. Box 58176, Tucson, AZ 85732-8176

Arkansas:

-Arkansas Christian Home Education Association, P.O. Box 501, Little Rock, AR 72203; (501) 753-9164

California:

-California Coalition--PALS, P.O. Box 92, Escondido, CA 92025; (619) 749-1522

-Center for Educational Guidance, P.O. Box 445, N San Juan, CA 95960; (916) 292-3623

-Christian Family Schools, P.O. Box 23068, San Jose, CA 95153-3068

-Christian Home Educators of CA, P.O. Box 28644, Santa Ana, CA 92799-8644; (714) 537-5121

-Community Education Gazette, P.O. Box 445, N San Juan, CA 95960

-East Valley Homeschoolers, 6046 Riverton Avenue, N Hollywood, CA 91606

-Monterey County Home Learners, P.O. Box 4667, Salinas, CA 93912; (408) 663-5324

-North Santa Clara Valley Homeschoolers, 795 Sheraton Drive, Sunnyvale, CA 94087

-Northern California Homeschoolers Association, 3345 Santa Paula Drive, Concord, CA 95418; (415) 674-1294

-Peninsula Homeschoolers, 4795 Lage, San Jose, CA 95130

San Diego Homeschoolers, 3581 Mt Aclare Avenue, San Diego, CA 92111

-Santa Clara Valley Homeschoolers Association, 795 Sheraton Drive, Sunnyvale, CA 94087

-Sonoma County Homeschoolers, 8600 Templeman Road, Forestville, CA 95436

-South St. Centre, Box 261, Boulder Creek, CA 95006 (resource center for families)

-South Valley Homeschoolers Association, Box 961, San Martin, CA 95046

-Yolo County Homeschoolers, P.O. Box 305, Esparto, CA 95627; (916) 787-3613

-Yosemite Area Homeschoolers, P.O. Box 74, Midpines, CA 95345

Colorado:

-Colorado Home Educators' Association, (303) 650-8833

-Colorado Home Schooling Network, 7490 W Apache, Sedalia, CO 80135; (303) 688-4136

-Colorado Springs Homeschoolers, 2906 Marilyn Road, Colorado Springs, CO 80909; (719) 598-8444

-Northern Colorado Home School Association, 4633 Skyline Drive, Ft. Collins, CO 80526

Connecticut:
-Connecticut Home Educators Association, 4 Hudson Street, Enfield, CT 06082; (203) 745-2848
Florida:
-Family Learning Exchange, 2020 Turpentine Rd., Mims, FL 32754
-Florida Association for Schools at Home, 1000 Devil's Dip, Tallahassee, FL 32308; 878-2793
-Florida Parent-Educators Association, 11801-5 28th St N, St. Petersburg, FL 33716
Georgia:
-Cobb County Homeschoolers, 813 Wyntuck Drive, Kennesaw, GA 30144
-Georgians for Freedom in Education, 209 Cobb Street, Palmetto, GA 30268; (404) 463-3719
-REACH, c/o Vicki Scott, 617 Colony Court, Woodstock, GA 30188
Hawaii:
-Christian Homeschoolers of Hawaii, 91084 Oama Street, Ewa Geach, HI 96706; 689-6398
-Friends Learning at Home, c/o Linda Inouye, 94-416 Ki'ilani Street, Mililani, HI 96789; 625-0445
-Hawaii Island Home Educators, 968-8076 or 965-9002
-Hawaii Homeschool Association, 66960 Kuewa Drive, Waialua, HI 96791
-Maui Home Educators, 777 Kolani Street, Wailuku, HI 96793; (808) 242-8225
Iowa:
-Iowa Families for Christian Education, RR 3 Box 143, Missouri Valley, IA 51555
-Iowa Home Educators Association, P.O. Box 213, Des Moines, IA 50301
Idaho:
-Home Educators of Idaho, 3618 Pine Hill Drive, Coeur d'Alene, ID 83814; (208) 667-2778
-Idaho Home Educators, P.O. Box 4022, Boise, ID 83711-4022; (208) 482-7336
Illinois:
-HOUSE, P.O. Box 578291, Chicago, IL 69657-8291; (312) 929-6723
-Illinois Christian Home Educators, P.O. Box 261, Zion, IL 60099 (Note: homeschoolers in Southern IL can also get support from the Southern Indiana Support Group, below.)
Indiana:
-Indiana Association of Home Educators, P.O. Box 50524, Indianapolis, IN 46250
-Southern Indiana Support Group, 118 E Water Street, Princeton, IN 47670; (812) 385-4176
Kansas:
-Hesston/Canton Home Educators Association, (316) 367-8205
-Kansans for Alternative Education, 19985 Renner Rd, Spring Hill, KS, 66083; (913) 686-2310
-Manhattan Parent Educators, (913) 539-3641
-Wichita Teaching Parents, (316) 264-9063
Kentucky:
-Kentucky Home Education Association, P.O. Box 81, Winchester, KY 40392-0081
-Kentucky Homeschoolers, 3310 Illinois Avenue, Louisville, KY 40213 (Note: Homeschoolers in Kentucky can also get support from the Southern Indiana Support Group, above.)
Louisiana:
-Louisiana Citizens for Home Education, 3404 Van Buren, Baker, LA 79714; (504) 775-5472
Maine:
-Maine Homeschool Association, P.O. Box 3283, Auburn, ME 04212; (207) 777-1700

-Southern Maine Home Education Support Group, 25 Belmeade Rd, Portland, ME 04101; (207) 774-7053

Maryland:

-Baltimore Homeschooling Contact, 2111 Eastern Avenue, Baltimore, MD 21231; 276-5130

-Christian Home Schools of Western MD, P.O. Box 564, Cumberland, MD 21502; (301) 759-9258

-Maryland Home Education Association, 9085 Flamepool Way, Columbia, MD 21045; (301) 730-0073

-Montgomery Co Support Group, 26824 Howard Chapel Drive, Damascus, MD 20872-1247; (301) 253-5467

-Parents For Home Education, 13020 Blairmore St, Beltsville, MD 20705; (301) 572-5827

-Prince Georges Support Group, 345-6487

Massachusetts:

-Apple Country Homeschooling Association, P.O. Box 246, Harvard, MA 01451; (508) 456-3688

-Franklin Co Families for Home Ed, (413) 625-6566

-Greater Boston Home Educators, (617) 246-2059 (Wakefield)

-Homeschoolers of Mass. Education Club (Boston area), 72 Dale St, Roslindale, MA 02131; (617) 323-1119

-Kitchen School Group, P.O. Box 96, W Boxford, MA 01885; (508) 352-2023

-Mass Home Learning Association, P.O. Box 1976, Lenox, MA 01240

-Metro West Homeschoolers, 379 Concord Road, Marlboro, MA 01752; (508) 485-2949

-North Shore Support Group, (508) 468-4663 or (508) 658-8970

-South Shore Homeschoolers, 87 Snell Avenue, Brockton, MA 02402; (508) 588-1529

-Worcester Area Homeschooling Organization, 246 May St #2, Worcester, MA 01602; (508) 755-9553

Michigan:

-Bay City Homeschooling Support Group, (517) 893-7608

-Information Network for Christian Homes, 4150 Ambrose NE, Grand Rapids, MI 49505

-Sunnyridge Alternative Learning Center, HCO 1 Box 134, Pelkie, MI 49958

Minnesota:

-Families Nurturing Lifelong Learners, 2452 Southcrest Avenue, Maplewood, MN 55199

-Fargo-Moorhead Homeschool Association, 1909-8th St South, Moorhead, MN 56560

-Home-Based Educators Accrediting Association, Rt. 1 Box 381, Cambridge, MN 55008

-Minnesota Association of Christian Home Educators, Box 14326, Minneapolis, MN 55414

-Minnesota Homeschool Alliance, P.O. Box 281, Maple Plain, MN 55359; (612) 479-4391

-Minnesota Home School Network, 9669 E 123rd, Hastings, MN 55033; (612) 437-3049

Mississippi:

-Mississippi Homeschoolers Association, Rt. 4 Box 436, Pass Christian, MS 39571

Missouri:

-Families for Home Education, 4400 Woods Rd, Sibley, MO 64088

-Springfield Area Homeschoolers, Rt 1 Box 193, Fair Grove, MO 65648

-St. Louis South County Support Group, 601 Madison, Arnold, MO 63010

Montana:

-Flathead Valley Homeschoolers Association, Kalispell, MT 892-4052

-The Grapevine (Montana Homeschool News), 1702 Hwy 83 North, Seeley Lake, MT 59868; (406) 754-2481

-Homeschoolers of Montana, Box 40, Billings, MT 59101

-Montana Homeschoolers Association, P.O. Box 95, UIM, MT 59485-0095

Nebraska:

-LEARN, 7741 E Avon Ln, Lincoln, NE 68505; (402) 464-8551

-Nebraska Independent Homeschoolers Network, 8010 Lillibridge St, Lincoln, NE 68506

-OPEN, 7930 Raven Oaks Drive, Omaha, NE 68152; (402) 572-8515

-Prairie Christian Home Schools, Rt 3 Box 73, Ord, NE 68862

Nevada:

-Home Schools United/Vegas Valley, P.O. Box 26811, Las Vegas, NV 89126; (702) 870-9566

New Hampshire:

-New Hampshire Home School Coalition, P.O. Box 2224, Concord, NH 03302

-New Hampshire Home Schools Newsletter, P.O. Box 97, Center Tuftonboro, NH 03816

New Jersey:

-Families Learning Together, 11 Bates Road, Jackson, NJ 08527; (201) 367-5012

-Homeschoolers of South Jersey, Rt 2 Burnt House Rd, Vincetown, NJ 08088

-Jersey Shore Christian Homeschoolers Association, 65 Middlesex Rd, Matawan, NJ 07747-3030

-NJ Family Schools Association, RD #2 Box 236, Califon, NJ 07830

-Sussex County Home Education Organization, 875-6178

-Unschoolers Network, 2 Smith St, Farmingdale 07727; (201) 938-2473

-Unschooling Families Support Group of Central NJ, RD 1 Box 713, Jobstown, NJ 08041; (609) 723-1524

New Mexico:

-New Mexico Family Educators, 678 Lisbon Avenue SE, Rio Rancho, NM 87124

-New Mexico Home Educators, P.O. Box 13383, Albuquerque, NM 87120

-Santa Fe Learning Cooperative, 2463 Camino Capitan, Santa Fe, NM 87505

New York:

-Fingerlakes Unschoolers Network, 607 Cascadilla St, Ithaca, NY 14850; (607) 277-6300

-Home Schoolers Exchange, RD 1, Box 172E, E Chatham, NY 12060; (518) 392-4277

-Long Island Homeschoolers Association, 4 Seville Place, Massapequa Park 11762; 516) 795-5554

-Loving Education At Home, PO Box 332, Syracuse, NY 13205-0332; (518) 337-6019

-New York City Home Educators Alliance, c/o Theresa Morris, 341 E 5th St, New York, NY 10003; (212) 473-7173

-St. Thomas More Catholic Home School Support Grp, 248 E 204 St, Bronx, NY 10458

-Western NY Homeschooling Network, 119 Cook Avenue, Jamestown, NY 14701; (716) 483-1839

North Carolina:

-Family Learning Exchange of North Carolina, Box 5825, Wrightsville Beach, NC 28450

-North Carolinans for Home Education, 204 North Person St, Raleigh, NC 27601; (919) 834-NCHE

North Dakota:

-North Dakota Home School Association, PO Box 539, Turtle Lake, NC 58575; (701) 448-9193 or 448-2602

Ohio:

-Christian Home Educators of Ohio, PO Box 1224, Kent, OH 44240

-Christian Parents Association, 310 Bluebonnet Drive, Findlay, OH 45840 (local only)

-Creative Thoughts from Ohio Home Schools, c/o Amy Vanorio, 2108 Kemper Ln, Cincinnati, OH 45206

-Growing Together, c/o Nancy McKibben, 1676 Trendril Ct, Columbus, OH 43229

-Home-Based Education League of Perrysburg, c/o Terry Endsley, 13947 5 Pt Rd, Perrysburg, OH 43551; (419) 874-2148

-Home School Resource Center, 1444 Gurley Avenue, Akron, OH 44310; (216) 633-3160

-Ohio Coalition of Educational Alternatives Now, P.O. Box 094, Thompson, OH 44086

Oklahoma:

-The Family Learning Connection, PO Box 1938, Durant, OK 74702

-OK Central Home Educators Consociation, PO Box 270601, Oklahoma City, OK 73137

-Oklahoma Christian Home Educators Association, PO Box 102, Jenks, OK 74037

Oregon:

-Avalos Learning Center, PO Box 70778, Eugene, OR 97401

-Central Oregon Homeschoolers, PO Box 9306, Bend, OR 97708; (503) 382-1547

-Douglas County Homeschoolers Connection, 4053 Hanna St, Roseburg, OR 97470

-Homeschoolers of Lane County, 38040 Pengra Rd, Fall Creek, OR 97438; (503) 937-2271

-The Learning Connection, PO Box 1091 #196, Grants Pass, OR 97526; (503) 476-5686

-Oregon Home Educators Association, c/o Kim Gordon, Oregon Yacht Club #D, Portland, OR 97202

-Parents Education Association, PO Box 1482, Beaverton, OR 97075, 503-645-3709

-Portland Area Tri-County Homeschoolers, c/o Susan Jorg, 28901 S. Davis Rd, Estacada 97023; (503) 630-4935

-Willamette Homeschoolers, 245 W 27th Avenue, Eugene, OR 97405

Pennsylvania:

-Chester County Homeschoolers, PO Box C, Paoli, PA 19301

Endless Mountains Homeschoolers, RD 6 Box 19B, Wellsboro, PA 16901

-Pennsylvania Home Education News, 411 N Duffy Rd, Butler, PA 16001

-Pennsylvania Homeschoolers, RD 2 Box 117, Kittanning, PA 16201; (412) 783-6512

Rhode Island:

-Home Spun News, 4 Sherwood Avenue, Warwick, RI 02888; (401) 781-5977

-Parent Educators of Rhode Island, PO Box 546, Coventry, RI 02816

-Rhode Island Guild of Home Teachers, 272 Pequot Avenue, Warwick, RI 02886; (401) 737-2265

-Rhode Islanders for Constitutional Education, 1 Solar St, Providence, RI 02903; (401) 861-9685

South Carolina:

-Carolina Family School Association, Rt 2 Box 17, St. Stephen, SC 29479

South Dakota:

-South Dakota Home School Association, 8801 E 38th St, Sioux Falls, SD 57103

Tennessee:

-Home Education Association of Tennessee (HEAT), 3677 Richbriar Ct, Nashville, TN 37211

-Homeschooling Families, 116 Richards Drive, Oliver Springs, TN 37840; 435-1667

Texas:
-Austin Area Homeschoolers, 6502 Bradley Drive, Austin, TX 78723
-Family Home Educators of Dallas, (214) 840-8342
-Home-Oriented Private Education for Texas, PO Box 43887, Austin, TX 78745-0018; (512) 280-4673
-Texas Homeschool Coalition, (806) 797-4927
Utah:
-FCLA Utah Spice Group, 1510 W 500 N, Provo, UT 84601; (801) 377-4728
-Utah Home Education Association, 1099 S 200 E, Farmington, UT 84054; (801) 488-3676
Vermont:
-Life is Valuable Education, RR 2 Box 289B, St. Albans, VT 05478; (802) 527-1674
-Vermont Homeschoolers Association, RR 1 Box 6680, Middletown Springs, VT 05757
Virginia:
-Home Educators Association of Virginia, PO Box 1810, Front Royal, VA 22630-1810; (793) 590-9048
-Home Educators Network, 3320 Waverly Drive, Fredericksburg, VA 22401
-Home Instruction Support Group, 217 Willow Terr, Sterling, VA 22170
-North Virginia Homeschoolers Newsletter, 2519 Buckelew Drive, Falls Church, VA 22046
-Northern Virginia Homeschoolers/LEARN, 4000 Terrace Drive, Annandale, VA 22003
Washington:
-Clark County Home Educators, 28823 NW Main St., Ridgefield, WA 98642; (206) 887-3042
-Families Learning Together, Box 10 Tiger Star Rt, Colville, WA 99114
-Family Academy, 146 SW 153rd #290, Seattle, WA 98166
Family Learning Organization, PO Box 7256, Spokane, WA 99207-0256; (509) 467-2552
-Homeschoolers' Support Association, PO Box 413, Maple Valley, WA 98038; (206) 432-9805
-Natural Learning Network, 5725 N Elgin, Spokane, WA 99205; 536-8110 (after 5 pm)
-Teaching Parents Association, 16427 28th Drive SE, Bothell, WA 98012; (206) 483-6642
-Washington Homeschool Organization, PO Box 938, Maple Valley, WA 98038; (206) 432-3935
-Whatcom Homeschool Association, 595 Trout Lake Rd, Bellingham, WA 98226
Wisconsin:
-Families in Schools at Home (FISH), 4639 Conestoga Trail, Cottage Grove, WI 53527
-HOME (Madison chapter), 5745 Bittersweet Place, Madison, WI 53705; (608) 238-3302
-HOME Network News, 1428 Woodland, Eau Claire, WI 57401
-Wisconsin Parents Association, PO Box 2502, Madison, WI 53701
West Virginia:
-Alternatives in Education, Rt 3 Box 305, Chloe, WV 25235; (304) 655-7232
-Christian Home Educators of West Virginia, PO Box 266, Glenville, WV 26351; (304) 462-8296
-West Virginia Home Educators Association, PO Box 7504, Charleston, WV 25356; (304) 733-4735
Wyoming:
-Wyoming Homeschoolers, Box 1386, Lyman, WY 82937; (307) 787-6728

Appendix C

helpful private schools, correspondence schools, mail order supplies

Helpful private schools

This list is taken from *Growing Without Schooling*'s annual directory. By the time you are reading it, it's probably partially out of date. However, *GWS* publishes frequent updates. Write and ask about their *Homeschooling Resource List*, which currently sells for $2.50. It lists not only helpful private schools, but also homeschooling support groups and organizations, correspondence schools, curriculum suppliers, homeschooling magazines, and related organizations. (Growing Without Schooling, 2269 Massachusetts Avenue, Cambridge, MA 02140, phone 617-864-3100.)

The schools here offer various kinds of help to homeschoolers. Some act as "umbrella schools" (see chapter 11); others offer curriculum only. As their names suggest, many have a religious emphasis. You probably don't *need* to deal with any of these schools unless you have a touchy legal situation, though you might *choose* to for a variety of reasons. Clonlara has an excellent reputation; I personally know little about any of the others. Many are small organizations with small budgets. Therefore, if you write to them, please include a stamped, self-addressed envelope.

Also, see the annual *National Directory of Alternative Schools*. Many of the alternative schools it describes are friendly and helpful to homeschoolers, and it includes a valuable section on homeschooling with descriptions of support groups all over the country. Order from National Coalition of Alternative Community Schools, 58 Schoolhouse Road, Summertown, TN 38483. Currently $12.50, or $7.50 with membership, which is $20 and includes a newsletter.

-Abbott Loop Christian Center, 2626 Abbott Rd, Anchorage, AK 99507

-Abington Academy, 176 Main St, Yarmouthport, MA 02675 (Cape Cod only)

-Aloha Kids Academy, 4640 SW 182, Aloha, OR 97007; (503) 642-4094 local

-Alpha Christian School, Rt 1, Perry, KS 66073; (913) 597-5822

-American Heritage Christian Academy, 9027 Calvine Road, Sacramento, CA 95829

-The Arches, P.O. Box 58176, Tucson, AZ 85732-8176

-Arivaca Community School, P.O. Box 24, Arivaca, AZ 85601

-Baldwin Park Christian School, 13940 E Merced, Baldwin Park, CA 91706; (916) 337-8828

-Cair Paravel Satellite Schools, (913) 232-9721 (Kansas)

-Calumet School, RD 1 Box 95, Smyrna, NY 13464

-Cascade Canyon School, 459-3464 (San Anselmo, CA)

-Christian Chapel Schools, 1920 S Brea Cyn Cut-off Rd, Walnut, CA 91789; (714) 598-9733

-Christian Family Educational Services, P.O. Box 47159, Phoenix, AZ 85068

-Clonlara Home Based Education Program, 1289 Jewett Street, Ann Arbor, MI 48104; (313) 769-4515

-Dayspring Christian Academy, P.O. Box 60956, Palo alto, CA 94306

-Discovery Christian School, 5547 Alabama Drive, Concord, CA 94521; (415) 672-5670

-G.A.T.E. School, 1725 N Dale #43, Mesa, AZ 85201; 969-4821

-Grassroots Free School, 2458 Grassroots Way, Tallahassee, FL 32301; (904) 656-3629

-High Meadow, 60 Gatehouse Rd, New Paltz, NY 12561; (914) 255-8842

-Home-Centered Learning, P.O. Box 92, Escondido, CA 92025; (619) 749-1522

-Independence Private School, c/o Principal: M. Black, 45 Albert St North, Orilla, ONT L3V 5K3, Canada

-The Learning Community, 9085 Flamepool Way, Columbia, MD 21045; (301) 730-0073

-Linden School, 572 Military, Battle Creek, MI 49015, (616) 963-3877

-Little Piney School, Rt 1 Box 20, Newburg, MO 65550

-Little Red Home School, 9669 E 123rd, Hastings, MN 55033; 437-3049

-Magic Meadow School, P.O. Box 29, N San Juan, CA 95960

-Meter Schools, P.O. Box 427, Rosharon, TX 77583

-Morning Glory Private School, P.O. Box 20, Ft. White, FL 32038

-Mount Vernon Academy, 184 Vine Street, Murray, UT 84107

-Mt. Carmel Academy, RD 1 Box 1737, Waterville, VT 05492

-Muncle Christian School, 230 S 65th, Kansas City, MO 66111; (913) 788-3018

-North Long Beach Calvary Chapel, 132 E Artesia Blvd, Long Beach, CA 90805; (213) 428-5166

-Pilgrim Christian School, 3759 E 57th St, Maywood, CA 90270; (213) 585-3167

-Pilgrim School, 531 N Balna, Porterville, CA 93257; (209) 782-0402

-Pinewood School, 112 Road D, Pine, CO 80470; (303) 838-4418

-Pittsburgh Urban Christian Coal. School, (412) 322-8324 (PA)

-Rocky Mountain High Academy, P.O. Box 418, Flora Vista, NM 87415

-Saddleback Valley Center, Box 912, El Toro, CA 92630; (714) 855-8003

-Santa Fe Community School, P.O. Box 2241, Santa Fe, NM 87501; (505) 471-6928

-Seedling, c/o Joy Reiter, 69 Sanderson Crescent, Richmond Hill, Ontario L4C 5L5, Canada

-Sidney Ledson School, 33 Overland Drive, Don Mills, Ontario, Canada, M3C 2C3; (416) 447-5355

-Snohomish County Christian School, 1215 Olympic Avenue, Edmonds, WA 98020; (206) 771-1793

-Stonemoor Hills School, 3 Stonemoor Drive, Pueblo, CO 81005; (719) 561-3510

-Summit Christian Academy, 13789 Noel Rd, Suite 100, Dallas, TX 75240

-Sycamore Tree, 2179 Meyer Place, Costa Mesa, CA 92627; (714) 650-4466

-TEACH, 4350 Lakeland Avenue, N, Robbinsdale, MN 55422

-Whole Earth Farm School, 3661 Seminole Rd NE, Silverton, OR 97381

Correspondence Schools

Generally, junior high or high school correspondence schools tend to be pretty much like regular school except that you work on your own schedule.

Also, they can be quite expensive. Therefore, I'm unenthusiastic. However, many teenaged homeschoolers find *college* level correspondence courses quite valuable, and begin earning college credit by taking them. Here are just a few trustworthy schools that operate at the junior high and high school level; for many more and for college level courses, see *Peterson's Independent Study Catalog*, available in libraries or from John Holt's Book and Music Store.

-American School, 850 E 58th, Chicago, IL 60637. High school level, excellent reputation.

-Calvert School, Tuscany Road, Baltimore, MD 21210. Through 8th grade only. Great reputation, but quite structured.

-High School Correspondence Courses, University Extension, University of California, Berkeley, CA 94720.

-University of Nebraska Independent Study High School, Continuing Education Center, Rm. 269, Lincoln, NE 68583.

Mail Order Supplies

Mail order suppliers for specific subjects, like science or foreign language, are described in the appropriate chapters. The companies listed here carry a *variety* of resources for the unschooler.

-Bluestocking Press sells a variety of homeschooling and other general educational books, with especially good coverage of economics and business. For their *Educational Spectrums Catalog*, send $1 to Bluestocking Press, PO Box 1014, Placerville, CA 95667-1014, (916) 621-1123.

-Home Education Press publishes *Home Education Magazine* (see bibliography) and several books, including Britt Barker's *Letters Home*. Their free catalog offers other homeschooling books also. Home Education Press, PO Box 1083, Tonasket, WA 98855.

-John Holt's Music and Book Store is by far my favorite mail order source for anything pertaining to homeschooling issues, and also for various "educational" books like David Macaulay's *The Way Things Work*. The same nice people who publish *Growing Without Schooling* magazine run this company: John Holt's Book and Music Store, 2269 Mass. Ave., Cambridge, MA 02140.

-Wilcox and Follett Book Company sells a tremendous variety of used textbooks, in case you can't find what you need through your school district. They carry all the major textbooks and textbook publishers, including Saxon math books. At one third to one half off, they're still expensive, but the savings are substantial. Wilcox and Follett Book Company, 1000 West Washington Blvd., Chicago, IL 60607.

Appendix D

Indexes

I. INDEX OF UNSCHOOLERS-- teenagers and parents

II. GENERAL INDEX

THE AUTHOR WOULD LOVE TO HEAR FROM YOU!

Do you have an unschooling experience that other people might learn from or be inspired by? If you write it down and send it to me, I may include it in my newsletter, *Unschooling Ourselves*, or in future editions of this book or other writings. Write to me at P.O. Box 1014, Eugene, OR 97440-1014. If you don't mind my writing about you or printing your letter (or parts of it), please include a signed, dated statement that goes something like this: "Grace Llewellyn has my permission to use this letter in any of her writings." Or "Grace Llewellyn has my permission to use this letter, but not my name, in future editions of *The Teenage Liberation Handbook* only." If you have any comments about this book and don't mind my using them (with or without your name) in advertising and publicity, please make a note of that also.

Of course, I'd also love to hear from you even if you don't want me to share your story or name. Keep in mind that I do get quite a bit of mail and am often slow to respond, so it's best not to rely on me for advice you need right away. If you are seeking advice and can't find it in this book, I'd suggest joining a local or regional support group or attending a homeschooling conference. Or, subscribe to *Growing Without Schooling* or *Home Education Magazine* and write your question in a letter to other readers. You can also call or write the *GWS* office and request to have back issues of the magazine chosen for you (currently $4.50 each) in order to help you deal with a particular issue in unschooling, such as college admissions, math, different ways to think about socialization, etc.

SPREADING THE WORD

Would you like to sell copies of this book or *Real Lives* at a festival, conference, party, fundraiser, or other event? Maybe you'd like to infiltrate back-to-school night? If you order 10 or more copies, you receive a 40% discount--you can earn approximately $5 for each copy you sell, or pass part of the savings along to your friends. Prepayment required--send a check to Lowry House for $8.97 x total number of copies, and you'll be billed for shipping costs.

GRACE'S ZINE

If you'd like to stay in touch with other people of all ages who are changing their lives in unschooly ways, you may also want to subscribe to my zine, or newsletter, *Unschooling Ourselves*. Readers are welcome to contribute stories about their own experiences (rather than about their children's homeschooling experiences). I also print photos, cartoons, and updates and additions to the resources and ideas in this book. One year subscription $12, sample issue $3. Make checks out to Lowry House Publishers and mail to Unschooling Ourselves, P.O. Box 1014, Eugene, OR 97440. Canadian and overseas orders: Pay in U.S. funds only: $16/subscription, $4/sample issue.

How to get another copy of *The Teenage Liberation Handbook* or *Real Lives*:

1. Ask a bookstore to order it.

2. Cut out or photocopy the order form below and mail it with a check or money order.

3. Send your name, address, name of the book(s) you want, and a check or money order for $16.95 for one copy ($14.95 + $2 shipping), $15.95 each for two or more copies ($1 shipping) to Lowry House Publishers, P.O. Box 1014, Eugene, OR 97440-1014.

Canadian orders enclose $17.95 U.S. funds for one book, $16.95 per copy for two or more books.

Please send

_____ copies of *The Teenage Liberation Handbook: how to quit school and get a real life and education*.
_____ copies of *Real Lives: eleven teenagers who don't go to school*.

Enclosed is a check or money order for _____ ($16.95 including shipping for 1 book; $15.95 each for more than one book mailed to the same address).

name_____

street address_____

city, state, ZIP_____

Mail to: Lowry House Publishers, P.O. Box 1014, Eugene, OR 97440-1014.
Thank you!